Teacher Edition

AUTHORS
Jacqueline Chanda
Kristen Pederson Marstaller

CONSULTANTS
Katherina Danko-McGhee
María Teresa García-Pedroche

Orlando Austin New York San Diego Toronto London

Visit *The Learning Site!*
www.harcourtschool.com

Printed in the United States of America

ISBN 0-15-336454-8
0-15-342014-6

2 3 4 5 6 7 8 9 10 030 13 12 11 10 09 08 07 06 05

Authors

Jacqueline Chanda

Chair, Division of Art Education and Art History, School of Visual Arts, University of North Texas; Co-Director, North Texas Institute for Educators on the Visual Arts

Research contributions: thematic instruction, literacy through art, art history

Kristen Pederson Marstaller

Instructional Coordinator of Fine Arts, Austin Independent School District; President, Texas Art Education Association, 2003–2005

Research contributions: teacher preparation, classroom management, creative expression

CONSULTANTS

Katherina Danko-McGhee

Early Childhood Art Education Coordinator, University of Toledo, Art Department—Center for the Visual Arts; Early Childhood Consultant, Toledo Museum of Art

Research contributions: aesthetic preferences of young children, museum studies

María Teresa García-Pedroche

Head of Family Programs and Community Outreach, Dallas Museum of Art; Visual Artist

Research contributions: school–home and community connections, museum studies, art and culture

How to Use
Art Everywhere

Art Everywhere **is a comprehensive program that teaches the elements of art, the principles of design, and other art concepts. Thirty lessons and twelve cross-curricular features are organized into six thematic units designed to help children think critically about art and the world around them.**

Plan

Use the **Planning Guide** and **Artist's Workshops Preview** to identify lesson objectives and plan production activities. Gather resources from a variety of options:

- Art Prints
- Teacher Resource Book
- Artist's Workshop Activities: English and Spanish
- Art Transparencies

Electronic Art Gallery CD-ROM, Primary

Visit *The Learning Site*
www.harcourtschool.com

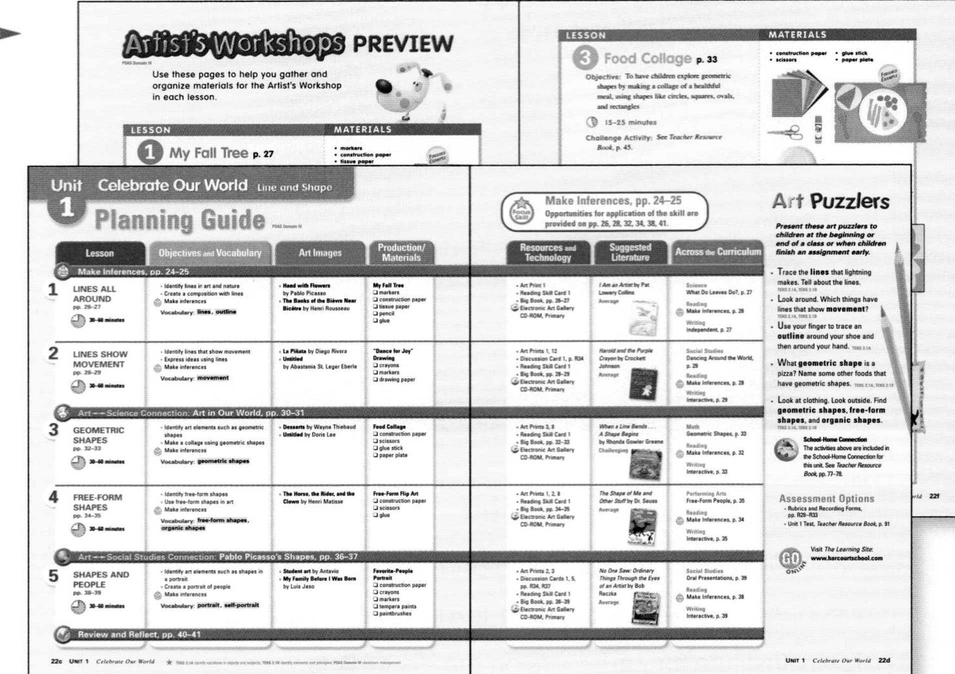

Provide Instruction

Teach the **elements of art**, the **principles of design**, and other **art concepts** through a variety of well-known and culturally diverse art images as well as student artworks. Encourage children's creativity and problem-solving skills through **Artist's Workshop** activities.

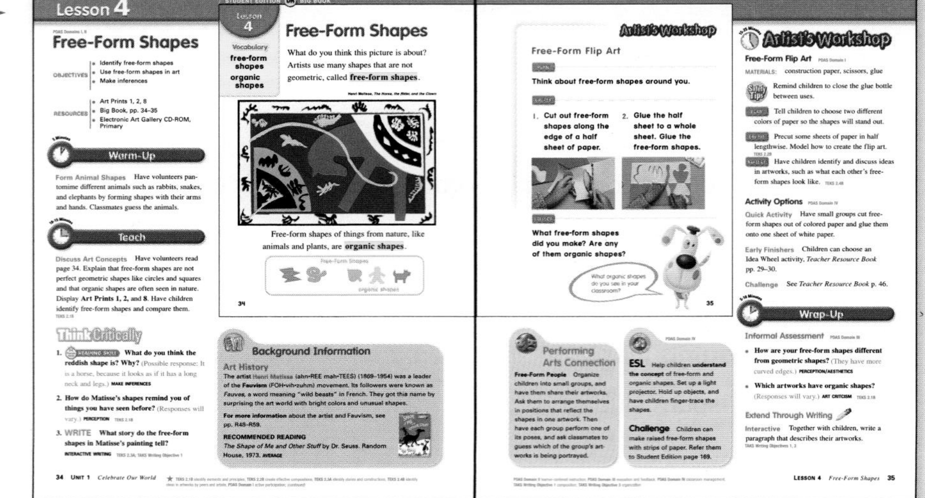

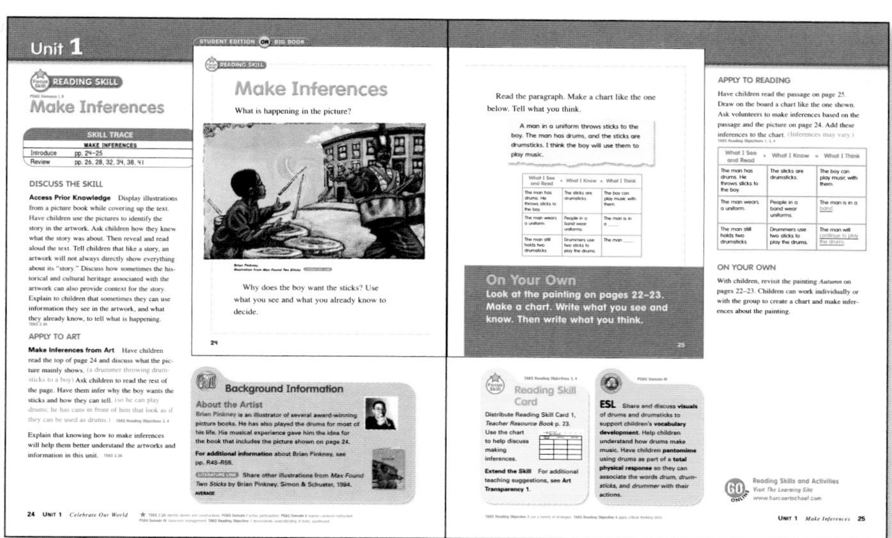

Support Reading

At the beginning of each unit, introduce a key **Reading Skill** that children will apply to artworks and to text throughout the unit.

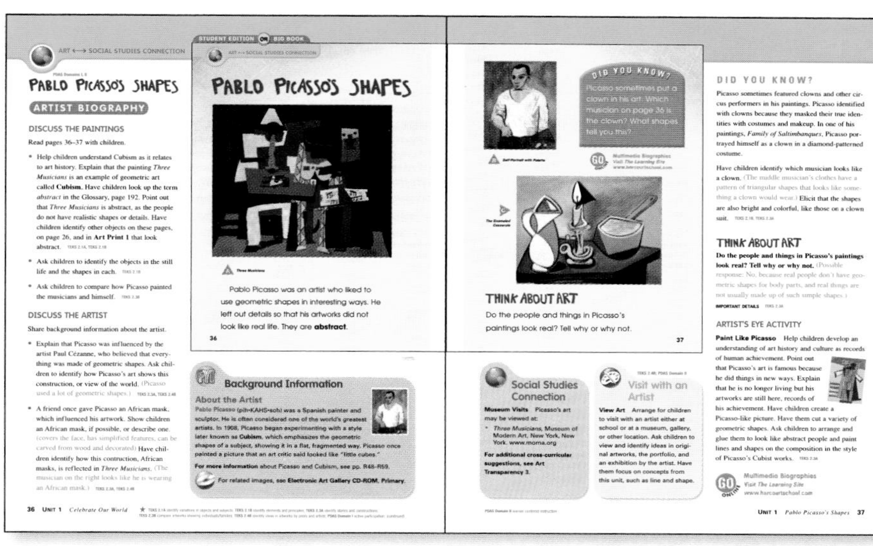

Make Connections

Make **meaningful cross-curricular connections** between art and other disciplines, including reading/literature, social studies, math, and science.

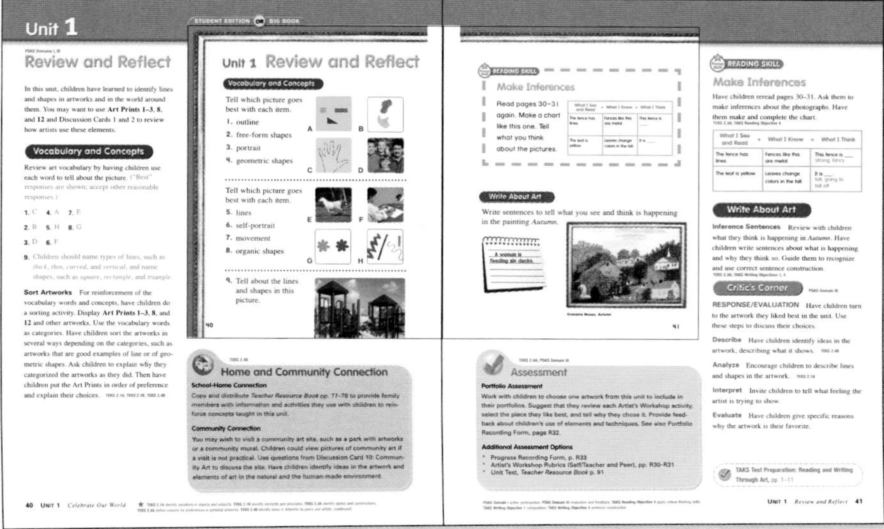

Review and Extend

Assess children's understanding of unit concepts with **Review and Reflect.** Extend the learning with additional **reading and writing** activities and opportunities for **response/evaluation.**

CONTENTS

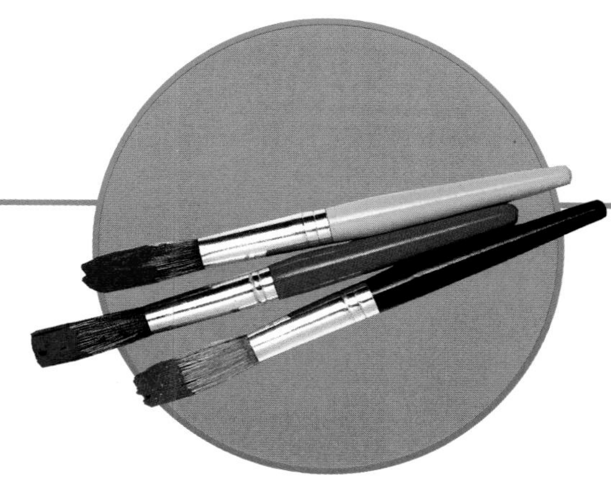

Unit 2 The Artist's Plan

Unit 3 Tell Your Story

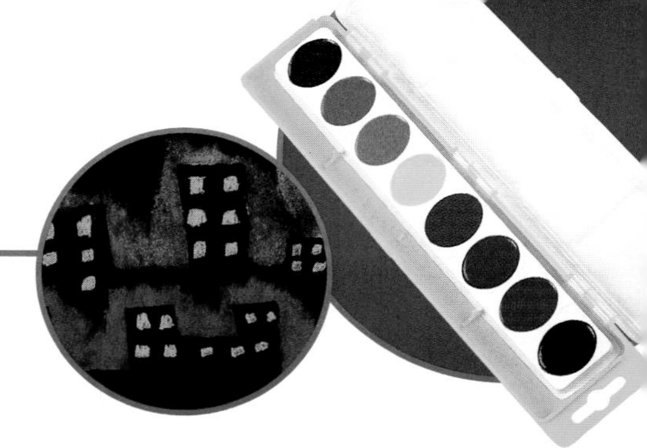

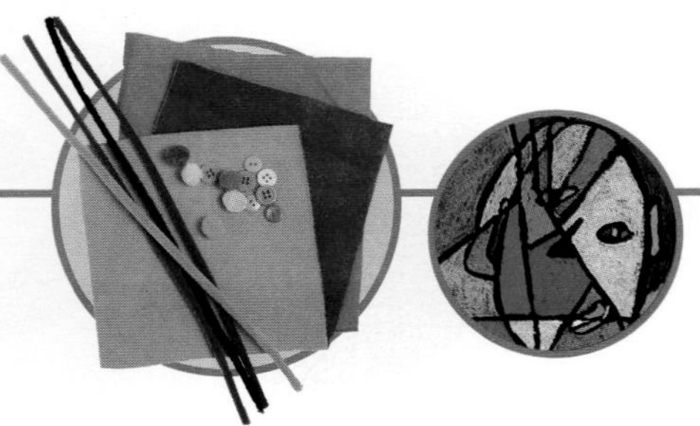

Unit 6 Old and New Ideas

RESOURCES

AUTHORS

Jacqueline Chanda
Kristen Pederson Marstaller

CONSULTANTS

Katherina Danko-McGhee
María Teresa García-Pedroche

Harcourt
SCHOOL PUBLISHERS
Orlando Austin New York San Diego Toronto London

Visit *The Learning Site!*
www.harcourtschool.com

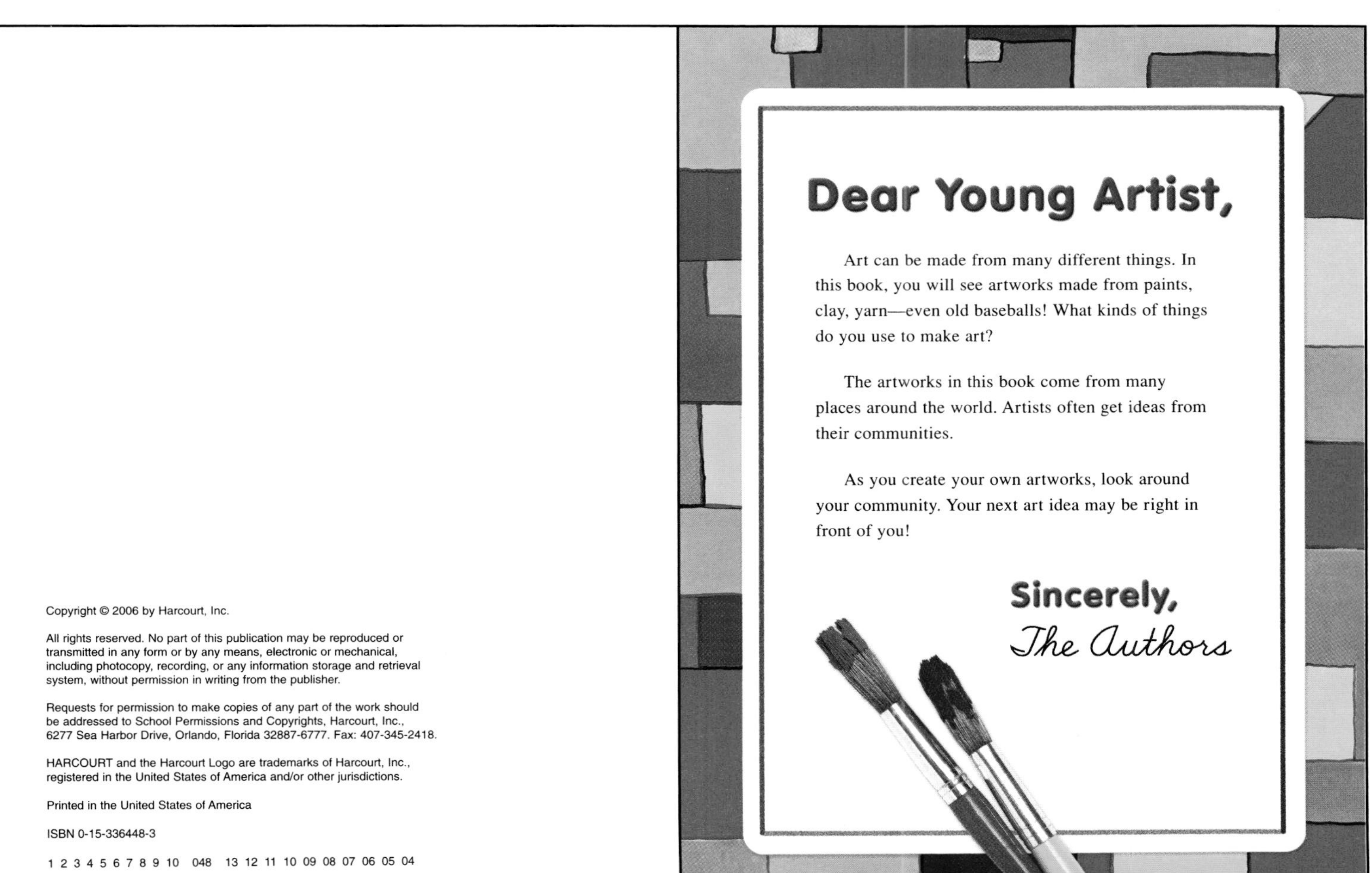

Printed in the United States of America

ISBN 0-15-336448-3

1 2 3 4 5 6 7 8 9 10 048 13 12 11 10 09 08 07 06 05 04

Dear Young Artist,

Art can be made from many different things. In this book, you will see artworks made from paints, clay, yarn—even old baseballs! What kinds of things do you use to make art?

The artworks in this book come from many places around the world. Artists often get ideas from their communities.

As you create your own artworks, look around your community. Your next art idea may be right in front of you!

Sincerely,
The Authors

3

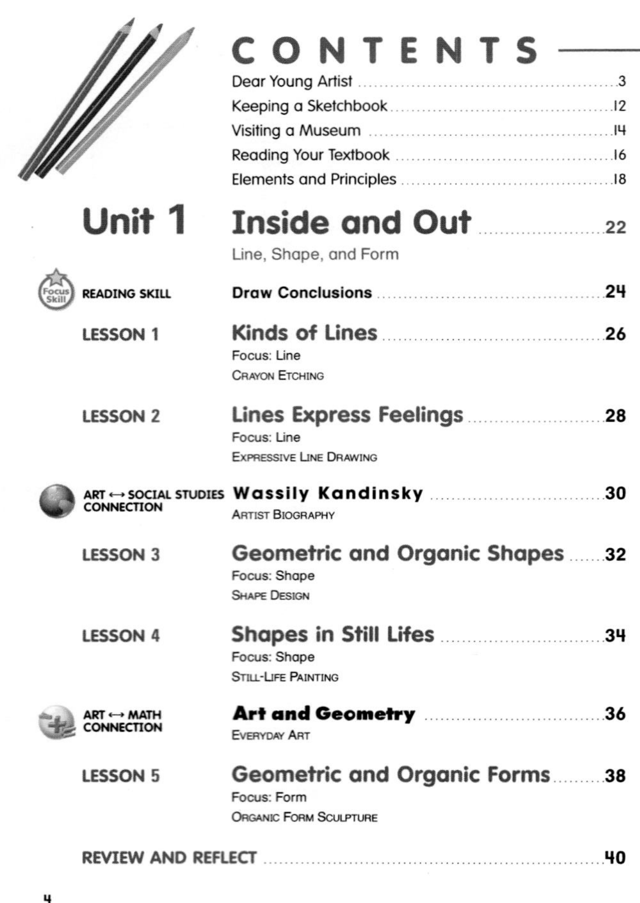

CONTENTS

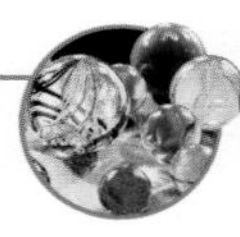
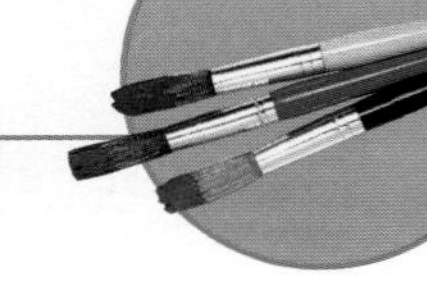

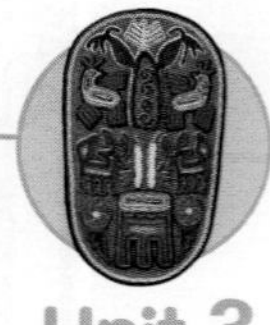

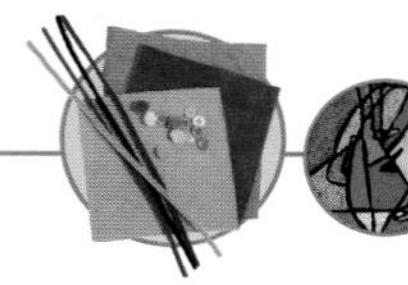
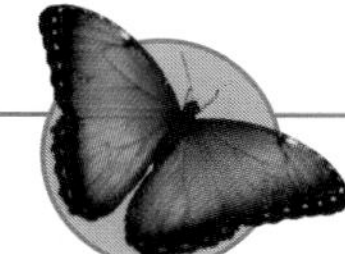

Unit 5 Surprising Viewpoints ... 102
Balance and Unity

8

Unit 6 Old and New Ideas ... 122
Variety and Rhythm

9

AT A GLANCE

Art Production

Elements and Principles

10

Cross-Curricular Connections

Media

11

Keeping a Sketchbook

Introduce Sketchbooks Share with students an example of a sketchbook or notebook that has sketches in it. Tell students that artists use sketchbooks to plan artworks, practice drawing parts of an artwork, try new styles, or help themselves remember what they see. Explain that a sketch, or rough drawing, is not meant to look like a finished artwork.

Discuss Pages 12–13 Have students read pages 12–13. Then discuss the photograph of Thomas Locker sketching a waterfall on page 12. Explain that a large river near Locker's home inspired him to create a book about the water cycle. He made sketches of water in its different forms, including clouds, mountain streams, and waterfalls. Locker then created paintings from the sketches and wrote the text for the book. Have students discuss other sketches that Locker might have made for this book. (Possible responses: rainstorm; ocean scene; snowy mountain) Point out the book cover for *Water Dance* at the bottom of page 12.

Share Ideas Draw students' attention to the drawings, pictures, and other images in the sketchbook pages shown on page 13. Ask students to share ideas about where they would like to take a sketchbook. Then ask them to discuss the kinds of pictures they would like to collect in a sketchbook.

Keeping a Sketchbook

A sketch is a rough drawing that shows an idea for an artwork. You can keep sketches together in a sketchbook. Make sketches of things you imagine and things you see.

Thomas Locker is an artist who enjoys nature. He plans his artworks by making sketches of different places in nature. Then he uses the sketches to create paintings.

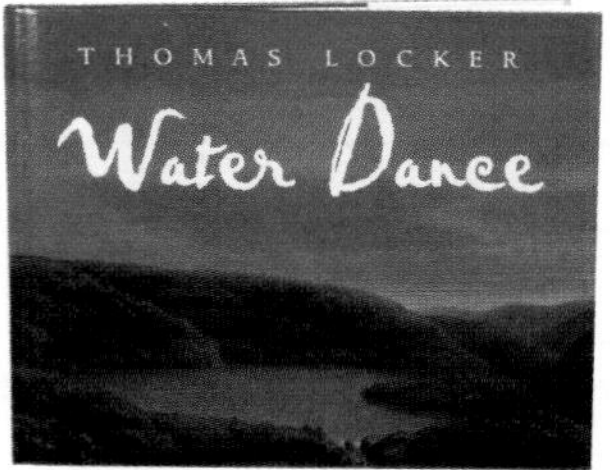

Locker is also an author. He writes words to go with his paintings. The paintings and words are made into books.

LITERATURE LINK

12

Background Information

FYI

About the Artist

Thomas Locker (1937–) lives in upstate New York at the edge of the Hudson River. The Hudson River and the Catskill Mountains are the backdrop for Locker's nature paintings. In 1984, Locker created his first picture book. He has since created more than twenty books about nature for children.

LITERATURE LINK *Water Dance* by Thomas Locker. Harcourt, 1997. AVERAGE

Use a sketchbook to plan your own artworks. Next to your drawings, write notes about colors or materials you might use.

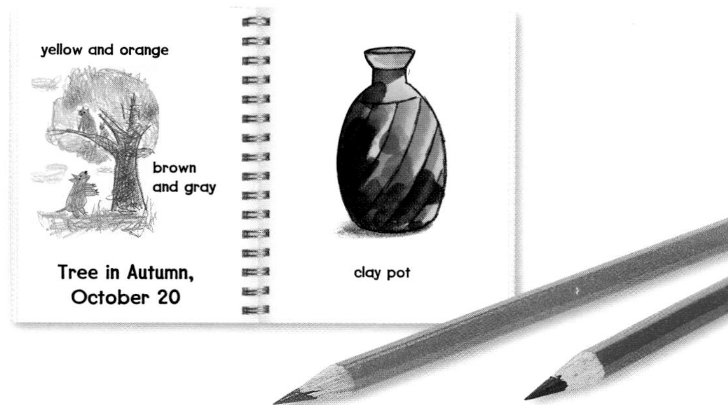

Collect pictures and other things in your sketchbook. Look at your sketchbook to get ideas for your art.

13

Student Self-Assessment

Have students make and keep several sketchbooks over the course of the school year. At the end of the year, they can look back at early sketchbooks and express ideas about their artwork and how they have grown as artists. See pages R28–R29 for assessment strategies.

MAKING A SKETCHBOOK

Model for students one way to make a sketchbook.

1. Staple a piece of construction paper to poster board or thin cardboard to create a pocket.

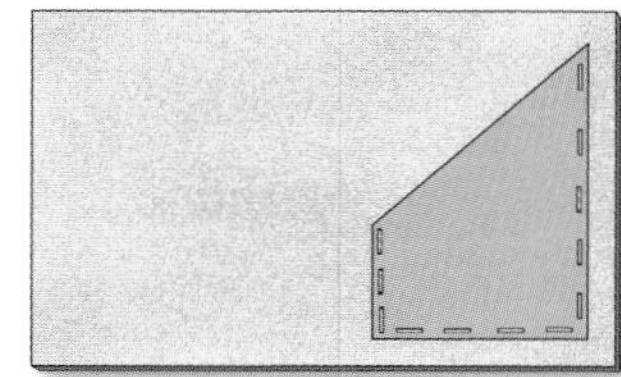

2. Staple a number of sheets of drawing paper to the poster board.

3. Make a cover, and use markers to decorate it.

USING A SKETCHBOOK

Encourage students to use their sketchbooks often. Share the following points about keeping and using a sketchbook.

- Imagine new ideas for art projects and sketch them in your sketchbook.
- Carry your sketchbook with you and sketch what you see.
- Use your sketchbook for projects in other subjects, such as recording observations in a science experiment or getting ideas for your writing.
- Tape or glue pictures, fabric scraps, or examples of things you like onto the pages, or keep them in the pocket.

Visiting a Museum

Access Prior Knowledge Have students share their experiences viewing art. Encourage them to talk about sculptures, murals, monuments, and other artworks in their community. Ask students to tell what kinds of artwork they like best and why. Then read page 14 with students.

Discuss Museum Features Help students brainstorm ways in which visiting a museum is different from viewing art in a book. You might use these ideas to get them started:

- You can see real artworks rather than photographs of them.
- You can look at sculptures from different sides.
- You can ask a docent, or museum guide, questions about the artworks.

Encourage volunteers to share their experiences visiting museums. Ask them where the museum was located and what they saw. Then tell students that the artworks shown in their *Student Editions* are located in museums around the world. Point out the museum names on pages 14 and 15, and read aloud the related Fast Facts.

Have students turn to *Student Edition* page 22, and point out the Locate It logo at the bottom of the page. Tell students that when they see this logo near an artwork, they can turn to the Maps of Museums and Art Sites on pages 144–147 to see where the artwork came from or where it is now located.

Visiting a Museum

An art museum is a place where artworks are collected and displayed. You can find art museums in cities and towns all over the world.

When you visit a museum, remember to

- **Walk** slowly and quietly. Note the artworks that catch your eye.
- **Look** closely at the artworks, but don't touch them.
- **Think** about what the artist's message might be.
- **Listen** carefully to what the docent, or guide, tells you about the artworks.
- **Speak** quietly, but don't be afraid to ask questions.

▲ High Museum of Art
Atlanta, Georgia

◀ The Museum of Fine Arts, Houston
Houston, Texas

Fast Fact More than 45,000 artworks are displayed in this museum. It is one of the largest museums in the United States.

Home and Community Connection

Visiting a Museum

Taking your class on a field trip to a museum in your region is a valuable way to enrich the art curriculum. Students can expand their ability to think critically about what they see by observing art and artifacts first-hand. Before your visit, talk with the museum education staff or with a docent. Prepare students for the visit by introducing the museum's major artists or exhibit themes.

Looking at Art

You may see artworks in museums, in books, or on websites. When you look at an artwork, you can follow these steps to better understand what you see:

- **DESCRIBE** Look closely at the artwork. How would you describe it to someone who has not seen it?
- **ANALYZE** Think about the way the artist organized the artwork. When you glance at it quickly, what catches your eye first?
- **INTERPRET** What do you think the artist's message is? Sometimes the title of an artwork can give you a clue.
- **EVALUATE** What is your opinion of the artwork? Think about why you do or do not like it. Do you think the artist was successful?

◀ National Gallery of Art
Washington, D.C.

Fast Fact The two buildings of this museum are connected by an underground walkway. The museum also features an outdoor sculpture garden.

15

Art Prints

Virtual Tour

If you are unable to arrange a museum visit, display the **Art Prints** to provide students with a similar experience. Refer to the backs of the **Art Prints** for discussion ideas.

For additional artworks, see **Electronic Art Gallery CD-ROM, Primary.**

ESL You can support students' **language acquisition** by using the additional teaching suggestions and resources in each lesson. See also Meeting Individual Needs, pages R24–R27, for ESL teaching strategies related to art education.

LOOKING AT ART

DISCUSS ART CRITICISM Tell students that art criticism is the process of describing the subject of an artwork and what the artwork means and then forming an opinion about it. Explain that they should try to use art vocabulary to tell about the artworks they see. See also page R34 for Discussion Cards 1 and 2.

MODEL

Display **Art Print 1**. Tell students that it shows a painting by Paul Gauguin (goh•GAN). Read the questions on *Student Edition* page 15 with students, and model the steps below, using the **Art Print**. Encourage students to share their own ideas for each step.

DESCRIBE Say: **This is a painting of three puppies drinking from a bowl. In front of the puppies, the artist painted three glasses and several kinds of fruit.**

ANALYZE Tell how the artist used the elements of art and the principles of design. Say: **The bright blue glasses in the center seem to stand out from the rest of the painting.** Students will become increasingly successful with this step as their art vocabulary grows. For more information about the elements of art and the principles of design, see *Student Edition* pages 18–21 and 166–177.

INTERPRET Say: **The bright colors and little puppies in this painting create a cheerful feeling.**

EVALUATE Say: **I like this painting because it makes me feel cheerful. I think the artist was successful because the different shapes and colors make me move my eyes around the artwork and notice every detail.** Encourage students to explain their opinions of the painting.

Reading Your Textbook

Access Prior Knowledge About Types of Text Display a fiction book that students are familiar with, and ask them to briefly describe what the book is about. Repeat with a familiar nonfiction book. Then use prompts like the ones below to help students distinguish between the kinds of text.

- Which book tells a story about made-up characters?
- Which book gives information about real people, things, events, or places?

Then discuss with students the genre of this book. (nonfiction; textbook; gives information)

Discuss Lesson Features Tell students that the lessons in their art textbook have special features to help them locate and remember facts and ideas. Point out and discuss the text features on page 16:

- **title** (tells the main topic)
- **vocabulary** (important terms or concepts)
- **captions** (give the artist's name and the title of the artwork)

Discuss Artist's Workshop Features Discuss with students why it is important to pay attention to the order of steps in directions. Then tell students that each Artist's Workshop activity in their *Student Edition* gives directions for making an art project. Point out the features on the reduced student page 53:

- **steps** (tell how to plan an artwork, create the artwork, and reflect on the finished product)
- **photographs** (show steps from the project)
- **tips** (give important information about techniques or safety)

Reading Your Textbook

Knowing how to read your art textbook will help you remember and enjoy what you read. Each lesson contains nonfiction text about artists, artworks, art techniques, and art history. Remember that nonfiction texts give facts about real people, things, events, or places.

The title tells the main topic of the lesson.

Highlighted words are art vocabulary.

You can identify the most important ideas in each lesson by becoming familiar with different features of your textbook. Look at this sample lesson from pages 52–53.

Lesson 8

Vocabulary
value
shades
tints

Color and Mood

Imagine a room with blue walls, blue furniture, and blue carpeting. Would the room give you a calm feeling or an excited feeling? Artists use color to create a certain mood, or feeling. What kind of mood do you feel when you look at the painting below?

Look for lighter and darker yellow in the painting. The lightness or darkness of a color is its **value**. Artists mix black paint with a color to make **shades**. They mix white paint with a color to make **tints**. Point out some shades and tints of green in the painting.

Diego Rivera, *Baile en Tehuantepec*

16

You can find more resources in the Student Handbook:

- Maps of Museums and Art Sites, pp. 144–147
- Art Safety, pp. 148–149
- Art Techniques, pp. 150–165
- Elements and Principles, pp. 166–177
- Gallery of Artists, pp. 178–188
- Glossary, pp. 189–197

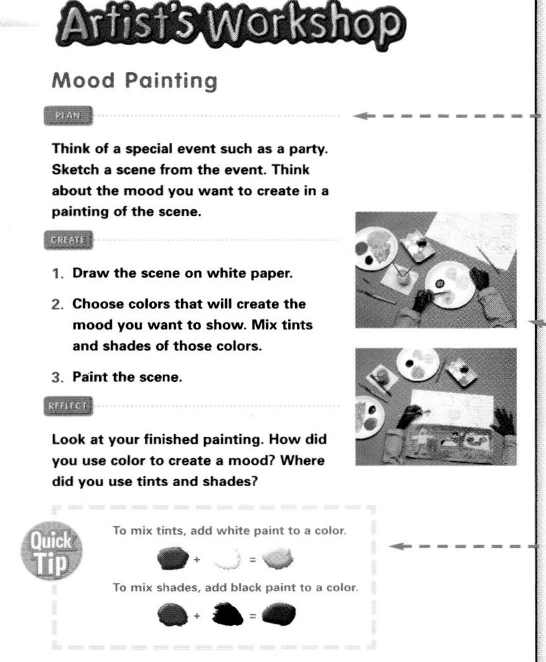

The Artist's Workshop activities are organized by the steps Plan, Create, and Reflect.

The photographs on this page show how an artwork can be made.

These are important tips about art techniques or safety.

17

Discuss Book Parts Tell students that their art textbook contains several resources to help them learn about art. Have them look at the list of resources on page 17.

As students look up each section in the back of their *Student Edition*, ask volunteers to tell what kinds of information each section gives.

- **Maps of Museums and Art Sites** (location of artworks shown in the book)
- **Art Safety** (guidelines for using materials)
- **Art Techniques** (instructions for making different kinds of art)
- **Elements and Principles** (photographs showing examples of each of the art elements and design principles)
- **Gallery of Artists** (pictures of artists and page numbers where their artworks appear)
- **Glossary** (definitions and pronunciations for vocabulary terms)

Technology

Tell students that they will be able to find more information about artists and art techniques online. Discuss with students rules for Internet safety.

Visit *The Learning Site*
www.harcourtschool.com

ESL Help students identify the parts of their book by **giving simple commands** and asking students to respond by pointing to the correct part of the page or section of the book. Then ask **yes/no questions** about the book parts.

Elements of Art

Access Prior Knowledge Play a game with students in which they invent and solve riddles about classroom objects. Use art elements such as line, color, and texture in a riddle to get them started. For example, "I am black and silver. I feel smooth and sharp. I have two holes in the shape of ovals. People use me to cut things. What am I?" (scissors) Tell students to use sensory knowledge as sources for ideas about visual symbols in their riddles by describing how an object looks, feels, smells, or sounds. Explain to students that they will learn more about ways of observing art and objects in the world around them. TEKS 3.1A

Discuss Pages 18–19 Have students read pages 18–19, and discuss how the elements of art are shown in the photographs. Then invite volunteers to identify shapes, forms, and textures in the classroom. Tell students that they will learn more about these elements of art throughout the year.

Elements and Principles

Elements of Art

The **elements of art** are the basic parts of an artwork. You can use them to describe art and to plan and create your own artworks. As you look at these photographs, think about other places where you have seen the elements of art.

COLOR ▲

what we see when light is reflected off objects

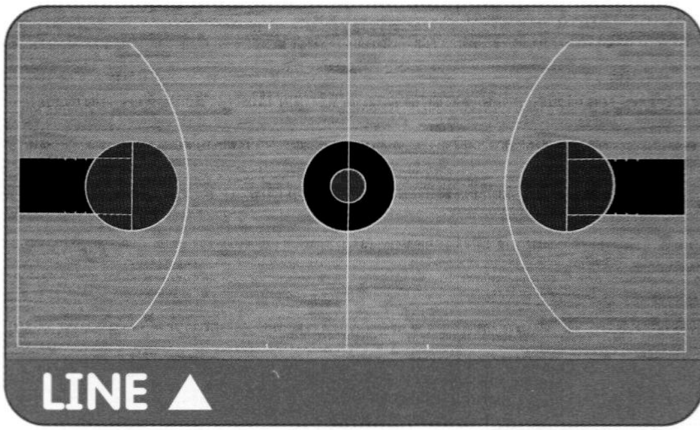

LINE ▲

a mark that begins at one point and continues for a certain distance

FORM ▲

an object that has height, width, and depth

18

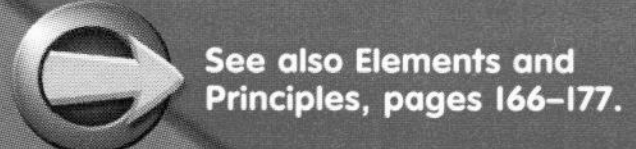
See also Elements and Principles, pages 166–177.

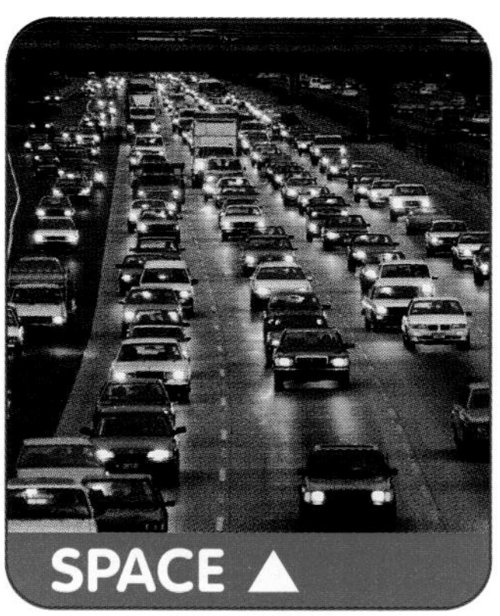

SPACE ▲
the area between and around objects

SHAPE ▲
an object that has height and width

VALUE ▲
the lightness or darkness of a color

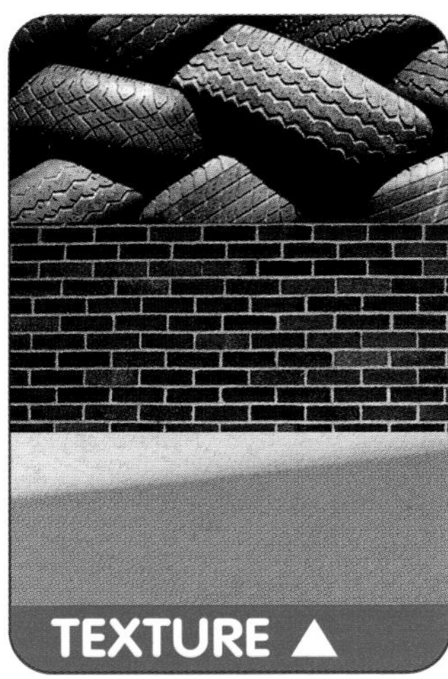

TEXTURE ▲
the way a surface looks or feels

19

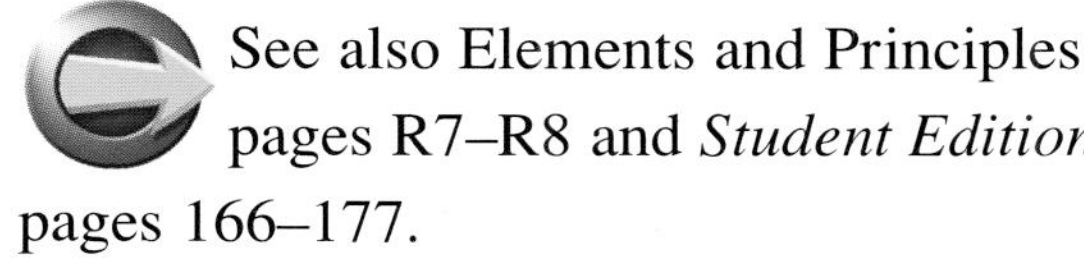
See also Elements and Principles pages R7–R8 and *Student Edition* pages 166–177.

Principles of Design

Discuss Pages 20–21 Have students read the top of page 20. Discuss how the principles of design are shown in the photographs. For example, read the definition of *pattern*, and have students point out repeating shapes in the photograph. Encourage students to describe patterns in their clothing or in other places around the classroom. Tell students that they will learn more about the principles of design as they look at and create artworks.

Principles of Design

Artists use the **principles of design** to arrange the elements in an artwork. Look at how the elements of art are arranged in these photographs.

PATTERN ▲

a design made with repeating lines, shapes, or colors

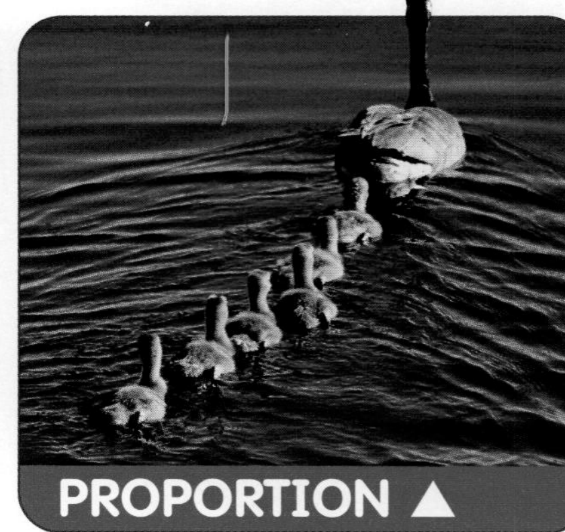

PROPORTION ▲

the size of one thing compared with another thing

BALANCE ▲

the arrangement of elements on each side of an artwork

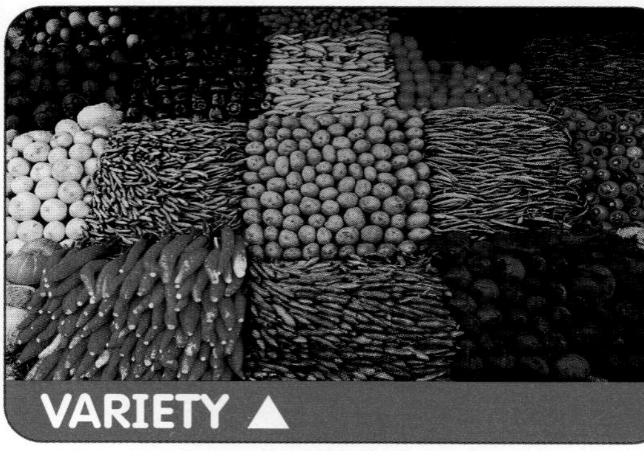

VARIETY ▲

the use of different elements in an artwork

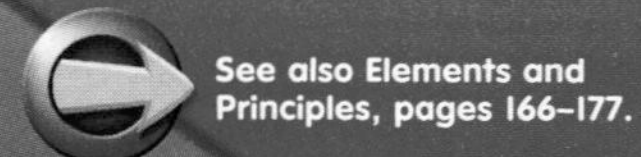

EMPHASIS ▲

importance given to a certain part of an artwork

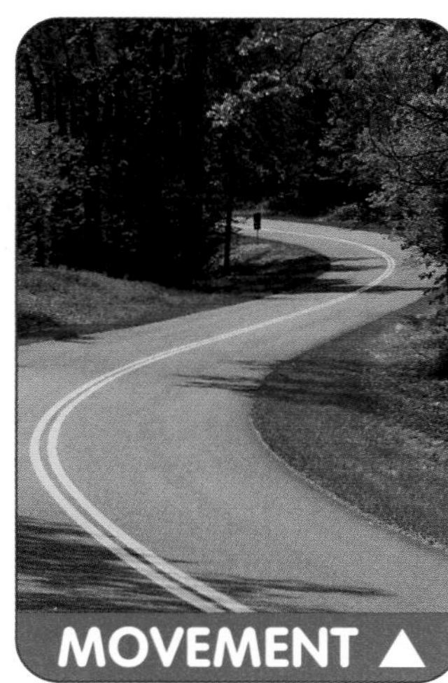

MOVEMENT ▲

the path your eyes take around an artwork

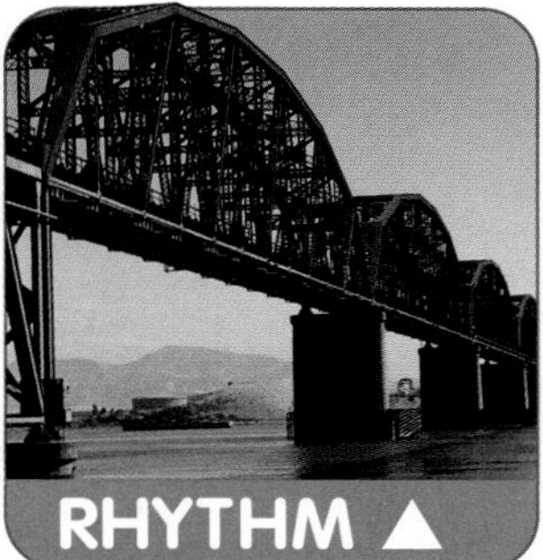

RHYTHM ▲

the use of repeating elements to create a visual beat

UNITY ▲

the sense that an artwork looks complete and that its parts go together

21

Picture File

Have students contribute to a classroom picture file with images they find in magazines and newspapers. Create labeled folders for each of the elements of art and the principles of design. You may also want to create folders for common subjects of artworks, such as ocean scenes and landscapes, for students to use as a reference for their own artworks.

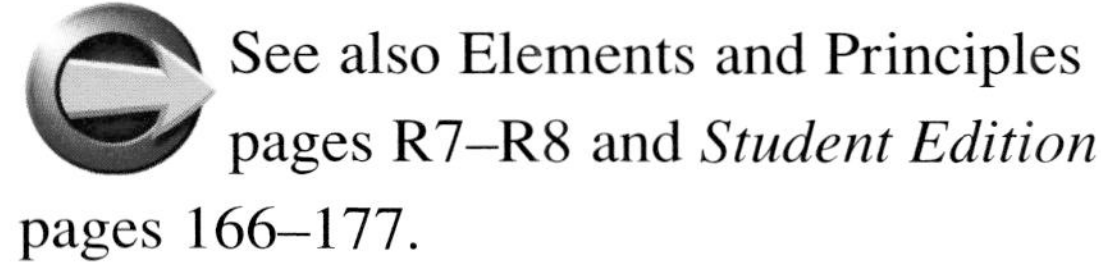

See also Elements and Principles pages R7–R8 and *Student Edition* pages 166–177.

Unit 1 Line, Shape, and Form

Inside and Out

Artworks are like windows to the ideas and experiences of other people. In this unit students will explore how artists use line, shape, and form to tell about themselves and their surroundings.

Resources

- Unit 1 Art Prints (1–3)
- Additional Art Prints (13, 14)
- Art Transparencies 1–3
- Test Preparation: Reading and Writing Through Art, pp. 1–21
- Artist's Workshop Activities: English and Spanish, pp. 1–10
- Encyclopedia of Artists and Art History, pp. R44–R59
- Picture Cards Collection, cards 14, 19, 53, 55, 58, 81, 89, 111

Using the Art Prints

- Discussion Cards, pp. R34–R38
- Teaching suggestions, backs of Art Prints
- Art Print Teaching Suggestions: Spanish

Teacher Resource Book

- Vocabulary Cards in English and Spanish, pp. 7–10
- Reading Skill Card 1, p. 31
- Copying Master, p. 44
- Challenge Activities, pp. 51–55
- School-Home Connection: English/Spanish, pp. 85–86
- Unit 1 Test, p. 99

Technology Resources

Electronic Art Gallery CD-ROM, Primary

Picture Card Bank CD-ROM

Visit *The Learning Site*
www.harcourtschool.com

- Multimedia Art Glossary
- Multimedia Biographies
- Reading Skills and Activities

Art Prints for This Unit

ART PRINT 2

Houses in Munich
by Wassily Kandinsky

ART PRINT 1

Still Life with Three Puppies
by Paul Gauguin

ART PRINT 13

Watermelons
by Rufino Tamayo

ART PRINT 3

Woman at the Piano
by Elie Nadelman

ART PRINT 14

Caprice in February
by Paul Klee

Unit 1 Inside and Out Line, Shape, and Form

Planning Guide

PDAS Domain IV

Lesson	Objectives and Vocabulary	Art Images	Production/ Materials
Focus Skill: Draw Conclusions, pp. 24–25			
1 KINDS OF LINES pp. 26–27 30–60 minutes	• Identify lines in artworks • Produce drawings with a variety of lines Focus Skill: Draw conclusions about artworks **Vocabulary: lines, contour lines**	• **Interior in Yellow and Blue** by Henri Matisse	**Crayon Etching** ❑ colored pencils ❑ white paper ❑ black crayons ❑ paper clip
2 LINES EXPRESS FEELINGS pp. 28–29 30–60 minutes	• Identify expressive qualities of lines in artworks • Produce drawings with expressive lines Focus Skill: Draw conclusions about artworks **Vocabulary: landscape, jagged lines**	• **Wild West** by Emil Armin	**Expressive Line Drawing** ❑ sketchbook ❑ pencil ❑ white paper ❑ colored pencils
Art ↔ Social Studies Connection: Wassily Kandinsky, pp. 30–31			
3 GEOMETRIC AND ORGANIC SHAPES pp. 32–33 30–60 minutes	• Identify shapes in artworks • Produce shape designs Focus Skill: Draw conclusions about artworks **Vocabulary: two-dimensional, geometric shapes, organic shapes**	• **Brazilian Tapestry (Six Patterns)** by Unknown artist	**Shape Design** ❑ sketchbook ❑ pencil ❑ construction paper ❑ scissors ❑ glue
4 SHAPES IN STILL LIFES pp. 34–35 30–60 minutes	• Identify shapes in artworks • Produce a still-life painting using design skills Focus Skill: Draw conclusions about artworks **Vocabulary: still life, composition**	• **Fruit** by Fernando Botero • **Flowers** by William H. Johnson • **Autumn Still Life** by Lauren, grade 3	**Still-Life Painting** ❑ various objects ❑ white paper ❑ pencil ❑ tempera paints ❑ paintbrushes ❑ water bowl
Art ↔ Math Connection: Art and Geometry, pp. 36–37			
5 GEOMETRIC AND ORGANIC FORMS pp. 38–39 30–60 minutes	• Identify forms in artworks • Produce ceramic sculptures Focus Skill: Draw conclusions about artworks **Vocabulary: three-dimensional, forms, sculpture**	• **Carrousel Pierrot** by Alexander Archipenko • **Lime Mist Ikebana with Cascading Oxblood Leaf** by Dale Chihuly	**Organic Form Sculpture** ❑ sketchbook ❑ pencil ❑ clay ❑ paper bag ❑ water bowl ❑ carving tools
Review and Reflect, pp. 40–41			

★ TEKS 3.2A create artworks; TEKS 3.2C produce various artworks; PDAS Domain IV classroom management

Draw Conclusions, pp. 24–25

Opportunities for application of the skill are provided on pp. 26, 28, 32, 34, 38, 40, and 41.

Resources and Technology	Suggested Literature	Across the Curriculum
• Art Print 1 • Reading Skill Card 1 Electronic Art Gallery CD-ROM, Primary	*Harold and the Purple Crayon* by Crockett Johnson 	**Performing Arts** Moving Like a Line, p. 27 **Reading** Draw Conclusions, p. 26 **Writing** Expository Paragraph, p. 27
• Art Print 14 • Discussion Card 6, p. R36 • Reading Skill Card 1 Electronic Art Gallery CD-ROM, Primary	*The Class Artist* by G. Brian Karas 	**Social Studies** The Wild West, p. 29 **Reading** Draw Conclusions, p. 28 **Writing** Descriptive Paragraph, p. 29
• Discussion Card 9, p. R38 • Reading Skill Card 1 Electronic Art Gallery CD-ROM, Primary	*The Life and Work of Wassily Kandinsky* by Paul Flux 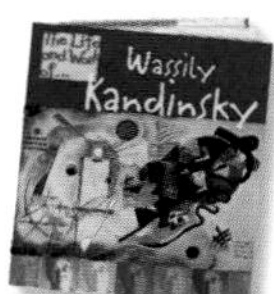	**Math** Geometric Shapes, p. 33 **Reading** Draw Conclusions, p. 32 **Writing** Compare-and-Contrast Paragraph, p. 33
• Art Print 13 • Reading Skill Card 1 Electronic Art Gallery CD-ROM, Primary	*Start with Art: Still Life* by Sue Lacey 	**Science** Variety in Nature, p. 35 **Reading** Draw Conclusions, p. 34 **Writing** Chart, p. 35
• Art Print 3 • Discussion Card 3, p. R35 • Reading Skill Card 1 Electronic Art Gallery CD-ROM, Primary	*Gugu's House* by Catherine Stock 	**Science** Glass, p. 39 **Reading** Draw Conclusions, p. 38 **Writing** Persuasive Letter, p. 39

Art Puzzlers

Present these art puzzlers to students at the beginning or end of a class or when students finish an assignment early.

- Sketch a simple object on paper. Glue pieces of yarn to the paper to show the object's **contour lines**. TEKS 3.2C
- Draw a picture of an object from observation. Use **expressive lines** to show your feelings about the object. TEKS 3.2A, TEKS 3.2C
- Design a traffic sign that has an **organic shape**. TEKS 3.2C
- Arrange a group of objects that tell something about you. Draw the **still life**. TEKS 3.2C
- Draw or sculpt a figure of your favorite animal. What **forms** did you use? TEKS 3.2C

School-Home Connection
The activities above are included in the School-Home Connection for this unit. See *Teacher Resource Book*, pp. 85–86.

Assessment Options

- Rubrics and Recording Forms, pp. R30–R33
- Unit 1 Test, *Teacher Resource Book*, p. 99

Visit *The Learning Site*: **www.harcourtschool.com**

Artist's Workshops PREVIEW

PDAS Domain IV

Use these pages to help you gather and organize materials for the production activity in each lesson.

LESSON	MATERIALS
1 Crayon Etching p. 27 **Objective:** Produce drawings with a variety of lines  **30–40 minutes** **Challenge Activity:** See *Teacher Resource Book,* page 51.	• colored pencils • white paper • black crayons • paper clip 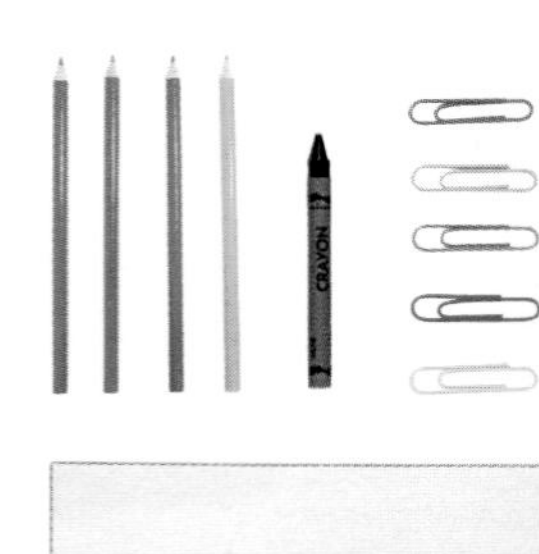 FINISHED EXAMPLE 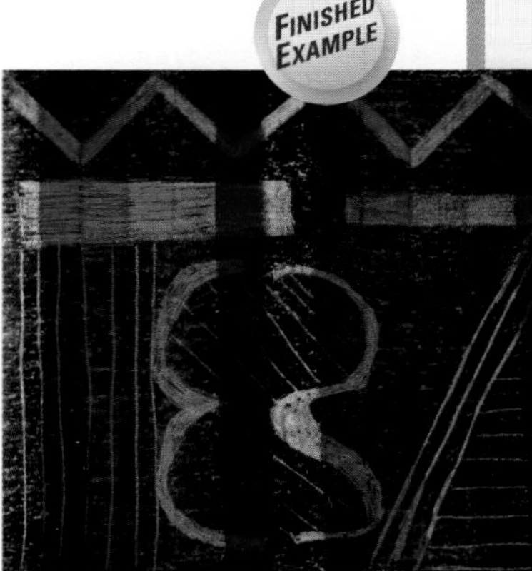
LESSON 2 Expressive Line Drawing p. 29 **Objective:** Produce landscape drawings with expressive lines  **30–40 minutes** **Challenge Activity:** See *Teacher Resource Book,* page 52.	• sketchbook • pencil • white paper • colored pencils  FINISHED EXAMPLE 

For safety information, see Art Safety, page R4; or the Art Safety Poster.

For information on media and techniques, see pp. R15–R23.

LESSON	MATERIALS

3 Shape Design p. 33

Objective: Produce designs with geometric and organic shapes

 **30–40 minutes**

Challenge Activity: See *Teacher Resource Book,* page 53.

- sketchbook
- pencil
- construction paper
- scissors
- glue

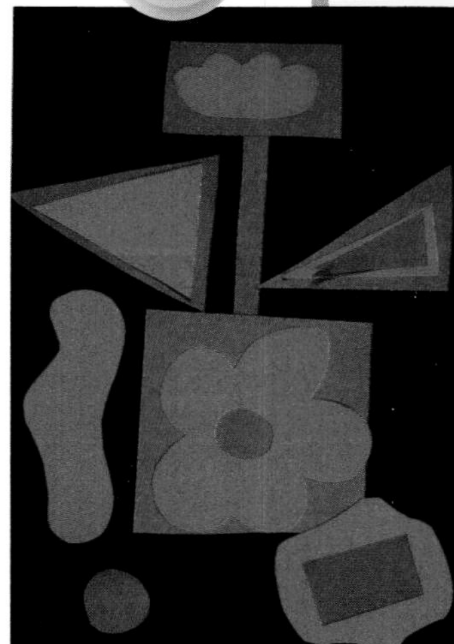

LESSON

4 Still-Life Painting p. 35

Objective: Produce a still-life painting with an interesting composition

 **30–40 minutes**

Challenge Activity: See *Teacher Resource Book,* page 54.

- various objects
- white paper
- pencil
- tempera paints
- paintbrushes
- water bowl

LESSON

5 Organic Form Sculpture p. 39

Objective: Produce ceramic sculptures based on natural objects

 **30–40 minutes**

Challenge Activity: See *Teacher Resource Book,* page 55.

- sketchbook
- pencil
- clay
- paper bag
- water bowl
- carving tools

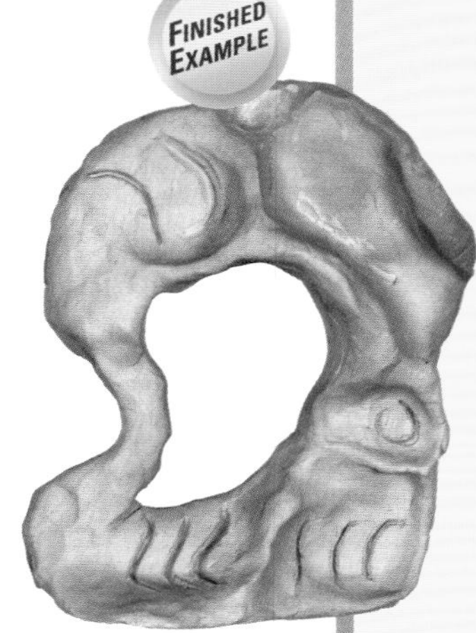

PDAS Domains I, II

Inside and Out

PREVIEW THE UNIT

Tell students that they will view and create artworks that express feelings. Read aloud the unit title, and ask students to predict what the artworks might show. Have students page through the unit to confirm or revise their predictions. Discuss using safety rules when creating art. (See Art Safety, *Student Edition*, pp. 148–149.)

SHARE THE POEM

Have students read aloud the poem on page 23 and view the painting.

How do the poem and the painting go together? (Possible response: The poem tells what happens inside and outside of a big room. The painting shows the inside of a big room. A window in the room shows a view outside.) DRAW CONCLUSIONS TAKS Reading Objective 4

STEP INTO THE ART

Have students look carefully at the painting and describe what they see.

Would you rather be inside or outside the room in the painting? Describe how the surroundings might feel and smell. (Responses will vary.) PERSONAL RESPONSE TEKS 3.1A

SHARE BACKGROUND INFORMATION

Tell students that Henri Matisse created *Harmony in Red* for the dining room of a famous Russian art collector. Explain that Matisse often used bright colors to show his personality. Have volunteers share what they think Matisse was like by looking at the painting. TEKS 3.1A

LOCATE IT See **Using the Maps of Museums and Art Sites,** p. R2.

Henri Matisse, *Harmony in Red*

LOCATE IT

This painting can be found at the Hermitage Museum in St. Petersburg, Russia.

See Maps of Museums and Art Sites, pages 144–147.

22

Background Information

About the Artist

Henri Matisse (ahn•REE mah•TEES) (1869–1954) was born in Le Cateau, France. He created many kinds of art, including sculptures, stained-glass windows, murals, and, near the end of his life, paper cutouts.

For additional information about Matisse, see the Encyclopedia of Artists and Art History, pp. R44–R59, and the Gallery of Artists, *Student Edition* pp. 178–188.

For related artworks, see **Electronic Art Gallery CD-ROM, Primary.**

★ **TEKS 3.1A** identify sources for ideas; **PDAS Domain I** active participation; **PDAS Domain II** learner-centered instruction; **TAKS Reading Objective 4** apply critical-thinking skills

Unit 1 Line, Shape, and Form

Inside and Out

Inside, Outside

Inside is a big, grand room.
Outside flowers are in bloom.

Inside it is quiet and still.
Outside sparrows chirp and trill.

Inside tables will be set,
but outside we are playing yet.

Anonymous

See Gallery of Artists, pages 178–188.

Unit Vocabulary

lines	organic shapes
contour lines	still life
landscape	composition
jagged lines	three-dimensional
two-dimensional	forms
geometric shapes	sculpture

Multimedia Art Glossary
Visit *The Learning Site*
www.harcourtschool.com

23

Unit Vocabulary

Read aloud the terms with students. Then use the Word Knowledge Chart below to assess and discuss their prior knowledge.

lines marks that begin at one point and continue for a certain distance in a certain direction

contour lines outlines drawn around shapes or objects

landscape an artwork that shows an outdoor scene

jagged lines lines that are uneven or ragged

two-dimensional having height and width; flat

geometric shapes shapes such as ovals, circles, squares, triangles, and rectangles that have a regular outline

organic shapes shapes with irregular borders like shapes that appear in nature

still life an artwork that shows a group of objects placed together in an interesting way

composition the way the parts of an artwork are put together

three-dimensional having height, width, and depth

forms objects that have height, width, and depth

sculpture a three-dimensional artwork

Vocabulary Resources

- Vocabulary Cards in English and Spanish: *Teacher Resource Book,* pp. 7–10
- Student Edition Glossary, pp. 189–197

Multimedia Art Glossary
Visit *The Learning Site*
www.harcourtschool.com

Language Arts Connection

Have students create a chart like the one below to identify familiar and unfamiliar vocabulary terms. Encourage them to add information to their charts as they work through this unit.

WORD KNOWLEDGE CHART		
I know this term.	I have seen this term before.	I have never seen this term.

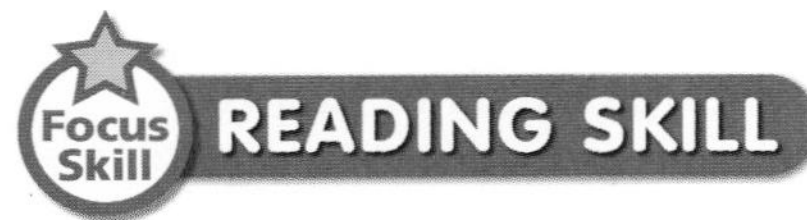

PDAS Domains I, II

Draw Conclusions

SKILL TRACE	
DRAW CONCLUSIONS	
Introduce	pp. 24–25
Review	pp. 26, 28, 32, 34, 38, 40, 41

DISCUSS THE SKILL

Access Prior Knowledge Tell students that their experiences and what they already know can help them understand things they are reading or seeing for the first time. Explain that they draw conclusions when they think about what they see and about what they already know.

Display Picture Card 111, and ask students to describe what they see. (trees covered in snow) Then have them share what they already know about snow. (Snow falls in winter in places that get cold weather.) Tell students they can use these clues to draw the conclusion that the picture shows a winter scene.

APPLY TO ART

Draw Conclusions in Art Have students read page 24 and look at the image. Then discuss the What You See and What You Already Know clues. Have students share other clues supporting the conclusion that the women in the painting are watching something funny. (Possible response: The woman in the back is hiding. People hide when they don't want to be seen. She is probably laughing at someone who doesn't see her.)

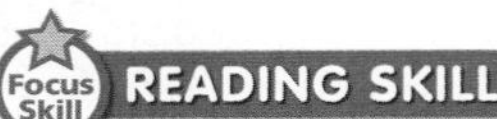

Draw Conclusions

Sometimes you need to use clues to understand what you see. You *draw conclusions* when you think about what you see and about what you already know.

Look at the image below. You can draw the conclusion that the women are watching something funny by using these clues:

- **What You See** The woman in the back is covering her mouth, and the woman in the front is smiling.
- **What You Already Know** People sometimes cover their mouths when they are laughing. People smile when they see something funny.

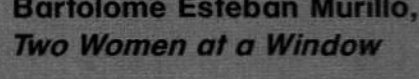

Bartolomé Esteban Murillo, *Two Women at a Window*

24

Background Information

About the Artist

Bartolomé Esteban Murillo (moo•REE•yoh) (1618–1682) was a Spanish painter who painted in the **Baroque** style. Artists using this style often included views seen through windows, doors, and mirrors. Art critics believe that the older woman in *Two Women at a Window* is the younger woman's chaperone.

For additional information about Murillo and the Baroque movement, see pp. R44–R59.

For related artworks, see **Electronic Art Gallery CD-ROM, Primary**.

★ **PDAS Domain I** active participation; **PDAS Domain II** learner-centered instruction; **PDAS Domain IV** classroom management; **TAKS Reading Objective 3** use a variety of strategies; **TAKS Reading Objective 4** apply critical-thinking skills

You can also draw conclusions to help you understand what you read. Read the passage below. Use what you read and what you already know to draw conclusions.

Bartolomé Esteban Murillo (moo•REE•yoh) was born in 1618. He was the first artist from Spain to become famous worldwide. Murillo made many paintings of people on the streets of Spain. He also made paintings for churches. In Spain today, a fine painting by any artist is often called a *Murillo*.

Do you think Murillo is still famous in Spain? Why or why not? Use a diagram like this to draw conclusions.

What I Read	What I Know
People in Spain often use the name *Murillo* to mean a fine painting.	

Conclusion

On Your Own

As you read the lessons in this unit, use diagrams like the one above to draw conclusions about the text and the artworks.

25

APPLY TO READING

Draw Conclusions in Text Explain to students that authors sometimes leave out details, but readers can use clues to draw conclusions about the information. Remind students that they should use information they read and what they already know to draw conclusions.

Have students read the passage on page 25. Work with them to complete the diagram to draw a conclusion about the Spanish artist Bartolomé Esteban Murillo. TAKS Reading Objectives 3, 4

What I Read	What I Know
People in Spain often use the name *Murillo* to mean a fine painting.	If people use a name a lot, the person with that name is probably famous.

Conclusion
Murillo must still be famous in Spain.

ON YOUR OWN

As students read the lessons in this unit, have them use their diagrams to draw conclusions about the text and the artworks.
TAKS Reading Objectives 3, 4

TAKS Reading Objectives 3, 4

Reading Skill Card

Distribute Reading Skill Card 1, *Teacher Resource Book* page 31. Have students use it to draw conclusions in this unit.

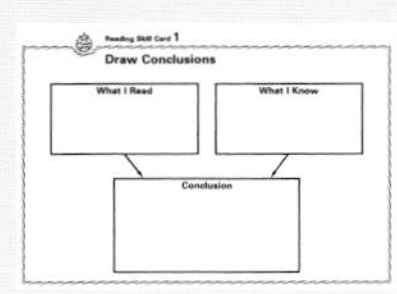

Extend the Skill For additional teaching suggestions, see **Art Transparency 1**.

PDAS Domain IV

ESL To aid in **oral language development**, pair students with fluent-English peers, and have them read the passage on page 25 together. Work with students to restate the paragraph in their own words.

Reading Skills and Activities
Visit *The Learning Site*
www.harcourtschool.com

Lesson 1

PDAS Domains I, II

Kinds of Lines

OBJECTIVES
- Identify lines in artworks
- Produce drawings with a variety of lines
- Draw conclusions about artworks

RESOURCES
- Art Print 1
- Electronic Art Gallery CD-ROM, Primary

5 Minutes

Warm-Up

Build Background Have students mark two points on a sheet of paper. Ask them to draw an interesting line that connects the points. Discuss the lines students drew. Tell them that artists use different kinds of lines in their artworks.

10-15 Minutes

Teach

Discuss Art Concepts Have students read page 26. Have them identify kinds of lines in the classroom and point out similar lines in the painting. Then read the top of page 27 with students. Point out the contour line that outlines the vase in the painting. Display **Art Print 1**, and ask students to identify the contour lines. TEKS 3.1B

Think Critically

1. READING SKILL **Why did the artist use curved lines to show watermelons in *Interior in Yellow and Blue?*** (He wanted the object to look real.) DRAW CONCLUSIONS
2. **What kinds of lines would you use to draw lightning?** (zigzag, diagonal) PERCEPTION/AESTHETICS
3. WRITE **Invent a new kind of line. Name the line, and describe what it looks like.** DESCRIPTIVE TAKS Writing Objective 1

Lesson 1

Vocabulary

lines

contour lines

Kinds of Lines

Look at the different kinds of **lines** on page 27, and find some of these lines in the objects around you. You may find lines on the pages of a notebook. You may also see lines that reach from the floor to the top of a door. What other kinds of lines do you see?

In the painting below, find lines that are straight, curved, and zigzag. What other kinds of lines do you see?

Henri Matisse, *Interior in Yellow and Blue*

26

Background Information

About the Artist

Henri Matisse is considered one of the greatest French painters of the twentieth century. Matisse was a leader of Fauvism, an art movement that stressed the use of pure colors and bold patterns. His travels to Morocco, Corsica, Italy, Spain, and Tahiti greatly influenced his artworks.

For additional information about Matisse and Fauvism, see pp. R44–R59.

RECOMMENDED READING

Harold and the Purple Crayon by Crockett Johnson. HarperCollins, 1955. EASY

★ **TEKS 3.1B** identify elements and principles; **TEKS 3.2C** produce various artworks; **PDAS Domain I** active participation; **PDAS Domain II** learner-centered instruction; **PDAS Domain III** evaluation and feedback; **PDAS Domain IV** classroom management; **TAKS Writing Objective 1** composition; **TAKS Writing Objective 3** organization

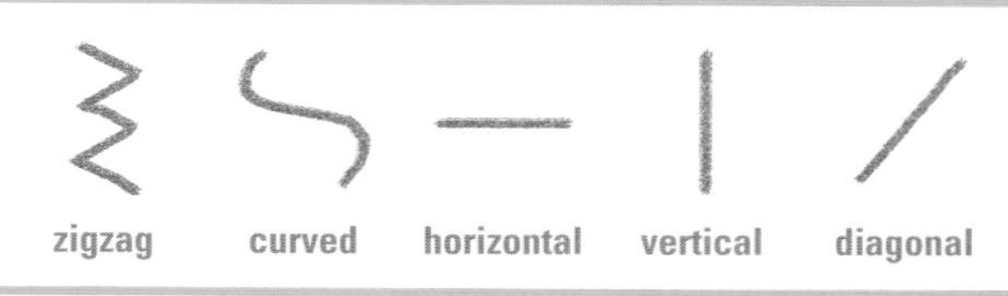

Lines that outline objects are called **contour lines**. Point out some objects in the painting on page 26 that have contour lines.

Artist's Workshop

Crayon Etching

1. **Use colored pencils to draw thick stripes on white paper. Cover all of the paper.**
2. **Use black crayon to color over the stripes. Cover all of the paper.**
3. **Think about a line design you would like to make.**
4. **Use a paper clip to scratch the design through the black crayon. The colors will show through in your design.**

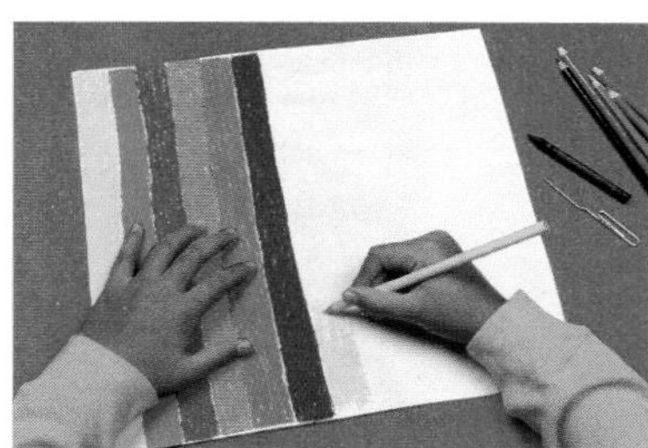

27

Artist's Workshop

Crayon Etching

MATERIALS: colored pencils, white paper, black crayons, paper clip

Quick Tip: Students can use the rounded edge of the paper clip to avoid tearing the paper.

PLAN Ask students to list the kinds of lines they will use.

CREATE Have students produce their etched drawings, using a variety of art materials appropriately. TEKS 3.2C

REFLECT Ask students to describe the lines they used.

Activity Options PDAS Domain IV

Quick Activity Have students fill in an outline of a simple shape with different lines.

Early Finishers Students may change their designs by coloring over the design with black crayon and etching new lines.

Challenge See *Teacher Resource Book*, p. 51.

5-10 Minutes

Wrap-Up

Informal Assessment PDAS Domain III

- **Where can you see curved lines in nature?** (Possible responses: flowers, ocean waves)
  PERCEPTION/AESTHETICS
- **What kinds of lines did you leave out of your drawing? Why?** (Responses will vary.)
  PERSONAL RESPONSE

Extend Through Writing

TAKS Writing Objectives 1, 3

Expository Paragraph Have students write about the steps of making a crayon etching. Tell them to explain the steps in order.

Performing Arts Connection

Moving Like a Line Divide the class into four groups. Name the groups according to kinds of lines: curved, zigzag, vertical, and diagonal. Then ask each group to make up a movement or dance to describe their kind of line.

PDAS Domain IV

ESL Create **visuals** by working with students to make a set of flash cards about kinds of lines. Each card should show a line and be labeled in English and in the student's first language.

Extra Support Select five kinds of lines for students to use in their drawings. Model how to draw each kind.

Lesson 2

PDAS Domains I, II

Lines Express Feelings

OBJECTIVES
- Identify expressive qualities of lines in artworks
- Produce drawings with expressive lines
- Draw conclusions about artworks

RESOURCES
- Art Print 14
- Discussion Card 6, p. R36
- Electronic Art Gallery CD-ROM, Primary

Warm-Up

Build Background Display **Art Print 14.** Explain that artists can use lines to show feelings. Have students discuss the feeling they think this artist wanted to show.

Teach

Discuss Art Concepts Read page 28 with students. Then have them trace a jagged line in the artwork with their finger. Suggest that the artist might have used straight lines if he had wanted to create a serious feeling. Have students discuss the feeling that curved lines would create. (calmness) TEKS 3.1B

Think Critically

1. READING SKILL **What do you think the Wild West was like?** (Possible response: an exciting place) DRAW CONCLUSIONS

2. **Would you use zigzag lines to show a lazy feeling? Why or why not?** (Responses will vary.) PERSONAL RESPONSE

3. WRITE **Write a story about the scene in *Wild West*.** NARRATIVE TAKS Writing Objective 1

Lesson 2

Vocabulary

landscape

jagged lines

Lines Express Feelings

The image below is a **landscape**, or outdoor scene. Read the title of the painting. What feeling about the Wild West do you think the artist wanted to show?

Emil Armin, *Wild West*

Artists can use lines to show how they feel about something. In the painting above, the artist used thick, **jagged lines** to create an exciting feeling. The jagged lines also show that the land is rough and bumpy. How would the painting be different if the artist had used many straight lines? What feeling do you think gently curving lines would create?

28

Background Information

About the Artist

Emil Armin (ay•MEEL AR•min) (1883–1971) grew up in Romania. When he was a child, Armin carved wood to make canes and ornaments. He emigrated to Chicago, Illinois, when he was 21 years old. He is best known for his paintings and woodblock prints of life in modern Chicago.

For additional information about Emil Armin, see pp. R44–R59.

RECOMMENDED READING

The Class Artist by G. Brian Karas. Greenwillow, 2001. CHALLENGING

★ **TEKS 3.1A** identify sources for ideas; **TEKS 3.1B** identify elements and principles; **TEKS 3.2A** create artworks; **TEKS 3.4A** identify intent in personal artworks; **PDAS Domain I** active participation; **PDAS Domain II** learner-centered instruction; **PDAS Domain III** evaluation and feedback; **PDAS Domain IV** classroom management; *(continued)*

Artist's Workshop

Expressive Line Drawing

PLAN

Choose an outdoor scene you would like to draw. Then think about the feelings you would like to express. What kinds of lines will you use? Sketch some ideas.

CREATE

1. Copy your best sketch onto white paper.
2. Add details to the landscape. Include different lines that show your feelings about the scene.
3. Use colored pencils to finish the drawing.

REFLECT

What kinds of lines did you use in your drawing? How do the lines show your feelings about the scene?

These lines can show different feelings. You may want to use some of them in your drawing.

curved	zigzag	jagged	vertical
calm	powerful	exciting	strong

29

Social Studies Connection

The Wild West Tell students that "Wild West" describes a time when pioneers created cities and towns in the western United States. Explain that it was an exciting period in United States history. Have students find one fact about the Wild West and share it with the class.

PDAS Domain IV

ESL Use **visuals** to support **comprehensible input** for kinds of outdoor scenes. Display ***Picture Cards Collection*** cards 58, 81, and 89 for students to use as a reference.

See also ***Picture Card Bank* CD-ROM,** Category: Places People Go.

30-40 Minutes

Artist's Workshop

Expressive Line Drawing

MATERIALS: sketchbook, pencil, white paper, colored pencils

Have students first draw the contour lines that show objects.

PLAN Have students select a scene based on an experience and identify sensory knowledge as the source for the life event. TEKS 3.1A

CREATE As students create artworks based on experiences, tell them to keep in mind the feeling they want to show. TEKS 3.2A

REFLECT Have students identify the expressive qualities of the lines they used in their artworks. TEKS 3.4A

Activity Options PDAS Domain IV

Quick Activity Have students sketch a landscape using three different kinds of lines.

Early Finishers Have students use Discussion Card 6 to discuss their finished drawings.

Challenge See *Teacher Resource Book*, p. 52.

5-10 Minutes

Wrap-Up

Informal Assessment PDAS Domain III

- **Are the lines in your landscape like the ones Emil Armin used? Explain.** (Responses will vary.) EVALUATION/CRITICISM TEKS 3.1B
- **How could you change your drawing to make it express a different feeling?** (Responses will vary.) PERCEPTION/AESTHETICS

Extend Through Writing

TAKS Writing Objective 1

Descriptive Paragraph Have students write a paragraph describing their landscape.

PDAS Domains I, II

Wassily Kandinsky

ARTIST BIOGRAPHY

DISCUSS THE IMAGES

Have students read pages 30–31.

- Discuss images A and B with students. Ask them to describe what makes these two paintings different from realistic paintings, which look more like photographs.
- Discuss with students the feeling of excitement in image A that's created by the different kinds of lines. Then ask students to identify sensory knowledge and life experiences as sources for ideas about visual symbols that could describe the kind of music that might have inspired Kandinsky to use these lines as visual symbols for feelings. TEKS 3.1A
- Display **Art Print 2,** an additional image by Kandinsky. Ask students to describe the subject of the painting and to compare it with images A and B. Explain that *Houses in Munich* was painted in 1908, *Yellow-Red-Blue* in 1925, and *Varied Rectangle* in 1929. Point out that these three paintings show how Kandinsky's style changed over many years.
- Ask students to discuss the feeling that Kandinsky tried to express with the straight horizontal and vertical lines in image B.

ART ⟷ SOCIAL STUDIES CONNECTION

Wassily Kan

Why do artists paint pictures that do not show real objects?

In 1895, Wassily Kandinsky (vuh•SEEL•yee kan•DIN•skee) saw an artwork that confused him. He could not figure out what the artist had painted. At the time, Kandinsky thought artists should make their artworks look almost like photographs. His first paintings had shown real objects — houses and outdoor scenes. Look at images **A** and **B**. How do you think Kandinsky's ideas about art changed?

Kandinsky saw ways in which art and music are alike. He used lines, shapes, and colors to express feelings the way instruments do in music. What feeling does image **A** express?

Wassily Kandinsky, *Yellow-Red-Blue*

Background Information

About the Artist

Wassily Kandinsky (vuh•SEEL•yee kan•DIN•skee) (1866–1944) was a Russian painter, stage designer, decorative artist, costume designer, teacher, and writer. Kandinsky and German painter Franz Marc founded an Expressionist art movement they named "The Blue Rider" after the title of one of Kandinsky's paintings.

For additional information about Kandinsky, see pp. R44–R59.

For related artworks, see **Electronic Art Gallery CD-ROM, Primary.**

★ **TEKS 3.1A** identify sources for ideas; **TEKS 3.2C** produce various artworks; **TEKS 3.4A** identify intent in personal artworks; **TEKS 3.4B** identify main ideas in artworks by peers and others; **PDAS Domain I** active participation; **PDAS Domain II** learner-centered instruction

dinsky

Kandinsky's style of painting became very popular with artists who wanted to try something new. These artists were called Expressionists because they used art to express feelings.

 Wassily Kandinsky, *Varied Rectangle (Variierte Rechtecke)*

DID YOU KNOW?

Many artists travel around the world to see new things and to learn from other artists. Kandinsky lived in Russia, France, and Germany. The image below is a picture of his studio in Germany.

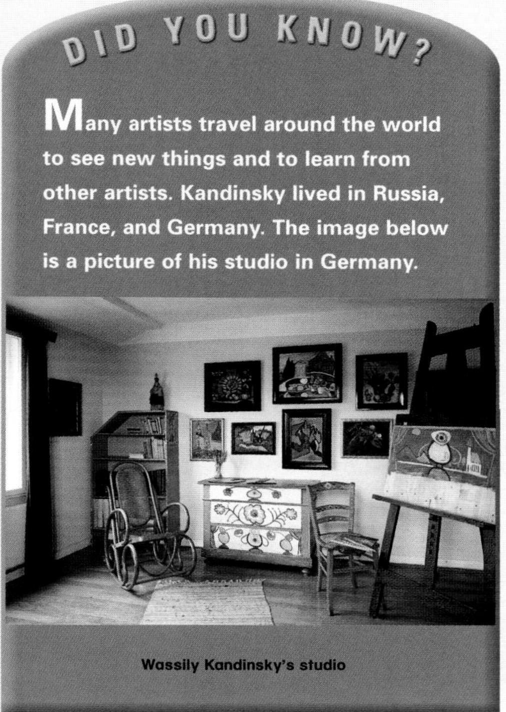

Wassily Kandinsky's studio

Think About Art

Think of a song that you enjoy. If you were to paint while listening to the song, what would your painting look like? What kinds of lines would you use?

Multimedia Biographies
Visit *The Learning Site*
www.harcourtschool.com

31

Performing Arts Connection

Musical Inspiration Kandinsky was inspired by the music of Richard Wagner, a German composer. Wagner's opera *Lohengrin* reminded Kandinsky of his childhood home.

For additional cross-curricular suggestions, see Art Transparency 2.

TEKS 3.4B

Visit with an Artist

Portfolios and Exhibitions Arrange for students to visit with a local artist, either at school or at a museum. Ask students to apply simple criteria they have learned from this unit to identify main ideas in the artist's original artworks, portfolio, and the exhibit.

DID YOU KNOW?

Tell students that Kandinsky, like many painters, created artworks inside his various studios. Use the facts below and the photograph of Kandinsky's studio to discuss artists' tools and materials.

- Point out the easel. Explain that an easel holds an artist's canvas.
- Tell students that a palette is a board on which artists mix paints. Have them find a palette on the chair in the photograph. Then ask students to find other artists' tools in the photograph.

Think About Art

Think of a song that you enjoy. If you were to paint while listening to the song, what would your painting look like? What kinds of lines would you use? (Responses will vary. Ask students to identify their sensory knowledge of the qualities of the music that would be a source for their ideas about visual symbols. Ask them to share feelings and life experiences that gave them their ideas.) PERSONAL RESPONSE TEKS 3.1A

ARTIST'S EYE ACTIVITY

Draw in Kandinsky's Style Have students use pencils and markers to draw a variety of lines that express similar and different feelings. If possible, have students choose music to listen to as they draw. Then have them identify the expressive qualities in their artworks and describe the feelings that the lines express. TEKS 3.2C, TEKS 3.4A

Multimedia Biographies
Visit *The Learning Site*
www.harcourtschool.com

Lesson 3

PDAS Domains I, II

Geometric and Organic Shapes

OBJECTIVES
- Identify shapes in artworks
- Produce shape designs
- Draw conclusions about artworks

RESOURCES
- Discussion Card 9, p. R38
- Electronic Art Gallery CD-ROM, Primary

Warm-Up

Build Background Have students name different kinds of shapes, and draw them on the board. Then have students look for examples of each shape in the classroom.

Teach

Discuss Art Concepts Read page 32 with students. Have them identify circles, triangles, and rectangles in the artwork. Then help them identify the organic shapes, such as the leaves, the bird, and the plants. TEKS 3.1B

Think Critically

1. READING SKILL **What kinds of shapes would you use to paint a garden? Why?** (Possible response: organic, because they are usually found in nature) DRAW CONCLUSIONS

2. **How are geometric shapes different from organic shapes?** (Geometric shapes have regular edges; organic shapes have irregular borders.) PERCEPTION/AESTHETICS

3. **WRITE** **Write a list of objects in your classroom that have geometric shapes.** DESCRIPTIVE

Lesson 3

Vocabulary

- two-dimensional
- geometric shapes
- organic shapes

Geometric and Organic Shapes

Shapes are **two-dimensional**, or flat. You can measure the height and width of a shape.

Artists use lines to make shapes. **Geometric shapes** such as squares, rectangles, and triangles can be drawn with straight lines. Circles and ovals are geometric shapes that have curved edges. What geometric shapes do you see in this artwork?

Unknown artist, Brazilian Tapestry (Six Patterns)

Organic shapes are found in nature. They show things such as flowers and can be drawn with wavy lines and irregular borders. Find some organic shapes in the artwork. What objects from nature do they show?

32

Background Information

Art History

Tapestries have been woven on hand looms since ancient times. Weavers in ancient China and Greece created tapestries of wool and silk. In medieval times, colorful tapestries were hung on the stone walls of European palaces. In the twentieth century, artists like Henri Matisse created tapestries with bold designs. Tapestries are made today in many cultures as a folk tradition.

RECOMMENDED READING

The Life and Work of Wassily Kandinsky by Paul Flux. Heinemann, 2002. AVERAGE

★ TEKS 3.1B identify elements and principles; PDAS Domain I active participation; PDAS Domain II learner-centered instruction; PDAS Domain III evaluation and feedback; PDAS Domain IV classroom management; TAKS Writing Objective 1 composition

Artist's Workshop

Shape Design

PLAN

Sketch a design made up of geometric and organic shapes. Draw smaller shapes inside larger shapes.

CREATE

1. **Copy the shapes from your sketch onto colored construction paper.**
2. **Cut out the shapes.**
3. **Use your sketch as a guide to place the shapes. Then glue them onto black paper.**

REFLECT

Look at your design. Describe the organic shapes. What kinds of geometric shapes did you use?

Quick Tip: Trace classroom objects or use a ruler to draw geometric shapes. You might trace the top of a cup to draw a circle.

33

Math Connection

Geometric Shapes Have students name and discuss the geometric shapes in their design, telling the number of sides and corners in each.

triangle	square	pentagon
3 sides	4 sides	5 sides

PDAS Domain IV

ESL Clarify words and phrases to give **language support** to students. Remind students that a sketch is a drawing. As students work, reinforce the names of shapes in their designs.

Special Needs Students with visual impairments may use precut shapes to create their designs.

30-40 Minutes

Artist's Workshop

Shape Design

MATERIALS: sketchbook, pencil, construction paper, scissors, glue

Quick Tip: Students can write the colors they will use on their sketch.

PLAN Remind students that shapes can be drawn with regular or irregular edges.

CREATE Encourage students to overlap some of the shapes in their arrangement.

REFLECT Have students point out and name the shapes in their designs. Ask them to describe their favorite part of the design. TEKS 3.1B

Activity Options PDAS Domain IV

Quick Activity Have students draw shape designs with markers.

Early Finishers Partners may use Discussion Card 9 to talk about their artworks.

Challenge See *Teacher Resource Book*, p. 53.

5-10 Minutes

Wrap-Up

Informal Assessment PDAS Domain III

- **How did the shapes in the tapestry help you create your own design?** (Responses will vary.) PERCEPTION/AESTHETICS
- **If you used a ruler to draw a shape, what kind of shape would you be drawing?** (geometric) DRAW CONCLUSIONS

Extend Through Writing

TAKS Writing Objective 1

Compare-and-Contrast Paragraph Have students write a paragraph comparing and contrasting geometric and organic shapes.

Lesson 4

PDAS Domains I, II

Shapes in Still Lifes

OBJECTIVES
- Identify shapes in artworks
- Produce a still-life painting using design skills
- Draw conclusions about artworks

RESOURCES
- Art Print 13
- Electronic Art Gallery CD-ROM, Primary

5 Minutes

Warm-Up

Build Background Display **Art Print 13**. Have students describe what they see and point out the geometric and organic shapes. Explain that they will learn about artworks that show groups of objects arranged by the artist. TEKS 3.1B

10-15 Minutes

Teach

Discuss Art Concepts Have students read page 34 and identify the fruits in image A as organic shapes. Ask them to describe how image A is arranged. Have students compare images B and C. Point out that each artist used similar shapes in a different way. TEKS 3.1B

Think Critically

1. READING SKILL **Why do you think an artwork that shows an arrangement of objects is called a still life?** (The objects do not move.) DRAW CONCLUSIONS
2. **How do artists make a composition?** (by arranging lines, shapes, and colors) PERCEPTION/AESTHETICS
3. WRITE **Describe an arrangement of objects that would make an interesting still life.** DESCRIPTIVE TAKS Writing Objective 1

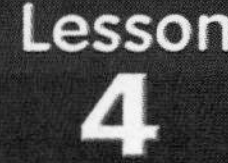

Lesson 4

Vocabulary

still life

composition

Shapes in Still Lifes

A **still life** is an artwork that shows a group of objects. Everyday objects are often the subjects of still lifes.

To create a still life, an artist arranges geometric and organic shapes into an interesting composition. A **composition** is the way an artist puts together lines, shapes, and colors in an artwork. What geometric and organic shapes do you see in image **A**? How would you describe this still life?

Image **B** is also a still life. Describe the composition the artist used. Now look at the still life in image **C**, and point out the geometric and organic shapes you see.

A Fernando Botero, *Fruit*

Background Information

About the Artists

A Fernando Botero (1932–) grew up in Colombia, South America. He owns the biggest collection of his own art because he hates to sell it!

B William H. Johnson (1901–1970) painted scenes from African American history and from his childhood in the South.

For additional information about the artists, see pp. R44–R59.

RECOMMENDED READING

Start with Art: Still Life by Sue Lacey. Copper Beech, 2000. CHALLENGING

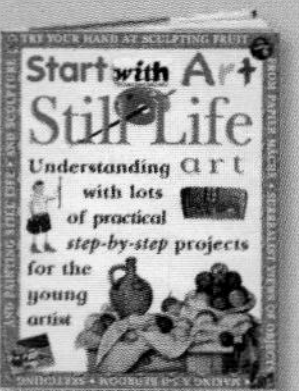

★ **TEKS 3.1B** identify elements and principles; **TEKS 3.2A** create artworks; **TEKS 3.2B** develop effective compositions; **TEKS 3.4A** identify intent in personal artworks; **PDAS Domain I** active participation; **PDAS Domain II** learner-centered instruction; **PDAS Domain III** evaluation and feedback; *(continued)*

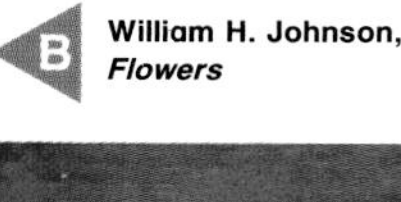

B William H. Johnson, *Flowers*

C Lauren, grade 3, *Autumn Still Life*

Artist's Workshop

Still-Life Painting

1. On a desk or table, arrange some objects that have different shapes and sizes. Create an interesting composition.
2. Sketch your still life by drawing the geometric and organic shapes you see.
3. Paint your still life.

35

Science Connection

Variety in Nature Have students choose an ecosystem and use online resources to research the fruits and flowers that grow in it. Then have students list the uses that humans have found for these plants.

PDAS Domain IV

ESL Use the Still-Life Painting activity as an opportunity for **vocabulary development.** Encourage peer interaction by having pairs of students discuss each of the steps in the project together. When students have completed their paintings, have them talk about the objects in their partner's artwork.

Still-Life Painting

MATERIALS: various objects, white paper, pencil, tempera paints, paintbrushes, water bowl

Tell students to place small objects in front of larger objects.

PLAN Have students look back at the still lifes in this lesson.

CREATE Tell students to arrange their objects to develop a variety of effective compositions using design skills. Then have them create their artworks based on personal observations. TEKS 3.2A, TEKS 3.2B

REFLECT Have students identify the general intent in their artworks. TEKS 3.4A

Activity Options PDAS Domain IV

Quick Activity Students may sketch a still-life arrangement.

Early Finishers Have students add to their paintings an object from their imagination.

Challenge See *Teacher Resource Book*, p. 54.

Wrap-Up

Informal Assessment PDAS Domain III

- **How did the images in this lesson help you arrange your still life?** (Responses will vary.) PERCEPTION/AESTHETICS
- **Describe the composition of a classmate's painting.** (Responses will vary.) EVALUATION/CRITICISM

Extend Through Writing

Chart Have students list the objects in their still life in a chart, under the headings Geometric Shapes and Organic Shapes.

PDAS Domain IV classroom management; TAKS Writing Objective 1 composition

PDAS Domains I, II

Art and Geometry

EVERYDAY ART

DISCUSS THE IMAGES

Have students read pages 36–37.

- Have students discuss the subject in image A and identify the shapes they see. Ask them to talk about why the triangles make the cat look sharp-edged instead of soft and furry. TEKS 3.1B
- Explain to students that flat shapes such as squares and rectangles can be made by combining two or more triangles. Have students look for shapes on the cat's head and tail that are not triangles. Have them use their fingers to trace diagonal lines in those shapes to show that the shapes are made up of triangles. TEKS 3.1B
- Discuss with students the objects in image B. Ask students how they can tell that the artwork is not flat. (The objects have shadows; the artwork doesn't look as if it was painted on a canvas or on paper.) Point out that flat objects would not cast the shadows shown in image B.

ART ⟷ MATH CONNECTION

Art and Geometry

Why is math important to artists?

Math has always been an important tool for artists. Shapes that are used in math can be found in almost every artwork. Look at the cat in image A. It was made almost completely with triangles. Does the cat look as soft and smooth as a real cat? Why or why not?

A Diana Ong, *Kat*

36

Background Information

About the Artists

A Diana Ong (1940–) creates art by using and combining many kinds of media, from woodcuts to computer art.

B Dame Barbara Hepworth (1903–1975) is known for creating sculptures with open or hollowed-out spaces.

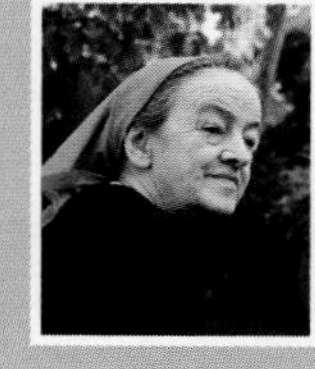

For additional information about the artists, see pp. R44–R59.

For related images, see **Electronic Art Gallery CD-ROM, Primary.**

★ **TEKS 3.1B** identify elements and principles; **TEKS 3.2C** produce various artworks; **TEKS 3.4B** identify main ideas in artworks by peers and others; **PDAS Domain I** active participation; **PDAS Domain II** learner-centered instruction

Image **B** shows an artwork that is not made up of flat shapes. The artwork can be viewed from different sides. Which part of it looks like a ball? Do the other parts look like objects you recognize?

DID YOU KNOW?

The artist of image A did not use paints or pencils. She created the image with a computer. In the past, artists had to use numbers to tell computers where to place lines and colors. Now artists can draw computer images more easily with a mouse.

Think About Art

Think of an animal you would like to draw. What geometric shapes could you use?

B Dame Barbara Hepworth, *Three Forms*

Science Connection

Marble Tell students that the sculpture in image B is carved from white marble, a metamorphic rock that has been changed by heat and pressure below the earth's surface.

For additional cross-curricular suggestions, see Art Transparency 3.

TEKS 3.4B

Student Art Show

Portfolios and Exhibitions Have students create an exhibit of their portfolios and finished artworks. Ask students to apply simple criteria related to line, shape, and form to identify main ideas in one another's original artworks and portfolios and in the exhibit as a whole.

DID YOU KNOW?

Use the facts below to discuss computer art with students.

- Computer-art software programs help an artist draw, color, shade, and move an image by using commands from the keyboard. The computer processes the images by using a mathematical language.
- An artist can use a mouse, a light pen, or a pressure-sensitive tablet to draw. The artist can also scan in other artwork or photographs to add to the image on the screen.
- Computer art is used to create animation and special effects in movies and video games.

Think About Art

Think of an animal you would like to draw. What geometric shapes could you use?
(Responses will vary.) PERSONAL RESPONSE

ARTIST'S EYE ACTIVITY

Geometric Sponge Prints Ask students to produce prints, using a variety of art materials appropriately. Have students cut out triangles, circles, and squares from household sponges. Have them dip the sponges in paint and use them to create prints. Ask them to try to combine their shapes to make a recognizable object. TEKS 3.2C

Lesson 5

PDAS Domains I, II

Geometric and Organic Forms

OBJECTIVES
- Identify forms in artworks
- Produce ceramic sculptures
- Draw conclusions about artworks

RESOURCES
- Art Print 3
- Discussion Card 3, p. R35
- Electronic Art Gallery CD-ROM, Primary

5 Minutes

Warm-Up

Build Background Have students compare a drawing of a circle with a ball. Point out that both are round, but the circle is a flat shape. Display **Art Print 3** and ask students if they think the artwork is two-dimensional.

10-15 Minutes

Teach

Discuss Art Concepts Have students read page 38. Then tell them to find the cones and spheres in image A. As students examine image B, encourage them to name other organic forms, such as fruits and plants. TEKS 3.1B

Think Critically

1. **READING SKILL** **Why do you think the artist displayed image B in a garden?** (It is an organic form, and gardens have organic forms in them.) DRAW CONCLUSIONS

2. **How is a sculpture different from a painting?** (A painting is two-dimensional, and a sculpture is three-dimensional.) PERCEPTION

3. **WRITE** **Describe the parts of image A.** DESCRIPTIVE TAKS Writing Objective 1

Lesson 5

Vocabulary
- three-dimensional
- forms
- sculpture

Geometric and Organic Forms

Objects that are **three-dimensional** have height, width, and depth. They are called **forms**. Which of these geometric forms do you see around you?

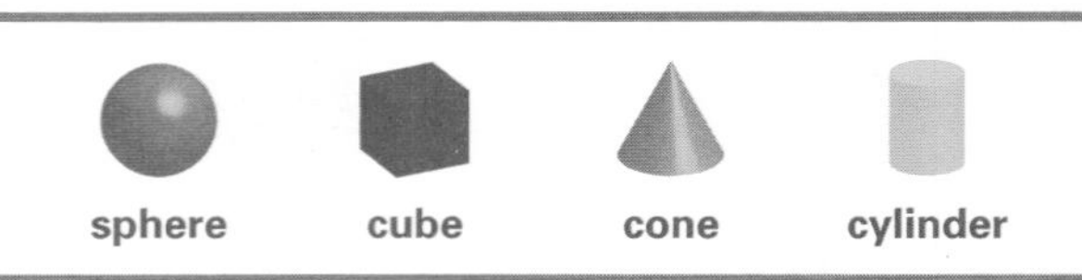

A **sculpture** is a three-dimensional artwork. Look at the sculpture in image A. What geometric forms did the artist use to show a person's head and body?

Image B shows an organic form. Organic forms are like the forms you see in nature. What object in nature does this form look like?

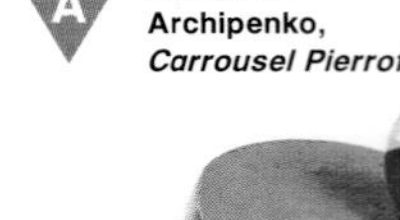
A Alexander Archipenko, *Carrousel Pierrot*

B Dale Chihuly, *Lime Mist Ikebana with Cascading Oxblood Leaf*

Background Information

About the Artist

Alexander Archipenko (ar•kih•PENG•koh) (1887–1964) was a Ukrainian sculptor. Of *Carrousel Pierrot,* Archipenko said he was inspired by a festival with "dozens of carrousels with horses, swings, gondolas, and airplanes. . . ."

For additional information about the artists in this lesson, see pp. R44–R59.

RECOMMENDED READING

Gugu's House by Catherine Stock. Clarion, 2001.
CHALLENGING

★ **TEKS 3.1A** identify sources for ideas; **TEKS 3.1B** identify elements and principles; **TEKS 3.2A** create artworks; **TEKS 3.2C** produce various artworks; **TEKS 3.4A** identify intent in personal artworks; **PDAS Domain I** active participation; **PDAS Domain II** learner-centered instruction; **PDAS Domain III** evaluation and feedback; *(continued)*

Artist's Workshop

Organic Form Sculpture

PLAN

Look at natural objects to get ideas for your sculpture. Sketch some ideas.

CREATE

1. **To get air bubbles out, put the clay on a paper bag and press down on it. Then fold the clay over and press down again.**
2. **Sculpt an organic form by pinching and pulling the clay.**
3. **Use carving tools to add details to your sculpture.**
4. **Let your sculpture dry completely.**

REFLECT

Describe the organic form you created. What object in nature does it look like?

Quick Tip: You can join two pieces of clay together by carving lines into both pieces. Then wet the pieces and press them together.

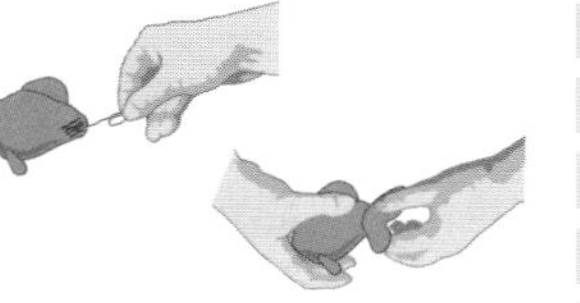

39

Science Connection

Glass Have students list several everyday objects made of glass, such as windows or lightbulbs. Then discuss reasons that glass is a useful material. Encourage students to recognize that glass is transparent and lets light through it.

PDAS Domain IV

ESL Use **visuals** to support **comprehensible input** for organic forms. Display ***Picture Cards Collection*** cards 14, 19, 53, and 55 for students to identify and use as reference.

See also ***Picture Card Bank* CD-ROM,** Category: Plants.

30-40 Minutes

Artist's Workshop

Organic Form Sculpture

MATERIALS: sketchbook, pencil, clay, paper bag, water bowl, carving tools

Quick Tip: Tell students to dampen their clay if it becomes dry.

PLAN Encourage students to keep their sketches simple.

CREATE Have students produce their ceramic sculpture, using a variety of art materials appropriately. TEKS 3.2A, TEKS 3.2C

REFLECT Have students explain how they were inspired by natural objects. TEKS 3.1A, TEKS 3.4A

Activity Options PDAS Domain IV

Quick Activity Distribute copies of the cube pattern on *Teacher Resource Book* page 44.

Early Finishers Have students discuss Art Print 3 with Discussion Card 3.

Challenge See *Teacher Resource Book*, p. 55.

5-10 Minutes

Wrap-Up

Informal Assessment PDAS Domain III

- **Why do you think clay is often used for organic sculptures?** (Possible response: It can be molded into forms with irregular edges.)
  PERCEPTION/AESTHETICS
- **How did looking at natural objects help you make your sculpture?** (Responses will vary.)
  PERSONAL RESPONSE

Extend Through Writing

TAKS Writing Objective 1

Persuasive Letter Have students write a letter that attempts to persuade a museum curator to exhibit their sculptures.

PDAS Domain IV classroom management; TAKS Writing Objective 1 composition

Unit 1

PDAS Domains I, III

Review and Reflect

Have students reflect on what they have learned about the ways artists use lines, shapes, and forms to create two-dimensional and three-dimensional artworks. Display **Art Prints 1, 2,** and **3**. Have students identify art elements such as line, shape, and form in the images. Encourage small groups of students to use their completed Word Knowledge Charts and Discussion Card 3, page R35, to discuss what they learned about line, shape, form, and other vocabulary and concepts in this unit. TEKS 3.1B

Vocabulary and Concepts

Have students read each sentence and choose the letter of the word or phrase that best completes it. (1. D; 2. C; 3. B; 4. D; 5. C)

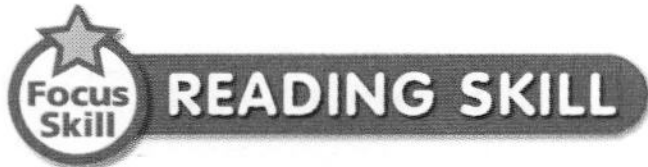

Draw Conclusions

Remind students that drawing a conclusion in art is like drawing a conclusion in reading. You use what you know and what you see to help you understand information. Tell students to use the information they read about Kandinsky, together with what they now know about how lines express feelings, to draw a conclusion about the style of the two paintings. Have partners work together to fill in their diagrams.
TAKS Reading Objectives 3, 4

What I Read
Kandinsky used lines to express feelings.

What I Know
The vertical lines in the paintings express strong feelings.

Conclusion
Kandinsky wanted his paintings to show strong feelings.

Unit 1 Review and Reflect

Vocabulary and Concepts

Choose the letter of the word or phrase that best completes each sentence.

1 Artists use ___ lines to outline objects.

A curved **C** wavy
B zigzag **D** contour

2 A ___ is a picture of an outdoor scene.

A still life **C** landscape
B composition **D** sculpture

3 A painting that shows a group of objects is a ___.

A sculpture **C** landscape
B still life **D** design

4 Shapes like those in nature are called ___.

A landscapes **C** forms
B geometric shapes **D** organic shapes

5 Shapes are flat, but forms are ___.

A two-dimensional **C** three-dimensional
B curved **D** straight

Focus Skill READING SKILL

Draw Conclusions

Reread pages 30–31. Use what you read and what you know to draw conclusions about Wassily Kandinsky's style of art. Use a diagram like the one shown here.

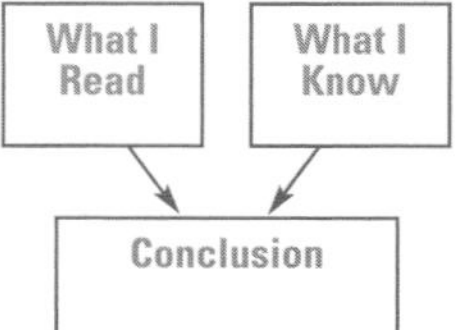

40

TEKS 3.1B

Home and Community Connection

School-Home Connection

Copy and distribute *Teacher Resource Book* pp. 85–86 to inform parents about upcoming art projects.

Community Connection

You may want to invite an artist from your community to share his or her portfolio with the class. Ask students to use simple criteria to identify important ideas in the artworks. For example, have them identify art elements such as line, shape, and form in the artworks.

★ **TEKS 3.1A** identify sources for ideas; **TEKS 3.1B** identify elements and principles; **TEKS 3.4B** identify main ideas in artworks by peers and others; **PDAS Domain I** active participation; **PDAS Domain III** evaluation and feedback; **TAKS Reading Objective 3** use a variety of strategies; *(continued)*

Write About Art

Choose an artwork from this unit. Then write a paragraph in which you draw conclusions about the artwork. Use a diagram to plan your writing.

REMEMBER—YOU SHOULD

- write about what you see and about what you already know.
- use correct grammar, spelling, and punctuation.

Critic's Corner

Look at *Prades, the Village* by Joan Miró (hoh•AHN mee•ROH) to answer the questions below.

DESCRIBE What do you see in the painting?

ANALYZE What kinds of lines did the artist use? Where do you see geometric and organic shapes?

INTERPRET What feeling do the lines express?

EVALUATE What do you think of the way the artist used lines and shapes to express a feeling? Explain your answer.

Joan Miró, *Prades, the Village*

41

PDAS Domain III

Assessment

Portfolio Assessment

Work with students to choose a piece of their artwork to include in their portfolios. Suggest that they decide which piece best fulfilled the assignment or which piece they liked best for another reason. You may want to provide specific feedback that targets students' use of the elements of art. See also Portfolio Recording Form, page R32.

Additional Assessment Options

- Progress Recording Form, p. R33
- Artist's Workshop Rubrics (Self/Teacher and Peer), pp. R30–R31
- Unit 1 Test, *Teacher Resource Book*, p. 99

Write About Art

Draw Conclusions Paragraph Read aloud the prompt with students. Suggest that they choose an artwork first and then reread the text about that artwork before they fill in the diagram. Remind them to use appropriate vocabulary words as they are writing. TAKS Reading Objective 4; TAKS Writing Objectives 1, 2, 5

Critic's Corner

RESPONSE/EVALUATION Use Discussion Card 2, page R34, and the steps below to guide students in analyzing *Prades, the Village* by Joan Miró.

DESCRIBE Students should describe the subject of the painting as a landscape, a village, or a town.

ANALYZE Tell students to identify straight, wavy, and zigzag lines. Point out the different lines the artist used to show the land. Students should recognize that the artist used geometric shapes on the buildings and organic shapes to show plants. TEKS 3.1B

INTERPRET Have students identify life experiences as sources for ideas about self to explain why the lines in the painting made them feel a certain way. TEKS 3.1A

EVALUATE Have students apply simple criteria to identify main ideas in the artworks. Remind students to support their opinions with reasons. You may want to model this step by stating your own opinion about the painting. TEKS 3.4B

TAKS Test Preparation: Reading and Writing Through Art, pp. 1–21

TAKS Reading Objective 4 apply critical-thinking skills; **TAKS Writing Objective 1** composition; **TAKS Writing Objective 2** conventions; **TAKS Writing Objective 5** usage

Unit 2

Color, Value, and Texture

The Artist's Plan

Artists choose colors and materials carefully to create a mood or to help viewers see something in a different way. In this unit students will see how artists can use color, value, and texture in their artworks.

Resources

- Unit 2 Art Prints (4–6)
- Additional Art Prints (2, 8)
- Art Transparencies 4–6
- Test Preparation: Reading and Writing Through Art, pp. 22–26
- Artist's Workshop Activities: English and Spanish, pp. 11–20
- Encyclopedia of Artists and Art History, pp. R44–R59
- Picture Cards Collection, cards 2, 29, 53, 67, 95, 111

Using the Art Prints

- Discussion Cards, pp. R34–R38
- Teaching suggestions, backs of Art Prints
- Art Print Teaching Suggestions: Spanish

Teacher Resource Book

- Vocabulary Cards in English and Spanish, pp. 11–14
- Reading Skill Card 2, p. 32
- Copying Master, p. 43
- Challenge Activities, pp. 56–60
- School-Home Connection: English/Spanish, pp. 87–88
- Unit 2 Test, p. 100

Technology Resources

Electronic Art Gallery CD-ROM, Primary

Picture Card Bank CD-ROM

Visit *The Learning Site*
www.harcourtschool.com

- Multimedia Art Glossary
- Multimedia Biographies
- Reading Skills and Activities

Art Prints for This Unit

ART PRINT 4

Water Lilies (Nympheas)
by Claude Monet

ART PRINT 5

Iris, Tulips, Jonquils and Crocuses
by Alma Woodsey Thomas

ART PRINT 6

From the Castle's Kitchen
by Patrick Dougherty

ART PRINT 2

Houses in Munich
by Wassily Kandinsky

ART PRINT 8

Taking in Laundry
by Grandma Moses

Unit 2 The Artist's Plan Color, Value, and Texture

Planning Guide

PDAS Domain IV

Lesson	Objectives and Vocabulary	Art Images	Production/ Materials
Main Idea, pp. 44–45			
6 **THE COLOR WHEEL** pp. 46–47 30–60 minutes	• Identify color in artworks • Produce paintings by mixing colors Identify main ideas **Vocabulary: primary colors, secondary colors, intermediate colors**	• **Woman pouring, Portuguese still life** by Robert Delaunay	**Indoor Scene Painting** ❑ white paper ❑ pencil ❑ tempera paints ❑ paintbrushes ❑ water bowl
7 **COLOR GROUPS** pp. 48–49 30–60 minutes	• Identify warm and cool colors in artworks • Produce drawings with warm or cool colors Identify main ideas **Vocabulary: warm colors, cool colors**	• **My Back Yard** by Georgia O'Keeffe • **Winter Palace** by Josephine Trotter	**Seasonal Drawing** ❑ white paper ❑ pencil ❑ markers or colored pencils
Art↔Social Studies Connection: Alma Woodsey Thomas, pp. 50–51			
8 **COLOR AND MOOD** pp. 52–53 30–60 minutes	• Identify value in artworks • Produce paintings with a variety of tints and shades Identify main ideas **Vocabulary: value, shades, tints**	• **Baile en Tehuantepec** by Diego Rivera	**Mood Painting** ❑ sketchbook ❑ pencil ❑ white paper ❑ tempera paints ❑ paintbrushes ❑ paper plate ❑ water bowl
9 **TACTILE TEXTURE** pp. 54–55 30–60 minutes	• Identify tactile texture in artworks and in the environment • Produce fiberart with different textures Identify main ideas **Vocabulary: tactile texture, weaving**	• **Object** by Meret Oppenheim • **Weaving** by Hailey, age 8	**Texture Weaving** ❑ 10 x 10-inch cardboard square ❑ ruler ❑ scissors ❑ tape ❑ string ❑ yarn and ribbons
Art↔Social Studies Connection: Traditions in Dance, pp. 56–57			
10 **VISUAL TEXTURE** pp. 58–59 30–60 minutes	• Identify visual texture in artworks • Produce rubbings with a variety of textures Identify main ideas **Vocabulary: photorealism, visual texture**	• **Dazzling Dozen** by Charles Bell • **Basket 26** by Jack Gunter	**Texture Rubbings** ❑ textured objects ❑ tracing paper ❑ peeled crayons ❑ scissors ❑ construction paper ❑ glue stick ❑ watercolors
Review and Reflect, pp. 60–61			

★ TEKS 3.2C produce various artworks; PDAS Domain IV classroom management

Main Idea, pp. 44-45

Opportunities for application of the skill are provided on pp. 46, 47, 48, 52, 54, 58, 59, 60, and 61.

Resources and Technology	Suggested Literature	Across the Curriculum
• Art Print 2 • Reading Skill Card 2  Electronic Art Gallery CD-ROM, Primary	*Color* by Ruth Heller 	**Science** Rainbow Colors, p. 47 **Reading** Main Idea, p. 46 **Writing** Expository Paragraph, p. 47
• Art Print 4 • Reading Skill Card 2 Electronic Art Gallery CD-ROM, Primary	*My Name is Georgia* by Jeanette Winter 	**Science** Weather Observations, p. 49 **Reading** Main Idea, p. 48 **Writing** Descriptive Paragraph, p. 49
• Art Print 8 • Reading Skill Card 2 Electronic Art Gallery CD-ROM, Primary	*How Artists Use Color* by Paul Flux 	**Social Studies** Mexican Geography, p. 53 **Reading** Main Idea, p. 52 **Writing** Song, p. 53
• Art Print 6 • Reading Skill Card 2 • Discussion Card 3, p. R35 Electronic Art Gallery CD-ROM, Primary	*Texture* by Rob Court 	**Science** Sense of Touch, p. 55 **Reading** Main Idea, p. 54 **Writing** How-to Paragraph, p. 55
• Discussion Card 3, p. R35 • Reading Skill Card 2 Electronic Art Gallery CD-ROM, Primary	*Micawber* by John Lithgow 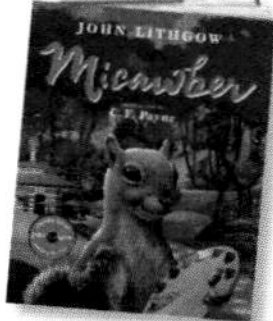	**Science** Magnification, p. 59 **Reading** Main Idea, p. 58 **Writing** List, p. 59

Art Puzzlers

Present these art puzzlers to students at the beginning or end of a class or when students finish an assignment early.

- Use surprising colors to paint a picture of an object. Mix **primary colors** to create all the colors in your painting. TEKS 3.2C
- Find a picture of an outdoor scene. Use **warm or cool colors** to draw or paint the scene in a different season. TEKS 3.2C
- Use **values** of one color to redesign the cover of a book you like. Paint your idea. TEKS 3.2C
- Find two objects with different **textures**. List several adjectives that describe each texture.
- Create a texture rubbing of a bumpy object. Then draw the object. Try to imitate the object's **visual texture** in your drawing. TEKS 3.2C

School-Home Connection

The activities above are included in the School-Home Connection for this unit. See *Teacher Resource Book*, pp. 87–88.

Assessment Options

- Rubrics and Recording Forms, pp. R30–R33
- Unit 2 Test, *Teacher Resource Book*, p. 100

Visit *The Learning Site*: **www.harcourtschool.com**

Artist's Workshops PREVIEW

PDAS Domain IV

Use these pages to help you gather and organize materials for the production activity in each lesson.

LESSON	MATERIALS
6 Indoor Scene Painting p. 47 **Objective:** Produce paintings by mixing primary colors to create secondary and intermediate colors  **30–40 minutes** **Challenge Activity:** See *Teacher Resource Book,* page 56.	• white paper • pencil • tempera paints • paintbrushes • water bowl 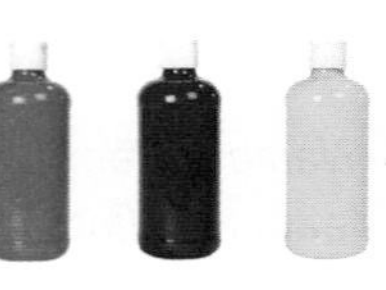
LESSON 7 Seasonal Drawing p. 49 **Objective:** Produce drawings with warm or cool colors  **30–40 minutes** **Challenge Activity:** See *Teacher Resource Book,* page 57.	• white paper • pencil • markers or colored pencils 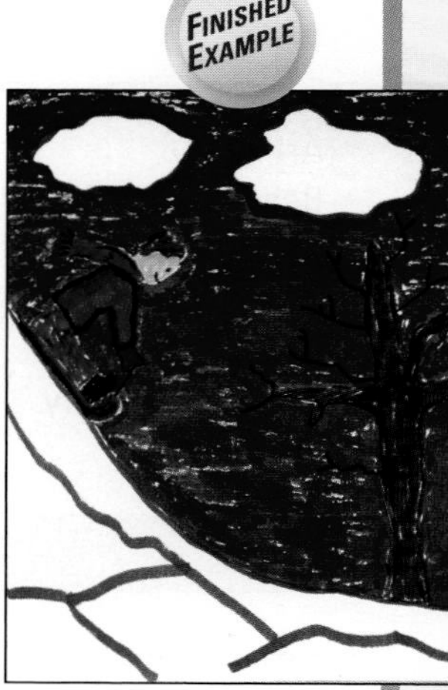

For safety information, see Art Safety, page R4; or the Art Safety Poster.

For information on media and techniques, see pp. R15–R23.

LESSON	MATERIALS

8 Mood Painting p. 53

Objective: Produce paintings with a variety of tints and shades

 **30–40 minutes**

Challenge Activity: See *Teacher Resource Book,* page 58.

- sketchbook
- pencil
- white paper
- tempera paints
- paintbrushes
- paper plate
- water bowl

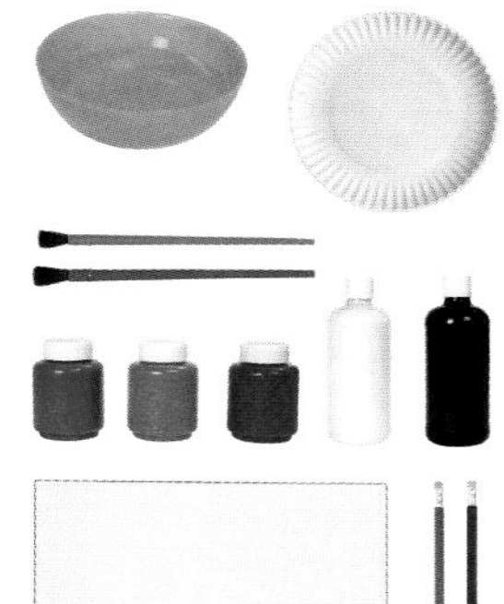

LESSON

9 Texture Weaving p. 55

Objective: Produce fiberart with different textures

 **30–40 minutes**

Challenge Activity: See *Teacher Resource Book,* page 59.

- 10 x 10-inch cardboard square
- ruler
- scissors
- tape
- string
- yarn
- ribbons

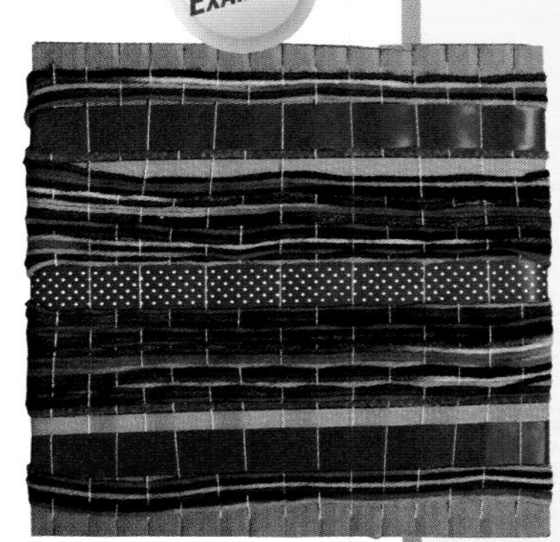

LESSON

10 Texture Rubbings p. 59

Objective: Produce an arrangement of rubbings with different textures

 **30–40 minutes**

Challenge Activity: See *Teacher Resource Book,* page 60.

- textured objects
- tracing paper
- peeled crayons
- pencil
- scissors
- construction paper
- glue stick
- watercolors
- paintbrushes
- water bowl

Unit 2

PDAS Domains I, II

The Artist's Plan

PREVIEW THE UNIT

Tell students that in this unit they will learn how artists can plan artworks. Have students page through the unit and predict some ways artists might plan an artwork. (make a sketch, select the materials, think about how to use line and shape)

SHARE THE POEM

Have students read aloud the poem on page 43 and then view the artwork.

How is the artwork like the objects in the poem? (The sculpture looks like a notebook with pages that have blown away; the objects in the poem have also been blown away by the wind.)

COMPARE AND CONTRAST

STEP INTO THE ART

Have students look carefully at the artwork and describe what they see.

Who do you think a notebook like this might belong to? What do you think the pages might say? (Responses will vary.)

PERSONAL RESPONSE

SHARE BACKGROUND INFORMATION

Tell students that *Torn Notebook* is a sculpture more than 22 feet tall. Explain that the notebook pages have handwritten notes describing the artists' observations about Lincoln, Nebraska, where the sculpture is located. The spiral binding represents a tornado moving across the plains.

LOCATE IT See **Using the Maps of Museums and Art Sites**, p. R2.

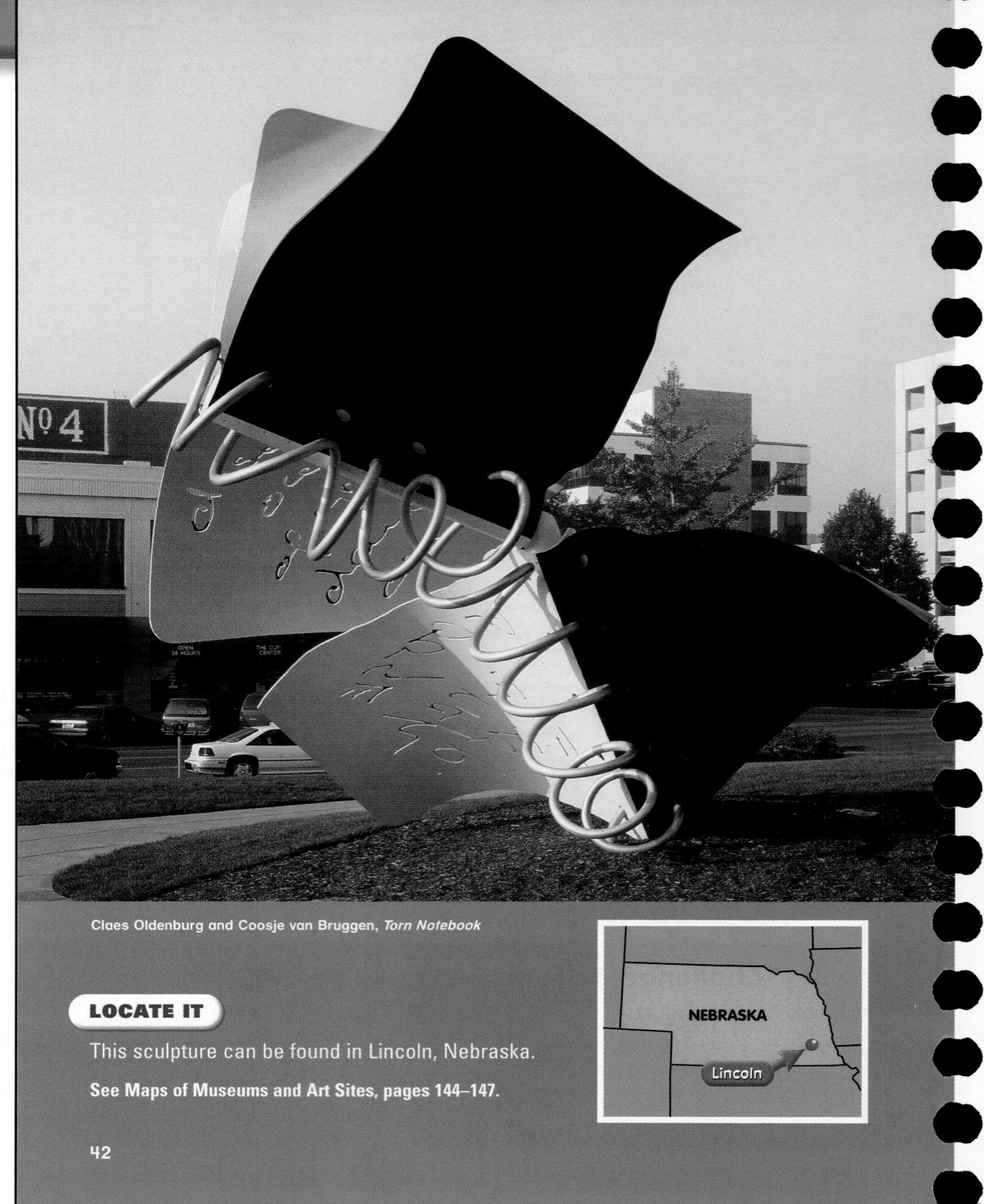

Claes Oldenburg and Coosje van Bruggen, *Torn Notebook*

LOCATE IT

This sculpture can be found in Lincoln, Nebraska.

See Maps of Museums and Art Sites, pages 144–147.

42

FYI

Background Information

About the Artists

In 1976, Claes Oldenburg (KLAS OHL•duhn•burg) (1929–) and Coosje van Bruggen (KOH•sha vahn BROO•guhn) (1942–) began collaborating to re-create everyday objects like an umbrella and a flashlight as huge metal sculptures.

For additional information about the artists, see the Encyclopedia of Artists and Art History, pp. R44–R59, and the Gallery of Artists, *Student Edition,* pp. 178–188.

For related artworks, see **Electronic Art Gallery CD-ROM, Primary.**

★ **PDAS Domain I** active participation; **PDAS Domain II** learner-centered instruction

Unit 2 Color, Value, and Texture

The Artist's Plan

Wind Tricks

The wind is full of tricks today,
He blew my daddy's hat away.
He chased our paper down the street.
He almost blew us off our feet.
He makes the trees and bushes dance.
Just listen to him howl and prance.

Anonymous

ABOUT THE ARTISTS

See Gallery of Artists, pages 178–188.

Unit Vocabulary

primary colors	shades
secondary colors	tints
intermediate colors	tactile texture
warm colors	weaving
cool colors	photorealism
value	visual texture

Multimedia Art Glossary
Visit *The Learning Site*
www.harcourtschool.com

43

Unit Vocabulary

Read aloud the terms with students, and use the Word Knowledge Chart below to assess and discuss their prior knowledge.

primary colors the colors red, yellow, and blue, which are mixed together to make other colors on the color wheel

secondary colors the colors orange, green, and violet, each of which is created by mixing two primary colors

intermediate colors colors that are created by mixing a primary color with a secondary color

warm colors the colors red, orange, and yellow, which appear on one half of the color wheel

cool colors the colors green, blue, and violet, which appear on one half of the color wheel

value the lightness or darkness of a color

shades dark values made by mixing black with a color

tints light values made by mixing white with a color

tactile texture the way a surface feels when you touch it

weaving an artwork made by lacing together fibers such as yarn, thread, or strips of fabric

photorealism a style of painting that looks almost like a photograph

visual texture the appearance of texture in an artwork

Language Arts Connection

Students may create a chart like the one below to identify familiar and unfamiliar vocabulary terms. Encourage them to add information to their charts as they work through this unit.

WORD KNOWLEDGE CHART		
I know this term.	I have seen this term before.	I have never seen this term.

Vocabulary Resources

- Vocabulary Cards in English and Spanish, *Teacher Resource Book,* pp. 11–14
- Student Edition Glossary, pp. 189–197

PDAS Domains I, II

Main Idea

SKILL TRACE	
MAIN IDEA	
Introduce	pp. 44–45
Review	pp. 46, 47, 48, 52, 54, 58, 59, 60, 61

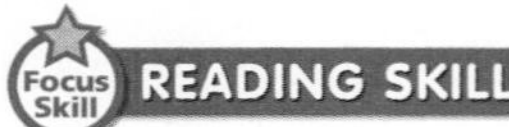

Main Idea

The *main idea* tells what something is mostly about. Details can help support the main idea.

The main idea of the painting below is that a train called the Ole '97 suddenly jumped off the tracks. You can tell this is the main idea by looking at these supporting details:

- what the title of the painting means
- why the people in the painting look surprised
- how the train tracks look

Thomas Hart Benton, *Wreck of the Ole '97*

44

DISCUSS THE SKILL

Access Prior Knowledge Explain to students that the main idea is what is most important about something. Point out that details support the main idea. Ask volunteers to share the name of a book they like. Then have them briefly tell what the book is mostly about, or give the main idea. Encourage students to share details that support the main idea, such as what the main characters are like or what they do. Classmates who have read the same books can add ideas.

APPLY TO ART

Identify Main Ideas in Art Have students read page 44. Then restate each of the bulleted points as a question to help students apply simple criteria to identify the main idea in this original artwork by a major artist. Discuss students' answers.

- What does the title mean? Point out that *ole* is a deliberate misspelling of the word *old*.
- Why do the people look surprised?
- How do the train tracks look?

Ask students to identify other details that support the main idea. (Possible response: Someone is falling out of the train; the train is tipping over; a woman has fallen off the wagon.) TEKS 3.4B

Background Information

About the Artist

Thomas Hart Benton (1889–1975) was influenced by the murals in the Capitol building in Washington, D.C., where his father was a member of Congress. Benton believed that American art should focus on the everyday lives of Americans, in a style that is easy to understand. He received praise for showing regional history in his murals in New York, Chicago, Indiana, and Missouri.

For additional information about Benton, see pp. R44–R59.

For related artworks, see **Electronic Art Gallery CD-ROM, Primary.**

★ **TEKS 3.4B** identify main ideas in artworks by peers and others; **PDAS Domain I** active participation; **PDAS Domain II** learner-centered instruction; **PDAS Domain IV** classroom management; **TAKS Reading Objective 1** demonstrate understanding of texts; **TAKS Reading Objective 3** use a variety of strategies

As you read, think about what the text is mostly about. This will help you understand what you are reading. Read the passage below. Look for details that support the main idea.

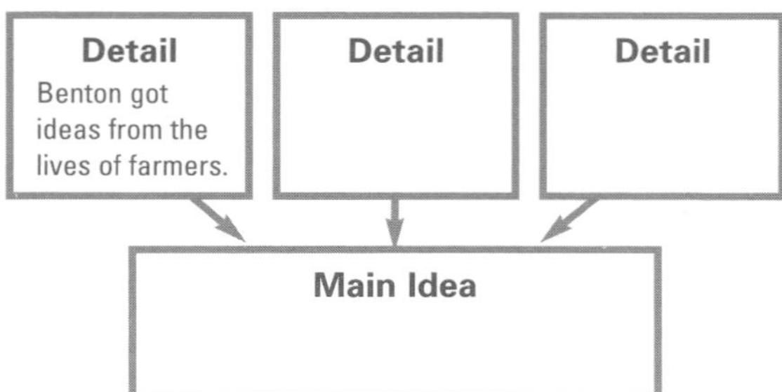
Thomas Hart Benton made paintings of scenes from American life. Benton got many of his ideas for paintings from the lives of farmers and railroad workers. He got other ideas from songs. He traveled around the country, making sketches of people living their lives. *Wreck of the Ole '97* is one of Benton's paintings. It is based on something that really happened.

What is this passage mostly about? What are some details in the passage? Use a diagram like this to help you.

Detail
Benton got ideas from the lives of farmers.

Detail

Detail

Main Idea

On Your Own

As you read the lessons in this unit, use diagrams like the one above to write about main ideas and details in the text and the artworks.

45

APPLY TO READING

Identify Main Ideas in Text Explain to students that identifying the main idea of a passage will help them check their understanding of the information. Point out that supporting details will often lead them to the main idea.

Have students read the passage about the artist Thomas Hart Benton on page 45. Work with them to complete the diagram to show the main idea and details. TAKS Reading Objectives 1, 3

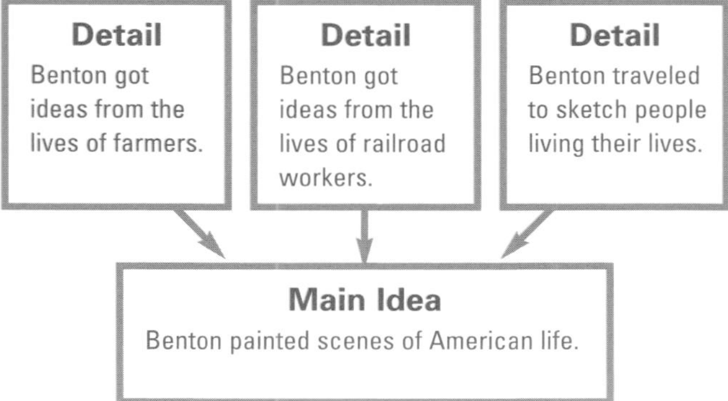

ON YOUR OWN

As students read the lessons in this unit, have them use diagrams to write about the main idea and details in the text and the artworks. TEKS 3.4B, TAKS Reading Objectives 1, 3

TAKS Reading Objectives 1, 3

Reading Skill Card

Distribute Reading Skill Card 2, *Teacher Resource Book,* page 32. Have students identify main ideas in this unit.

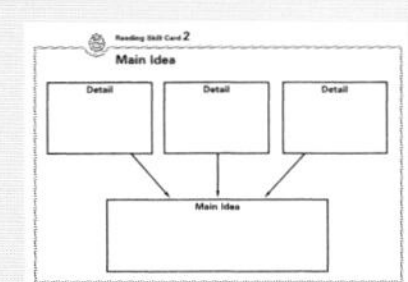

Extend the Skill For additional teaching suggestions, see **Art Transparency 4.**

PDAS Domain IV

ESL Pair **less fluent speakers** with more fluent peers to read the passage on page 45 together. Have partners work together to restate the passage in their own words and then complete Reading Skill Card 2 with the main idea and details. Have partners reread their completed diagrams together.

Reading Skills and Activities
Visit *The Learning Site*
www.harcourtschool.com

Lesson 6

PDAS Domains I, II

The Color Wheel

OBJECTIVES
- Identify color in artworks
- Produce paintings by mixing colors
- Identify main ideas

RESOURCES
- Art Print 2
- Electronic Art Gallery CD-ROM, Primary

5 Minutes

Warm-Up

Build Background Display **Art Print 2,** and ask volunteers to identify the colors they see in the artwork. List them on the board. Explain that many paint colors come from *pigments,* powders that are mixed with liquids to make paints. TEKS 3.1B

10-15 Minutes

Teach

Discuss Art Concepts Have students read page 46 and identify each of the primary colors in the painting. Then ask them to read page 47 and find details in the painting that are painted in secondary and intermediate colors. Point out that in the names of intermediate colors, the primary color is always named first. TEKS 3.1B

Think Critically

1. READING SKILL **Why are the primary colors important?** (They are the only colors you need to make any other color.) MAIN IDEA

2. **What colors would you mix to paint a realistic plum?** (red and blue to make violet) PERCEPTION/AESTHETICS

3. WRITE **Describe the color red for someone who has never seen it.** DESCRIPTIVE
TAKS Writing Objective 1

Lesson 6

Vocabulary
- primary colors
- secondary colors
- intermediate colors

The Color Wheel

Artists may use a color wheel to help them plan artworks. Look at the color wheel on page 47. Find the colors red, blue, and yellow. These are the **primary colors**. They can be mixed to make any other color on the color wheel. Now look at the painting below. Where do you see primary colors in this painting?

Robert Delaunay,
Woman pouring, Portuguese still life

Background Information

About the Artist

Robert Delaunay (duh•loh•NAY) (1885–1941) began his art career by painting theater scenery in France. His characteristic painting style is marked by the use of bold, bright colors. Delaunay is most famous for his series of paintings of the Eiffel Tower.

For additional information about Delaunay, see pp. R44–R59.

RECOMMENDED READING

Color by Ruth Heller. Putnam & Grosset, 1995.

AVERAGE

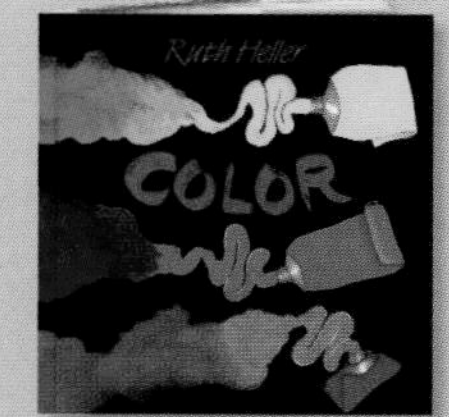

★ **TEKS 3.1A** identify sources for ideas; **TEKS 3.1B** identify elements and principles; **TEKS 3.2A** create artworks; **TEKS 3.2C** produce various artworks; **TEKS 3.4A** identify intent in personal artworks; **TEKS 3.4B** identify main ideas in artworks by peers and others; **PDAS Domain I** active participation; *(continued)*

Secondary colors are made by mixing two primary colors together. Orange, violet, and green are secondary colors. Find them on the color wheel. Red and yellow mixed together make orange. Which two primary colors mixed together make violet? What about green? Point out the secondary colors in the painting.

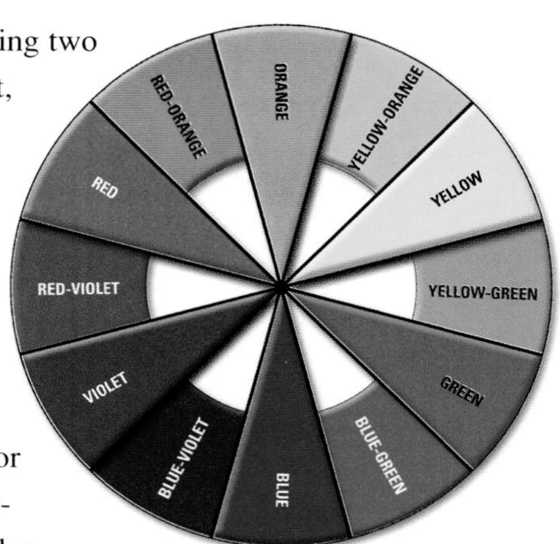

Now find blue and violet on the color wheel. The color between them is blue-violet. **Intermediate colors** are made by mixing a primary color with a secondary color that is next to it on the color wheel. Name the other intermediate colors on the color wheel.

Artist's Workshop

Indoor Scene Painting

1. **Use a pencil to draw a scene from a room you know well.**
2. **Decide what colors of paint you will use. Look at the color wheel above to help you mix your colors.**
3. **Paint the scene.**

47

Artist's Workshop

30-40 Minutes

Indoor Scene Painting

MATERIALS: white paper, pencil, tempera paints, paintbrushes, water bowl

Quick Tip Remind students to clean the brush in water before changing colors.

PLAN Ask students to identify life experiences as sources for ideas about self to show why the room is important to them. TEKS 3.1A

CREATE As students produce their paintings based on an experience, remind them to use art materials appropriately. TEKS 3.2A, TEKS 3.2C

REFLECT Have students identify the general intent in their own artworks. TEKS 3.4A

Activity Options PDAS Domain IV

Quick Activity Have students mix paints to make their own color wheels. See *Teacher Resource Book*, p. 43.

Early Finishers Have students paint an imaginary indoor scene.

Challenge See *Teacher Resource Book*, p. 56.

Wrap-Up

5-10 Minutes

Informal Assessment PDAS Domain III

- **What is the main idea of the painting on page 46?** (A woman is standing next to a group of objects.) MAIN IDEA TEKS 3.4B
- **What intermediate colors did you use in your painting?** (Responses will vary.) PERCEPTION/AESTHETICS

Extend Through Writing

TAKS Writing Objective 1

Expository Paragraph Have students write a paragraph that explains what the color wheel is.

Science Connection

Rainbow Colors Point out the similarities between a rainbow and the color wheel. Then have students research how a rainbow appears in the sky.

PDAS Domain IV

ESL Before beginning the activity, review the color wheel with students to help them **identify cognates.** Say each of the following words, and have students identify the related English word: *violeta, colores, primario, secundario,* and *intermedio.*

Lesson 7

PDAS Domains I, II

Color Groups

OBJECTIVES
- Identify warm and cool colors in artworks
- Produce drawings with warm or cool colors
- Identify main ideas

RESOURCES
- Art Print 4
- Electronic Art Gallery CD-ROM, Primary

5 Minutes

Warm-Up

Build Background Display **Art Print 4,** and ask students to identify the main colors. Ask if the painting makes them feel cool or warm. Explain that colors like green and blue are often used to paint water and that these colors can make viewers feel a certain way. TEKS 3.1B

10-15 Minutes

Teach

Discuss Art Concepts Have students read pages 48–49. Then ask them to identify the warm and cool colors in image B. Discuss reasons the artist might have used warm colors in a winter scene. (They show a warm sunset.) TEKS 3.1B

Think Critically

1. READING SKILL **How can artists use color groups to show weather?** (by using warm colors for warm weather and cool colors for cold weather) MAIN IDEA
2. **What colors would you use to show a rainy day?** (Responses will vary.) PERCEPTION/AESTHETICS
3. **WRITE** **Tell a short story about the scene in image B.** NARRATIVE TAKS Writing Objective 1

Lesson 7

Vocabulary

warm colors

cool colors

Color Groups

Look at images **A** and **B**. What kind of weather do you see in these paintings? What colors did the artist use in image **A**?

Artists often use colors such as red, orange, and yellow to show warm places. Red, orange, and yellow are **warm colors**. Find them on the color wheel on page 47. In image **A** the artist used mostly warm colors to create the hot feeling of a desert.

Georgia O'Keeffe, *My Back Yard*

48

Background Information

About the Artist

Georgia O'Keeffe (1887–1986) was inspired by the stark New Mexico landscape from the time she first painted there in 1929. She referred to the land as "the faraway" and felt that the thin, dry desert air helped her see farther.

For additional information about the artists, see pp. R44–R59.

RECOMMENDED READING

My Name is Georgia by Jeanette Winter. Harcourt, 1998. AVERAGE

★ **TEKS 3.1A** identify sources for ideas; **TEKS 3.1B** identify elements and principles; **TEKS 3.2A** create artworks; **TEKS 3.2C** produce various artworks; **TEKS 3.4B** identify main ideas in artworks by peers and others; **PDAS Domain I** active participation; **PDAS Domain II** learner-centered instruction; *(continued)*

Cool colors are found opposite warm colors on the color wheel. Green, blue, and violet are cool colors. For the painting in image B, the artist used mostly cool colors to show a cold day. What other details in the painting tell you it is a winter scene? Where do you see warm colors in image B? Why do you think the artist used them?

B Josephine Trotter, *Winter Palace*

Artist's Workshop

Seasonal Drawing

1. **Think of an outdoor scene in summer or winter. Draw it on white paper.**
2. **Use either warm colors or cool colors to show weather in your scene.**
3. **Add details to your drawing that help show the kind of weather.**

49

30-40 Minutes Artist's Workshop

Seasonal Drawing

MATERIALS: white paper, pencil, markers or colored pencils

Quick Tip Have students refer to a color wheel as they choose colors.

PLAN Have students identify sensory knowledge and life experiences as sources for ideas to show a life event in their drawings. TEKS 3.1A

CREATE Tell students to use only warm or cool colors in their drawings. TEKS 3.2A, TEKS 3.2C

REFLECT Display drawings that show the same season together. Have students identify the main idea in each mini-exhibit. TEKS 3.4B

Activity Options PDAS Domain IV

Quick Activity Have students draw objects in both warm and cool colors and compare them.

Early Finishers Have students redraw their scene to show it in another season.

Challenge See *Teacher Resource Book*, p. 57.

5-10 Minutes Wrap-Up

Informal Assessment PDAS Domain III

- **How are the paintings in this lesson alike?** (Both use color groups to show weather.) PERCEPTION/AESTHETICS
- **How could you change your drawing to show a different season?** (Responses will vary.) EVALUATION/CRITICISM

Extend Through Writing TAKS Writing Objective 1

Descriptive Paragraph Have students write about how it feels to be outdoors in the weather pictured in their drawing.

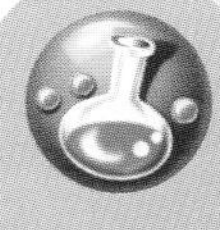

Science Connection

Weather Observations Have students work together to make a chart of the day's weather. Have them note the temperature, the amount of sunshine, and any precipitation or wind. Have students compare the weather outdoors with the weather in their Artist's Workshop drawings.

PDAS Domain IV

ESL Use **visuals** to support **comprehensible input** for weather terms. Display ***Picture Cards Collection*** cards 29, 95, and 111 for students to use as reference.

See also ***Picture Card Bank*** **CD-ROM**, Category: Weather.

PDAS Domain III evaluation and feedback; **PDAS Domain IV** classroom management; **TAKS Writing Objective 1** composition

PDAS Domains I, II

ALMA WOODSEY THOMAS

ARTIST BIOGRAPHY

DISCUSS THE IMAGES

Have students read pages 50–51.

- Have students describe the colors they see in image A. Ask them if the artist used warm or cool colors. Invite volunteers to tell what they think the patches of color represent. Then ask students to read the title of the painting. Discuss how the painting shows what fall is like. TEKS 3.1B
- Have students discuss experiences they have had looking at the ground from the window of an airplane or a tall building. Point out that details disappear from a vantage point that high, but colors are still visible. Ask them to identify sensory knowledge and life experiences to describe how they would use colors and shapes as visual symbols to show a forest in summer. TEKS 3.1A
- As students view image B, have them speculate about why the center of the painting is round. (Possible response: It is a view from a spacecraft window.)
-  Display **Art Print 5,** a painting of a garden from above, and ask students to compare it with image B. Then have them identify primary, secondary, and intermediate colors in **Art Print 5**. TEKS 3.1B

How do artists get ideas for their artworks?

Alma Woodsey Thomas was an artist for most of her life. As a child, she used clay from a river near her home to make sculptures. Her memories of the flowers outside her home became part of her paintings many years later.

Thomas saw nature in a special way. From her window, she watched patches of color change with the seasons. In her paintings, she used patches of color, too. She sometimes used them to show how the ground might look from an airplane. Look at the shapes and colors in image A. What season do you think they show?

Alma Woodsey Thomas, *Fall Begins*

50

Background Information

About the Artist

Alma Woodsey Thomas (1891–1978) was eighty years old when she became the first African American woman to have a solo show at the Whitney Museum of Art in New York City. She is best known for large, irregularly patterned works painted with thick, bright colors.

For additional information about Thomas, see pp. R44–R59.

 For related artworks, see **Electronic Art Gallery CD-ROM, Primary.**

★ **TEKS 3.1A** identify sources for ideas; **TEKS 3.1B** identify elements and principles; **TEKS 3.2C** produce various artworks; **TEKS 3.4B** identify main ideas in artworks by peers and others; **PDAS Domain I** active participation; **PDAS Domain II** learner-centered instruction

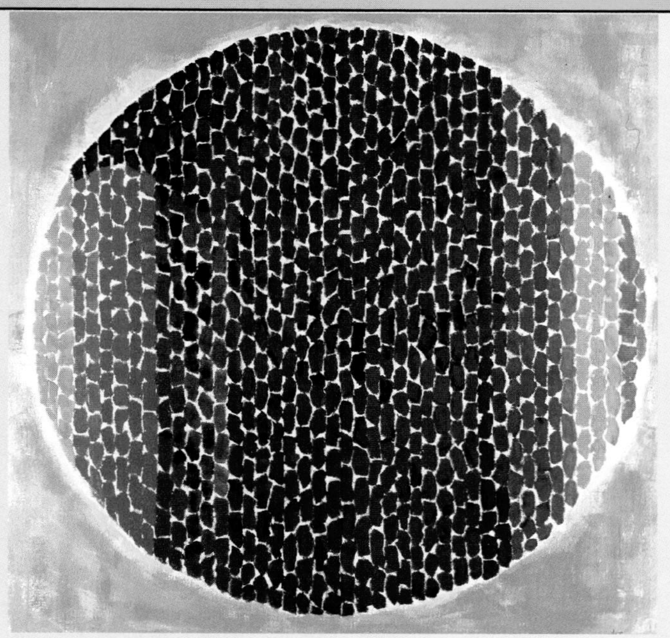

Alma Woodsey Thomas, *Snoopy—Early Sun Display on Earth*

Thomas also used art to show her interest in space. Look at the title of image B. *Snoopy* was the nickname for a real spacecraft. Thomas imagined what the astronauts saw looking out from space. What do you see in image B?

THINK ABOUT ART

What would you like to paint from a spacecraft view? What colors would you use?

DID YOU KNOW?

Snoopy was part of the *Apollo 10* space mission in 1969. The astronauts on the mission went closer to the moon than anyone had been before. They took pictures to help other astronauts get ready for a moon landing later that year.

Multimedia Biographies
Visit *The Learning Site*
www.harcourtschool.com

51

DID YOU KNOW?

Use the facts below to discuss Alma Woodsey Thomas's interest in the space program.

- Inspired by the Apollo mission's space explorations, Alma Woodsey Thomas began a group of paintings called *Space Series.*
- The paintings do not show any realistic images of planets or space, but the colors and shapes suggest the mysterious wonder of space.
- Thomas used photographs taken from satellites as inspiration for some of her images.

What would you like to paint from a spacecraft view? What colors would you use?

(Responses will vary.) PERSONAL RESPONSE

ARTIST'S EYE ACTIVITY

View from a Spacecraft Window Have students produce paintings of their imagined spacecraft view, using a variety of art materials appropriately. Have them refer to a color wheel to mix primary colors to create secondary and intermediate colors. Before students begin, suggest that they look at color photographs taken from space. TEKS 3.2C

Science Connection

Apollo 10 *Apollo 10* consisted of the Command and Service Module, named *Charlie Brown*, and the Lunar Module, named *Snoopy*. These are names from the *Peanuts* comic strip.

For additional cross-curricular suggestions, see Art Transparency 5.

TEKS 3.4B

View an Artist's Work

Portfolios and Exhibitions Arrange for students to visit a museum or gallery to view original artworks in a major artist's portfolio or exhibition. Students should apply simple criteria they learned in this unit to identify main ideas.

Multimedia Biographies
Visit *The Learning Site*
www.harcourtschool.com

Lesson 8

PDAS Domains I, II

Color and Mood

OBJECTIVES
- Identify value in artworks
- Produce paintings with a variety of tints and shades
- Identify main ideas

RESOURCES
- Art Print 8
- Electronic Art Gallery CD-ROM, Primary

5 Minutes

Warm-Up

Build Background Display **Art Print 8,** and ask students what feeling they get from looking at the colors in the painting. Point out that part of the sky is dark and stormy and part is sunlit. Explain that in this lesson they will learn how artists choose colors to create a feeling.

10-15 Minutes

Teach

Discuss Art Concepts Have students read page 52. Students should recognize that Rivera used mostly warm colors to create a cheerful, festive mood. Have students find the darkest shade and lightest tint of yellow and green in the painting. TEKS 3.1B

Think Critically

1. READING SKILL **How do artists make shades and tints?** (by mixing a color with black or white) MAIN IDEA

2. **Why do paintings of the ocean often make people feel peaceful and calm?** (Possible response: They are painted with tints and shades of cool colors.) PERCEPTION/AESTHETICS

3. WRITE **Describe the mood that blue can create.** DESCRIPTIVE TAKS Writing Objective 1

Lesson 8

Vocabulary
- value
- shades
- tints

Color and Mood

Imagine a room with blue walls, blue furniture, and blue carpeting. Would the room give you a calm feeling or an excited feeling? Artists use color to create a certain mood, or feeling. What kind of mood do you feel when you look at the painting below?

Look for lighter and darker yellow in the painting. The lightness or darkness of a color is its **value**. Artists mix black paint with a color to make **shades**. They mix white paint with a color to make **tints**. Point out some shades and tints of green in the painting.

Diego Rivera, *Baile en Tehuantepec*

Background Information

About the Artist

Diego Rivera (DYAY•goh ree•VAY•rah) (1886–1957) created artworks about the history, customs, and daily lives of Mexican people. He was influenced by ancient Aztec and Mayan art. Rivera created portraits, prints, murals, and sculptures.

For additional information about Rivera, see pp. R44–R59.

RECOMMENDED READING

How Artists Use Color by Paul Flux. Heinemann, 2001.

CHALLENGING

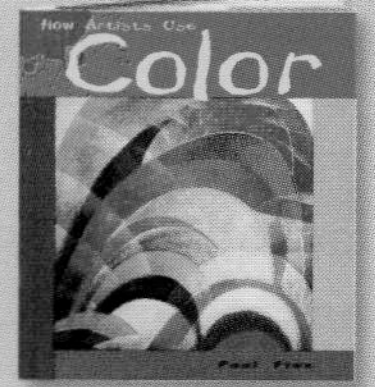

★ **TEKS 3.1A** identify sources for ideas; **TEKS 3.1B** identify elements and principles; **TEKS 3.2A** create artworks; **TEKS 3.2C** produce various artworks; **TEKS 3.4A** identify intent in personal artworks; **PDAS Domain I** active participation; *(continued)*

Artist's Workshop

Mood Painting

PLAN

Think of a special event such as a party. Sketch a scene from the event. Think about the mood you want to create in a painting of the scene.

CREATE

1. **Draw the scene on white paper.**
2. **Choose colors that will create the mood you want to show. Mix tints and shades of those colors.**
3. **Paint the scene.**

REFLECT

Look at your finished painting. How did you use color to create a mood? Where did you use tints and shades?

Quick Tip

To mix tints, add white paint to a color.

To mix shades, add black paint to a color.

53

30–40 Minutes

Artist's Workshop

Mood Painting

MATERIALS: sketchbook, pencil, white paper, tempera paints, paintbrushes, paper plate, water bowl

PLAN Have students identify a special event from their own life experiences to plan a scene of a life event. TEKS 3.1A

CREATE Ask students to produce their paintings based on experiences, using a variety of art materials appropriately. Have them use tints and shades of only two or three colors. TEKS 3.2A, TEKS 3.2C

REFLECT Ask students to identify the expressive qualities in their artworks. TEKS 3.4A

Activity Options PDAS Domain IV

Quick Activity Have students create a mood drawing with crayons.

Early Finishers Have students paint a scene that has a different mood.

Challenge See *Teacher Resource Book*, p. 58.

5–10 Minutes

Wrap-Up

Informal Assessment PDAS Domain III

- **What do you think of the way Diego Rivera showed a mood in his painting?** (Responses will vary.) EVALUATION/CRITICISM
- **How did your classmates use color to show a mood in their paintings?** (Responses will vary.) PERCEPTION/AESTHETICS

Extend Through Writing

TAKS Writing Objective 1

Song Have students write a song about the special event in their painting.

TAKS Reading Objective 1

Social Studies Connection

Mexican Geography The title of the painting on page 52 means *"Dance in Tehuantepec"* (tay•WAHN•tay•pek). *Tehuantepec* is the name of a town, a river, and an isthmus on the Pacific Coast of Mexico. Have students research the geographic location of that area and the customs of the people who live there.

PDAS Domain IV

ESL Before students begin the activity, familiarize them with the materials and instructions. **Create visuals** by working with students to make a set of flash-cards for the names of art materials. Each card should show a different material with its name in English and in the student's first language.

PDAS Domain II learner-centered instruction; **PDAS Domain III** evaluation and feedback; **PDAS Domain IV** classroom management; **TAKS Reading Objective 1** demonstrate understanding of texts; **TAKS Writing Objective 1** composition

Lesson 9

PDAS Domains I, II

Tactile Texture

OBJECTIVES
- Identify tactile texture in artworks and in the environment
- Produce fiberart with different textures
- Identify main ideas

RESOURCES
- Art Print 6
- Discussion Card 3, p. R35
- Electronic Art Gallery CD-ROM, Primary

5 Minutes

Warm-Up

Build Background Display **Art Print 6** and tell students that the jugs and teapots are made of willow trees. Help them brainstorm words that describe what the artwork might feel like. (scratchy, rough, bumpy, prickly)

10-15 Minutes

Teach

Discuss Art Concepts Have students read page 54 and describe the textures of the images. Students should use words like *soft, furry, fuzzy, smooth,* and *silky* for image A and words like *lumpy, bumpy, fuzzy,* and *soft* for image B. TEKS 3.1B

Think Critically

1. READING SKILL **Why is the tactile texture in image A surprising?** (These objects are usually smooth, not furry.) MAIN IDEA
2. **How would you describe the tactile texture of a marble statue?** (Possible responses: smooth, shiny, hard) PERCEPTION/AESTHETICS
3. WRITE **Describe how the tactile textures of coins and paper dollars are different.** DESCRIPTIVE TAKS Writing Objective 1

Lesson 9

Vocabulary
tactile texture
weaving

Tactile Texture

Have you ever felt the fuzzy skin of a peach or the smooth skin of an apple? **Tactile texture** is the way an object feels when you touch it. Touch some of the things around you. Describe the textures you feel.

Tactile texture can make an artwork more interesting or surprising. Look at image A. What do you see? The artist covered smooth objects with a surprising texture. What do you think the artwork feels like?

Image B is a **weaving** made of yarn. Rugs and baskets are also kinds of weavings. What do you think image B feels like?

B Hailey, age 8, *Weaving*

A Meret Oppenheim, *Object*

54

Background Information

Art History

Meret Oppenheim's *Object* is an example of **Surrealism**, an art movement that mixes reality with fantasy. Artworks from this movement often show impossible scenes or have an unexpected twist.

For additional information about Oppenheim and about Surrealism, see pp. R44–R59.

RECOMMENDED READING

Texture by Rob Court. The Child's World, 2003.
AVERAGE

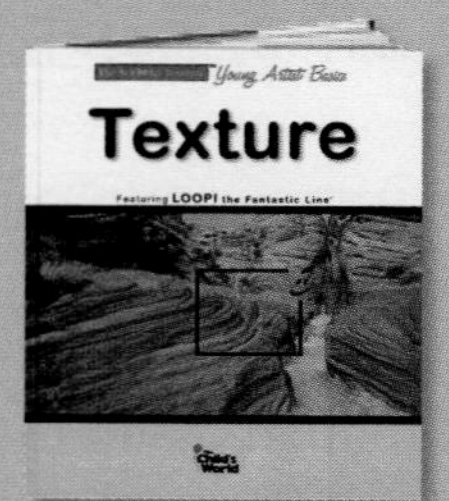

★ **TEKS 3.1B** identify elements and principles; **TEKS 3.2C** produce various artworks; **TEKS 3.4A** identify intent in personal artworks; **PDAS Domain I** active participation; **PDAS Domain II** learner-centered instruction; **PDAS Domain III** evaluation and feedback; **PDAS Domain IV** classroom management; **TAKS Writing Objective 1** composition

Artist's Workshop

Texture Weaving

PLAN

Think about the kind of texture you want in your weaving. Choose materials with textures and colors that you like.

CREATE

1. **Cut fifteen ½-inch slits along the top and bottom of a cardboard square. Try to put equal space between each slit.**
2. **Wrap string through each slit around the cardboard. Tape the ends of the string to the back of the cardboard.**
3. **Weave the yarn and the ribbon over and under the string to create your weaving. Tie the ends in a knot on the back of the cardboard.**

How would you describe the texture in your weaving?

Use a ruler to mark where you will cut the slits on your cardboard.

55

Science Connection

Sense of Touch Have pairs of students conduct an experiment about touch by using a box with a hole large enough for a hand to go through. Have one partner place objects—such as a block, spoon, sponge, and leaf—in the box. Have the other partner try to guess each object.

PDAS Domain IV

ESL Encourage both **peer interaction** and **oral language development** by having partners talk about the textures in their weavings.

Challenge Have students string beads onto several pieces of yarn before weaving.

30-40 Minutes

Artist's Workshop

Texture Weaving

MATERIALS: 10 × 10-inch cardboard square, ruler, scissors, tape, string, yarn, ribbons

Using several pieces of yarn at one time will create wider bands of color.

PLAN Have students cut the materials to the correct length, about 24 inches.

CREATE Tell students to produce their fiberart weavings, using a variety of art materials appropriately. Tell them to tie the yarn and ribbons in a knot on the back after they finish weaving a row. TEKS 3.2C

REFLECT Ask students to describe textures in their artwork and identify the general intent. TEKS 3.4A

Activity Options PDAS Domain IV

Quick Activity Have partners work together to create one weaving.

Early Finishers Students may use Discussion Card 3 to describe texture in their weavings.

Challenge See *Teacher Resource Book,* p. 59.

Wrap-Up

Informal Assessment PDAS Domain III

- **How did looking at image B help you plan your weaving?** (Responses will vary.) PERCEPTION/AESTHETICS
- **Compare the textures you used with those that your classmates used.** (Responses will vary.) EVALUATION/CRITICISM

Extend through Writing

TAKS Writing Objective 1

How-To Paragraph Have students write instructions for making a cardboard loom.

PDAS Domains I, II

Traditions in Dance

COMMUNITY ART

DISCUSS THE IMAGES

Have students read pages 56–57.

- Encourage students to discuss what they see in image A. Point out that the fringe on the dancers' clothing moves and sways with their movements. Have students point out the colors and details in the clothing. TEKS 3.1B
- Point out the fans and the dancers' outstretched arms in image B. Explain to students that in traditional Korean dance, the dancers use the upper half of their bodies—their head, shoulders, and hands—much more than their legs. Ask students to discuss why fans would accent that kind of dance movement. Have students describe the pink and red colors of the embroidered costumes and headdresses.
- Ask students to compare the traditional clothing of the Native American Shoshone dancers and the Korean dancers. Students should compare how these selected artworks from different cultures help to tell a story in a dance and are designed to emphasize the movement of the dancer. Then have them compare how the clothing documents the history and traditions of the two cultures. TEKS 3.3A, TEKS 3.3B

Background Information

Powwow was originally the term used for Native American healing ceremonies. In modern times, powwows have become social gatherings where large numbers of Native American participants from different tribes dance, sing, and play the drum. Powwows begin with a procession through the arena with the American, state, and tribal flags, followed by the most important male and female dancers, the honored tribes or guest, and finally all the other dance participants.

For related artworks, see **Electronic Art Gallery CD-ROM, Primary.**

★ **TEKS 3.1A** identify sources for ideas; **TEKS 3.1B** identify elements and principles; **TEKS 3.2C** produce various artworks; **TEKS 3.3A** compare artworks from the past and present; **TEKS 3.3B** compare artworks from different cultures; **TEKS 3.4B** identify main ideas in artworks by peers and others; **PDAS Domain I** active participation; **PDAS Domain II** learner-centered instruction

B Traditional dancers in Korea

Image B shows a group of dancers in Korea. They are using objects and simple hand movements to tell stories from their culture. What do you notice about the dancers' clothing in image B?

DID YOU KNOW?

***B**allet Folklórico* is the name of traditional Mexican dance groups. The dancers wear colorful clothing and perform on Mexican holidays such as Cinco de Mayo. The dancers in the image below are at a festival in Austin, Texas.

Teenagers dancing at an Austin festival

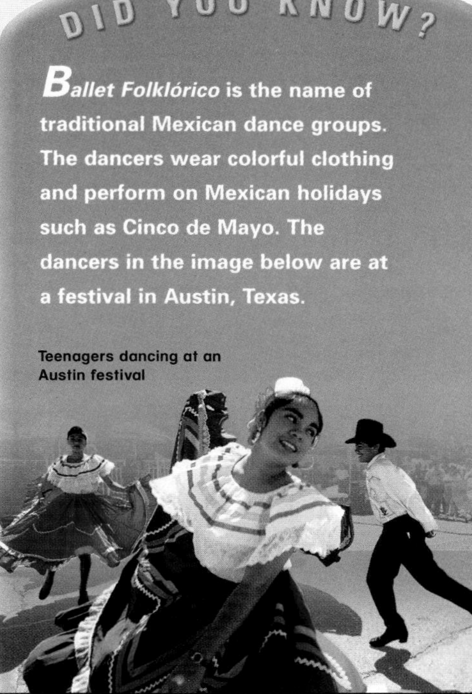

Think About Art

What kind of clothing would you wear for a dance about your community? What kind of music would you use?

Performing Arts Connection

Dance to the Music Collect some music from Native American, Korean, or Mexican dance traditions for students to listen to. Then have students invent a few dance steps to accompany their choice of music.

For additional cross-curricular suggestions, see Art Transparency 6.

TEKS 3.4B

Student Art Show

Portfolios and Exhibitions Periodically during this unit, have students create a display or exhibition of their portfolios or other finished artworks. Ask students to use simple criteria to identify main ideas in one another's original artworks and portfolios and in the exhibit as a whole.

DID YOU KNOW?

Use the facts below to discuss traditional dance with students.

- Ballet Folklórico groups in the United States and Mexico perform traditional regional dances from different Mexican states. Each region of Mexico has developed unique folkloric styles of dance steps, costumes, and music.
- Cinco de Mayo, the Fifth of May, marks the victory of the Mexicans over the French army in 1862. In the United States it is celebrated with traditional folklórico dancing, mariachi music, and parades.

Think About Art

What kind of clothing would you wear for a dance about your community? What kind of music would you use? (Responses will vary; ask students to identify life experiences as sources for ideas about how the clothing would be a visual symbol for important things in their community.)

PERSONAL RESPONSE TEKS 3.1A

ARTIST'S EYE ACTIVITY

Dance Painting Have students choose one of the photographs on pages 56–57 and create a design inspired by the colors and shapes in the traditional dance outfits. Have students choose colors that reflect the mood of the performance. TEKS 3.2C

Lesson 10

PDAS Domains I, II

Visual Texture

OBJECTIVES
- Identify visual texture in artworks
- Produce rubbings with a variety of textures
- Identify main ideas

RESOURCES
- Discussion Card 3, p. R35
- Electronic Art Gallery CD-ROM, Primary

Warm-Up

Build Background Display a photograph of an object and ask students if the object was photographed or painted. Tell students they will learn about paintings that look like photographs.

Teach

Discuss Art Concepts Have students read pages 58–59. Discuss how image A shows the smooth texture of marbles in a painting. Then ask students to point out objects in image B and identify their visual textures. TEKS 3.1B

Lesson 10

Vocabulary

photorealism

visual texture

Visual Texture

Look at image **A**. Does it show a photograph or a painting? Image **A** is an example of **photorealism**. Paintings in this style look almost like photographs.

How would you describe the tactile texture of real marbles? The artist of image **A** painted the marbles to look smooth. He gave them visual texture. **Visual texture** shows the way a real object would feel if you touched it. What color did the artist use to show light shining on the tops of the marbles?

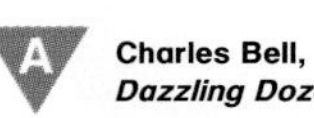

A Charles Bell, *Dazzling Dozen*

58

Think Critically

1.  READING SKILL **Why is visual texture important in photorealism?** (It shows the way something real would feel.) MAIN IDEA

2. **What is the difference between visual texture and tactile texture?** (Visual texture shows the way a real object would feel; tactile texture is the way something actually feels.) PERCEPTION/AESTHETICS

3. WRITE **Do you think a photograph of marbles or a painting of marbles is more interesting? Write about your opinion.** EXPOSITORY TAKS Writing Objective 1

FYI

Background Information

About the Artists

A Charles Bell (1935–1995) chose toys, gumball machines, marbles, and pinball machines as the subjects of his photorealistic still lifes.

B Jack Gunter has created many series of paintings of Native American baskets and vintage airplanes.

For additional information about the artists and photorealism, see pp. R44–R59.

RECOMMENDED READING

Micawber by John Lithgow. Simon & Schuster, 2002. AVERAGE

★ **TEKS 3.1B** identify elements and principles; **TEKS 3.2B** develop effective compositions; **TEKS 3.2C** produce various artworks; **PDAS Domain I** active participation; **PDAS Domain II** learner-centered instruction; **PDAS Domain III** evaluation and feedback; **PDAS Domain IV** classroom management; **TAKS Writing Objective 1** composition

Compare the visual textures of the baskets in image B and the marbles in image A. Notice how the artist of the painting in image B used many tiny lines to create the visual texture of grass. What other objects in image B have visual texture?

Jack Gunter, ***Basket 26***

Artist's Workshop

Texture Rubbings

1. **Find some objects with different textures. Cover each object with tracing paper. Rub peeled crayons on the paper to show the objects' textures.**
2. **Draw some organic or geometric shapes on the rubbings. Cut out the shapes.**
3. **Arrange the shapes on construction paper in an interesting way. Glue the shapes to the paper.**
4. **Paint the rubbings with watercolors.**

59

Science Connection

Magnification Point out that artists who paint photorealistic paintings often show objects enlarged or magnified. Have students experiment with magnifying glasses to observe the kinds of details they see when they magnify common objects like pencils, paper, and shoelaces.

PDAS Domain IV

ESL Use **visuals** to support **language acquisition** for adjectives that describe textures. Have students brainstorm words that describe textures in ***Picture Card Collection*** cards 2, 53, and 67.

See also ***Picture Card Bank*** **CD-ROM,** Category: Animals/Wild.

30-40 Minutes

Artist's Workshop

Texture Rubbings

MATERIALS: textured objects, tracing paper, peeled crayons, pencil, scissors, construction paper, glue stick, watercolors, paintbrushes, water bowl

PLAN Have students select about five objects with different textures.

CREATE Tell students to develop a variety of effective compositions using different cutout shapes. Then have them choose a composition for their finished artwork. TEKS 3.2B, TEKS 3.2C

REFLECT Ask students to identify the visual texture of each shape in their artwork. TEKS 3.1B

Activity Options PDAS Domain IV

Quick Activity Have students create rubbings of two or three textures and compare them.

Early Finishers Have students use Discussion Card 3 to talk about their artwork with a partner.

Challenge See *Teacher Resource Book*, p. 60.

Wrap-Up

Informal Assessment PDAS Domain III

- **How would you show the visual texture of a mirror?** (Responses will vary.) PERCEPTION/AESTHETICS
- **What title would you give your artwork?** (Responses will vary.) MAIN IDEA

Extend Through Writing

List Have students make a list of adjectives that describe textures.

PDAS Domains I, III

Review and Reflect

Have students reflect on what they have learned about the ways artists use color, value, and texture to create two-dimensional and three-dimensional works of art. Display **Art Prints 2, 4, 5, 6,** and **8**. Have students identify art elements in the images. Encourage small groups of students to use Discussion Card 3, page R35, and their completed Word Knowledge Charts to discuss what they learned about color, value, texture, and other vocabulary and concepts in this unit. TEKS 3.1B

Vocabulary and Concepts

Have students read each sentence and choose the letter of the word or phrase that best completes it. (1. A; 2. A; 3. B; 4. C; 5. C)

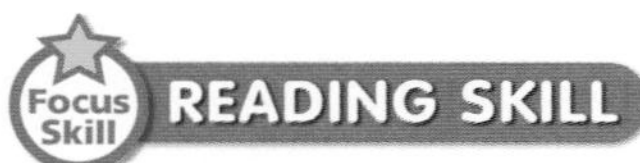

Main Idea

Remind students that the main idea tells what something is mostly about and that details support the main idea. Have students look for the main idea and details in the first paragraph on page 47 and then copy and fill out the diagram.
TAKS Reading Objectives 1, 3

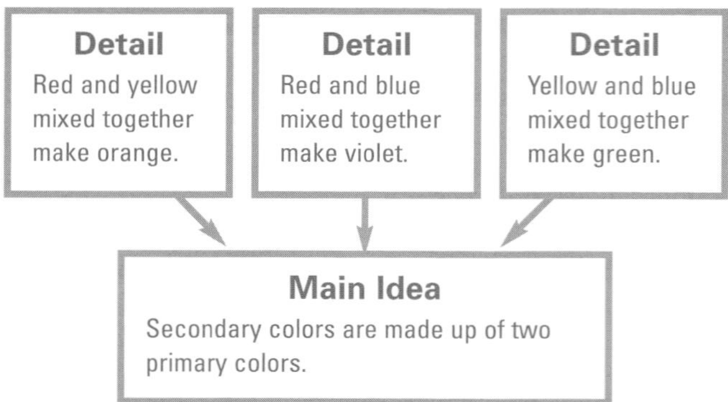

Unit 2 Review and Reflect

Vocabulary and Concepts

Choose the letter of the word or phrase that best completes each sentence.

1 Artists mix white paint with a color to make ___.

A tints **C** moods
B shades **D** textures

2 Artists make ___ colors by mixing a primary color with a secondary color.

A intermediate **C** warm
B lighter **D** cool

3 Artists often use ___ colors to show cold weather.

A warm **C** secondary
B cool **D** darker

4 ___ colors can be mixed to make all the other colors on the color wheel.

A Warm **C** Primary
B Cool **D** Secondary

5 ___ is the way an object feels when you touch it.

A Visual texture **C** Tactile texture
B Photorealism **D** Value

Focus Skill READING SKILL

Main Idea

Reread the first paragraph on page 47. Write details and the main idea in a diagram like the one shown here.

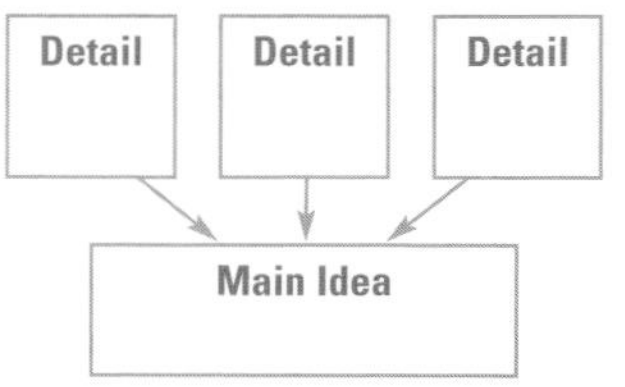

60

TEKS 3.4B

Home and Community Connection

School-Home Connection

Copy and distribute *Teacher Resource Book* pp. 87–88 to inform parents about upcoming art projects. Also, have students work with a parent to make rubbings of objects at home. Encourage students to explore textures they find indoors and outdoors.

Community Connection

You may want to obtain a list of public sculptures in your community. Organize a sculpture tour or share photos of the sculptures so that students can view and discuss the local public art. Have them identify the main idea in each artwork.

★ **TEKS 3.1B** identify elements and principles; **TEKS 3.4A** identify intent in personal artworks; **TEKS 3.4B** identify main ideas in artworks by peers and others; **PDAS Domain I** active participation; **PDAS Domain III** evaluation and feedback; **TAKS Reading Objective 1** demonstrate understanding of texts; *(continued)*

Write About Art

Write a paragraph that tells the main idea in one of your own artworks. Include the title of the artwork in your paragraph. Use a diagram to plan your writing.

REMEMBER—YOU SHOULD

- write about the main idea.
- use details that support the main idea.
- use correct grammar, spelling, and punctuation.

Critic's Corner

Look at *Ice and Clouds* by Arthur G. Dove to answer the questions below.

DESCRIBE What do you see in the painting?

ANALYZE What colors did the artist use? Where do you see tints and shades of blue?

INTERPRET What kind of mood did the artist of this painting create?

EVALUATE Do you like the way the artist used color to show a mood? Why or why not?

Arthur G. Dove, *Ice and Clouds*

61

PDAS Domain III

Assessment

Portfolio Assessment

Work with students to choose one of their artworks to include in their portfolio. Suggest that they decide which piece best fulfilled the assignment or which piece they liked best for another reason. You may want to provide specific feedback that targets students' use of the elements of art and techniques. See also Portfolio Recording Form, page R32.

Additional Assessment Options

- Progress Recording Form, p. R33
- Artist's Workshop Rubrics (Self/Teacher and Peer), pp. R30–R31
- Unit 2 Test, *Teacher Resource Book*, p. 100

Write About Art

Main Idea Paragraph Read aloud the prompt with students. Suggest that they use the main-idea-and-details diagram on page 60 to help them plan their paragraphs and describe the general intent of their artwork. Tell students to choose an artwork that includes enough details to write about. Remind students to use appropriate vocabulary words as they write. TEKS 3.4A; TAKS Writing Objectives 1, 2

Critic's Corner

RESPONSE/EVALUATION Use Discussion Card 2, page R34, and the steps below to guide students in analyzing *Ice and Clouds* by Arthur G. Dove.

DESCRIBE Have students describe the subject of the artwork. If they have difficulty, discuss how the title gives a clue.

ANALYZE Students should identify brown, blue, and white in the painting. Have students identify value by pointing out the tints and shades of blue in the sky. TEKS 3.1B

INTERPRET Students should explain that the cool color blue creates a calm mood.

EVALUATE Ask students to support their opinions by telling whether or not the artist effectively depicted ice and clouds.

TAKS Test Preparation: Reading and Writing Through Art, pp. 22–26

TAKS Reading Objective 3 use a variety of strategies; TAKS Writing Objective 1 composition; TAKS Writing Objective 2 conventions

Unit 3 Proportion, Movement, and Pattern

Tell Your Story

Artists share their stories by showing a single moment in time. An artwork can tell how people lived, what they did, and what they were like. In this unit students will be challenged to look for proportion, movement, and pattern in artworks that tell a story.

Resources

- Unit 3 Art Prints (7–9)
- Additional Art Prints (3, 16)
- Art Transparencies 7–9
- Test Preparation: Reading and Writing Through Art, pp. 27–47
- Artist's Workshop Activities: English and Spanish, pp. 21–30
- Encyclopedia of Artists and Art History, pp. R44–R59
- Picture Cards Collection, cards 14, 17, 26, 42, 45, 82, 84, 92

Using the Art Prints

- Discussion Cards, pp. R34–R38
- Teaching suggestions, backs of Art Prints
- Art Print Teaching Suggestions: Spanish

Teacher Resource Book

- Vocabulary Cards in English and Spanish, pp. 15–18
- Reading Skill Card 3, p. 33
- Copying Master, p. 42
- Challenge Activities, pp. 61–65
- School-Home Connection: English/Spanish, pp. 89–90
- Unit 3 Test, p. 101

Technology Resources

Electronic Art Gallery CD-ROM, Primary
Picture Card Bank CD-ROM

Visit *The Learning Site*
www.harcourtschool.com

- Multimedia Art Glossary
- Multimedia Biographies
- Reading Skills and Activities

Art Prints for This Unit

ART PRINT 7

George Washington (Lansdowne Portrait)
by Gilbert Stuart

ART PRINT 8

Taking in Laundry
by Grandma Moses

ART PRINT 9

Mother and Child
by Henry Moore

ART PRINT 16

Unveiling of the Statue of Liberty
by Katherine Westphal

ART PRINT 3

Woman at the Piano
by Elie Nadelman

Unit 3 Tell Your Story Proportion, Movement, and Pattern

Planning Guide

PDAS Domain IV

Lesson	Objectives and Vocabulary	Art Images	Production/ Materials
Focus Skill: Narrative Elements, pp. 64–65			
11 PORTRAITS pp. 66–67 30–60 minutes	• Identify proportion in artworks • Produce self-portrait drawings Focus Skill: Identify narrative elements **Vocabulary: portrait, proportion, self-portrait**	• **Portrait of Virginia** by Frida Kahlo • **I Myself Portrait-Landscape** by Henri Rousseau	**Self-Portrait** ❑ pencil ❑ mirror ❑ white paper ❑ colored pencils
12 FAMILY SCENES pp. 68–69 30–60 minutes	• Identify movement in artworks • Produce drawings of family scenes Focus Skill: Identify narrative elements **Vocabulary: seascape, movement**	• **Play in the Surf** by Edward Potthast	**Family Scene Drawing** ❑ white paper ❑ pencil ❑ oil pastels
Art ↔ Social Studies Connection: Henry Moore, pp. 70–71			
13 PATTERNS IN MASKS pp. 72–73 30–60 minutes	• Identify patterns in artworks • Produce yarn masks with symmetry Focus Skill: Identify narrative elements **Vocabulary: patterns, symmetry**	• **African Mask** by Unknown artist • **Huichol yarn mask** by Unknown artist	**Mexican Yarn Mask** ❑ sketchbook ❑ pencil ❑ yarn ❑ glue ❑ tagboard ❑ scissors ❑ craft stick
14 PATTERNS IN CLOTH pp. 74–75 30–60 minutes	• Identify patterns in artworks • Produce fiberart Focus Skill: Identify narrative elements **Vocabulary: mola**	• **Mola panel** by Unknown artist	**Bird Mola** ❑ magazines ❑ paper ❑ pencil ❑ marker ❑ colored felt pieces ❑ scissors ❑ glue
Art ↔ Social Studies Connection: Western Wear, pp. 76–77			
15 MURAL ART pp. 78–79 30–60 minutes	• Identify movement in artworks • Produce mural paintings Focus Skill: Identify narrative elements **Vocabulary: mural**	• **The Market** by Diego Rivera • **Mural (America)** by Unknown artists	**Community Mural** ❑ sketchbook ❑ pencil ❑ butcher paper ❑ tempera paints ❑ paintbrushes ❑ water bowl
Review and Reflect, pp. 80–81			

★ **TEKS 3.2A** create artworks; **TEKS 3.2C** produce various artworks; **PDAS Domain IV** classroom management

Narrative Elements, pp. 64–65

Opportunities for application of the skill are provided on pp. 66, 67, 68, 69, 72, 74, 78, 79, 80, and 81.

Resources and Technology	Suggested Literature	Across the Curriculum
• Art Prints 3 and 7 • Reading Skill Card 3 • Electronic Art Gallery CD-ROM, Primary	*Portraits* by Penny King and Clare Roundhill 	**Math** Facial Fractions, p. 67 **Reading** Narrative Elements, p. 66 **Writing** Friendly Letter, p. 67
• Art Print 8 • Discussion Card 7, p. R37 • Reading Skill Card 3 • Electronic Art Gallery CD-ROM, Primary	*Peter's Painting* by Sally Moss 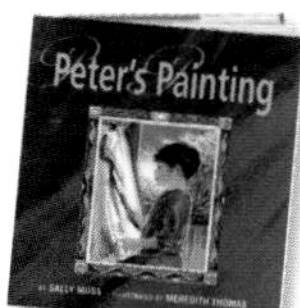	**Health** Safety Rules, p. 69 **Reading** Narrative Elements, p. 68 **Writing** Poem, p. 69
• Discussion Cards 1 and 4, pp. R34–R35 • Reading Skill Card 3 • Electronic Art Gallery CD-ROM, Primary	*Start with Art: Animals* by Sue Lacey 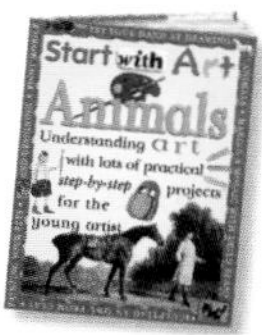	**Science** Symmetry in Nature, p. 73 **Reading** Narrative Elements, p. 72 **Writing** Compare-and-Contrast Paragraph, p. 73
• Art Print 16 • Reading Skill Card 3 • Electronic Art Gallery CD-ROM, Primary	*Nature's Paintbrush* by Susan Stockdale 	**Social Studies** Fabric Artists, p. 75 **Reading** Narrative Elements, p. 74 **Writing** Descriptive Paragraph, p. 75
• Discussion Card 10, p. R38 • Reading Skill Card 3 • Electronic Art Gallery CD-ROM, Primary	*Diego* by Jeanette Winter 	**Social Studies** Mural Search, p. 79 **Reading** Narrative Elements, p. 78 **Writing** Letter, p. 79

Art Puzzlers

Present these art puzzlers to students at the beginning or end of a class or when students finish an assignment early.

- Use **proportion** to draw a family **portrait**. TEKS 3.2A; TEKS 3.2C
- Find several magazine pictures or advertisements. Describe the **movement** in each picture.
- Draw and color a picture of an animal from your imagination. Include **patterns** in your drawing. TEKS 3.2C
- Design a shirt with **patterns** that you would like to wear. Use crayons to draw your idea. TEKS 3.2C
- Draw an idea for a **mural** about your school. Include school colors to show school pride. TEKS 3.2C

School-Home Connection
The activities above are included in the School-Home Connection for this unit. See *Teacher Resource Book,* pp. 89–90.

Assessment Options

- Rubrics and Recording Forms, pp. R30–R33
- Unit 3 Test, *Teacher Resource Book,* p. 101

Visit *The Learning Site*:
www.harcourtschool.com

Artist's Workshops PREVIEW

PDAS Domain IV

Use these pages to help you gather and organize materials for the production activity in each lesson.

LESSON	MATERIALS
11 Self-Portrait p. 67 **Objective:** Produce self-portrait drawings using correct proportions  **30–40 minutes** **Challenge Activity:** See *Teacher Resource Book*, page 61.	• pencil • mirror • white paper • colored pencils FINISHED EXAMPLE 
LESSON  **12 Family Scene Drawing** p. 69 **Objective:** Produce family scene drawings that show movement  **30–40 minutes** **Challenge Activity:** See *Teacher Resource Book*, page 62.	• white paper • pencil • oil pastels FINISHED EXAMPLE 

For safety information, see Art Safety, page R4; or the Art Safety Poster.

For information on media and techniques, see pp. R15–R23.

LESSON	MATERIALS

13 Mexican Yarn Mask p. 73

Objective: Produce yarn masks with symmetry and patterns

30–40 minutes

Challenge Activity: See *Teacher Resource Book,* page 63.

- sketchbook
- pencil
- yarn
- glue
- tagboard (8 in. x 10 in.)
- scissors
- craft stick

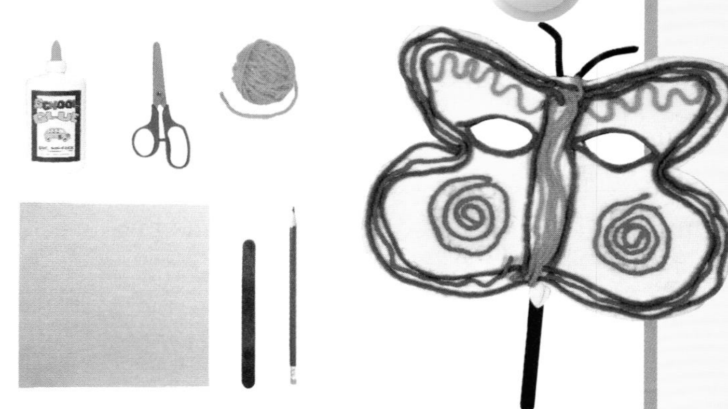

LESSON

14 Bird Mola p. 75

Objective: Produce fiberart molas

30–40 minutes

Challenge Activity: See *Teacher Resource Book,* page 64.

- magazines
- paper
- pencil
- marker
- 4 different-colored felt pieces
- scissors
- glue

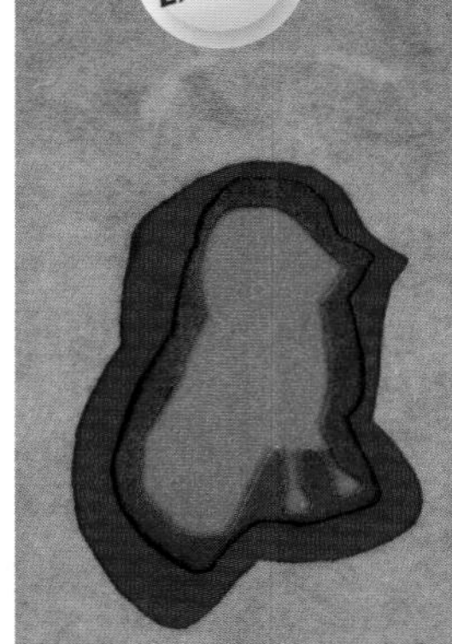

LESSON

15 Community Mural p. 79

Objective: Produce mural paintings that show movement

30–40 minutes

Challenge Activity: See *Teacher Resource Book,* page 65.

- sketchbook
- pencil
- butcher paper
- tempera paints
- paintbrushes
- water bowl

PDAS Domains I, II

Tell Your Story

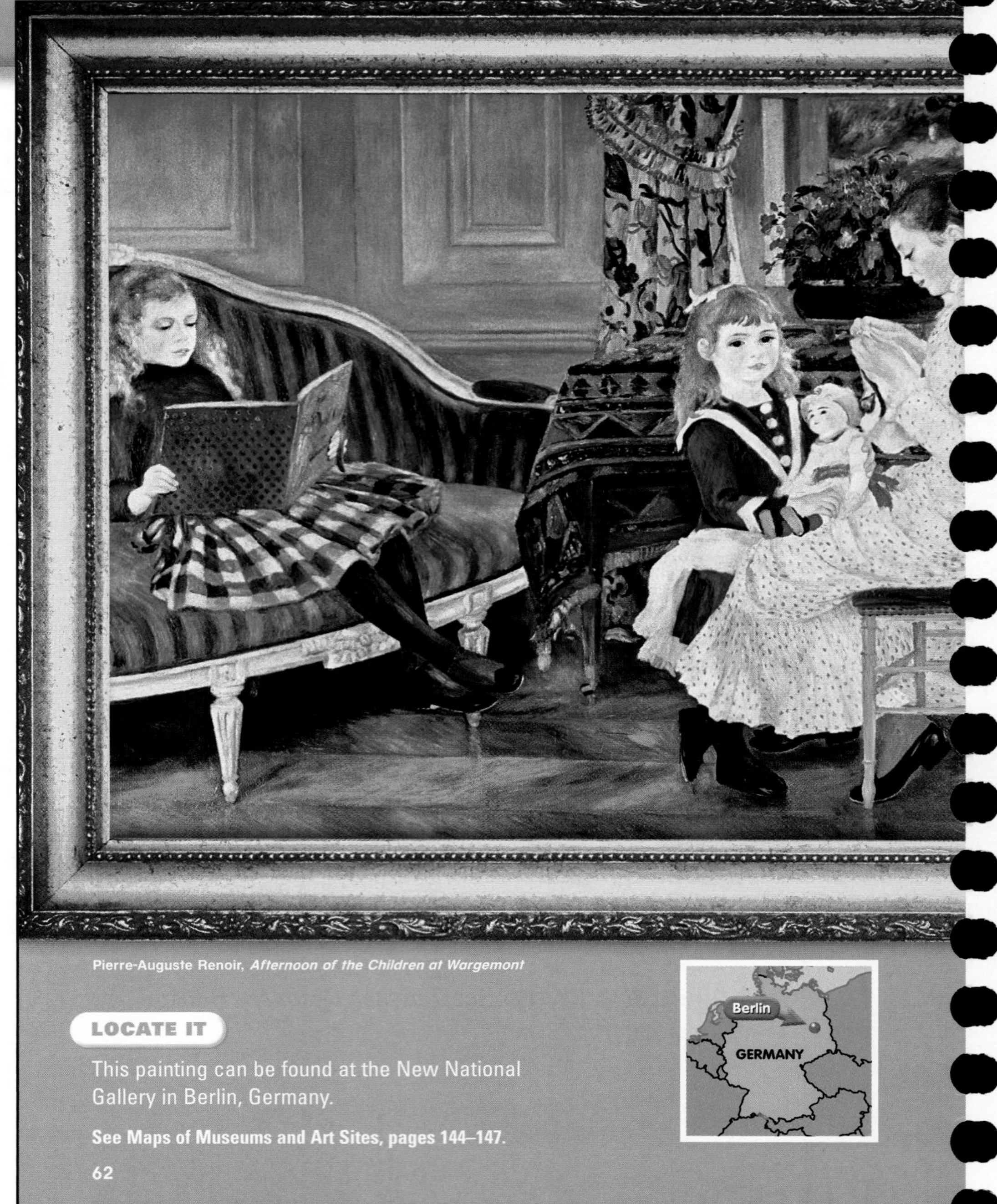

PREVIEW THE UNIT

Tell students that in this unit they will view and create artworks that tell a story. Read aloud the unit title, *Tell Your Story*, and have students preview the artworks. Ask students to predict the kind of story each artist may be telling.

SHARE THE POEM

Have students read the poem and then view the art.

How do the poem and painting go together? (Possible response: The poem tells how a book can take the reader to other worlds. In the painting, one girl is reading a book.) **DRAW CONCLUSIONS** TAKS Reading Objective 4

STEP INTO THE ART

Have students look carefully at the painting on pages 62–63 and use sensory knowledge and life experiences as sources for ideas about self to answer the questions below.

How would you change the room in the painting to make it a place for you to enjoy? How would the room look, feel, and smell? (Responses will vary.) **PERSONAL RESPONSE** TEKS 3.1A

SHARE BACKGROUND INFORMATION

Tell students that Renoir is famous for his paintings of people. Explain that this painting was created in Wargemont, near the coast of Normandy, France. Point out that Renoir painted all kinds of people, from shopkeepers' and circus performers' children to the daughters of wealthy families.

LOCATE IT See **Using the Maps of Museums and Art Sites**, p. R2.

Background Information

About the Artist

Pierre-Auguste Renoir (PYAIR•oh•GOOST REN•wahr) (1841–1919) changed his style of painting several times throughout his life, though he is best known as an **Impressionist** painter. These artists used quick brush strokes and bright colors.

For additional information about Renoir and Impressionism, see the Encyclopedia of Artists and Art History, pp. R44–R59, and the Gallery of Artists, *Student Edition*, pp. 178–188.

For related images, see **Electronic Art Gallery CD-ROM, Primary.**

★ **TEKS 3.1A** identify sources for ideas; **PDAS Domain I** active participation; **PDAS Domain II** learner-centered instruction; **TAKS Reading Objective 4** apply critical-thinking skills

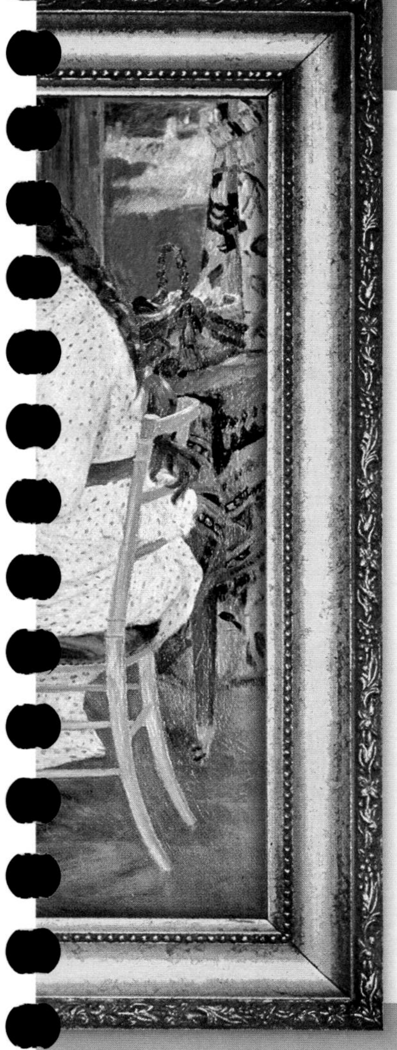

Unit 3 Proportion, Movement, and Pattern

Tell Your Story

A Book

Closed, I am a mystery.
Open, I will always be
a friend with whom you think and see.

Closed, there's nothing I can say.
Open, we can dream and stray
to other worlds, far and away.

Myra Cohn Livingston

Unit Vocabulary

portrait
proportion
self-portrait
seascape
movement
patterns
symmetry
mola
mural

ABOUT THE ARTIST

See Gallery of Artists, pages 178–188.

Multimedia Art Glossary
Visit *The Learning Site*
www.harcourtschool.com

63

Unit Vocabulary

Read aloud the terms with students, and use the Word Knowledge Chart below to assess and discuss their prior knowledge.

portrait a picture that shows what a person, a group of people, or an animal looks like

proportion the size and placement of one thing compared with the size and placement of other things

self-portrait a portrait of an artist made by himself or herself

seascape an artwork that shows a view of an ocean or a sea

movement a design principle used to guide the viewer's eye around an artwork

patterns designs made up of repeated lines, shapes, or colors

symmetry an arrangement in which one half of an artwork is a mirror image of the other half

mola an artwork made by sewing together layers of brightly colored cloth

mural a very large painting that covers a wall

Vocabulary Resources

- Vocabulary Cards in English and Spanish, *Teacher Resource Book,* pp. 15–18
- Student Edition Glossary, pp. 189–197

Multimedia Art Glossary
Visit *The Learning Site*
www.harcourtschool.com

Language Arts Connection

Students may create a chart like the one below to identify familiar and unfamiliar vocabulary terms. Encourage them to add information to their charts as they work through this unit.

WORD KNOWLEDGE CHART		
I know this term.	I have seen this term before.	I have never seen this term.

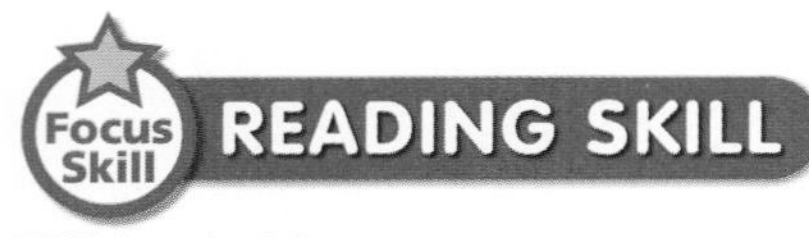

PDAS Domains I, II

Narrative Elements

SKILL TRACE	
NARRATIVE ELEMENTS	
Introduce	pp. 64–65
Review	pp. 66, 67, 68, 69, 72, 74, 78, 79, 80, 81

DISCUSS THE SKILL

Access Prior Knowledge Name a story that students are familiar with, and ask volunteers to briefly retell it. As students discuss the plot, write on the board the names of the characters as they are mentioned. Then ask students to tell where the story takes place, and write it on the board. Tell students that keeping track of the important parts of a story can help them better understand it.

APPLY TO ART

Narrative Elements in Art Have students read page 64 and look at the illustration. Explain that the illustration is for a Native American folktale about the Southwest. Ask students to discuss what the picture shows. (a group of animals facing a coyote in a canyon at night) Then have students give more details about the characters, setting, and plot. Help them name the additional animals. (bison, lizards, porcupine, squirrel, deer) Point out that the setting shows the unique geography in one part of the country.

Have students compare content in artworks from the present for the purpose of telling stories. Display an illustration from a familiar picture book, and ask students to describe how characters, setting, and plot are different from those in the illustration on page 64. TEKS 3.3A

Narrative Elements

***Narrative elements* are the parts of a story. They include characters, setting, and plot. *Characters* are the people or animals. The *setting* is where and when a story takes place. The *plot* is what happens.**

Artists may also tell stories in their artworks. Look at the narrative elements in the image below.

- The characters are a coyote, an eagle, a bear, rabbits, and many other animals.
- The setting is a canyon at night.
- The plot seems to be that the coyote is telling the other animals something important.

Harriet Peck Taylor, Illustration from *Coyote Places the Stars* LITERATURE LINK

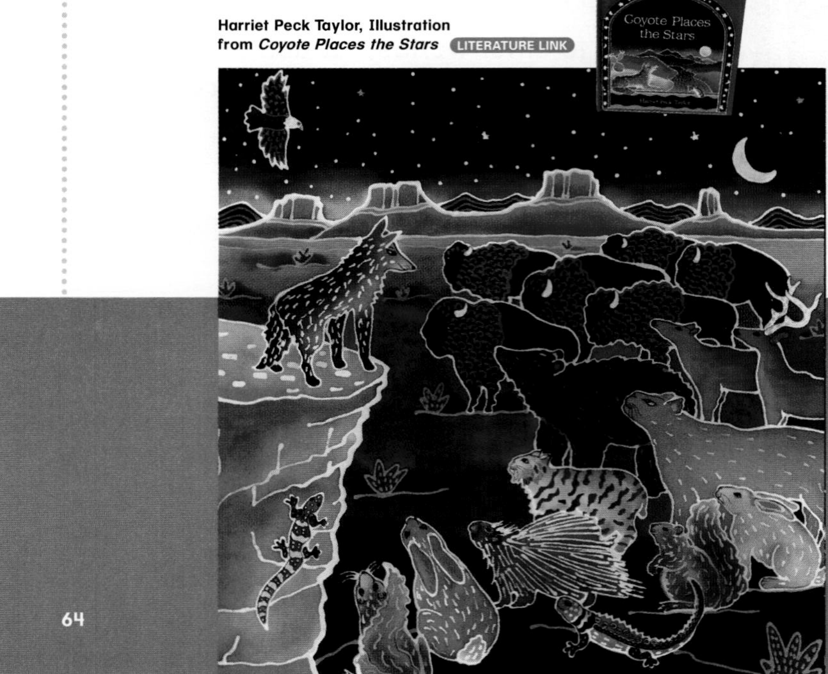

64

Background Information

About the Artist

Harriet Peck Taylor (1954–) is a writer and an artist. Many of her artworks appear in her own stories, which are retellings of Native American folktales about animals. Peck uses a technique called *batik* to create her artwork. Batik is an ancient artform for decorating fabric with hot wax and dyes.

For additional information about Taylor, see pp. R44–R59.

LITERATURE LINK *Coyote Places the Stars* by Harriet Peck Taylor. Aladdin Library, 1997. AVERAGE

★ **TEKS 3.3A** compare artworks from the past and present; **PDAS Domain I** active participation; **PDAS Domain II** learner-centered instruction; **PDAS Domain IV** classroom management; **TAKS Reading Objective 2** apply knowledge of literary elements; **TAKS Reading Objective 3** use a variety of strategies

Thinking about the characters, setting, and plot can help you understand the stories you read. Read the story below.

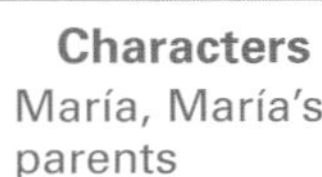

"Are we almost there?" María asked her parents from the back seat of the car.

María always looked forward to family vacations. She had helped plan this trip to Big Bend National Park by researching things to do there. Along with her clothes, María had packed her sketchbook. She wanted to draw the plants and animals she would see. When the car finally stopped, María was filled with excitement.

"Let's go exploring!" she shouted.

Who are the characters in the story, and where are they? What are the characters doing? Use a story map like this to describe the characters, setting, and plot of the story.

Characters	Setting
María, María's parents	

Plot (Story Events)
1.
2.
3.

On Your Own

As you look at the artworks in this unit, think about the stories the artists are trying to tell. Use story maps to write about what you see.

65

APPLY TO READING

Identify Narrative Elements in Text Explain to students that as they read a story, they should think about the characters, setting, and plot. Have students read the passage on page 65. Work with them to identify the narrative elements in the story and record the information in the story map. TAKS Reading Objectives 2, 3

Characters	Setting
María, María's parents	Big Bend National Park

Plot (Story Events)
1. María and her parents are traveling by car.
2. María thinks about what she will draw in her sketchbook.
3. The family arrives at Big Bend, and María is ready to go.

ON YOUR OWN

As students read the lessons in this unit, have them use story maps to identify the narrative elements in the artworks. TAKS Reading Objectives 2, 3

TAKS Reading Objectives 2, 3

Reading Skill Card

Distribute Reading Skill Card 3, *Teacher Resource Book*, p. 33. Have students think about the narrative elements in this unit.

Extend the Skill For additional teaching suggestions, see **Art Transparency 7**.

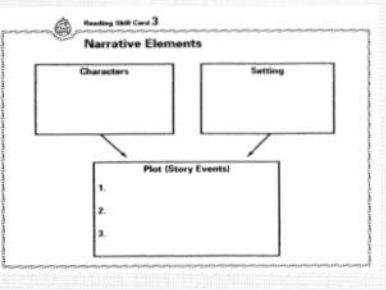

PDAS Domain IV

ESL **Rephrase** the terms *characters, setting,* and *plot* as *people* (or *animals*), *places,* and *things that happen.* Then page through a familiar picture book with students, calling attention to illustrations that show examples of the three narrative elements.

Reading Skills and Activities
Visit *The Learning Site*
www.harcourtschool.com

Lesson 11

PDAS Domains I, II

Portraits

OBJECTIVES
- Identify proportion in artworks
- Produce self-portrait drawings
- Identify narrative elements

RESOURCES
- Art Prints 3, 7
- Electronic Art Gallery CD-ROM, Primary

5 Minutes

Warm-Up

Build Background Explain to students that artworks may tell stories about people and about the time and place in which they lived. Display **Art Prints 3** and **7**. Ask students to describe what they can learn about each subject from the artworks and to compare the stories in these two artworks from the past. TEKS 3.3A

10-15 Minutes

Teach

Discuss Art Concepts Have students read page 66. Then use image A to discuss proportion. Students should identify that the girl's nose is halfway between her eyes and her chin and that her mouth is halfway between the bottom of her nose and her chin. Have students point out objects in image B, such as the paint and paintbrush, that tell about the artist. TEKS 3.1B

Think Critically

1. READING SKILL **Who is the character in image B? What is he doing?** (the artist, Henri Rousseau; holding paints) NARRATIVE ELEMENTS
2. **Why is proportion important in a portrait?** (to make it look lifelike) PERCEPTION/AESTHETICS
3. WRITE **Write a short story about the scene in image B.** NARRATIVE TAKS Writing Objective 1

Lesson 11

Vocabulary

portrait

proportion

self-portrait

Portraits

A **portrait** is a picture of a person. Artists can use proportion to make portraits look lifelike. **Proportion** is the size and placement of some things compared with other things. Look at the portrait in image A. Notice that the girl's eyes are halfway between her chin and the top of her head. Where is her nose compared with her eyes and chin? What do you notice about where her mouth and ears are placed?

Image B is a **self-portrait**. The artist painted a portrait of himself. Artists sometimes include things in self-portraits to tell about themselves. What can you tell about this artist from his self-portrait?

A Frida Kahlo, *Portrait of Virginia*

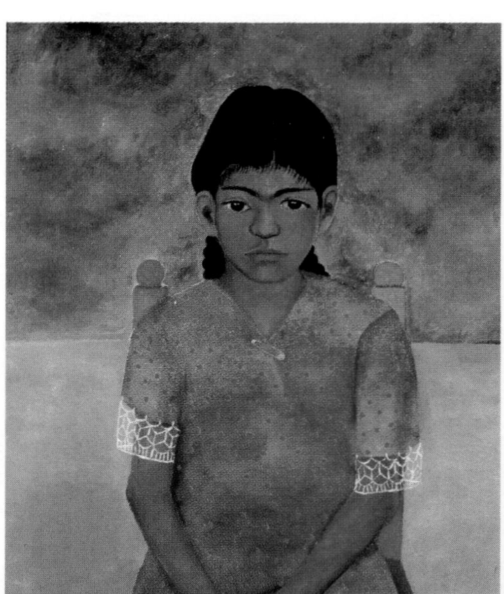

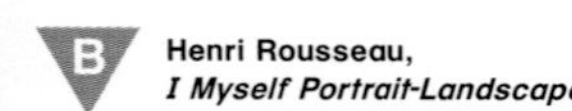
B Henri Rousseau, *I Myself Portrait-Landscape*

66

Background Information

About the Artist

Frida Kahlo (FREE•dah KAH•loh) (1907–1954) was a Mexican artist best known for her self-portraits, painted with symbols of Mexican history. She often painted herself wearing colorful clothing and jewelry.

For additional information about Kahlo, see pp. R44–R59.

RECOMMENDED READING

Portraits by Penny King and Clare Roundhill. Crabtree, 1996. CHALLENGING

★ **TEKS 3.1A** identify sources for ideas; **TEKS 3.1B** identify elements and principles; **TEKS 3.2A** create artworks; **TEKS 3.2C** produce various artworks; **TEKS 3.3A** compare artworks from the past and present; **TEKS 3.4A** identify intent in personal artworks; **PDAS Domain I** active participation; *(continued)*

Artist's Workshop

Self-Portrait

PLAN

Think of some objects that tell something about you. Decide how you could include them in a self-portrait.

CREATE

1. Look at yourself in a mirror. Sketch your face on white paper.
2. Make sure you use proportion in your drawing. Use the diagram below to help you draw your eyes, nose, ears, and mouth.
3. Add details to your self-portrait with colored pencils. Include at least one object that tells something about you.

REFLECT

How did you use proportion in your self-portrait? What can people learn about you from your self-portrait?

- The eyes are halfway between the top of the head and the bottom of the chin.
- The nose is halfway between the eyes and the chin, and the mouth is halfway between the nose and the chin.

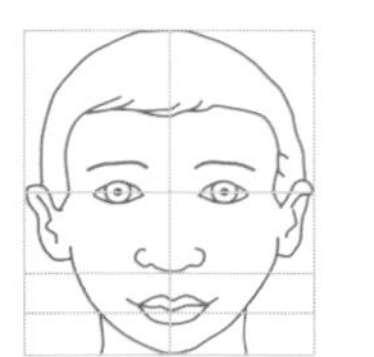

67

30–40 Minutes

Artist's Workshop

Self-Portrait

MATERIALS: pencil, mirror, white paper, colored pencils

PLAN Ask students to use life experiences and hobbies as sources for ideas about self. TEKS 3.1A

CREATE Have students use personal observation to examine the shape of their face, draw the outline, and lightly draw the proportion diagram to help them produce their drawings. TEKS 3.2A, TEKS 3.2C

REFLECT Have students identify the general intent and expressive qualities in their artwork by telling about the objects they included. TEKS 3.4A

Activity Options PDAS Domain IV

Quick Activity Have students sketch their self-portraits using the proportion diagram. See *Teacher Resource Book*, p. 42.

Early Finishers Have students sketch a partner's portrait.

Challenge See *Teacher Resource Book*, p. 61.

5–10 Minutes

Wrap-Up

Informal Assessment PDAS Domain III

- **How did understanding proportion help you draw your self-portrait?** (Responses will vary.) PERCEPTION/AESTHETICS
- **What setting would you choose for a self-portrait like image B?** (Responses will vary.) NARRATIVE ELEMENTS

Extend Through Writing

TAKS Writing Objective 1

Friendly Letter Have students write a letter to introduce themselves to a penpal.

Math Connection

Facial Fractions Have students copy the proportion diagram from page 67 and annotate it with fractions relating each section to the whole head. For example, the section between the eyes and the top of the head is one-half of the entire face.

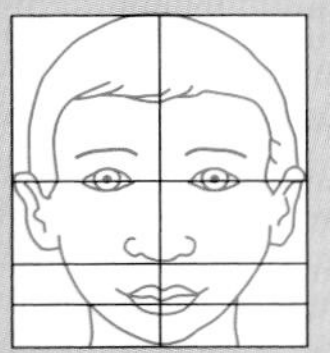

PDAS Domain IV

ESL Use **visuals** to support **comprehensible input** for the names of facial features. Display ***Picture Cards Collection,*** cards 42, 45, 82, and 84 for students to discuss and use as reference.

See also ***Picture Card Bank* CD-ROM,** Category: My Body.

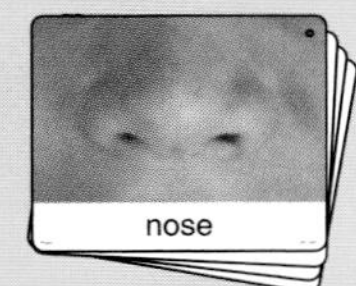

PDAS Domain II learner-centered instruction; **PDAS Domain III** evaluation and feedback; **PDAS Domain IV** classroom management; **TAKS Writing Objective 1** composition

Lesson 12

PDAS Domains I, II

Family Scenes

OBJECTIVES
- Identify movement in artworks
- Produce drawings of family scenes
- Identify narrative elements

RESOURCES
- Art Print 8
- Discussion Card 7, p. R37
- Electronic Art Gallery CD-ROM, Primary

5 Minutes

Warm-Up

Build Background Display **Art Print 8** and read the title. Have students point out details that explain why the family is gathering the laundry. (rain in distance, blowing trees) Then have students share their life experiences in preparing for a storm. TEKS 3.1A

10-15 Minutes

Teach

Discuss Art Concepts Have students read pages 68–69. They should describe movement in the painting by pointing out that they notice the tallest standing children first, the smaller child squatting in the sand next, and the children in the upper left last. TEKS 3.1B

Lesson 12

Vocabulary

seascape
movement

Family Scenes

A **seascape** is an artwork that shows a view of an ocean or a sea. Look at the seascape below. How would you describe this family scene? What do you think the people are doing?

Edward Potthast, *Play in the Surf*

68

Think Critically

1. READING SKILL **Who are the most important characters in this painting? How do you know?** (the three largest girls because you notice them first) NARRATIVE ELEMENTS
2. **What is one way artists create movement?** (by showing objects of different sizes) PERCEPTION/AESTHETICS
3. WRITE **Describe the setting of the seascape.** DESCRIPTIVE TAKS Writing Objective 1

FYI

Background Information

About the Artist

Edward Potthast (1857–1927) was an Impressionist painter originally from Cincinnati, Ohio. He painted many seascapes of children playing at New York City-area beaches.

For additional information about Potthast and Impressionism, see pp. R44–R59.

RECOMMENDED READING

Peter's Painting by Sally Moss. Mondo, 1995. EASY

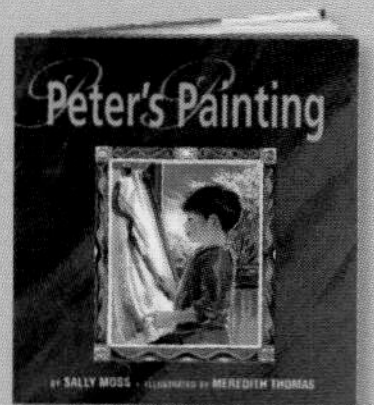

★ **TEKS 3.1A** identify sources for ideas; **TEKS 3.1B** identify elements and principles; **TEKS 3.2A** create artworks; **TEKS 3.2B** develop effective compositions; **TEKS 3.2C** produce various artworks; **TEKS 3.3A** compare artworks from the past and present; **TEKS 3.4A** identify intent in personal artworks; **PDAS Domain I** active participation; *(continued)*

Artists create **movement** in an artwork to guide a viewer's eyes around the artwork. On the seascape on page 68, trace with your finger the path your eyes take around the artwork. What do you notice first? What do you notice next? Now trace the path to the part you notice last. One way artists create movement is by showing objects of different sizes. Did you notice small objects or large objects first?

Artist's Workshop

Family Scene Drawing

1. **Think about a time when your family worked together on something. Sketch your ideas.**
2. **Lightly trace a line to show how you want to guide viewers' eyes around the artwork. Draw the largest objects in the part of the artwork you want viewers to look at first.**
3. **Erase the guide line, and color your drawing.**

69

Artist's Workshop

Family Scene Drawing

30-40 Minutes

MATERIALS: white paper, pencil, oil pastels

Quick Tip Students can use a tissue to blend colors.

PLAN Have students brainstorm activities from their life experiences as sources for ideas about life events. TEKS 3.1A

CREATE After students have developed an effective composition, ask them to produce their drawings based on experiences. TEKS 3.2A, TEKS 3.2B, TEKS 3.2C

REFLECT Have students tell how they intended viewers' eyes to move around the artwork. TEKS 3.4A

Activity Options PDAS Domain IV

Quick Activity Have students draw three simple objects in different sizes to show movement.

Early Finishers Have partners use Discussion Card 7 to discuss their finished drawings.

Challenge See *Teacher Resource Book*, p. 62.

Wrap-Up

5-10 Minutes

Informal Assessment PDAS Domain III

- **Why do artists create movement in their artworks?** (to guide viewers' eyes)
  PERCEPTION/AESTHETICS
- **Compare the story in your drawing to the story in Potthast's painting.** (Responses will vary.) NARRATIVE ELEMENTS TEKS 3.3A

Extend Through Writing

Poem Have students write a poem to accompany their family scene.

Health Connection

Safety Rules Tell students that obeying rules at the beach or a pool is important for their safety. Have students research safety rules and make a poster for a community pool or beach. Students may illustrate their posters with pictures that show examples of safe behavior.

PDAS Domain IV

ESL Help students **build confidence** in their **oral language development** by having them describe their drawings in small groups.

Extra Support Review with students comparison words such as *big, bigger,* and *biggest* to help them describe objects in their artworks.

PDAS Domain II learner-centered instruction; PDAS Domain III evaluation and feedback; PDAS Domain IV classroom management; TAKS Writing Objective 1 composition

PDAS Domains I, II

Henry Moore

ARTIST BIOGRAPHY

DISCUSS THE IMAGES

Have students read pages 70–71.

- As students discuss the subjects in image A, ask them to point out details in the artwork that support their ideas. Help students recognize that the rocker and the figure of the mother are one form. To explain why Moore may have done this, encourage students to compare the parts of a rocking chair to the parts of a person. (Both have arms, legs, and a back.)
- Have students point out the two adults and two children in image B. Ask them to describe how the composition creates the feeling that the people are part of the same family. As they compare and contrast images A and B, have students explain how they think Moore created movement in each artwork. TEKS 3.1B
-  Display **Art Print 9.** Ask students to look at the sculpture along with those shown in images A and B as a portfolio of Moore's work. Read aloud the titles of the artworks, and ask students to point out the common theme. (family) Then have students use this simple criteria along with what they see to identify the main idea in the portfolio. TEKS 3.4B

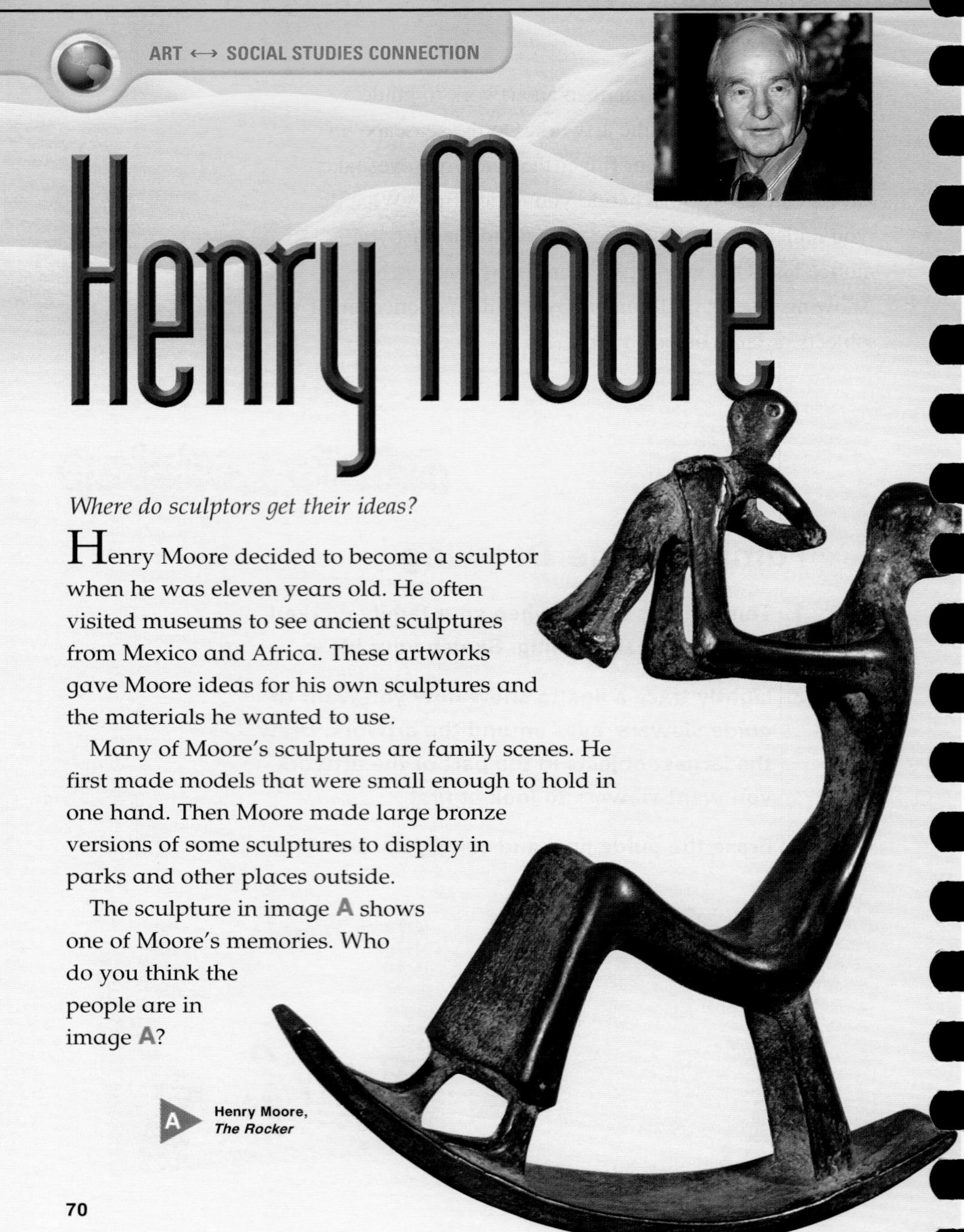

Where do sculptors get their ideas?

Henry Moore decided to become a sculptor when he was eleven years old. He often visited museums to see ancient sculptures from Mexico and Africa. These artworks gave Moore ideas for his own sculptures and the materials he wanted to use.

Many of Moore's sculptures are family scenes. He first made models that were small enough to hold in one hand. Then Moore made large bronze versions of some sculptures to display in parks and other places outside.

The sculpture in image **A** shows one of Moore's memories. Who do you think the people are in image **A**?

A Henry Moore, *The Rocker*

70

Background Information

About the Artist

Henry Moore (1898–1986) was an important twentieth-century British sculptor. Most of his sculptures show abstract human figures, often a mother and a child or larger family groups. Many of Moore's sculptures are larger than life, so they are often shown in outdoor parks and outside public buildings.

For additional information about Moore, see pp. R44–R59.

 For related artworks, see **Electronic Art Gallery CD-ROM, Primary.**

★ **TEKS 3.1A** identify sources for ideas; **TEKS 3.1B** identify elements and principles; **TEKS 3.2C** produce various artworks; **TEKS 3.4B** identify main ideas in artworks by peers and others; **PDAS Domain I** active participation; **PDAS Domain II** learner-centered instruction; **TAKS Writing Objective 1** composition

Henry Moore, *Study for a Family Group*

DID YOU KNOW?

Sculptors who work with hard materials use special carving tools. For large sculptures, they remove material by hitting a sharp tool with a hammer. They use smaller hand tools to carve details. The photograph below shows Henry Moore carving a small sculpture.

Henry Moore carving

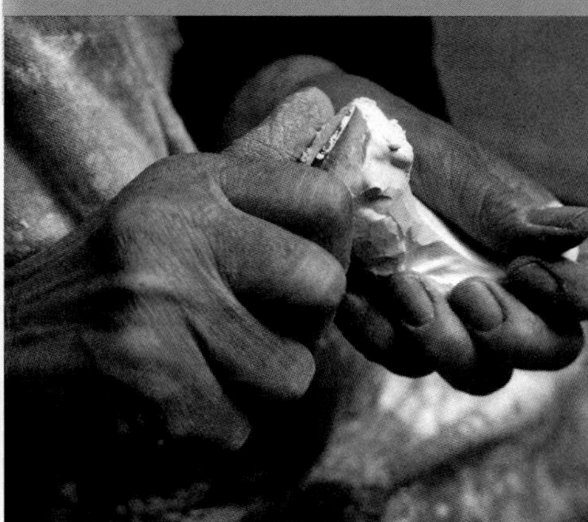

The sculpture in image B is a family scene. What family members do you see? How is image B different from image A? How are they alike?

Think About Art

What happy family memory might you show in a sculpture of your own? What materials would you use?

Multimedia Biographies
Visit *The Learning Site*
www.harcourtschool.com

71

DID YOU KNOW?

Use the facts below to elaborate on the process Henry Moore used to make sculptures.

- For many of his largest bronze sculptures, Moore began by making a small model of the subject. These models were usually made of clay or plaster.
- Moore and his assistants would then make larger plaster models that sometimes became the actual artwork.
- Moore used tools such as files and cheese graters to add texture to the working models.
- When Moore was pleased with the carving on the model, he would send it to a foundry, a place where metal is melted and poured into molds. Some of Moore's small models were also cast in bronze.

Think About Art

What happy family memory might you show in a sculpture of your own? What materials would you use? (Responses will vary. Students should identify life experiences as sources for ideas about self and life events.) **PERSONAL RESPONSE**
TEKS 3.1A

ARTIST'S EYE ACTIVITY

Model a Moore Have students use a slab of clay to produce a small ceramic sculpture of an animal in Henry Moore's style, using a variety of art materials appropriately. Tell them to omit details but to use carving tools to add textures and to smooth out the edges. TEKS 3.2C

Multimedia Art Biographies
Visit *The Learning Site*
www.harcourtschool.com

Science Connection

What Is Bronze? Explain to students that many ancient and modern sculptures are made of bronze. Bronze is an alloy, or combination, of copper and tin. It is commonly used in casting sculptures.

For additional cross-curricular suggestions, see Art Transparency 8.

TEKS 3.4B; TAKS Writing Objective 1

View an Artist's Work

Portfolios and Exhibitions
Have students locate additional images by a major artist in this unit. Students should write a paragraph that tells the names of the artworks and identifies the main idea of the artist's work. You may also want to have students visit an exhibition at a local museum.

Lesson 13

PDAS Domains I, II

Patterns in Masks

OBJECTIVES
- Identify patterns in artworks
- Produce yarn masks with symmetry
- Identify narrative elements

RESOURCES
- Discussion Cards 1, 4, pp. R34–R35
- Electronic Art Gallery CD-ROM, Primary

5 Minutes

Warm-Up

Build Background Have students discuss occasions when people might wear masks that tell a story. (in a dance or play) Point out that some masks have features or designs that help identify the culture they are from.

10-15 Minutes

Teach

Discuss Art Concepts Have students read page 72 and identify patterns in image A such as those made by triangles and by curved lines under the eyes. Have students find the pattern made from small shells. Then discuss exact symmetry in both masks. Use Discussion Card 1 to guide further discussion. TEKS 3.1B

Lesson 13

Vocabulary
patterns
symmetry

Patterns in Masks

People from many different cultures make masks. The mask in image A is from Africa. Describe the lines, shapes, and colors you see on the mask. Artists use repeating lines, shapes, and colors to create **patterns**. Point out a pattern of triangles in image A. Where on the mask do you see a pattern of curved lines?

The mask from Mexico in image B was made by gluing pieces of yarn to wood. Compare one side of the mask to the other side. The artist created **symmetry** by making one side of the mask match the other side. Does image A have symmetry? How can you tell?

A Unknown artist, African mask

B Unknown artist, Huichol yarn mask

72

Think Critically

1. READING SKILL What story do you think the mask in image B might tell? (Responses will vary.) NARRATIVE ELEMENTS
2. **How are these masks from different cultures alike and different?** (Both have symmetry, but they are made from different materials.) ART HISTORY AND CULTURE TEKS 3.3B
3. **WRITE** **List the geometric shapes in image A and the organic shapes in image B.** EXPOSITORY

FYI Background Information

Art History

The **Huichol** (WEE•chol) Indians live in remote areas of the Sierra Madre mountains in west-central Mexico. They are well known for two unique artforms—beadwork and yarn paintings—which they use to communicate their culture to people inside and outside of the community. The shapes and colors in Huichol yarn masks often stand for important ideas and beliefs.

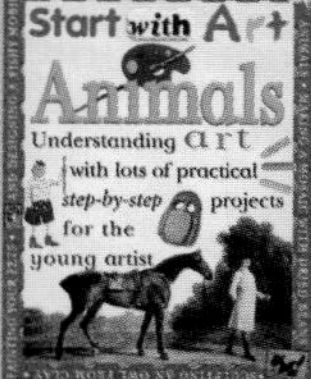

RECOMMENDED READING

Start with Art: Animals by Sue Lacey. Copper Beech Books, 1999. CHALLENGING

★ TEKS 3.1B identify elements and principles; TEKS 3.2C produce various artworks; TEKS 3.3B compare artworks from different cultures; PDAS Domain I active participation; PDAS Domain II learner-centered instruction; PDAS Domain III evaluation and feedback; PDAS Domain IV classroom management; *(continued)*

Artist's Workshop

Mexican Yarn Mask

PLAN

Sketch some ideas for a mask that has symmetry. Repeat lines and shapes to make patterns.

CREATE

1. **Draw your best idea on tagboard. Cut out the mask.**
2. **Outline the lines and shapes with glue. Press yarn onto the glue.**
3. **Glue a craft stick to the back to make a holder for your mask.**

REFLECT

Describe the patterns on your mask. How did you show symmetry?

Quick Tip: Draw a straight line down the center of your mask. Match the patterns on each side of the line to show symmetry.

73

Artist's Workshop

30-40 Minutes

Mexican Yarn Mask

MATERIALS: sketchbook, pencil, yarn, glue, tagboard (8 in. × 10 in.), scissors, craft stick

Have students add beads, buttons, or shells to their masks.

PLAN If students plan to wear their masks, have them measure the tagboard against their faces to place the openings.

CREATE Have students produce their fiberart masks, using yarn and other art materials appropriately. TEKS 3.2C

REFLECT Ask students to identify the elements of art that make up each pattern. TEKS 3.1B

Activity Options PDAS Domain IV

Quick Activity Have students use colored pencils to draw a mask with a pattern.

Early Finishers Have students use Discussion Card 4 to discuss the patterns in their masks.

Challenge See *Teacher Resource Book*, p. 63.

5-10 Minutes

Wrap-Up

Informal Assessment PDAS Domain III

- **How did the masks in this lesson give you ideas for your mask?** (Responses will vary.) EVALUATION/CRITICISM
- **What shapes or lines did you use most in your patterns?** (Responses will vary.) PERCEPTION/AESTHETICS

Extend Through Writing

TEKS 3.3B; TAKS Writing Objective 1

Compare-and-Contrast Paragraph Have students compare their masks with images A and B.

Science Connection

Symmetry in Nature Have students identify objects in nature that have symmetry. Have them use nature magazines, science books, and encyclopedias to find photographs of the objects.

PDAS Domain IV

ESL As you read aloud the directions, use simple gestures to **pantomime** each step. Then model each step before students begin that part of the activity. Draw attention to words that may be unfamiliar.

Lesson 14

PDAS Domains I, II

Patterns in Cloth

OBJECTIVES
- Identify patterns in artworks
- Produce fiberart
- Identify narrative elements

RESOURCES
- Art Print 16
- Electronic Art Gallery CD-ROM, Primary

5 Minutes

Warm-Up

Build Background Display **Art Print 16** and explain that it shows a quilt, a kind of fiber-art. Ask students to identify patterns in the quilt and name the shapes that make up each pattern. TEKS 3.1B

10-15 Minutes

Teach

Discuss Art Concepts Have students read page 74 and point out the astronaut, the American flag, and other details. Help students identify the triangle pattern along the edge of the spacecraft, as well as the repeated pattern of colored contour lines around the objects. TEKS 3.1B

Lesson 14

Vocabulary

mola

Patterns in Cloth

The image below shows a cloth panel called a **mola**. The Cuna people of Panama have been making molas for more than one hundred years. The colorful panels often show famous scenes. This mola shows a moon landing. What details do you see?

Artists make molas by sewing together layers of cloth. Each layer is a different color. Look at the edges of the spacecraft in the image below. What shape did the artist repeat to make a pattern? What other patterns do you see?

Unknown artist, Mola panel

74

Think Critically

1. Focus Skill **READING SKILL** **What is the setting of the story shown on the mola?** (the moon) NARRATIVE ELEMENTS
2. **How did the artist create patterns in the cloth?** (by cutting shapes into the layers of cloth) PERCEPTION/AESTHETICS
3. WRITE **Compare the content in the mola and the quilt. Explain how these present-day artworks tell a story and show a moment in United States history.** EXPOSITORY TEKS 3.3A; TAKS Writing Objective 1

FYI

Background Information

Art History

The **Cuna** people live on more than 365 islands and a strip of land on the eastern coast of Panama. A mola takes many hours to design and sew. Cuna women are proud of their ability to create fine molas, which are judged by the choice of design and color combinations, the quality of the stitching, the number of layers, and any details that have been added with embroidery.

RECOMMENDED READING

Nature's Paintbrush by Susan Stockdale. Simon & Schuster, 1999. AVERAGE

★ **TEKS 3.1A** identify sources for ideas; **TEKS 3.1B** identify elements and principles; **TEKS 3.2C** produce various artworks; **TEKS 3.3A** compare artworks from the past and present; **PDAS Domain I** active participation; **PDAS Domain II** learner-centered instruction; **PDAS Domain III** evaluation and feedback; *(continued)*

Artist's Workshop

Bird Mola

PLAN

Find a picture of a bird you like. Draw the shape of the bird in three different sizes. Cut out the shapes.

CREATE

1. Set aside one color of felt material for the bottom layer of your mola.
2. Use a marker to trace each shape onto a different color of felt material.
3. Cut out each shape from the center.
4. Glue the piece with the smallest cutout onto your bottom layer first. Glue down the piece with the medium cutout next and the piece with the largest cutout last.

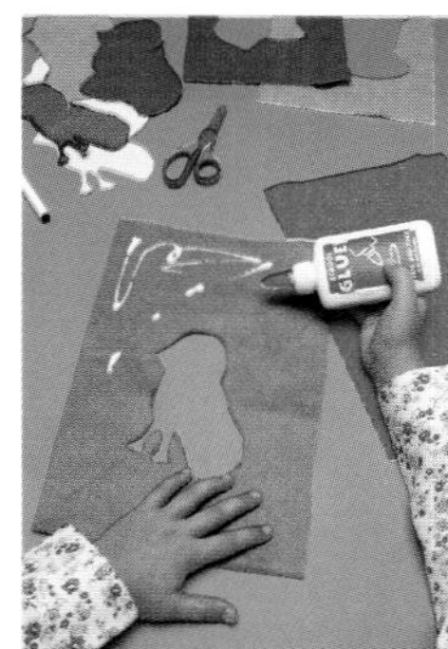

REFLECT

How did the layers of your mola make the design interesting?

Safety Tips As you cut, point the scissors away from your body.

75

Social Studies Connection

Fabric Artists Tell students that in almost every culture, artworks made out of fabric have been created for clothing and household use. In the United States, quilts are a traditional fabric art. Have students research common quilt patterns and present their findings, with illustrations.

MEETING INDIVIDUAL NEEDS PDAS Domain IV

ESL Use **visuals** to support **comprehensible input** for the features of birds. Display ***Picture Cards Collection,*** card 14, for students to discuss and use as a reference.

See also ***Picture Card Bank*** **CD-ROM,** Category: Animals/Wild.

30-40 Minutes

Artist's Workshop

Bird Mola

MATERIALS: magazines, paper, pencil, marker, 4 different-colored felt pieces, scissors, glue

Quick Tip Have students place bright colors next to each other for more interest.

PLAN Have students make sure the sizes of their shapes vary so that each bird will show.

CREATE As students produce their fiberart, model how to cut the shapes from the middle of the felt. TEKS 3.2C

REFLECT Have students compare their molas, noting the features that make them unique.

Activity Options PDAS Domain IV

Quick Activity Have students create molas with construction paper.

Early Finishers Have students add beads or other materials to create a design along the edges of their molas.

Challenge See *Teacher Resource Book*, p. 64.

5-10 Minutes

Wrap-Up

Informal Assessment PDAS Domain III

- **Why do you think molas have layers?** (Responses will vary.) PERCEPTION/AESTHETICS
- **Do you prefer making artworks on paper or with cloth?** (Responses will vary.) PERSONAL RESPONSE

Extend Through Writing

TEKS 3.1A; TAKS Writing Objective 1

Descriptive Paragraph Have students describe a design for a mola, identifying life experiences as sources for ideas about self and life events.

PDAS Domain IV classroom management; TAKS Writing Objective 1 composition

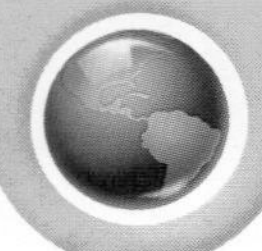

ART ⟷ SOCIAL STUDIES CONNECTION

PDAS Domains I, II

Western Wear

COMMUNITY ART

DISCUSS THE IMAGES

Have students read pages 76–77.

- Tell students that the boots in image A are full of visual symbols from Eisenhower's life experiences. Have students identify the U.S. Capitol; the Great Seal of the United States; sunflowers, the Kansas state flower; and the President's nickname, *Ike*. Explain that these boots were given to Eisenhower in 1953 when he was President. Tell students that President Eisenhower was a big fan of Western movies and books about the Wild West. TEKS 3.1A
- As students discuss the boot in image B, ask them to speculate about what kind of person might own boots like this one. (a person from Texas who has state pride)
- Ask students to describe and point out the kinds of lines the artist used in image C, such as wavy, horizontal, and diagonal. TEKS 3.1B

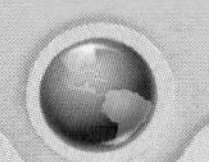

Western Wear

How have cowboy boots changed over many years?

The first cowboys in the United States wore boots to make their jobs easier. The boots reached halfway up the cowboy's legs to protect him from snow, mud, and thorns. The toes of the boots were pointed so that cowboys could easily slip their feet into stirrups.

Zeferino and Eli Rios, Cowboy boots A

Over time, cowboy boots have become popular with people who do not work on ranches or compete in rodeos. Artists have made special boots to show things that are important to the person who wears them. The boots in image **A** were a gift to President Dwight Eisenhower. The pictures on the boots tell about Washington, D.C., and Kansas, where President Eisenhower grew up.

Background Information

Art History

Cowboy boots are a symbol of the United States recognized all over the world. Some cowboy boots are considered "wearable art" and are part of museum exhibits and private collections. The design of cowboy boots combines practical and decorative details. The stitching on the upper parts stiffens them; the toe and heel caps protect the leather; the fancy stitching across the instep, called *wrinkles*, makes the top of the boot more flexible; and the bootstraps help with pulling on the boots.

For related artworks, see **Electronic Art Gallery CD-ROM, Primary.**

★ **TEKS 3.1A** identify sources for ideas; **TEKS 3.1B** identify elements and principles; **TEKS 3.2C** produce various artworks; **TEKS 3.4B** identify main ideas in artworks by peers and others; **PDAS Domain I** active participation; **PDAS Domain II** learner-centered instruction

Texas cowboy boot

The boot in image B has the Texas flag on it. Why do you think someone might wear boots like this one?

The artist of image C used different kinds of lines to create a pattern. How would you describe this drawing to someone who has not seen it?

DID YOU KNOW?

The design of the American cowboy hat was borrowed from Mexican sombreros like the one shown below. Sombreros were made with wide brims to protect Mexican cowboys, or vaqueros, from the hot sun.

Mexican sombrero

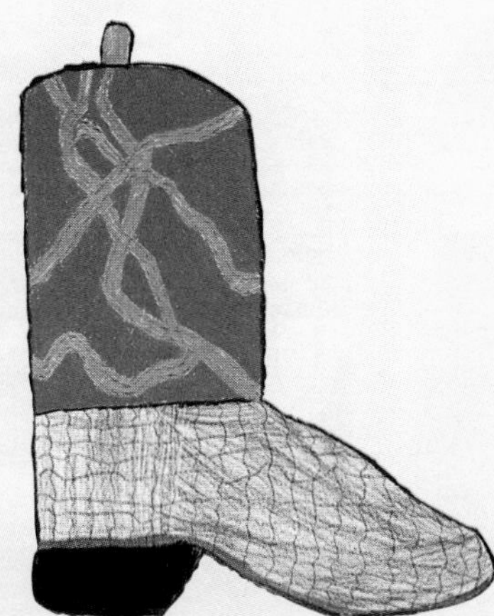

Think About Art

Imagine you are designing a pair of boots for yourself. What would you include to show what is important to you?

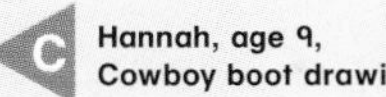
Hannah, age 9, Cowboy boot drawing

77

DID YOU KNOW?

Use the facts below to discuss what cowboys wore in the past and what many still wear today.

- Cowboys' hats protected them from sun, wind, rain, and snow. The space between a cowboy's head and the top of his hat kept his head cool.
- Cowboys wore leather pants called *chaps* over their canvas or denim jeans. The chaps protected their legs from thorns and cacti. The design was borrowed from *chaparajos* (shap•ah•RAY•ohs) that Mexican cowboys wore.
- Cowboys wore spurs on their boots to help them guide their horses. The spurs had wheels that the cowboy would press against the horse's side to control it.
- Cowboys today still wear special boots, hats, chaps, and spurs to help them in their jobs and to make them look like authentic Western cowboys.

Think About Art

Imagine you are designing a pair of boots for yourself. What would you include to show what is important to you? (Responses will vary. Students should identify life experiences as sources for ideas about visual symbols and self.)

PERSONAL RESPONSE TEKS 3.1A

ARTIST'S EYE ACTIVITY

Ceramic Boot Point out to students that cowboys and their clothing have been made popular by movies and television shows about the West. Have students imagine they are costume designers for a cowboy movie, and have them sculpt a small ceramic cowboy boot, using clay and other art materials appropriately. Tell them to use carving tools to add textures and other interesting details. TEKS 3.2C

Social Studies Connection

Cowboy Museums Tell students that they can find Western art and cowboy clothing at many museums in the United States, including the Texas Cowboy Hall of Fame in Forth Worth, Texas.

For additional cross-curricular suggestions, see Art Transparency 9.

TEKS 3.4B

Student Art Show

Portfolios and Exhibitions Periodically during this unit, have students create a display or exhibition of their portfolios or other finished artworks. Ask students to use simple criteria to identify main ideas in peers' artworks. See *Teacher Edition* page 142 for information on planning and preparing a student art show.

Lesson 15

PDAS Domains I, II

Mural Art

OBJECTIVES
- Identify movement in artworks
- Produce mural paintings
- Identify narrative elements

RESOURCES
- Discussion Card 10, p. R38
- Electronic Art Gallery CD-ROM, Primary

5 Minutes

Warm-Up

Build Background Ask students to imagine that they could paint directly onto the walls of a public building in your community. Have students brainstorm the subjects they would choose.

10-15 Minutes

Teach

Discuss Art Concepts Have students read pages 78–79. Students should note the way the viewer's eye moves in an arc around the actual doorway in image A. In image B, students should identify the patterns created by the stars and stripes on the American flag and by the repeated shapes of the children. Discuss American symbols in the mural. TEKS 3.1B

Think Critically

1. READING SKILL **What story do you think image A tells?** (a busy day at the market) NARRATIVE ELEMENTS
2. **Images A and B show artworks from different cultures. How are they alike?** (Both show people in an activity together.) ART HISTORY AND CULTURE TEKS 3.3B
3. WRITE **Write the beginning of the story you see in image B.** NARRATIVE TAKS Writing Objective 1

Lesson 15

Vocabulary

mural

Mural Art

A **mural** is a large painting that covers a wall on the inside or the outside of a building. Image **A** shows a mural on a building in Mexico City, Mexico. Why do you think an artist would choose to paint murals instead of smaller paintings?

Murals often show people doing everyday things. Look at the crowded street in image **A**. How did the artist create movement in his mural? What path do your eyes take around it?

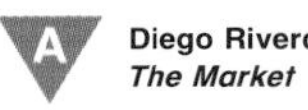

A Diego Rivera, *The Market*

FYI

Background Information

About the Artist

Diego Rivera (DYAY•goh ree•VAY•rah) (1886–1957) was an important painter in the Mexican mural movement. He painted his murals using the fresco technique—painting directly onto a wall surface. Rivera's artworks show everyday lives of Mexican people, as well as events from Mexican history.

For additional information about Rivera, see pp. R44–R59.

RECOMMENDED READING

Diego by Jeanette Winter. Alfred A. Knopf, 1991. AVERAGE

★ **TEKS 3.1A** identify sources for ideas; **TEKS 3.1B** identify elements and principles; **TEKS 3.2A** create artworks; **TEKS 3.2C** produce various artworks; **TEKS 3.3B** compare artworks from different cultures; **TEKS 3.4A** identify intent in personal artworks; **PDAS Domain I** active participation; **PDAS Domain II** learner-centered instruction; *(continued)*

Image B is part of a large mural made by a group of children. What story do you think it tells about the United States? What kinds of patterns did the artists create in image B?

Unknown artists, *Mural (America)*

Artist's Workshop

Community Mural

1. **Work with a partner to brainstorm ideas for a mural about your community or another community. Then sketch one idea.**
2. **Transfer your sketch to a large sheet of butcher paper.**
3. **Think about how you want viewers' eyes to move around the mural. Place objects in the mural to create movement.**
4. **Paint your mural.**

79

30-40 Minutes

Artist's Workshop

Community Mural

MATERIALS: sketchbook, pencil, butcher paper, tempera paints, paintbrushes, water bowl

Quick Tip Tell students to paint their murals in sections, from top to bottom.

PLAN Students should identify life experiences, local landmarks, or cultural celebrations as their subjects. TEKS 3.1A

CREATE Have students draw a faint line on the butcher paper to indicate the path they want viewers' eyes to take and then produce their paintings. TEKS 3.2A, TEKS 3.2C

REFLECT Have students identify the general intent in their artwork. TEKS 3.4A

Activity Options PDAS Domain IV

Quick Activity Students can each make one small drawing and join them to make a mural.

Early Finishers Have students use Discussion Card 10 to discuss their murals.

Challenge See *Teacher Resource Book*, p. 65.

5-10 Minutes

Wrap-Up

Informal Assessment PDAS Domain III

- **How did you create movement in your mural?** (Responses will vary.) PERCEPTION/AESTHETICS
- **What story does your mural tell?** (Responses will vary.) NARRATIVE ELEMENTS

Extend Through Writing

TAKS Writing Objective 1

Letter Have students write a letter to persuade city officials to commission a mural for a specific site.

Social Studies Connection

Mural Search Many communities have murals on the outside or inside of public buildings. Have students research public art in your community. Ask them to describe the artworks and their significance. Students may also brainstorm sites where they would like to see a mural created.

PDAS Domain IV

ESL Use **visuals** to support **comprehensible input** for words associated with neighborhoods and communities. Display ***Picture Cards Collection,*** cards 17, 26, and 92, for students to discuss and use as reference.

See also ***Picture Card Bank*** **CD-ROM,** Category: At Work.

PDAS Domain III evaluation and feedback; **PDAS Domain IV** classroom management; **TAKS Writing Objective 1** composition

Unit 3

PDAS Domains I, III

Review and Reflect

Have students reflect on what they have learned about the ways artists tell stories in artworks. Display **Art Prints 3, 7, 8, 9,** and **16.** Have students identify art principles such as proportion, movement, and pattern in the images. Ask small groups to use their completed Word Knowledge Charts and Discussion Cards 3 and 4, page R35, to discuss what they learned about the vocabulary and concepts in this unit. TEKS 3.1B

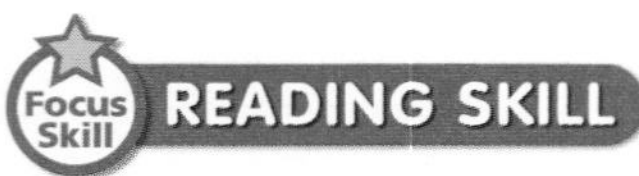

Vocabulary and Concepts

Have students read each sentence and choose the letter of the word or phrase that best completes it. (1. B; 2. C; 3. B; 4. A; 5. B)

READING SKILL

Narrative Elements

Remind students that the narrative elements of a story or an artwork are the characters, the setting, and the plot. Have students look for the narrative elements in the mola on page 74 and then complete a story map. For the plot, ask students to imagine what happened before and after the scene in the mola. You may want to have volunteers or students who are interested in space travel share their ideas with the class.

Characters
3 astronauts

Setting
on the moon

Plot (Story Events)
1. Astronauts travel to the moon.
2. They make discoveries about space.
3. They return to Earth to share what they learned.

Unit 3 Review and Reflect

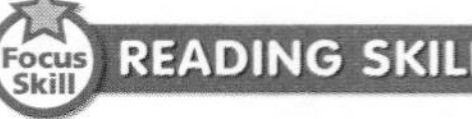

Vocabulary and Concepts

Choose the letter of the word or phrase that best completes each sentence.

1 A ___ is an artwork that an artist paints of himself or herself.

A portrait **C** mural
B self-portrait **D** mola

2 ___ is the size and placement of some things compared with other things.

A Movement **C** Proportion
B Pattern **D** Symmetry

3 Artists create ___ to guide your eyes around an artwork.

A portraits **C** proportion
B movement **D** murals

4 Artists repeat lines, shapes, and colors to make ___.

A patterns **C** molas
B proportion **D** sculptures

5 A ___ is a large painting that covers a wall.

A portrait **C** seascape
B mural **D** mola

READING SKILL

Narrative Elements

Look at the image on page 74. What story is the artist trying to tell? Use a story map like the one shown here to record your ideas.

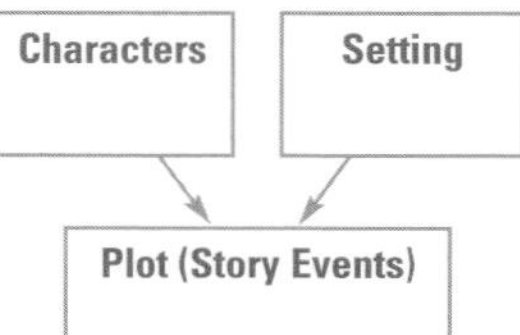

80

TEKS 3.3C

Home and Community Connection

School-Home Connection

Copy and distribute *Teacher Resource Book* pp. 89–90 to inform parents about upcoming art projects. Encourage students to share what they have learned about public art with their families.

Community Connection

Have students relate art to different kinds of jobs in everyday life. Use prompts such as these to get them started: *Who makes costumes for plays and movies? Who designs the covers of books?* Ask students to think about how some art careers have changed over time due to new technology or other factors.

★ **TEKS 3.1B** identify elements and principles; **TEKS 3.3C** relate art to different jobs; **TEKS 3.4B** identify main ideas in artworks by peers and others; **PDAS Domain I** active participation; **PDAS Domain III** evaluation and feedback; **TAKS Writing Objective 1** composition; **TAKS Writing Objective 2** conventions; *(continued)*

Write About Art

Write a story for one of your own artworks. Use a story map to plan your writing.

REMEMBER—YOU SHOULD

- describe the characters and setting of your story.
- tell the events in the plot.
- use correct grammar, spelling, and punctuation.

Critic's Corner

Look at the mural to answer the questions below.

Unknown artist,
Mural showing waterfront activities

DESCRIBE What are the people in the artwork doing?

ANALYZE How did the artist use proportion? What do you think the artist wanted viewers to see first?

INTERPRET Do you think the artist wanted to create a calm feeling or a busy feeling? Why do you think so?

EVALUATE Do you like the way this artwork shows people doing different activities? Why or why not?

81

PDAS Domain III

Assessment

Portfolio Assessment

Work with students to choose a piece of their artwork to include in their portfolios. Suggest that they decide which piece best fulfilled the assignment or which piece they liked best for another reason. You may want to provide specific feedback that targets students' use of elements, principles, and techniques. See also Portfolio Recording Form, page R32.

Additional Assessment Options

- Progress Recording Form, p. R33
- Artist's Workshop Rubrics (Self/Teacher and Peer), pp. R30–R31
- Unit 3 Test, *Teacher Resource Book* p. 101

Write About Art

Story Read aloud the prompt with students. Suggest that students use the story map on page 80 to help them plan their stories. Tell students to choose an artwork that shows characters and a setting. Remind students to organize the events of the plot in order. TAKS Writing Objectives 1, 2, 3, 5

Critic's Corner

RESPONSE/EVALUATION Use Discussion Card 2, page R34, and the steps below to guide students in analyzing the mural.

DESCRIBE Discuss with students the characters in the artwork. Have students describe what the characters are doing.

ANALYZE Students should point out that the artist used proportion to place facial features. Ask students to describe the path their eyes take around the mural. TEKS 3.1B

INTERPRET Students should use details to support the idea that the mural has a busy feeling. Point out the many activities going on at the same time.

EVALUATE Ask students to think about whether the artist succeeded in showing a busy scene of people doing different things. Have them share their opinions about the main idea of the mural. TEKS 3.4B

TAKS Test Preparation: Reading and Writing Through Art, pp. 27–47

TAKS Writing Objective 3 organization; TAKS Writing Objective 5 usage

Unit 4 Space and Emphasis

Special Places

From the calm ocean waters to the streets of a busy city, artists have unique ways of interpreting their environment. In this unit students will examine space and emphasis in artworks that show special places around the world.

Resources

- Unit 4 Art Prints (10–12)
- Additional Art Prints (2, 6)
- Art Transparencies 10–12
- Test Preparation: Reading and Writing Through Art, pp. 48–52
- Artist's Workshop Activities: English and Spanish, pp. 31–40
- Encyclopedia of Artists and Art History, pp. R44–R59
- Picture Cards Collection, cards 26, 29, 48, 65, 89, 98, 115

Using the Art Prints

- Discussion Cards, pp. R34–R38
- Teaching suggestions, backs of Art Prints
- Art Print Teaching Suggestions: Spanish

Teacher Resource Book

- Vocabulary Cards in English and Spanish, pp. 19–22
- Reading Skill Card 4, p. 34
- Copying Masters, pp. 46, 47
- Challenge Activities, pp. 66–70
- School-Home Connection: English/Spanish, pp. 91–92
- Unit 4 Test, p. 102

Technology Resources

Electronic Art Gallery CD-ROM, Primary

Picture Card Bank CD-ROM

Visit *The Learning Site*
www.harcourtschool.com

- Multimedia Art Glossary
- Multimedia Biographies
- Reading Skills and Activities

Art Prints for This Unit

ART PRINT 6

From the Castle's Kitchen
by Patrick Dougherty

ART PRINT 2

Munich Houses
by Wassily Kandinsky

ART PRINT 10

Marine Landscape
by Stuart Davis

ART PRINT 11

Poinciana Tree #150
by Mary Ann Carroll

ART PRINT 12

Snap the Whip
by Winslow Homer

Unit 4 Special Places Space and Emphasis

Planning Guide

PDAS Domain IV

Lesson	Objectives and Vocabulary	Art Images	Production/ Materials
Cause and Effect, pp. 84–85			
16 HORIZON LINE pp. 86–87 30–60 minutes	• Identify space in artworks • Produce watercolor paintings Focus Skill: Identify cause-and-effect relationships in artworks **Vocabulary: horizon line, space, depth**	• **Boats Together at the Sea** by Arturo Gordon • **Valley Pasture** by Robert Scott Duncanson	**Saltwater Seascape** ❑ watercolor paper ❑ pencil ❑ watercolors ❑ paintbrushes ❑ water bowl ❑ table salt
17 DEPTH IN LANDSCAPES pp. 88–89 30–60 minutes	• Identify depth in artworks • Produce landscape drawings Focus Skill: Identify cause-and-effect relationships in artworks **Vocabulary: foreground, background**	• **Fuji from Kogane-Ga-Hara, Shimosa** by Ando Hiroshige	**Landscape Drawing** ❑ magazines ❑ sketchbook ❑ pencil ❑ white paper ❑ colored pencils
Art↔Science Connection: Forces in Nature, pp. 90–91			
18 OVERLAPPING LINES AND SHAPES pp. 92–93 30–60 minutes	• Identify how overlapping lines and shapes create depth in artworks • Paint a cityscape that shows depth Focus Skill: Identify cause-and-effect relationships in artworks **Vocabulary: cityscape, overlapping**	• **Looking Along Broadway Towards Grace Church** by Red Grooms • **City Lights** by Laura, grade 3	**Cityscape Painting** ❑ magazines ❑ books ❑ construction paper ❑ tempera paints ❑ paintbrushes ❑ water bowl ❑ markers
19 CENTER OF INTEREST pp. 94–95 30–60 minutes	• Identify emphasis in artworks • Produce drawings with a center of interest Focus Skill: Identify cause-and-effect relationships in artworks **Vocabulary: center of interest, emphasis, contrast**	• **The Cozy Coupe** by Reynard Milici	**Outdoor Scene** ❑ sketchbook ❑ pencil ❑ white paper ❑ colored pencils
Art↔Social Studies Connection: Winslow Homer, pp. 96–97			
20 ART IN NATURE pp. 98–99 30–60 minutes	• Identify emphasis in artworks • Produce a garden design Focus Skill: Identify cause-and-effect relationships in artworks **Vocabulary: earthworks**	• **Ornamental Municipal Gardens in Angers, France** • **Surrounded Islands** by Christo and Jeanne-Claude	**Garden Design** ❑ white paper ❑ pencil ❑ crayons or colored pencils
Review and Reflect, pp. 100–101			

★ **TEKS 3.2A** create artworks; **TEKS 3.2C** produce various artworks; **PDAS Domain IV** classroom management

Cause and Effect pp. 84–85

Opportunities for application of the skill are provided on pp. 86, 88, 92, 94, 98, 100, and 101.

Resources and Technology	Suggested Literature	Across the Curriculum
• Art Print 2 • Reading Skill Card 4 Electronic Art Gallery CD-ROM, Primary	*Going to the Getty* by J. Otto Seibold and Vivian Walsh	**Science** Sunrise, Sunset, p. 87 **Reading**  Cause and Effect, p. 86 **Writing** Postcard, p. 87
• Art Print 12 • Discussion Card 6, p. R36 • Reading Skill Card 4 Electronic Art Gallery CD-ROM, Primary	*Hokusai: The Man Who Painted a Mountain* by Deborah Kogan Ray	**Social Studies** Mount Fuji, p. 89 **Reading**  Cause and Effect, p. 88 **Writing** Poem, p. 89
• Art Print 10 • Reading Skill Card 4 Electronic Art Gallery CD-ROM, Primary	*Art Dog* by Thacher Hurd  	**Health** Traffic Safety, p. 93 **Reading** Cause and Effect, p. 92 **Writing** Compare-and-Contrast Paragraph, p. 93
• Art Print 11 • Discussion Card 4, p. R35 • Reading Skill Card 4 Electronic Art Gallery CD-ROM, Primary	*Lunchtime for a Purple Snake* by Harriet Ziefert 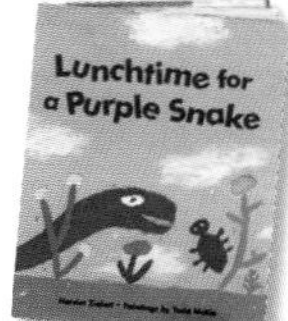 	**Math** Finding the Center, p. 95 **Reading** Cause and Effect, p. 94 **Writing** Story Starter, p. 95
• Art Print 6 • Reading Skill Card 4 Electronic Art Gallery CD-ROM, Primary	*Sunflower Sal* by Janet S. Anderson  	**Science** Gardens, p. 99 **Reading** Cause and Effect, p. 98 **Writing** Advertisement, p. 99

Art Puzzlers

Present these art puzzlers to students at the beginning or end of a class or when students finish an assignment early.

- Cut a square from the middle of a piece of paper to create a viewfinder. Go outside and look at the **horizon line** through the hole in your paper. Draw what you see. TEKS 3.2A, TEKS 3.2C
- Draw a landscape that shows **depth** for a calendar page. Include objects related to a fall or a winter month. TEKS 3.2C
- Use construction paper and a shoe box to make a diorama of a city scene. Create depth in your scene by **overlapping** shapes and objects. TEKS 3.2C
- Create a line design that shows **emphasis**. Use contrasting lines and colors to make one part of your drawing stand out. TEKS 3.2C
- Find natural objects such as sticks and pebbles to create an **earthwork** construction. TEKS 3.2C

School-Home Connection

The activities above are included in the School-Home Connection for this unit. See *Teacher Resource Book* pp. 91–92.

Assessment Options

- Rubrics and Recording Forms, pp. R30–R33
- Unit 4 Test, *Teacher Resource Book*, p. 102

Visit *The Learning Site*: *www.harcourtschool.com*

Artist's Workshops PREVIEW

PDAS Domain IV

Use these pages to help you gather and organize materials for the production activity in each lesson.

LESSON	MATERIALS
16 Saltwater Seascape p. 87	• watercolor paper • pencil • watercolors • paintbrushes • table salt • water bowl
Objective: Produce watercolor paintings that show space and depth	
 **30–40 minutes**	
Challenge Activity: See *Teacher Resource Book,* page 66.	

LESSON

LESSON	MATERIALS
17 Landscape Drawing p. 89	• magazines • sketchbook • pencil • white paper • colored pencils
Objective: Produce landscape drawings that show space and depth	
 **30–40 minutes**	
Challenge Activity: See *Teacher Resource Book,* page 67.	

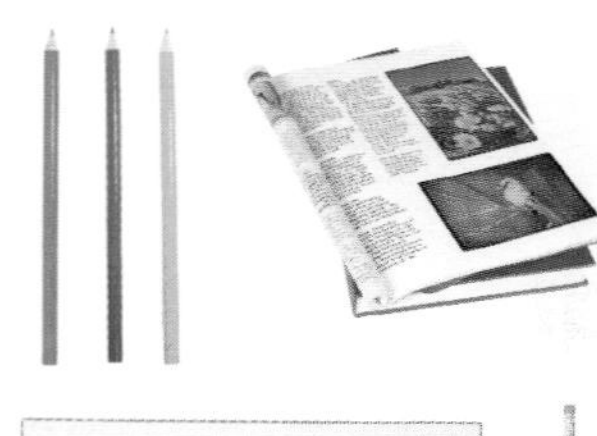

For safety information, see Art Safety, page R4; or the Art Safety Poster.

For information on media and techniques, see pp. R15–R23.

LESSON	MATERIALS

18 Cityscape Painting p. 93

Objective: Paint a cityscape that uses overlapping to show depth

 **30–40 minutes**

Challenge Activity: See *Teacher Resource Book,* page 68.

Materials:

- magazines
- books
- sketchbook
- pencil
- construction paper
- tempera paints
- paintbrushes
- water bowl
- markers

LESSON

19 Outdoor Scene p. 95

Objective: Produce drawings that use contrast to show a center of interest

 **30–40 minutes**

Challenge Activity: See *Teacher Resource Book,* page 69.

Materials:

- sketchbook
- pencil
- white paper
- colored pencils

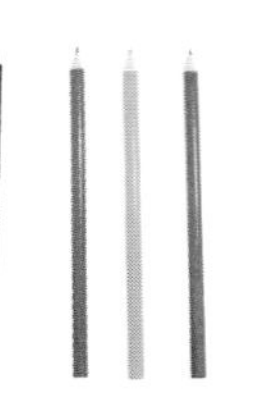

LESSON

20 Garden Design p. 99

Objective: Produce a garden design drawing that shows emphasis

 **30–40 minutes**

Challenge Activity: See *Teacher Resource Book,* page 70.

Materials:

- white paper
- pencil
- crayons or colored pencils

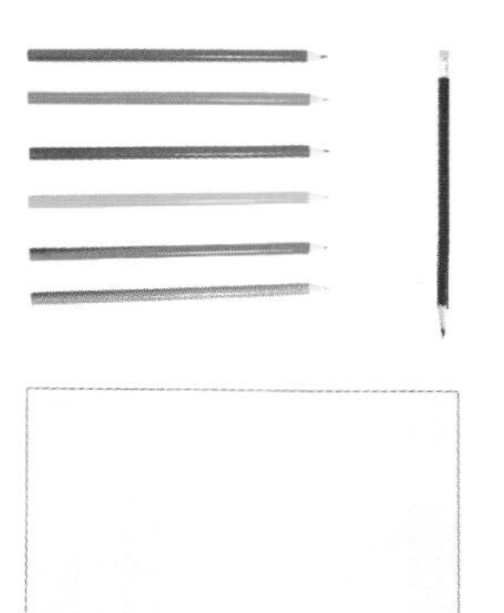

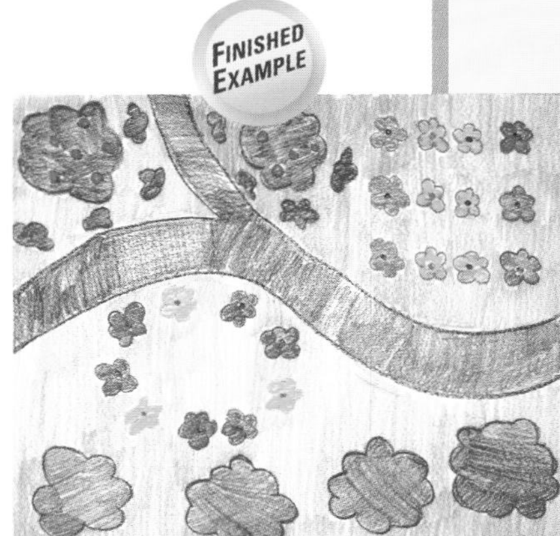

PDAS Domains I, II

Special Places

PREVIEW THE UNIT

Tell students that in this unit they will view and create artworks that show the beauty of different places in the world. Ask volunteers to describe a place that is special to them. Then have students page through the unit and preview the images.

SHARE THE POEM

Have students read aloud the poem on page 83 and then view the painting.

How is the lighthouse in the painting like the lighthouse described in the poem? What would you see looking out from the lighthouse at night? (Possible responses: Both are white; sailing ships.) COMPARE AND CONTRAST

STEP INTO THE ART

Have students look carefully at the painting and identify sensory knowledge as sources for ideas to describe how their life events would be different if they lived near a lighthouse.

What would it be like to live in the house attached to this lighthouse? What looks special about this place to you? (Responses will vary.) PERSONAL RESPONSE TEKS 3.1A

SHARE BACKGROUND INFORMATION

Tell students that Edward Hopper painted *The Lighthouse at Two Lights* in Cape Elizabeth, Maine. Explain that Hopper spent many summers in Maine. In 1929, he painted three oil paintings and several watercolors of this 120-foot-tall lighthouse tower.

LOCATE IT See **Using the Maps of Museums and Art Sites**, p. R2.

Edward Hopper, *The Lighthouse at Two Lights*

LOCATE IT

This painting can be found at The Metropolitan Museum of Art in New York City.

See Maps of Museums and Art Sites, pages 144–147.

82

Background Information

About the Artist

Edward Hopper (1882–1967) discovered his love of boats and water while growing up near the Hudson River in New York. Hopper is best known for his realistic paintings of rural and city life, called American Scene Paintings.

For additional information about Hopper and American Scene Painting, see the Encyclopedia of Artists and Art History, pp. R44–R59, and the Gallery of Artists, *Student Edition* pp. 178–188.

For related artworks, see **Electronic Art Gallery CD-ROM, Primary.**

★ **TEKS 3.1A** identify sources for ideas; **PDAS Domain I** active participation; **PDAS Domain II** learner-centered instruction

Unit 4 Space and Emphasis

Special Places

I'd Like to Be a Lighthouse

I'd like to be a lighthouse
  And scrubbed and painted white.
I'd like to be a lighthouse
  And stay awake all night
To keep my eye on everything
  That sails my patch of sea;
I'd like to be a lighthouse
  With the ships all watching me.

Rachel Field

Unit Vocabulary

horizon line	overlapping
space	center of interest
depth	emphasis
foreground	contrast
background	earthworks
cityscape	

ABOUT THE ARTIST

See Gallery of Artists, pages 178–188.

Multimedia Art Glossary
Visit *The Learning Site*
www.harcourtschool.com

83

Unit Vocabulary

Read aloud the terms with students. Then use the Word Knowledge Chart below to assess and discuss their prior knowledge.

horizon line a line in the distance where the sky seems to meet land or water

space the distance or area between or around objects

depth the appearance of space or distance in a two-dimensional artwork

foreground the part of an artwork that seems to be closest to the viewer

background the part of an artwork that seems to be farthest away from the viewer

cityscape an artwork that shows a view of a city

overlapping the placement of some objects to partly cover other objects to show which objects are closest to the viewer

center of interest the part of an artwork that the viewer notices first

emphasis a design principle used to show which part of an artwork is most important

contrast a difference between two parts of an artwork that makes one or both stand out

earthworks artworks that are made of natural materials and placed in a natural setting

Vocabulary Resources

- Vocabulary Cards in English and Spanish: *Teacher Resource Book*, pp. 19–22
- Student Edition Glossary, pp. 189–197

Language Arts Connection

Have students create a chart like the one below to identify familiar and unfamiliar vocabulary terms. Encourage them to add information to their charts as they work through this unit.

WORD KNOWLEDGE CHART		
I know this term.	I have seen this term before.	I have never seen this term.

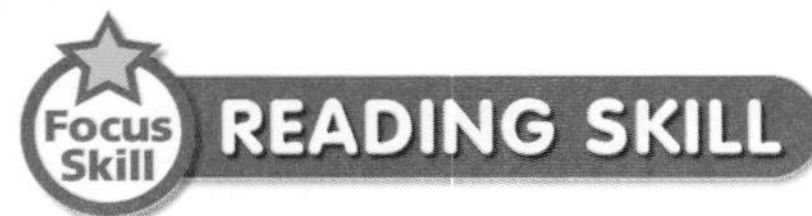

PDAS Domains I, II

Cause and Effect

SKILL TRACE	
CAUSE AND EFFECT	
Introduce	pp. 84–85
Review	pp. 86, 88, 92, 94, 98, 100, 101

DISCUSS THE SKILL

Access Prior Knowledge Display Picture Card 65, and ask students to describe the picture. (A girl is smiling.) Then ask them why they think she is smiling. (Something has made her happy.) Tell students that the girl is smiling *because* something happened that made her happy. Explain that what happened is the cause, and feeling happy and smiling is the effect.

APPLY TO ART

Cause and Effect in Art Have students read page 84 and look at the images. Tell students that the paintings show haystacks, or large piles of hay that are stored for feeding farm animals. Then explain that the paintings look different from each other because they were painted in different seasons and in different light. Point out that the changing weather and light caused the scene to look different at different times of the year. Have students share other effects in image A that were caused by winter weather. (There is snow on the haystacks.) Then tell students to look for details in image B that are effects of warm weather. (The grass and trees are green.)

Cause and Effect

A *cause* is the reason something happens. What happens is an *effect*.

Look at the images below. The artist painted the same subject at different times of the year.

- In image **A**, the cold weather and dim light caused the colors to look pale. The pale blues, grays, and white are effects of the cold and the dim light.
- In image **B**, the warm weather and bright sunlight caused the colors to be bright. The bright colors are effects of the bright sunlight.

Claude Monet, ***Landscape—Haystacks in the Snow***

Claude Monet, ***Grainstacks in Bright Sunlight***

Background Information

About the Artist

Claude Monet (KLOHD moh•NAY) (1840–1926) is often called the founder of **Impressionism**. He painted the haystacks in a farmer's field near his home in France. Monet often worked on five or six haystack paintings at the same time, switching canvases when the light or the weather changed.

For additional information about Monet and Impressionism, see pp. R44–R59.

For related artworks, see **Electronic Art Gallery CD-ROM, Primary.**

★ **PDAS Domain I** active participation; **PDAS Domain II** learner-centered instruction; **PDAS Domain IV** classroom management; **TAKS Reading Objective 3** use a variety of strategies; **TAKS Reading Objective 4** apply critical-thinking skills

You can also look for causes and effects to help you understand what you read. Find clues that tell what happened or why something happened. Read the passage below to find causes and effects.

> Claude Monet (moh•NAY) was a painter from France. He painted outdoors because he wanted to see how light and colors changed between different seasons and different times of the day. Beginning in 1890, Monet made more than thirty paintings of haystacks near his home. He also created many paintings of his own garden.

Why did Claude Monet paint outdoors? Use a diagram like this to write the cause and the effect.

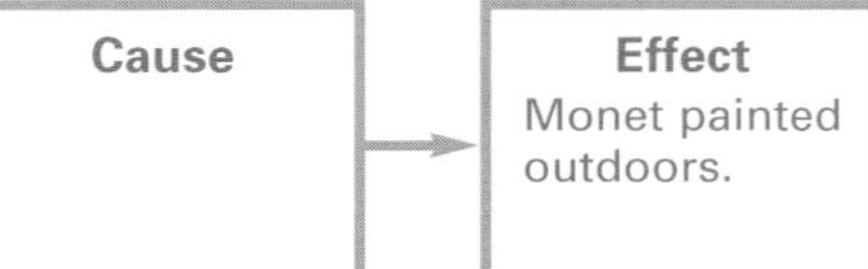

On Your Own

As you read the lessons in this unit, use diagrams like the one above to write causes and effects that you find in the text and in the artworks.

APPLY TO READING

Cause and Effect in Text Tell students that looking for causes and effects when they read will help them understand why things happen or why characters did certain things. Explain to students that signal words such as *because, so,* and *so that* will help them identify causes and effects.

Have students read the passage on page 85. Tell them to look for signal words. Then have students complete the diagram to tell why Monet painted outdoors. TAKS Reading Objectives 3, 4

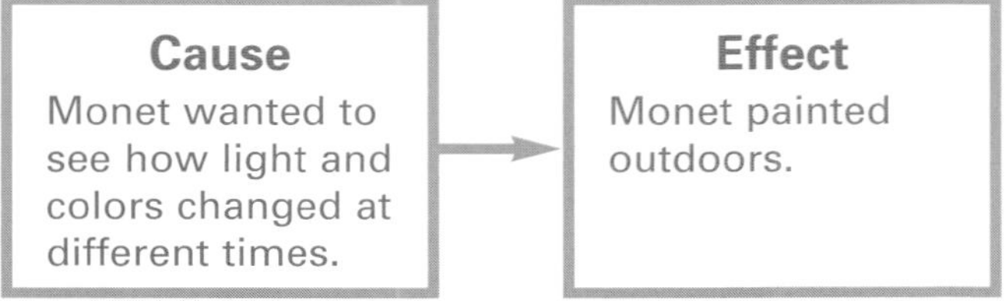

ON YOUR OWN

As students read the lessons in this unit, have them use diagrams to write causes and effects they find in the text and in the artworks.
TAKS Reading Objectives 3, 4

Focus Skill — TAKS Reading Objectives 3, 4

Reading Skill Card

Distribute Reading Skill Card 4, *Teacher Resource Book,* p. 34. Have students use it to look for causes and effects in this unit.

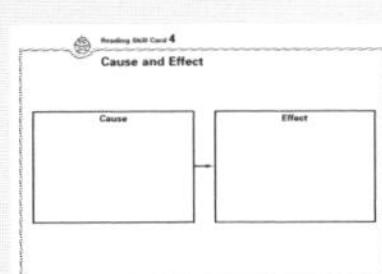

Extend the Skill
For additional teaching suggestions, see **Art Transparency 10.**

PDAS Domain IV

ESL **Modify instruction** for students by reading the paragraph aloud. Stop as necessary to **paraphrase** the text. Then pair students with English-fluent peers to identify the sentence that shows a cause-and-effect relationship.

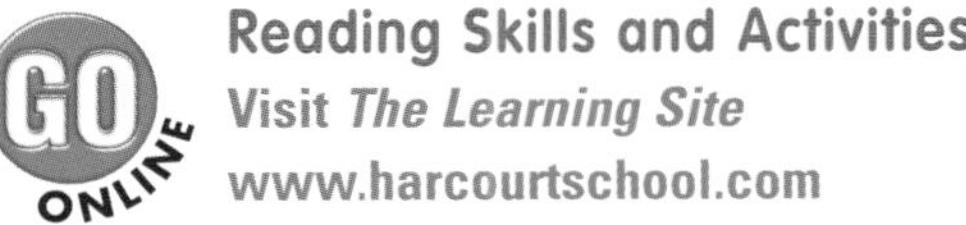

Reading Skills and Activities
Visit *The Learning Site*
www.harcourtschool.com

Lesson 16

PDAS Domains I, II

Horizon Line

OBJECTIVES
- Identify space in artworks
- Produce watercolor paintings
- Identify cause-and-effect relationships in artworks

RESOURCES
- Art Print 2
- Electronic Art Gallery CD-ROM, Primary

5 Minutes

Warm-Up

Build Background Display Picture Card 29. Ask students to find the line that shows where the sky meets the land. Ask them to think about why an artist would show that line in a painting. (to make it look realistic; to show what is far away)

10-15 Minutes

Teach

Discuss Art Concepts Ask students to read pages 86–87. Have them identify the horizon lines in images A and B. Students should identify space by pointing out that the smaller boat in image A and the rocks in image B appear closest to the viewer because they are placed farther below the horizon line. Display **Art Print 2**, and have students point out the high horizon line. TEKS 3.1B

Think Critically

1. READING SKILL **Why might an artist place an object close to the horizon line?** (to show that it is far away) CAUSE AND EFFECT
2. **What mood did the artist create in image B?** (Responses will vary.) PERCEPTION/AESTHETICS
3. WRITE **Would you rather visit the scene in image A or image B? Write a paragraph that explains why.** EXPOSITORY TAKS Writing Objective 1

Lesson 16

Vocabulary
- horizon line
- space
- depth

Horizon Line

The place in an artwork where sky meets land or water is called the **horizon line**. In image A, the horizon line appears near the top of the painting. Find the horizon line in image B.

Space is the area between and around objects. In two-dimensional artworks, artists create the feeling of space, or **depth**, by making some objects seem to be closer to the viewer than others. An object that is placed farther below the horizon line seems to be closer to the viewer. Look at image A. Which boat seems to be closer to the viewer?

Arturo Gordon, *Boats Together at the Sea*

Background Information

Art History

The **Hudson River School** was a group of nineteenth-century artists, including **Robert Scott Duncanson,** who painted the natural features of the American landscape. Many of these paintings showed scenes in New York state.

For additional information about Duncanson and the Hudson River School, see pp. R44–R59.

RECOMMENDED READING

Going to the Getty by J. Otto Seibold and Vivian Walsh. The J. Paul Getty Museum, 1997. CHALLENGING

★ **TEKS 3.1B** identify elements and principles; **TEKS 3.2C** produce various artworks; **TEKS 3.4B** identify main ideas in artworks by peers and others; **PDAS Domain I** active participation; **PDAS Domain II** learner-centered instruction; **PDAS Domain III** evaluation and feedback; **PDAS Domain IV** classroom management; *(continued)*

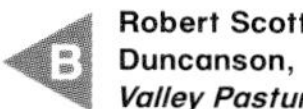

B Robert Scott Duncanson, *Valley Pasture*

Point out the large rocks and the water in image B. Do the rocks or the water seem to be closer to you? How can you tell?

Artist's Workshop

Saltwater Seascape

1. **Draw your seascape on watercolor paper. Think about how much sky you want to show in your painting.**
2. **To create depth, draw an object near the horizon line and another object far below it.**
3. **Paint your seascape with watercolors.**
4. **Before the paint dries, create texture by sprinkling salt on the part of your painting that shows water.**

87

Science Connection

Sunrise, Sunset Ask students to think about times they have seen a setting or rising sun on the horizon. Point out that long ago, people first observed that the sun rose in the east and crossed the sky to set in the west. Have partners research the characteristics of the sun and present one sun fact to the class.

PDAS Domain IV

ESL Support **language acquisition** by helping students make vocabulary word cards for the names of objects in their paintings. Students may use the cards as they describe their paintings.

Special Needs If students have difficulty holding paintbrushes, wrap modeling clay around the brushes to help students grip them.

30-40 Minutes

Artist's Workshop

Saltwater Seascape

MATERIALS: watercolor paper, pencil, watercolors, paintbrushes, water bowl, table salt

Quick Tip Tell students to paint the sea last so that it's wet when they apply the salt.

PLAN Have students practice drawing boats or other objects they will include in their watercolor paintings.

CREATE Tell students to produce their paintings, using a variety of art materials appropriately. They should draw lightly so that their marks will not show through the paint. TEKS 3.2C

REFLECT Have students display their paintings and describe how they created space or depth.

Activity Options PDAS Domain IV

Quick Activity Have students use colored pencils to draw a seascape that shows depth.

Early Finishers Ask students to draw a seascape with the horizon line in a different place.

Challenge See *Teacher Resource Book*, p. 66.

5-10 Minutes

Wrap-Up

Informal Assessment PDAS Domain III

- **Describe the main idea in a classmate's painting.** (Responses will vary.) EVALUATION/CRITICISM TEKS 3.4B
- **How is your painting different from image A?** (Responses will vary.) PERCEPTION/AESTHETICS

Extend Through Writing

TAKS Writing Objective 1

Postcard Have students imagine they are visiting the place in their painting. Ask them to write a postcard from there to a friend.

TAKS Writing Objective 1 composition

Lesson 17

PDAS Domains I, II

Depth in Landscapes

OBJECTIVES
- Identify depth in artworks
- Produce landscape drawings
- Identify cause-and-effect relationships in artworks

RESOURCES
- Art Print 12
- Discussion Card 6, p. R36
- Electronic Art Gallery CD-ROM, Primary

5 Minutes

Warm-Up

Build Background Display **Art Print 12**. Have students compare the height of the largest boy with the height of the barn in the background. Ask them to tell why they think the barn appears to be smaller than the boy.

10-15 Minutes

Teach

Discuss Art Concepts Have students read page 88. Students should point out the flowers, the stream, and the larger horse in the foreground. As students focus on the background of the artwork, they should note that objects in this section are smaller and placed higher in the composition.

Think Critically

1. READING SKILL **Why did the artist make the horse in the background so small?** (to make it look far away) CAUSE AND EFFECT
2. **Do you think the artist created this scene exactly as he saw it? Explain.** (Responses will vary.) PERCEPTION/AESTHETICS
3. WRITE **Explain how Hiroshige showed depth in his artwork.** EXPOSITORY TAKS Writing Objective 1

Lesson 17

Vocabulary

foreground

background

Depth in Landscapes

When you look out your window, do faraway objects seem smaller or larger than nearby objects? Artists can create the feeling of depth by changing the size of objects in their artworks.

Look at the image below. The area at the bottom of the artwork is the **foreground**. The foreground is the part of the artwork that seems closest to the viewer. What do you see in the foreground of this image?

Ando Hiroshige,
Fuji from Kogane-Ga-Hara, Shimosa

Now look at the area near the horizon line. This is the **background**. The background is the part of the artwork that seems farthest away. What objects do you see in the background? Does the horse in the foreground seem smaller or larger than the horse in the background?

Background Information

About the Artist

Ando Hiroshige (hee•roh•shee•gay) (1797–1858) was one of the masters of Japanese woodblock prints, called Ukiyo-e (oo•kee•oh•ay). Hiroshige was called "the artist of the sweeping brush." He often used just a few lines to indicate an entire landscape.

For additional information about Hiroshige and Japanese Ukiyo-e, see pp. R44–R59.

RECOMMENDED READING

Hokusai: The Man Who Painted a Mountain by Deborah Kogan Ray. Farrar, Straus & Giroux, 2001. CHALLENGING

★ **TEKS 3.2A** create artworks; **TEKS 3.2C** produce various artworks; **PDAS Domain I** active participation; **PDAS Domain II** learner-centered instruction; **PDAS Domain III** evaluation and feedback; **PDAS Domain IV** classroom management; **TAKS Writing Objective 1** composition

Artist's Workshop

Landscape Drawing

PLAN

Look at pictures of outdoor scenes to sketch ideas for a landscape.

CREATE

1. Fold a sheet of paper into three equal sections. Then open it up.
2. Draw a line in pencil along the highest fold. This will be your horizon line.
3. The lowest section of your paper is the foreground. Draw the largest objects in the foreground.
4. The middle section of your paper is the background. Draw the smallest objects in the background.
5. Use colored pencils to add details.

REFLECT

Look at your completed landscape. How did you create depth?

Quick Tip: You can also add depth to your drawing by using light values in the background and dark values in the foreground.

89

Social Studies Connection

Mount Fuji Have students use an encyclopedia to find facts about Mount Fuji, the mountain in the background of Hiroshige's artwork. Students should note that Mount Fuji is considered an active volcano, although it last erupted in 1707.

PDAS Domain IV

ESL Use **visuals** to support **comprehensible input** for kinds of landscapes. Display ***Picture Cards Collection,*** cards 48, 89, and 98. Suggest that students use one of the pictures as an inspiration for their drawing.

See also ***Picture Card Bank* CD-ROM,** Category: Places People Go.

30-40 Minutes

Artist's Workshop

Landscape Drawing

MATERIALS: magazines, sketchbook, pencil, white paper, colored pencils

PLAN Have students look for pictures of outdoor scenes in magazines.

CREATE Have students produce their drawings, using a variety of art materials appropriately, based on personal observations of pictures or actual outdoor scenes. TEKS 3.2A, TEKS 3.2C

REFLECT Students should point out the differences in size and placement between objects in the foreground and background.

Activity Options PDAS Domain IV

Quick Activity Distribute copies of *Teacher Resource Book*, pp. 46–47, to have students show how sized objects should be placed in a scene.

Early Finishers Have students use Discussion Card 6 to compare their landscape drawings with Hiroshige's artwork.

Challenge See *Teacher Resource Book*, p. 67.

5-10 Minutes

Wrap-Up

Informal Assessment PDAS Domain III

- **How did the ideas in this lesson help you create your landscape drawing?** (Responses will vary.) EVALUATION/CRITICISM
- **How would you change your drawing to show greater depth?** (move the horizon line up) PERCEPTION/AESTHETICS

Extend Through Writing

TAKS Writing Objective 1

Poem Have students write a poem about the scene in their drawings.

ART ⟷ SCIENCE CONNECTION

PDAS Domains I, II

Forces in Nature

ART AND NATURE

DISCUSS THE IMAGES

Have students read pages 90–91.

- Tell students that when Powell explored the Grand Canyon, most of the area hadn't even been mapped. He explored the area for nearly ten years and led a group of geologists who mapped the canyon.
- Have students discuss the photograph in image A. Ask them to identify sensory knowledge as sources for ideas to explain why they think the Grand Canyon is a visual symbol to different artists. Discuss with students the size of the canyon, the textures of the rock, and the sounds of the flowing river or animals that one might hear. Prompt students to explain what the Grand Canyon might stand for to these artists. (Possible responses: the power of nature, freedom, peacefulness) TEKS 3.1A
- Discuss image B. Students should identify the artist's use of space and depth by pointing out that the peak on the right side of the painting is in the foreground and seems closest to the viewer, while the peaks on the left side of the painting are in the background and seem the farthest away. TEKS 3.1B
- Tell students that image A is a modern photograph and that image B is a painting from the past. Have students compare the content in these artworks to describe which gives a stronger impression of the great size of the canyon and what it might feel like to be standing at the rim. TEKS 3.3A

ART ⟷ SCIENCE CONNECTION

Forces in Nature

How was the Grand Canyon formed?

The Grand Canyon in Arizona is a popular subject of artworks. The Colorado River, shown in image A, cut into layers of rock to form the deep canyon.

Few people knew about the Grand Canyon until 1869. At that time, an explorer named John Wesley Powell traveled by boat along the Colorado River and saw how the river had cut through the land.

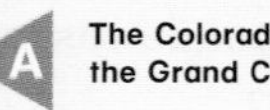

A The Colorado River in the Grand Canyon

Background Information

About the Artist

Carl Oscar Borg (1879–1947) was born in Sweden. When Borg was 22, he walked 450 miles from San Francisco to Los Angeles, where he found someone to teach him painting. Later, he traveled through the American West, painting pictures of Native Americans and the Grand Canyon.

For additional information about Borg, see pp. R44–R59.

For related artworks, see **Electronic Art Gallery CD-ROM, Primary.**

★ **TEKS 3.1A** identify sources for ideas; **TEKS 3.1B** identify elements and principles; **TEKS 3.2A** create artworks; **TEKS 3.2B** develop effective compositions; **TEKS 3.2C** produce various artworks; **TEKS 3.3A** compare artworks from the past and present; **TEKS 3.4B** identify main ideas in artworks by peers and others; *(continued)*

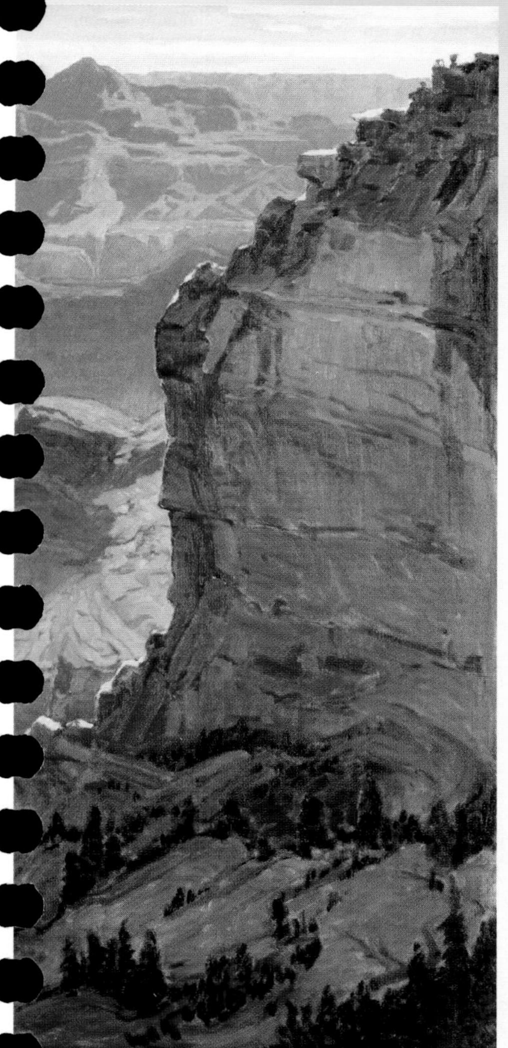

DID YOU KNOW?

The colors of the rock layers in the Grand Canyon seem to change throughout the day. For example, red and brown layers stand out at sunset. During what time of day do you think image B was painted?

Carl Oscar Borg, *Grand Canyon*

Powell took artists to the Grand Canyon to paint pictures for many people to see. Artists are still painting the canyon. In image B, what part of the canyon seems closest to the viewer? What part seems farthest away?

Think About Art

Would you rather paint the Grand Canyon from the bottom of the canyon looking up or from the top looking down? How would these views be different?

91

Social Studies Connection

The Grand Canyon Tell students that the Grand Canyon is part of a national park that was established by the United States government in 1919. The park is almost 1¼ million acres.

For additional cross-curricular suggestions, see Art Transparency 11.

TEKS 3.4B

Student Art Show

Portfolios and Exhibitions Have students create an exhibit of their portfolios and finished artworks. Ask students to apply simple criteria, such as determining the subject of the artwork, to identify main ideas in one another's original artworks and portfolios and in the exhibit as a whole.

DID YOU KNOW?

Use the facts below to discuss the Grand Canyon with students.

- Scientists study the canyon's rock layers to find information about Earth's history. Rock layers can be identified by their different colors, including gray, green, red, and violet.
- The canyon is 277 miles long, 1 mile deep, and 18 miles across in some places.
- Ancient peoples once lived in the canyon. There are many Pueblo and cliff-dweller ruins.

Think About Art

Would you rather paint the Grand Canyon from the bottom of the canyon looking up or from the top looking down? How would these views be different? (Responses will vary. Encourage students to identify how the horizon lines, the colors of the rock layers, and the amount of light would be affected by the artist's point of view.) PERSONAL RESPONSE

ARTIST'S EYE ACTIVITY

Painting Our National Parks Provide photographs of America's national parks from books or magazines for students to use as a reference. Have students develop and sketch a variety of effective compositions, using design skills, based on personal observation of the photographs. Help students choose a composition to paint, and have them produce their paintings using watercolors or tempera paints appropriately. TEKS 3.2A, TEKS 3.2B, TEKS 3.2C

Lesson 18

PDAS Domains I, II

Overlapping Lines and Shapes

OBJECTIVES
- Identify how overlapping lines and shapes create depth in artworks
- Paint a cityscape that shows depth
- Identify cause-and-effect relationships in artworks

RESOURCES
- Art Print 10
- Electronic Art Gallery CD-ROM, Primary

5 Minutes

Warm-Up

Build Background Display **Art Print 10.** Point out objects in the foreground that seem close to the viewer. Tell students that artists may cover shapes with parts of other shapes to show that one object is in front of another object.

10-15 Minutes

Teach

Discuss Art Concepts Have students read pages 92–93. Students should point out that the buildings in the foreground of image A seem closest because they overlap buildings in the background. Have students describe how overlapping creates depth in image B.

Think Critically

1. READING SKILL **Why does the scene in image A look crowded?** (It is filled with cars, people, and buildings.) CAUSE AND EFFECT
2. **What would you like to show in a cityscape?** (Responses will vary.) PERSONAL RESPONSE
3. WRITE **Describe the sounds you would hear if you were walking in image A.** DESCRIPTIVE TAKS Writing Objective 1

Lesson 18

Vocabulary
- cityscape
- overlapping

Overlapping Lines and Shapes

A **cityscape** is an artwork that shows a city view. Look at the cityscapes in images A and B. What time of day does each one show?

Now look at the buildings in image A. Find one building that overlaps, or partly covers, part of another building. Artists can use **overlapping** to show that one object is closer to the viewer than another object. Which buildings in image A seem closest to the viewer? Find lines, such as the tall streetlights, that also cover parts of the artwork.

A Red Grooms, *Looking Along Broadway Towards Grace Church*

Background Information

About the Artist

Red Grooms (1937–) is best known for his mixed-media constructions that celebrate New York City. His style, called **Pop Art,** is often full of humor. Some of Grooms's life-sized pieces look like three-dimensional comic strips, filled with characters painted in bright, clashing colors.

For additional information about Grooms and Pop Art, see pp. R44–R59.

RECOMMENDED READING

Art Dog by Thacher Hurd. HarperCollins, 1996. AVERAGE

★ **TEKS 3.2C** produce various artworks; **TEKS 3.3B** compare artworks from different cultures; **TEKS 3.4A** identify intent in personal artworks; **PDAS Domain I** active participation; **PDAS Domain II** learner-centered instruction; **PDAS Domain III** evaluation and feedback; **PDAS Domain IV** classroom management; *(continued)*

The artist of image **B** also used overlapping. Which objects in image **B** seem closest to the viewer? Why?

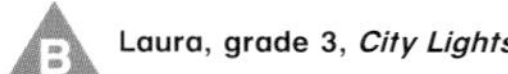

Laura, grade 3, *City Lights*

Artist's Workshop

Cityscape Painting

1. Look at pictures of buildings and cities to get ideas for your cityscape. Sketch one idea.
2. Draw your cityscape on construction paper. Use overlapping to show the buildings that are closest to the viewer.
3. Paint your cityscape. Then add details with markers.

93

Health Connection

Traffic Safety Call students' attention to the cars and people on the city street in image A. Have them work in groups to create a Bike and Pedestrian Safety Chart, with rules for walking and biking safely near busy streets and intersections.

PDAS Domain IV

ESL Use **visuals** to support **comprehensible input** for city scenes. Display ***Picture Cards Collection,*** cards 26 and 115. Suggest that students use one or more of these objects in their paintings.

See also ***Picture Card Bank*** **CD-ROM,** Category: Places People Go.

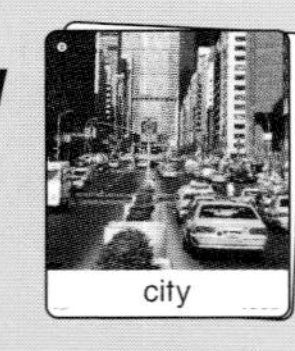

30-40 Minutes

Artist's Workshop

Cityscape Painting

MATERIALS: magazines, books, sketchbook, pencil, construction paper, tempera paints, paintbrushes, water bowl, markers

PLAN Have students look at pictures of cities from different cultures for inspiration.

CREATE Tell students to produce their paintings, using a variety of art materials appropriately. They should use markers after the paint dries. TEKS 3.2C

REFLECT Have students identify the general intent in their artworks and point out overlapping. TEKS 3.4A

Activity Options PDAS Domain IV

Quick Activity Have students use colored markers to draw several overlapping buildings.

Early Finishers Have students use overlapping to add cutout shapes to their paintings.

Challenge See *Teacher Resource Book*, p. 68.

5-10 Minutes

Wrap-Up

Informal Assessment PDAS Domain III

- **How did the cityscapes in this lesson inspire your painting?** (Responses will vary.) EVALUATION/CRITICISM
- **Which objects in your painting appear to be farthest from the viewer?** (Responses will vary.) PERCEPTION/AESTHETICS

Extend Through Writing

TEKS 3.3B; TAKS Writing Objective 1

Compare-and-Contrast Paragraph Have students compare their paintings with a classmate's painting that shows a different culture. Tell them to describe buildings or other objects that illustrate how people in each city might live.

Lesson 19

PDAS Domains I, II

Center of Interest

OBJECTIVES
- Identify emphasis in artworks
- Produce drawings with a center of interest
- Identify cause-and-effect relationships in artworks

RESOURCES
- Art Print 11
- Discussion Card 4, p. R35
- Electronic Art Gallery CD-ROM, Primary

5 Minutes

Warm-Up

Build Background Display **Art Print 11**. Ask students to name the object they notice first in the painting. Tell students that the artist has made the tree stand out by painting it a bright color.

10-15 Minutes

Teach

Discuss Art Concepts Have students read page 94. Then ask them to point out the painting's center of interest. (toy car) Students should identify emphasis in the painting by pointing out how the bright colors on the toy car contrast with dark, dull colors in the background. TEKS 3.1B

Lesson 19

Vocabulary
- center of interest
- emphasis
- contrast

Center of Interest

Look at the painting below. What do you notice first? Why do you think this is so?

The part of an artwork that an artist wants you to see first is called the **center of interest**. Artists use **emphasis** to make the viewer look at the center of interest. One way to create emphasis in an artwork is to use contrast. Lines, shapes, textures, and colors that are very different from each other have **contrast**.

Look at how the artist used contrasting colors to create emphasis in the painting below. The bright colors on the toy car make it stand out. How are these colors different from the colors in the background?

Reynard Milici, *The Cozy Coupe*

Think Critically

1. Focus Skill READING SKILL **Why did the artist make the toy car the center of interest?** (to show its importance in the scene) CAUSE AND EFFECT
2. **How does using contrast create emphasis?** (Things that are very different from what is around them stand out.) PERCEPTION/AESTHETICS
3. WRITE **Write a story about why the toy car was left on the path.** NARRATIVE
TAKS Writing Objective 1

FYI

Background Information

About the Artist

Reynard Milici (1942–) was born in Brooklyn, New York. He is best known for his photorealistic paintings, which have been displayed in numerous galleries in the northeastern United States.

For additional information about Milici and photorealism, see pp. R44–R59.

RECOMMENDED READING

Lunchtime for a Purple Snake by Harriet Ziefert. Houghton Mifflin, 2003. AVERAGE

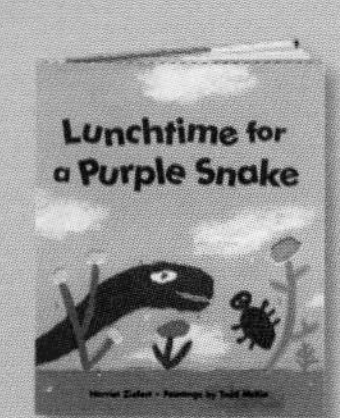

★ **TEKS 3.1B** identify elements and principles; **TEKS 3.2A** create artworks; **TEKS 3.2C** produce various artworks; **PDAS Domain I** active participation; **PDAS Domain II** learner-centered instruction; **PDAS Domain III** evaluation and feedback; **PDAS Domain IV** classroom management; **TAKS Writing Objective 1** composition

Artist's Workshop

Outdoor Scene

PLAN

Sketch an idea for an outdoor scene. Choose one object in the scene to be your center of interest.

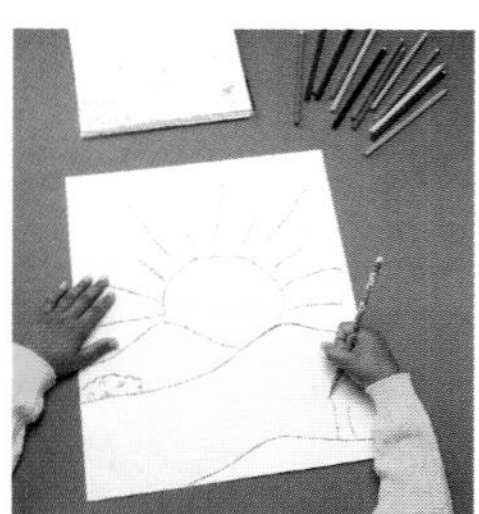

CREATE

1. **Copy your sketch onto white paper.**
2. **Think about your center of interest. Create emphasis by using contrasting lines, shapes, textures, or colors.**
3. **Add details to your drawing with colored pencils.**

REFLECT

Look at your finished drawing. How did you show emphasis?

Quick Tip You can show emphasis by using contrasting shapes. For example, you can make a geometric shape stand out by placing it in a scene with many organic shapes.

95

Math Connection

Finding the Center Ask students to find out if Milici placed the center of interest in the actual center of his painting. Have students cover the painting with tracing paper. Then have them use a ruler to measure the sides and mark the center of the painting.

PDAS Domain IV

ESL Before beginning the activity, **provide language support** by helping students connect new ideas with prior knowledge. Review vocabulary for different lines, shapes, colors, and textures. Then have students use the vocabulary to discuss the image in this lesson.

Outdoor Scene

MATERIALS: sketchbook, pencil, white paper, colored pencils

PLAN Review kinds of lines, shapes, textures, and colors to help students plan contrasting elements in the scenes they will draw.

CREATE Have students produce their drawings by developing an idea based on experiences, such as a visit to a familiar park or playground. TEKS 3.2A, TEKS 3.2C

REFLECT Have students identify the center of interest in their drawings and describe how they created emphasis. TEKS 3.1B

Activity Options PDAS Domain IV

Quick Activity Have students sketch a still life and use emphasis to make one object stand out.

Early Finishers Have students use Discussion Card 4 to evaluate how they used emphasis in their finished artworks.

Challenge See *Teacher Resource Book*, p. 69.

Wrap-Up

Informal Assessment PDAS Domain III

- **What parts of your drawing show contrast?** (Responses will vary.) EVALUATION/CRITICISM
- **How is your scene different from the scene in the painting on page 94?** (Responses will vary.) PERCEPTION/AESTHETICS

Extend Through Writing

TAKS Writing Objective 1

Story Starter Have students write the beginning of a story, using their drawing as the setting.

PDAS Domains I, II

Winslow Homer

ARTIST BIOGRAPHY

DISCUSS THE IMAGES

Have students read pages 96–97.

- Have students discuss what they see in image A and point out where the artist created emphasis. Ask them to identify life experiences as sources for ideas about the kinds of conversations they might have in the peaceful setting in image A. TEKS 3.1A, TEKS 3.1B
- Explain to students that although Winslow Homer lived in New York City, he painted most of his pictures of the Northeast countryside. Ask students to describe the environment they would most like to paint in. Have students identify sensory knowledge as sources for ideas about self by telling how the sights and sounds of the environment reflect their personality. TEKS 3.1A
- In image B, students should identify space by recognizing that the real sailboat looks smaller than the toy sailboat because it is far in the distance. They should note that Homer may have included both sailboats to show that the children are interested in the world around them. TEKS 3.1B
-  Display **Art Print 12**, another painting by Homer. Ask students to discuss the similarities in the subjects of the three images. (All three paintings show children enjoying themselves in nature.) Ask students to compare content in these artworks from the past for various purposes, such as how they document the history and traditions of children in Homer's time. TEKS 3.3A

ART ⟷ SOCIAL STUDIES CONNECTION

Winslow Homer

What were Winslow Homer's favorite subjects to paint?

As a child, Winslow Homer enjoyed playing outdoors in the Massachusetts countryside. His mother was a painter, and Homer was interested in art from an early age.

Homer became known for his paintings of children and nature. In many of Homer's paintings, you can see his childhood memories. Look at image **A**. What might the children in this painting be thinking about?

A Winslow Homer, *Boys in a Pasture*

Background Information

About the Artist

Winslow Homer (1836–1910) is best known for his oil and watercolor paintings of the sea and nature. He often traveled to the Adirondack Mountains and to Florida, Bermuda, and the Bahamas, returning to his studio in Maine to turn the sketches made on his travels into paintings.

For additional information about Homer, see pp. R44–R59.

For related artworks, see **Electronic Art Gallery CD-ROM, Primary.**

★ **TEKS 3.1A** identify sources for ideas; **TEKS 3.1B** identify elements and principles; **TEKS 3.2A** create artworks; **TEKS 3.2B** develop effective compositions; **TEKS 3.2C** produce various artworks; **TEKS 3.3A** compare artworks from the past and present; **TEKS 3.4B** identify main ideas in artworks by peers and others; *(continued)*

 Winslow Homer, *The Boat Builders*

The children in image B are building toy boats. Look at the background of the painting. Why do you think Homer showed a toy boat overlapping a real sailboat? What do you notice when you compare the sizes of the toy boat and the real sailboat?

DID YOU KNOW?

Children in nearly every culture play with the same kinds of toys. Even children in ancient times had toys such as dolls, balls, and toy animals. Most toys are small copies of larger objects. Why do you think the same kinds of toys have been popular with children for many years?

Think About Art

Why do you think Winslow Homer made many paintings of the same subject? What subject would you like to paint in different ways?

 Multimedia Biographies
Visit *The Learning Site*
www.harcourtschool.com

97

DID YOU KNOW?

Use the facts below to discuss children's toys with students.

- Throughout time, toys have imitated everyday objects that adults use, such as boats, tools, and trains.
- Ancient toys were often made from materials like wood, metal, and ivory. The invention of new materials has allowed toymakers to create toys that are more lifelike and detailed.
- The children in Homer's paintings would not have had toy telephones or computers because the real versions had not been invented yet.

Think About Art

Why do you think Winslow Homer made many paintings of the same subject? What subject would you like to paint in different ways?
(Responses will vary.) PERSONAL RESPONSE

ARTIST'S EYE ACTIVITY

Favorite Toys Have students list their favorite toys and match them with objects that adults use. Then ask them to develop an effective composition that shows both a toy and the adult version of the object. Students may enjoy making the sketch a self-portrait based on an experience that shows them playing with the toy. TEKS 3.2A, TEKS 3.2B, TEKS 3.2C

Social Studies Connection

Shipbuilding Explain that Homer painted image B as part of a series about the shipbuilding industry in and around Gloucester (GLAW•ster), Massachusetts.

For additional cross-curricular suggestions, see Art Transparency 12.

TEKS 3.4B

Visit with an Artist

Portfolios and Exhibitions
Arrange a museum visit for students to view artworks by a major artist. Ask students to use simple criteria they have learned from this unit to identify main ideas in the artist's original artworks, portfolio, and the exhibit.

PDAS Domain I active participation; **PDAS Domain II** learner-centered instruction

Lesson 20

PDAS Domains I, II

Art in Nature

OBJECTIVES
- Identify emphasis in artworks
- Produce a garden design
- Identify cause-and-effect relationships in artworks

RESOURCES
- Art Print 6
- Electronic Art Gallery CD-ROM, Primary

5 Minutes

Warm-Up

Build Background Display **Art Print 6**. Explain that artworks made from natural materials, such as sticks, are often temporary and are designed to be viewed outdoors.

10-15 Minutes

Teach

Discuss Art Concepts Have students read pages 98–99. They should point out that in image A, the artist created emphasis by placing red flowers in a garden that is mostly green. Students should also identify the circles as shapes and the cones as forms. In image B, discuss how the color and texture of the fabric makes it stand out from the trees and the blue, glassy water. TEKS 3.1B

Think Critically

1. READING SKILL **Why do you think many earthworks are temporary?** (Weather might cause them to break down.) CAUSE AND EFFECT
2. **Which of these two artworks would you like to visit? Why?** (Responses will vary.) PERSONAL RESPONSE
3. WRITE **Describe what you might see if you were in the center of the larger island in image B.** DESCRIPTIVE TAKS Writing Objective 1

Lesson 20

Vocabulary

earthworks

Art in Nature

Earthworks are artworks that are designed to be outdoors and are made of natural materials. Artists who make earthworks arrange their materials in natural environments. They can create emphasis by using contrasting lines, shapes, colors, forms, or textures.

Look at the garden in image A. How did the artist create emphasis? What kinds of lines, shapes, and forms did the artist who designed this garden use?

A Ornamental Municipal Gardens in Angers, France

98

Background Information

About the Artists

Christo (1935–) and Jeanne-Claude (1935–) are known for their huge temporary outdoor artworks. The artists have used fabric to wrap huge structures like the German Parliament building and to hang a curtain across a valley in the Rocky Mountains.

For additional information about the artists, see pp. R44–R59.

RECOMMENDED READING

Sunflower Sal by Janet S. Anderson. Albert Whitman & Company, 1997. AVERAGE

★ TEKS 3.1B identify elements and principles; TEKS 3.2C produce various artworks; PDAS Domain I active participation; PDAS Domain II learner-centered instruction; PDAS Domain III evaluation and feedback; PDAS Domain IV classroom management; TAKS Writing Objective 1 composition

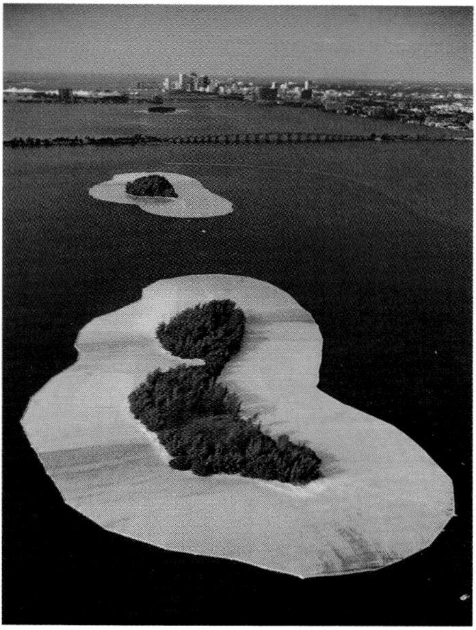

Now look at image B. The artists surrounded real islands with floating fabric. Why do you think the artists used the color pink? Would you notice this artwork from a distance if the artist had used blue fabric instead?

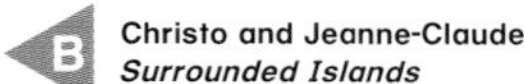

B Christo and Jeanne-Claude, *Surrounded Islands*

Artist's Workshop

Garden Design

1. **Think of a garden design you would like to create. Picture what the garden would look like from above.**
2. **Draw your garden design on white paper. Draw different shapes to show how the plants would be arranged.**
3. **Include a path for people to walk on in your garden.**
4. **Use crayons or colored pencils to color your garden design.**

99

Science Connection

Gardens Explain to students that most gardens are planted with *perennials*, plants that live through the winter and continue to grow for years, and *annuals*, plants that must be replanted every spring. Have students research familiar plants to place them in the correct category.

PDAS Domain IV

ESL Encourage students to **share cultures** by having them describe plants and flowers native to their home culture.

Challenge Have students research the variety of colors of specific plants and flowers and incorporate that information into their garden designs.

30-40 Minutes

Artist's Workshop

Garden Design

MATERIALS: white paper, pencil, crayons or colored pencils

Quick Tip Tell students to rub color over a rough surface to add texture to the walking path.

PLAN If possible, show students a landscape plan or overhead garden views.

CREATE Tell students to create emphasis in their drawings by using contrasting shapes and colors. TEKS 3.2C

REFLECT Have students describe how their garden designs show emphasis.

Activity Options PDAS Domain IV

Quick Activity Have students sketch a simple design for a backyard garden.

Early Finishers Have students draw a close-up view of one plant in their garden.

Challenge See *Teacher Resource Book*, p. 70.

5-10 Minutes

Wrap-Up

Informal Assessment PDAS Domain III

- **How is your garden design different from the garden in image A?** (Responses will vary.) PERCEPTION/AESTHETICS
- **What is your favorite part of your design?** (Responses will vary.) PERSONAL RESPONSE

Extend Through Writing

TAKS Writing Objective 1

Advertisement Have students write an advertisement that tries to persuade people to visit their garden. Tell them to explain where the garden is located and what viewers will experience during their visit.

PDAS Domains I, III

Review and Reflect

Have students reflect on what they have learned about the ways artists use space and emphasis to create artworks about special places. Display **Art Prints 2, 6, 10, 11,** and **12**. Have students identify art elements such as space and design principles such as emphasis in the images. Encourage small groups of students to use their completed Word Knowledge Charts and Discussion Cards 3 and 4, page R35, to discuss what they learned about space, emphasis, and other vocabulary and concepts in this unit. TEKS 3.1B

Vocabulary and Concepts

Have students read each sentence and choose the letter of the word or phrase that best completes it. (1. A; 2. D; 3. B; 4. B; 5. B)

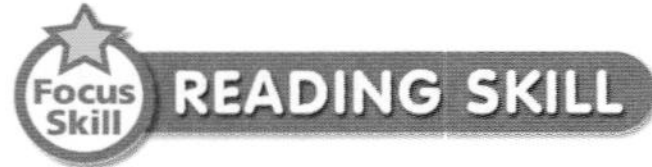

Cause and Effect

Remind students that a cause is why something happens and that an effect is what happens as a result. As students reread page 90, tell them to look for information that tells how the Grand Canyon became so deep over many years. Then have students restate the information in their diagrams in one sentence, using a signal word such as *because*. For example, *The Grand Canyon is a deep canyon because the Colorado River cut through the layers of rock.* TAKS Reading Objectives 3, 4

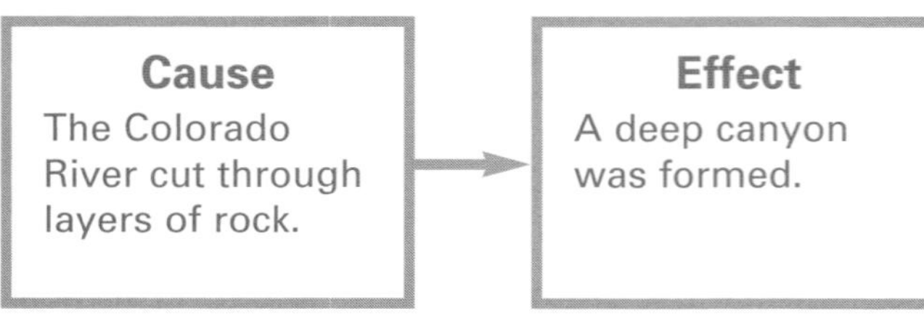

Unit 4 Review and Reflect

Vocabulary and Concepts

Choose the letter of the word or phrase that best completes each sentence.

1 ___ is the area between and around objects.

A Space **C** Depth

B Emphasis **D** Symmetry

2 The ___ is the place in an artwork where the sky meets the land.

A foreground **C** background

B emphasis **D** horizon line

3 Artists place smaller objects in the background of a painting to show ___.

A overlapping **C** emphasis

B depth **D** pattern

4 Artists use ___ to show that one object is in front of another object.

A proportion **C** contrast

B overlapping **D** movement

5 Artworks that are set outdoors and made of natural materials are ___.

A cityscapes **C** seascapes

B earthworks **D** murals

Focus Skill READING SKILL

Cause and Effect

Reread the information on page 90. Then use a cause-and-effect diagram to tell how the Grand Canyon was formed.

Cause	→	Effect

100

TEKS 3.3C, TEKS 3.4B

Home and Community Connection

School-Home Connection

Invite parents or members of the community to view an exhibition of student artworks from this unit. Help students collaborate to create a flyer that tells the names of the artists and the titles of the artworks and identifies the main idea of the exhibition. Copy and distribute *Teacher Resource Book* pp. 91–92 to inform parents about upcoming art projects.

Community Connection

Have students relate art to different kinds of jobs in everyday life by inviting a garden designer to your classroom. Ask him or her to explain how to take a garden from initial design to a planted landscape.

★ **TEKS 3.1A** identify sources for ideas; **TEKS 3.1B** identify elements and principles; **TEKS 3.3C** relate art to different jobs; **TEKS 3.4B** identify main ideas in artworks by peers and others; **PDAS Domain I** active participation; **PDAS Domain III** evaluation and feedback; **TAKS Reading Objective 3** use a variety of strategies; (continued)

Write About Art

Write a story about the artwork on page 92. Tell what caused the street to become so busy. Then tell the effect of the busy street on people who live in the city. Use a diagram to plan your writing.

REMEMBER—YOU SHOULD

- explain at least one cause and one effect.
- use correct grammar, spelling, and punctuation.

Critic's Corner

Look at *Boats on the Beach* by Vincent van Gogh to answer the questions below.

DESCRIBE What is the subject of this painting?

ANALYZE How did the artist show depth? How did he create emphasis?

INTERPRET Why do you think the artist wanted to show this place?

EVALUATE Does the painting show a place you would like to visit? Why or why not?

Vincent van Gogh, *Boats on the Beach*

101

PDAS Domain III

Assessment

Portfolio Assessment

Work with students to choose a piece of their artwork to include in their portfolios. Suggest that they decide which piece best fulfilled the assignment or which piece they liked best for another reason. You may want to provide specific feedback that targets students' use of elements, principles, and techniques. See also Portfolio Recording Form, page R32.

Additional Assessment Options

- Progress Recording Form, p. R33
- Artist's Workshop Rubrics (Self/Teacher and Peer), pp. R30–R31
- Unit 4 Test, *Teacher Resource Book*, p. 102

Write About Art

Cause-and-Effect Story Read aloud the prompt with students. Suggest that they think about the kinds of events that could cause a traffic jam on a big-city street. Point out that one way to tell the story is to imagine they were there. Have students organize the events of their stories in time order. TAKS Writing Objectives 1, 2, 3, 5

Critic's Corner

RESPONSE/EVALUATION Use Discussion Card 2, page R34, and the steps below to guide students in analyzing *Boats on the Beach* by Vincent van Gogh.

DESCRIBE Students should note that the painting is a seascape and that there are boats on the shore and in the water.

ANALYZE Have students discuss the placement of the boats in relation to the horizon line, as well as the overlapping lines and shapes. Students should point out that the artist created emphasis by contrasting the bright colors of the boats on the shore with the paler colors of the boats in the water. TEKS 3.1B

INTERPRET Students may suggest that this place was important to the artist and that he wanted to share its beauty with viewers.

EVALUATE Ask students to identify sensory knowledge and their life experiences as sources for ideas about self to explain why the painting does or does not show a place they would like to visit. TEKS 3.1A

TAKS Test Preparation: Reading and Writing Through Art, pp. 48–52

TAKS Reading Objective 4 apply critical-thinking skills; **TAKS Writing Objective 1** composition; **TAKS Writing Objective 2** conventions; **TAKS Writing Objective 3** organization; **TAKS Writing Objective 5** usage

Unit 5

Balance and Unity

Surprising Viewpoints

Artists often show ordinary objects in ways that viewers might not expect. In this unit students will learn how artists can use balance and unity to show surprising viewpoints.

Resources

- Unit 5 Art Prints (13–15)
- Additional Art Prints (16, 17)
- Art Transparencies 13–15
- Test Preparation: Reading and Writing Through Art, pp. 53–57
- Artist's Workshop Activities: English and Spanish, pp. 41–50
- Encyclopedia of Artists and Art History, pp. R44–R59
- Picture Cards Collection, cards 19, 68, 72

Using the Art Prints

- Discussion Cards, pp. R34–R38
- Teaching suggestions, backs of Art Prints
- Art Print Teaching Suggestions: Spanish

Teacher Resource Book

- Vocabulary Cards in English and Spanish, pp. 23–26
- Reading Skill Card 5, p. 35
- Copying Master, p. 41
- Challenge Activities, pp. 71–75
- School-Home Connection: English/Spanish, pp. 93–94
- Unit 5 Test, p. 103

Technology Resources

Electronic Art Gallery CD-ROM, Primary

Picture Card Bank CD-ROM

Visit *The Learning Site*
www.harcourtschool.com

- Multimedia Art Glossary
- Multimedia Biographies
- Reading Skills and Activities

Art Prints for This Unit

ART PRINT 13

Watermelons
by Rufino Tamayo

ART PRINT 14

Caprice in February
by Paul Klee

ART PRINT 15

Brass Section (Jamming at Minton's)
by Romare Bearden

ART PRINT 16

Unveiling of the Statue of Liberty
by Katherine Westphal

ART PRINT 17

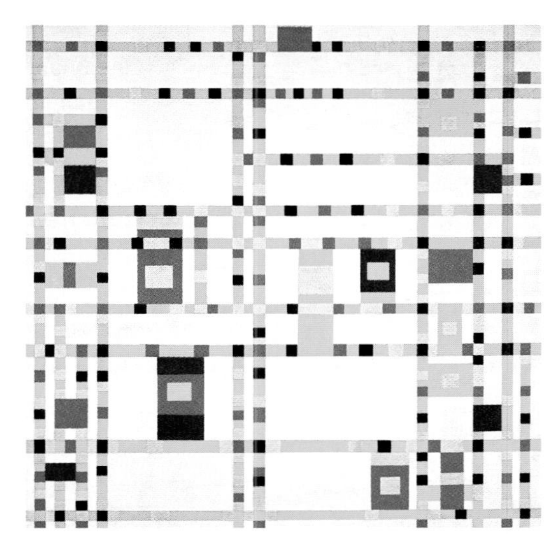

Broadway Boogie Woogie
by Piet Mondrian

Unit 5 Surprising Viewpoints Balance and Unity

Planning Guide

PDAS Domain IV

Lesson	Objectives and Vocabulary	Art Images	Production/ Materials
Fact and Opinion, pp. 104–105			
21 SYMMETRICAL BALANCE pp. 106–107 30–60 minutes	• Identify symmetrical balance in artworks • Produce grid drawings • Identify facts and opinions **Vocabulary: grid, symmetrical balance**	• **Red House Painting** by Jennifer Bartlett • **Fenye's House Dining Room** by Patssi Valdez	**Grid Drawing** ❑ sketchbook ❑ pencil ❑ graph paper ❑ colored pencils
22 ASYMMETRICAL BALANCE pp. 108–109 30–60 minutes	• Identify asymmetrical balance in artworks • Produce drawings that show asymmetrical balance • Identify facts and opinions **Vocabulary: asymmetrical balance**	• **The Pigeons** by Pablo Picasso	**Window View Drawing** ❑ sketchbook ❑ pencil ❑ white paper ❑ oil pastels ❑ cotton swabs
Art ↔ Literature Connection: Patricia Polacco: Storyteller, pp. 110–111			
23 ABSTRACT PORTRAITS pp. 112–113 30–60 minutes	• Identify balance and shape in artworks • Produce abstract paintings • Identify facts and opinions **Vocabulary: abstract art, distortion**	• **Clown** by Juan Gris • **Untitled** by Taylor, grade 3	**Abstract Self-Portrait** ❑ sketchbook ❑ pencil ❑ white paper ❑ tempera paints ❑ paintbrushes ❑ paper plate ❑ water bowl
24 ABSTRACT DESIGNS pp. 114–115 30–60 minutes	• Identify unity and color in artworks • Produce an abstract design • Identify facts and opinions **Vocabulary: unity, complementary colors, neutral colors**	• **Composition** by Sonia Delaunay	**Abstract Painting** ❑ sketchbook ❑ pencil ❑ white paper ❑ tempera paints ❑ paper plate ❑ water bowl ❑ paintbrushes
Art ↔ Social Studies Connection: Romare Bearden, pp. 116–117			
25 COLLAGE pp. 118–119 30–60 minutes	• Identify unity and texture in artworks • Produce collages • Identify facts and opinions **Vocabulary: collage**	• **Still Life #25** by Tom Wesselmann • **Merz Picture 32A. (The Cherry Picture)** by Kurt Schwitters	**Multi-Texture Collage** ❑ sketchbook ❑ pencil ❑ scraps with different textures ❑ scissors ❑ glue ❑ tagboard
Review and Reflect, pp. 120–121			

★ **TEKS 3.2A** create artworks; **TEKS 3.2C** produce various artworks; **PDAS Domain IV** classroom management

Fact and Opinion, pp. 104–105

Opportunities for application of the skill are provided on pp. 106, 108, 112, 114, 118, 119, 120, and 121.

Resources and Technology	Suggested Literature	Across the Curriculum
• Discussion Card 4, p. R35 • Reading Skill Card 5 • Electronic Art Gallery CD-ROM, Primary	*In Blue Mountains* by Thomas Locker 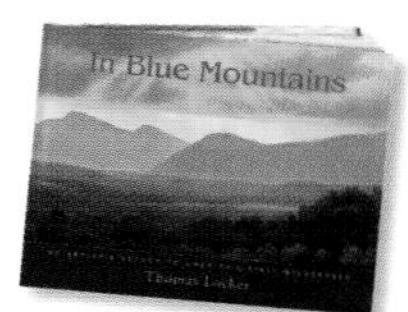 	**Math** Area, p. 107 **Reading** Fact and Opinion, p. 106 **Writing** Compare-and-Contrast Paragraph, p. 107
• Art Print 13 • Reading Skill Card 5 • Electronic Art Gallery CD-ROM, Primary	*Pablo Picasso* by Ibi Lepscky  	**Science** Simple Machines, p. 109 **Reading** Fact and Opinion, p. 108 **Writing** Poem, p. 109
• Art Print 14 • Discussion Card 8, p. R37 • Reading Skill Card 5 • Electronic Art Gallery CD-ROM, Primary	*Matthew's Dream* by Leo Lionni  	**Social Studies** Map Reading, p. 113 **Reading** Fact and Opinion, p. 112 **Writing** Art Review, p. 113
• Art Prints 16 and 17 • Color Wheel Poster • Reading Skill Card 5 • Electronic Art Gallery CD-ROM, Primary	*Hello, Red Fox* by Eric Carle  	**Language Arts** Homophones, p. 115 **Reading** Fact and Opinion, p. 114 **Writing** E-mail, p. 115
• Discussion Card 3, p. R35 • Reading Skill Card 5 • Electronic Art Gallery CD-ROM, Primary	*Me and Uncle Romie: A Story Inspired by the Life and Art of Romare Bearden* by Claire Hartfield 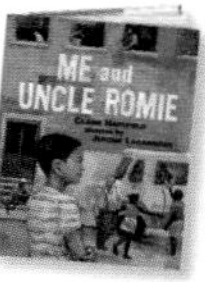 	**Science** Recycling, p. 119 **Reading** Fact and Opinion, p. 118 **Writing** Letter, p. 119

Art Puzzlers

Present these art puzzlers to students at the beginning or end of a class or when students finish an assignment early.

- Find a magazine picture of an object that has **symmetrical balance**. Cut the picture in half, and glue one half to white paper. Draw the other half of the picture. TEKS 3.2A, TEKS 3.2C
- Design a building with **asymmetrical balance**. Think about what the building will be used for. Sketch your idea. TEKS 3.2C
- Produce an **abstract construction**. Use cardboard tubes and other art materials appropriately to design your fantasy car. TEKS 3.2C
- Tear up pieces of construction paper in **complementary colors**. Arrange them in an interesting design and glue them to a sheet of white paper.
- Using magazine pictures, create a **collage** based on an experience you enjoyed. TEKS 3.2A

School-Home Connection
The activities above are included in the School-Home Connection for this unit. See *Teacher Resource Book,* pp. 93–94.

Assessment Options

- Rubrics and Recording Forms, pp. R30–R33
- Unit 5 Test, *Teacher Resource Book,* p. 103

Visit *The Learning Site:* **www.harcourtschool.com**

Artist's Workshops PREVIEW

PDAS Domain IV

Use these pages to help you gather and organize materials for the production activity in each lesson.

LESSON	MATERIALS
21 Grid Drawing p. 107 **Objective:** Produce grid drawings that show symmetrical balance  **30–40 minutes** **Challenge Activity:** See *Teacher Resource Book,* page 71.	• sketchbook • pencil • graph paper • colored pencils 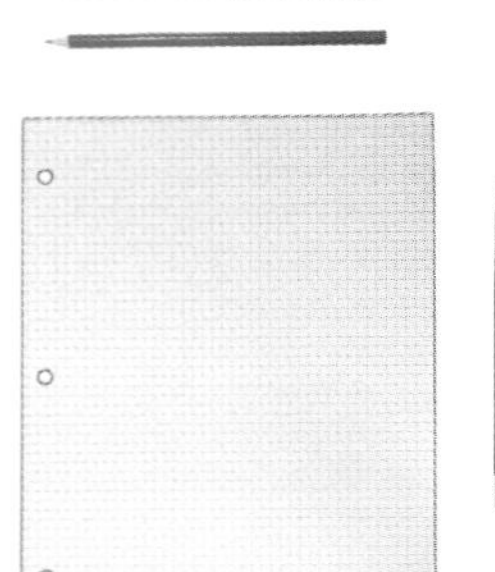 FINISHED EXAMPLE 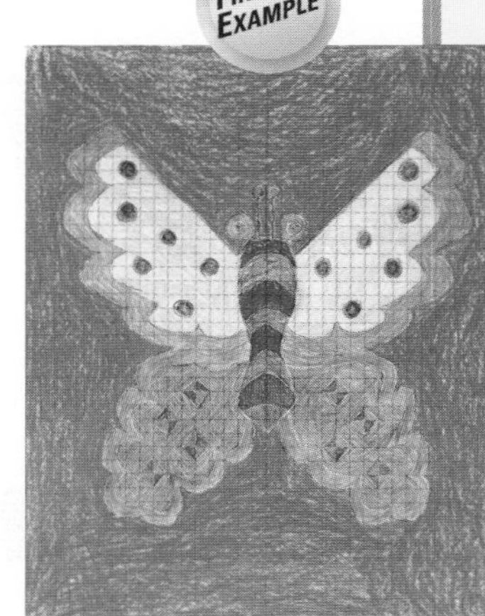
LESSON **22 Window View Drawing** p. 109 **Objective:** Produce drawings that show asymmetrical balance  **30–40 minutes** **Challenge Activity:** See *Teacher Resource Book,* page 72.	• sketchbook • pencil • white paper • oil pastels • cotton swabs 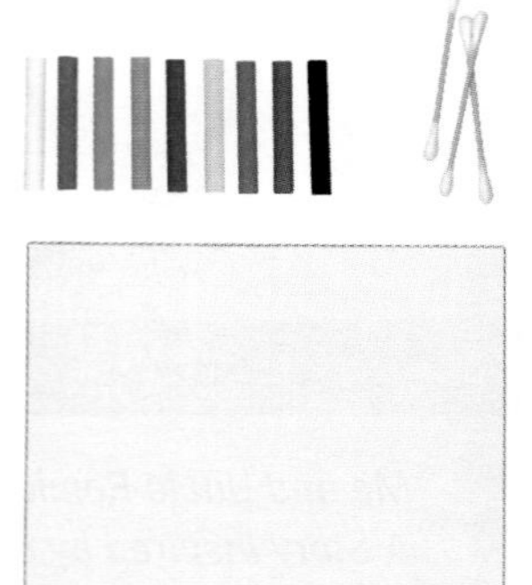 FINISHED EXAMPLE 

For safety information, see Art Safety, page R4; or the Art Safety Poster.

For information on media and techniques, see pp. R15–R23.

LESSON	MATERIALS

23 Abstract Self-Portrait p. 113

Objective: Produce abstract self-portraits that show distortion and expressive qualities

30–40 minutes

Challenge Activity: See *Teacher Resource Book,* page 73.

- sketchbook
- pencil
- white paper
- tempera paints
- paintbrushes
- paper plate
- water bowl

LESSON

24 Abstract Painting p. 115

Objective: Produce abstract paintings with complementary colors and neutral colors

30–40 minutes

Challenge Activity: See *Teacher Resource Book,* page 74.

- sketchbook
- pencil
- white paper
- tempera paints
- paper plate
- water bowl
- paintbrushes

FINISHED EXAMPLE

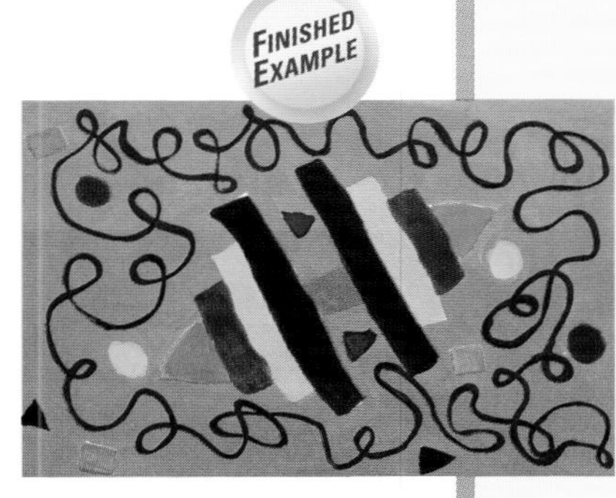

LESSON

25 Multi-Texture Collage p. 119

Objective: Produce collages that show unity and different textures

30–40 minutes

Challenge Activity: See *Teacher Resource Book,* page 75.

- sketchbook
- pencil
- scraps with different textures
- scissors
- glue
- tagboard

FINISHED EXAMPLE

Unit 5

PDAS Domains I, II

Surprising Viewpoints

PREVIEW THE UNIT

Tell students that in this unit they will learn how artists show subjects in ways that might surprise the viewer. Read aloud the unit title, *Surprising Viewpoints*, and tell students that a viewpoint is the way someone sees something. Have students preview the images in this unit and point out one image that they think shows an artist's surprising viewpoint of a subject.

SHARE THE POEM

Have students read the poem on page 103 and view the painting. Tell students to think about the poet's and the artist's viewpoint of their subjects.

How are the poem and the painting alike? (The poet gives her viewpoint of how waves of the sea sound. The painting shows an unusual viewpoint of the sea.) COMPARE AND CONTRAST

STEP INTO THE ART

Have students look carefully at the painting and describe what they see.

What would it be like to sail on the sea in this painting? (Responses will vary.) PERSONAL RESPONSE TEKS 3.1A

SHARE BACKGROUND INFORMATION

Tell students that Paul Klee painted many images of nature, including many paintings of fish. Explain that he was often inspired by children's drawings. Ask students to find examples of child-like representations of boats, fish, and people in the painting.

LOCATE IT See **Using the Maps of Museums and Art Sites,** p. R2.

Background Information

About the Artist

Paul Klee (KLAY) (1879–1940) wanted his artwork to illustrate the world of the imagination. Klee created his own unique style that combined caricature, symbols, bold colors, and humor.

For additional information about Klee, see the Encyclopedia of Artists and Art History, pp. R44–R59, and the Gallery of Artists, *Student Edition* pp. 178–188.

For related artworks, see **Electronic Art Gallery CD-ROM, Primary.**

★ **TEKS 3.1A** identify sources for ideas; **PDAS Domain I** active participation; **PDAS Domain II** learner-centered instruction

Unit 5 Balance and Unity

Surprising Viewpoints

Waves of the Sea

Waves of the sea
make the sound of thunder
when they break against rocks
and somersault under.

Waves of the sea
make the sound of laughter
when they run down the beach
and birds run after.

Aileen Fisher

Unit Vocabulary

grid	distortion
symmetrical balance	unity
asymmetrical balance	complementary colors
abstract art	neutral colors
	collage

Multimedia Art Glossary
Visit *The Learning Site*
www.harcourtschool.com

ABOUT THE ARTIST

See Gallery of Artists, pages 178–188.

103

Unit Vocabulary

Read aloud the terms with students, and use the Word Knowledge Chart below to assess and discuss their prior knowledge.

grid a pattern of squares of equal size

symmetrical balance a kind of balance in which the same lines, shapes, and colors are placed on both sides of an artwork

asymmetrical balance a kind of balance in which different lines, shapes, and colors are used on both sides of an artwork to make both sides seem equal

abstract art art that does not look realistic; may show either distorted objects or no real objects at all

distortion the changing of the way an object looks by bending or stretching its shape

unity the sense that an artwork looks whole or complete

complementary colors pairs of colors that are opposite each other on the color wheel

neutral colors colors, such as brown and gray, that can be created by mixing two complementary colors

collage an artwork made by gluing bits of paper, fabric, scraps, photographs, or other materials to a flat surface

Vocabulary Resources

- Vocabulary Cards in English and Spanish: *Teacher Resource Book*, pp. 23–26
- Student Edition Glossary, pp. 189–197

Language Arts Connection

Students may create a chart like the one below to identify familiar and unfamiliar vocabulary terms. Encourage them to add information to their charts as they work through this unit.

WORD KNOWLEDGE CHART		
I know this term.	I have seen this term before.	I have never seen this term.

Multimedia Art Glossary
Visit *The Learning Site*
www.harcourtschool.com

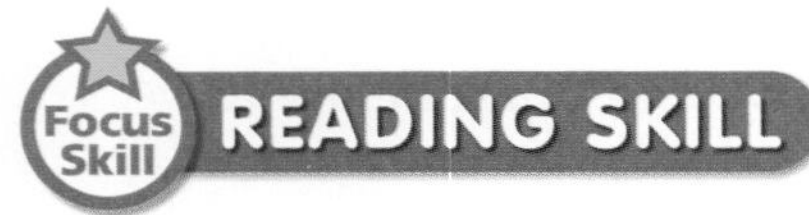

PDAS Domains I, II

Fact and Opinion

SKILL TRACE	
FACT AND OPINION	
Introduce	pp. 104–105
Review	pp. 106, 108, 112, 114, 118, 119, 120, 121

DISCUSS THE SKILL

Access Prior Knowledge Have volunteers share the name of their favorite color and describe why they like it or what it reminds them of. Point out that they have different ideas or beliefs about colors. Then help students understand the difference between beliefs and information that can be proved.

APPLY TO ART

Identify Fact and Opinion in Art Have students read page 104. Explain that facts are statements that can be proved by observation or by checking a reference source, such as a textbook or an encyclopedia. Ask students to use observation to state other facts about the artwork. (It was created by Alexander Calder. It is called *Myxomatose*. It has a black base. It has seven circle shapes.)

Discuss the opinion with students, pointing out that people have different opinions about what makes a fine artwork. Have students give other opinions about the sculpture by asking questions such as these: *Do you like the colors? Do you think the sculpture belongs in a museum?* Encourage students to support their opinions with facts about the artwork.

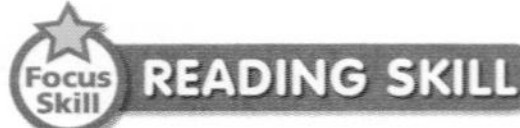

Fact and Opinion

A *fact* is something that can be proved. An *opinion* is a person's own belief or feeling.

You can discuss artworks by sharing facts and your own opinions. Look at the artwork in the image below. Then read the facts and opinion about it.

- **Facts** The artwork is a sculpture. The artist painted it black, red, and blue.
- **Opinion** The artwork is one of the finest in the world.

Do you agree with the opinion? What are some other facts about the artwork?

Alexander Calder, *Myxomatose*

Background Information

About the Artist

Alexander Calder's (CAWL•der) (1898–1976) background in mechanical engineering helped him when he designed his moving artworks. One of Calder's first artworks with movable parts was a miniature circus that included animals and performers made of wood, cork, and wire. Calder could move the characters to make them "perform."

For additional information about Calder, see pp. R44–R59.

For related artworks, see **Electronic Art Gallery CD-ROM, Primary.**

★ **PDAS Domain I** active participation; **PDAS Domain II** learner-centered instruction; **PDAS Domain IV** classroom management; **TAKS Reading Objective 3** use a variety of strategies; **TAKS Reading Objective 4** apply critical-thinking skills

You can look for facts and opinions to help you understand what you read. Read the passage below. Look for facts and opinions about the artist.

A mobile is a sculpture that has moving parts. Alexander Calder was one of the first artists to become known for making mobiles. In some of his mobiles, parts are moved by a small motor. In others, parts are moved by the wind or by air blowing on them. Many other artists have created wonderful mobiles. However, Calder's are the best.

What information in the passage can be proved? What opinions did the author include? Use a chart like this one to write facts and opinions.

Facts	Opinions
A small motor moves parts in some of Calder's mobiles.	

On Your Own

As you read the lessons in this unit, use charts like the one above to write facts and opinions about the text and the artworks.

105

TAKS Reading Objectives 3, 4

Reading Skill Card

Distribute Reading Skill Card 5, *Teacher Resource Book* page 35. Ask students to identify facts and opinions in this unit.

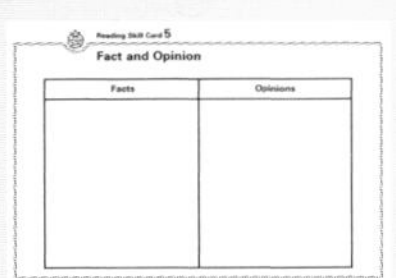

Extend the Skill For additional teaching suggestions, see **Art Transparency 13.**

PDAS Domain IV

ESL To aid in **oral language development,** pair students with English-fluent peers to read the passage on page 105 together. Have partners **paraphrase** the paragraph and then complete Reading Skill Card 5 with facts and opinions. Have partners reread their completed charts together.

APPLY TO READING

Identify Facts and Opinions in Text Explain to students that as they read, they should try to figure out whether a statement can be proved true or if it expresses the writer's own belief or opinion. Point out that words like *finest, worst,* and *best* and phrases such as *I think, I believe,* and *I feel* are clues that the writer is stating his or her opinion.

Have students read the passage about mobiles on page 105. Work with them to find facts and opinions in the passage and to complete the chart. Students should find facts in each of the first four sentences and opinions in the last two.

TAKS Reading Objectives 3, 4

Facts	Opinions
A small motor moves parts in some of Calder's mobiles. Mobiles are sculptures that have moving parts.	Many artists have created wonderful mobiles. Calder's mobiles are the best.

ON YOUR OWN

As students read the lessons in this unit, have them create fact-and-opinion charts that include information about the text and the artworks.

TAKS Reading Objectives 3, 4

Reading Skills and Activities
Visit *The Learning Site*
www.harcourtschool.com

Lesson 21

PDAS Domains I, II

Symmetrical Balance

OBJECTIVES
- Identify symmetrical balance in artworks
- Produce grid drawings
- Identify facts and opinions

RESOURCES
- Discussion Card 4, p. R35
- Electronic Art Gallery CD-ROM, Primary

5 Minutes

Warm-Up

Build Background Demonstrate what happens when two objects of equal weight are placed on each side of a scale. Then replace one of the objects with a heavier object. Point out that this makes the scale unbalanced.

10-15 Minutes

Teach

Discuss Art Concepts Have students read pages 106–107. Students should note that the dots in image A are small circles that are placed in a grid to make the left and right sides of the artwork match. In image B, discuss with students the tidy feeling that symmetrical balance creates.
TEKS 3.1B

Think Critically

1. READING SKILL **What is your opinion of artworks created on a grid?** (Responses will vary.) FACT AND OPINION

2. **How would image A be different if all of the dots were red?** (You wouldn't see the house.) PERCEPTION/AESTHETICS

3. WRITE **Write a story about visiting the room in image B.** NARRATIVE TAKS Writing Objective 1

Lesson 21

Vocabulary

grid

symmetrical balance

Symmetrical Balance

Look closely at image **A**. What is unusual about this painting? The artist created image **A** on a **grid**, a pattern of squares of equal size. She placed dots of color in each space on the grid. What shapes do the dots make?

grid

Trace your finger down the middle of image **A**. What do you notice about the two sides? Artists can create **symmetrical balance** by using lines, shapes, and colors to make one side of an artwork match the other side.

A Jennifer Bartlett, *Red House Painting*

106

Background Information

About the Artists

A Jennifer Bartlett (1941–) creates many of her artworks on grids. Her subjects often include simple objects such as houses and trees.

B Patssi Valdez is a Los Angeles-based artist who paints colorful still lifes of rooms full of objects she loves.

For additional information about the artists, see pp. R44–R59.

RECOMMENDED READING
In Blue Mountains by Thomas Locker. Bell Pond Books, 2000. CHALLENGING

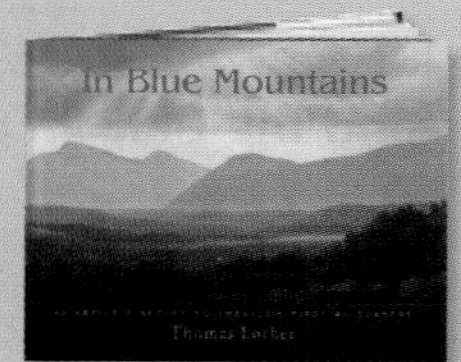

★ TEKS 3.1B identify elements and principles; TEKS 3.2C produce various artworks; PDAS Domain I active participation; PDAS Domain II learner-centered instruction; PDAS Domain III evaluation and feedback; PDAS Domain IV classroom management; TAKS Writing Objective 1 composition

Artists can also create symmetrical balance by placing similar objects on opposite sides of the artwork. What does the painting in image **B** show? Choose one object in the painting. Then look for a similar object on the other side of the painting. Does symmetrical balance create a tidy feeling or messy feeling in this painting?

Patssi Valdez, *Fenye's House Dining Room*

Artist's Workshop

Grid Drawing

1. **Think of an object or scene that has symmetrical balance. Sketch some ideas.**
2. **Draw a line down the middle of a sheet of graph paper.**
3. **Lightly draw your picture. Count the number of boxes in each shape to make sure you have symmetrical balance.**
4. **Color in the boxes. Use the same colors for matching shapes on each side of the middle line.**

107

Math Connection

Area Have students draw a square or rectangle on graph paper, and help them figure out the area of the figure. Have them count the number of grid boxes for length and width. Then tell students to multiply the length by the width.

PDAS Domain IV

ESL Use **visuals** to support **comprehensible input** for images with symmetrical balance. Display ***Picture Cards Collection***, cards 19, 68, and 72 for students to discuss and use as reference.

See also ***Picture Card Bank* CD-ROM.**

30-40 Minutes

Artist's Workshop

Grid Drawing

MATERIALS: sketchbook, pencil, graph paper (*Teacher Resource Book* p. 41), colored pencils

PLAN Tell students to keep their objects simple. Have them page through magazines for objects with symmetrical balance.

CREATE Have students find the center line on the graph paper. Tell them to draw one half of the image and then make a mirror image of the drawing on the other half of the paper. TEKS 3.2C

REFLECT Have students evaluate how well they showed symmetrical balance in their drawings.

Activity Options PDAS Domain IV

Quick Activity Have students fold colored paper in half and cut shapes from the paper to create a symmetrical design.

Early Finishers Have students use Discussion Card 4 to discuss balance in their drawings.

Challenge See *Teacher Resource Book*, p. 71.

5-10 Minutes

Wrap-Up

Informal Assessment PDAS Domain III

- **Name some objects in nature that have symmetrical balance.** (Responses will vary.) PERCEPTION/AESTHETICS
- **How did image A help you plan your grid drawing?** (Responses will vary.) EVALUATION/CRITICISM

Extend Through Writing

TAKS Writing Objective 1

Compare-and-Contrast Paragraph Have students write a paragraph that compares two objects that have symmetrical balance.

PDAS Domains I, II

Asymmetrical Balance

OBJECTIVES
- Identify asymmetrical balance in artworks
- Produce drawings that show asymmetrical balance
- Identify facts and opinions

RESOURCES
- Art Print 13
- Electronic Art Gallery CD-ROM, Primary

Warm-Up

Build Background Display **Art Print 13.** Have students discuss whether the artist created symmetrical balance and share their reasoning.

Teach

Discuss Art Concepts Read page 108 with students and have them identify balance in the painting. They should notice that the organic shape of the tall tree is balanced by the geometric shape of the column of squares. Discuss how the artist also created balance by using warm colors on the left side and cool colors on the right side. TEKS 3.1B

Think Critically

1. READING SKILL **What are three facts about the painting?** (Responses will vary.) FACT AND OPINION

2. **How would you change this painting to show symmetrical balance?** (Responses will vary.) PERCEPTION/AESTHETICS

3. **WRITE Tell how symmetrical and asymmetrical balance are different.** EXPOSITORY TAKS Writing Objective 1

Lesson 22

Vocabulary

asymmetrical balance

Asymmetrical Balance

When the two sides of an artwork do not match each other, the artwork can still be balanced. Artists can use different lines, shapes, and colors to give the artwork **asymmetrical balance**.

Look at the painting below. Notice that the window frame is not in the middle of the painting. The tall tree on the right is balanced by the column of squares on the left. How are the shapes of these objects different?

Now look at the colors the artist used. What part of the painting shows mostly warm colors? Where do you see mostly cool colors?

Pablo Picasso, *The Pigeons*

Background Information

About the Artist

Spanish artist **Pablo Picasso** (pih•KAHS•soh) (1881–1973) is one of the most well-known names in art history. He created more than 22,000 works of art, including paintings, prints, sculptures, ceramics, mosaics, and set designs. Picasso created several paintings with pigeons as the subject.

For additional information about Picasso, see pp. R44–R59.

RECOMMENDED READING

Pablo Picasso by Ibi Lepscky. Barron's, 1984. AVERAGE

★ TEKS 3.1B identify elements and principles; TEKS 3.2C produce various artworks; PDAS Domain I active participation; PDAS Domain II learner-centered instruction; PDAS Domain III evaluation and feedback; PDAS Domain IV classroom management; TAKS Writing Objective 1 composition

Artist's Workshop

Window View Drawing

PLAN

Imagine how a city at night might look from the window of a tall building. Sketch your ideas.

CREATE

1. Draw a window frame on the left or right side of your paper. Then draw a city scene inside the window frame.
2. Draw some objects inside the room. Use different shapes to create asymmetrical balance.
3. Add color to your drawing with oil pastels. Blend the colors with a cotton swab.

REFLECT

What shapes and colors did you use to create asymmetrical balance?

You may want to use geometric shapes to show tall buildings outside the window. Balance these shapes by using organic shapes for objects inside the room.

109

30-40 Minutes

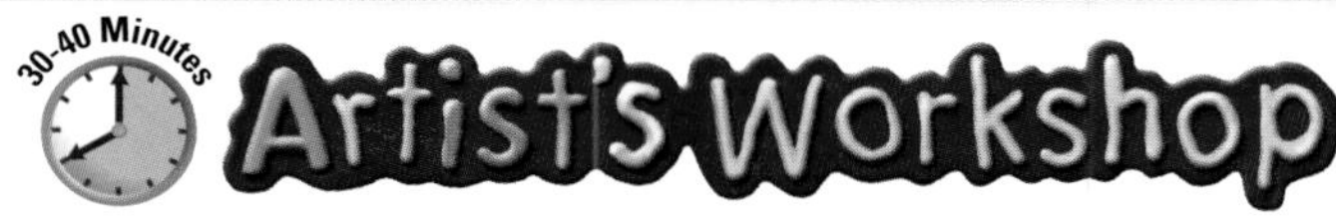

Window View Drawing

MATERIALS: sketchbook, pencil, white paper, oil pastels, cotton swabs

Have students blend colors with a cotton swab to show value changes.

PLAN Tell students to think about how they can use overlapping to show depth.

CREATE As students produce their drawings using oil pastels appropriately, tell them to consider using warm and cool colors to balance objects on either side of their drawing. TEKS 3.2C

REFLECT Students should identify shapes and colors that balance each other. TEKS 3.1B

Activity Options PDAS Domain IV

Quick Activity Have students sketch a still life with asymmetrical balance.

Early Finishers Have students draw a shape design with asymmetrical balance.

Challenge See *Teacher Resource Book*, p. 72.

5-10 Minutes

Wrap-Up

Informal Assessment PDAS Domain III

- **How could you change your drawing to make it symmetrically balanced?** (Responses will vary.) PERCEPTION/AESTHETICS
- **Compare your drawing with a classmate's drawing.** (Responses will vary.) EVALUATION/CRITICISM

Extend Through Writing

TAKS Writing Objective 1

Poem Have students write a poem about a city at night.

Science Connection

Simple Machines Tell students that a balance scale and a seesaw are examples of levers, a kind of simple machine used to perform work. Have students use their science textbook or another resource to name and sketch two other kinds of simple machines.

PDAS Domain IV

ESL Support **language acquisition** by having students describe their drawing, using prepositions to tell about the placement of objects in the scene. Provide these words for students to use in their description: *above, below, beside.* Use **total physical response** to demonstrate the meaning of each word.

PDAS Domains I, II

Patricia Polacco: Storyteller

CAREERS IN ART

DISCUSS THE IMAGES

Have students read pages 110–111.

- Have students discuss the illustration on page 111. Explain that the boy on the ground is Appelemando. Help students understand that the colorful birds and animals floating above Appelemando's head show his dreams and his vivid imagination.
- Discuss Polacco's use of color to show the difference between Appelemando's dreams and what is real. Students should note that the dreams are shown in bright, cheerful colors and that the rest of the image is mostly brown, gray, black, and white. Have students use this simple criteria to identify Polacco's main idea or message in this original artwork. (Possible response: Wonderful ideas come from the imagination.) TEKS 3.1B, TEKS 3.4B
- Have students relate art to jobs in everyday life by discussing how an illustrator plays an important role in telling a story. Ask students to share experiences reading textbooks or trade books when an illustration clarified information in the text or made the text more enjoyable. TEKS 3.3C

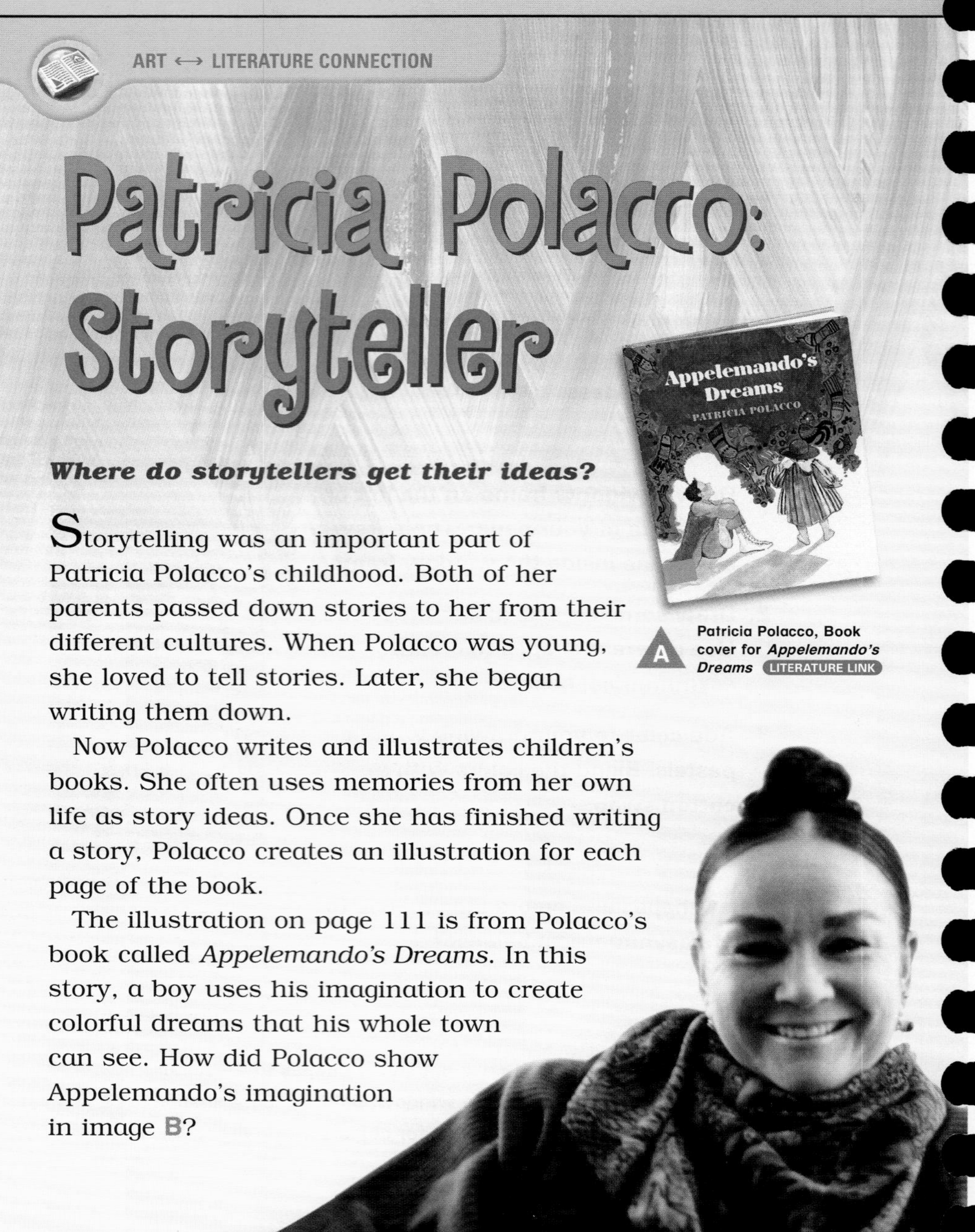

ART ⟷ LITERATURE CONNECTION

Patricia Polacco: Storyteller

Where do storytellers get their ideas?

Storytelling was an important part of Patricia Polacco's childhood. Both of her parents passed down stories to her from their different cultures. When Polacco was young, she loved to tell stories. Later, she began writing them down.

Now Polacco writes and illustrates children's books. She often uses memories from her own life as story ideas. Once she has finished writing a story, Polacco creates an illustration for each page of the book.

The illustration on page 111 is from Polacco's book called *Appelemando's Dreams*. In this story, a boy uses his imagination to create colorful dreams that his whole town can see. How did Polacco show Appelemando's imagination in image B?

A Patricia Polacco, Book cover for *Appelemando's Dreams* LITERATURE LINK

110

Background Information

About the Artist

Patricia Polacco (1944–) was a skillful artist at a very young age, but because of a learning disability, she didn't read until she was fourteen years old. With the help of a teacher, Polacco overcame her disability and succeeded in school. Her close relationship with her sets of Russian and Irish grandparents influenced her art and her writing.

For additional information about Polacco, see pp. R44–R59.

LITERATURE LINK *Appelemando's Dreams* by Patricia Polacco. Paper Star, 1997.

★ **TEKS 3.1A** identify sources for ideas; **TEKS 3.1B** identify elements and principles; **TEKS 3.2A** create artworks; **TEKS 3.2C** produce various artworks; **TEKS 3.3C** relate art to different jobs; **TEKS 3.4B** identify main ideas in artworks by peers and others; **PDAS Domain I** active participation; *(continued)*

DID YOU KNOW?

Artists and writers often work for months or even years on a book. Once Patricia Polacco gets an idea for a book, a year and a half might go by before you can buy that book in a bookstore. Polacco spends about five months writing and illustrating a story. Another year or more is needed to make the stories and pictures into a book.

B Patricia Polacco, Illustration from *Appelemando's Dreams*

Think About Art

What life experiences would you include in a story about yourself? What would the illustrations look like?

111

DID YOU KNOW?

Use the facts below to discuss how books are published.

- Many people help to prepare a book before it is sold in stores.
- Editors read and correct the text. They make sure all of the facts are accurate and change or rewrite parts that are not clear. Editors also check the text for correct grammar, spelling, and punctuation.
- Designers plan how a book will look. They arrange the text and illustrations on the pages. Then the book is sent to a printer.
- Sales people try to get people to buy the book. They create advertisements to tell about it.

Think About Art

What life experiences would you include in a story about yourself? What would the illustrations look like? (Responses will vary. Students should identify life experiences as sources for ideas about self and life events.) PERSONAL RESPONSE
TEKS 3.1A

ARTIST'S EYE ACTIVITY

Be an Illustrator Have students think about a story or life event from their own cultural traditions or life experiences. Ask students to sketch one scene from a story for an artwork based on experiences. Then have them use markers to add color to their illustration. When students are finished, have them relate art to different kinds of jobs in everyday life by discussing how being an illustrator is different from other careers in art.
TEKS 3.1A, TEKS 3.2A, TEKS 3.2C, TEKS 3.3C

Social Studies Connection

Books from Long Ago Tell students that some of the first books were written in Egypt on *papyrus*, a paper-like material made from the papyrus plant.

For additional cross-curricular suggestions, see Art Transparency 14.

TEKS 3.4B

Student Art Show

Portfolios and Exhibitions Periodically during this unit, have students create a display or exhibition of their portfolios or other finished artworks. Ask students to use simple criteria to identify main ideas in peers' artworks. See *Teacher Edition* page 142 for information on planning and preparing a student art show.

Lesson 23

PDAS Domains I, II

Abstract Portraits

OBJECTIVES
- Identify balance and shape in artworks
- Produce abstract paintings
- Identify facts and opinions

RESOURCES
- Art Print 14
- Discussion Card 8, p. R37
- Electronic Art Gallery CD-ROM, Primary

5 Minutes

Warm-Up

Build Background Display **Art Print 14,** and ask students to describe what they see. Tell them to find a person's legs, arms, and eyes in the painting.

10-15 Minutes

Teach

Discuss Art Concepts Have students read page 112. They should point out that in image A, the artist used geometric shapes to show the subject's eyes and mouth. Students should also identify how the artist created asymmetrical balance. For image B, have students describe the distortion of the subject's eyes and mouth. TEKS 3.1B

Think Critically

1.  READING SKILL **Which painting do you like better—image A or image B? Explain.** (Responses will vary.) FACT AND OPINION

2. **How did the artist use distortion in image A?** (Possible response: The eyes are different shapes.) PERCEPTION/AESTHETICS

3. WRITE **Describe a subject that you would like to paint in an abstract style.** DESCRIPTIVE TAKS Writing Objective 1

Lesson 23

Vocabulary

abstract art

distortion

Abstract Portraits

An artwork that shows something exactly as it looks in real life is realistic art. **Abstract art** is not realistic. The painting in image A is an abstract portrait. Find the subject's eyes, nose, mouth, and hands. What shapes and colors did the artist use to paint these features? Does the painting have symmetrical or asymmetrical balance?

Distortion can be seen in many abstract artworks. When artists use **distortion**, they change the way an object looks by bending or stretching its shape. Look at the abstract portrait in image B. Where has the artist used distortion?

A Juan Gris, *Clown*

B Taylor, grade 3, Untitled

Background Information

About the Artist

In 1906, Juan Gris (GREES) (1887–1927) moved from Spain to Paris, France. There he witnessed Pablo Picasso and Georges Braque develop **Cubism,** in which subjects are distorted in surprising ways. Gris later began experimenting with Cubism himself.

For additional information about Gris and Cubism, see pp. R44–R59.

RECOMMENDED READING

Matthew's Dream by Leo Lionni. Alfred A. Knopf, 1991.

AVERAGE

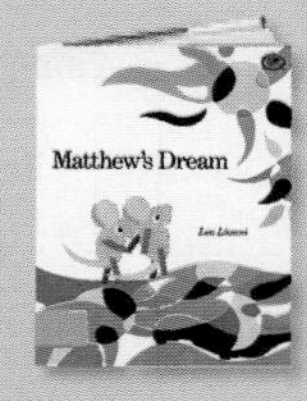

★ TEKS 3.1A identify sources for ideas; TEKS 3.1B identify elements and principles; TEKS 3.2C produce various artworks; TEKS 3.4A identify intent in personal artworks; PDAS Domain I active participation; PDAS Domain II learner-centered instruction; PDAS Domain III evaluation and feedback; *(continued)*

Artist's Workshop

Abstract Self-Portrait

PLAN

Sketch a self-portrait. Think about how you can add distortion by changing the shapes of your facial features.

CREATE

1. Copy your sketch onto white paper.
2. Use geometric shapes for the parts of your face. Erase parts of your sketch, and change or break up the shapes to create distortion.
3. Add different kinds of lines to the background to show your feelings.
4. Paint your self-portrait.

REFLECT

What shapes did you use in your painting? How did you show distortion?

Mix tints and shades of your favorite color to show your personality in your painting.

113

Abstract Self-Portrait

MATERIALS: sketchbook, pencil, white paper, tempera paints, paintbrushes, paper plate, water bowl

PLAN Have students begin by sketching a realistic self-portrait.

CREATE Have students identify sensory knowledge as sources for ideas about self to describe the feeling they want to show. Students should use the ideas they generated as they produce their paintings. TEKS 3.1A, TEKS 3.2C

REFLECT Ask students to point out where they used distortion and identify the expressive qualities in their artwork. TEKS 3.4A

Activity Options PDAS Domain IV

Quick Activity Have students use distortion to sketch an abstract portrait.

Early Finishers Have students use Discussion Card 8 to evaluate their finished paintings.

Challenge See *Teacher Resource Book*, p. 73.

Wrap-Up

Informal Assessment PDAS Domain III

- **How did you use lines to express a feeling in your abstract portrait?** (Responses will vary.) EVALUATION/CRITICISM TEKS 3.4A
- **Would you rather paint an abstract portrait or a realistic portrait? Explain.** (Responses will vary.) PERSONAL RESPONSE

Extend Through Writing  TAKS Writing Objective 1

Art Review Have students imagine they are art critics and write a review of image A.

Social Studies Connection

Map Reading Tell students that Juan Gris grew up in Madrid, Spain, and then moved to Paris, France, the center for modern art at the time. Have students locate a map of Europe and use the mileage scale to measure how far Gris traveled from Madrid to Paris to start his new life as a painter.

PDAS Domain IV

ESL Promote **oral language development** by asking questions about students' paintings as they work. Use yes/no questions or why/how questions, depending on the student's level of language acquisition.

Extra Support To demonstrate distortion, mold a familiar form with clay and then distort it.

PDAS Domain IV classroom management; TAKS Writing Objective 1 composition

Lesson 24

PDAS Domains I, II

Abstract Designs

OBJECTIVES
- Identify unity and color in artworks
- Produce an abstract design
- Identify facts and opinions

RESOURCES
- Art Prints 16 and 17
- Color Wheel Poster
- Electronic Art Gallery CD-ROM, Primary

5 Minutes

Warm-Up

Build Background Display **Art Prints 16** and **17,** and tell students that both images are abstract artworks. Have students identify the subject of the quilt. Then discuss the ideas or feelings these abstract artists may have wanted to express.

10-15 Minutes

Teach

Discuss Art Concepts Have students read page 114, and discuss how deleting any of the shapes would make the painting seem incomplete. Then display the **Color Wheel Poster.** Have students find complementary colors placed side by side in the painting. Students should identify the neutral gray shapes in the artwork. TEKS 3.1B

Think Critically

1. READING SKILL **What are some facts about the painting?** (Responses will vary.) FACT AND OPINION

2. **Why do artists place complementary colors next to each other in an artwork?** (to create a lively feeling) PERCEPTION/AESTHETICS

3. **WRITE Think of another title for this painting. Write a paragraph that explains your thinking.** DESCRIPTIVE TAKS Writing Objective 1

Lesson 24

Vocabulary

unity

complementary colors

neutral colors

Abstract Designs

The painting below has an abstract design. It does not show any objects from real life. Look at the repeated lines, shapes, and colors. When the parts of an artwork seem to belong together, the artist has created a feeling of **unity**. Would this painting look complete if some of the shapes were missing? Why or why not?

Now find places in the painting where the colors red and green are next to each other. Red and green are complementary colors. **Complementary colors** are opposite each other on the color wheel. When complementary colors are placed side by side in an artwork, they create a lively feeling. What other complementary colors do you see in this painting?

Artists can create **neutral colors**, such as brown and gray, by mixing complementary colors. Where do you see neutral colors in this painting?

Sonia Delaunay, *Composition*

114

Background Information

About the Artist

Sonia Delaunay (duh•loh•NAY) (1885–1979) was a pioneer in abstract art. She used what she had learned about color and abstract art to create designs for textiles and clothing. She also worked with her husband, Robert Delaunay, to design huge murals for the Paris Exposition of 1937.

For additional information about Delaunay, see pp. R44–R59.

RECOMMENDED READING

Hello, Red Fox by Eric Carle. Aladdin, 1998. AVERAGE

★ **TEKS 3.1B** identify elements and principles; **TEKS 3.2B** develop effective compositions; **TEKS 3.2C** produce various artworks; **PDAS Domain I** active participation; **PDAS Domain II** learner-centered instruction; **PDAS Domain III** evaluation and feedback; **PDAS Domain IV** classroom management; *(continued)*

Artist's Workshop

Abstract Painting

PLAN

Sketch repeated lines and shapes to create an abstract design. Then choose a pair of complementary colors to use in your painting.

CREATE

1. **Copy your sketch onto white paper. You may need to add lines and shapes to create a feeling of unity.**
2. **Mix small amounts of your complementary colors to create neutral colors.**
3. **Paint your design. Use only the two complementary colors and the neutral colors you have mixed.**

REFLECT

What complementary colors and neutral colors did you use? How did you show unity in your painting?

Quick Tip: You can make tints and shades of neutral colors by mixing them with black and white.

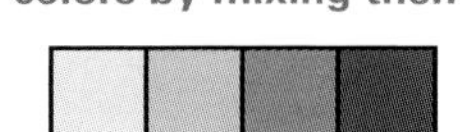

115

Artist's Workshop

30-40 Minutes

Abstract Painting

MATERIALS: sketchbook, pencil, white paper, tempera paints, paper plate, water bowl, paintbrushes

PLAN Have students refer to the **Color Wheel Poster** to choose complementary colors.

CREATE Tell students to focus on unity to create an effective composition using design skills. Have students experiment with mixing colors until they achieve a pleasing neutral. TEKS 3.2B, TEKS 3.2C

REFLECT Have students identify neutrals and complementary colors in their paintings and explain how they created unity. TEKS 3.1B

Activity Options PDAS Domain IV

Quick Activity Have students draw a pattern with complementary colors.

Early Finishers Have students make a color strip that shows how a color changes when different amounts of its complement are added.

Challenge See *Teacher Resource Book*, p. 74.

Language Arts Connection

Homophones Tell students that homophones are words with the same pronunciation but different meanings and spellings. Write the words *complement* and *compliment* on the board, and have students use a dictionary to define the words. Then have students list other homophone pairs they know.

PDAS Domain IV

ESL Encourage **language acquisition** by having students make vocabulary cards for colors on the color wheel. Tell them to label the cards with the name of the color and other descriptors, such as *primary color* or *cool color.*

5-10 Minutes

Wrap-Up

Informal Assessment PDAS Domain III

- **How would your painting change if you used only neutral colors?** (Responses will vary.) EVALUATION/CRITICISM
- **How do artists create neutrals?** (by mixing complementary colors) PERCEPTION/AESTHETICS

Extend Through Writing

TAKS Writing Objective 1

E-mail Have students write an e-mail to a friend describing their experience of creating their abstract painting.

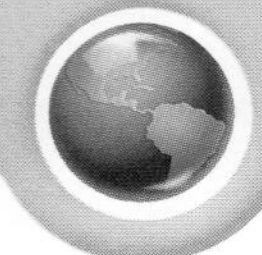

PDAS Domains I, II

Romare Bearden

ARTIST BIOGRAPHY

DISCUSS THE IMAGES

Have students read pages 116–117.

- Tell students that many of Romare Bearden's artworks represent his life experiences. Explain that music, family, and the experiences of African Americans were strong influences in his work. Have students brainstorm ideas for one or two major themes in artworks they could create. Ask them to identify sensory knowledge and life experiences as sources for theme ideas about visual symbols, self, and life events. Students may respond with ideas such as sports, a particular kind of music, or the people in their community. TEKS 3.1A
- Help students recognize that the subject in image A is a guitar player. Ask students to share their ideas of what kind of music the person is playing by discussing the title of the artwork. TEKS 3.1A
- Have students compare the mood in image B with the mood in image A. Then display **Art Print 15**, a third artwork by Bearden with music as the subject. Help students evaluate this portfolio of Bearden's work by asking questions such as these: *What is the subject of each artwork? How did the artist use line and color in each artwork?* Then have students apply simple criteria to identify the main idea in this portfolio by a major artist. TEKS 3.4B

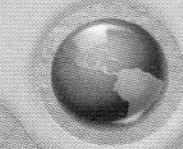

Romare Bearden

Romare Bearden, *Gospel Song*

What inspired many of Romare Bearden's artworks?

Romare Bearden grew up listening to the sounds of jazz music. Bearden's father had many friends who were musicians, and they gathered at the Bearden home to play music together. Bearden also heard the musicians who played on the street corners near his home in Harlem, New York.

Background Information

About the Artist

Romare Bearden (roh•MAIR BEER•duhn) (1911–1988) experimented with a variety of art media and styles, though he is best known for his collages. As a **Harlem Renaissance** artist, Bearden tried to show what life was like for African American people in his community.

For additional information about Bearden and the Harlem Renaissance, see pp. R44–R59.

For related artworks, see **Electronic Art Gallery CD-ROM, Primary.**

★ **TEKS 3.1A** identify sources for ideas; **TEKS 3.2A** create artworks; **TEKS 3.2C** produce various artworks; **TEKS 3.4A** identify intent in personal artworks; **TEKS 3.4B** identify main ideas in artworks by peers and others; **PDAS Domain I** active participation; **PDAS Domain II** learner-centered instruction

Romare Bearden,
The Piano Lesson (Homage to Mary Lou)

Bearden's interest in music can be seen in many of his artworks. He often created artworks that have musicians and instruments as subjects. Look at image **A**. What is the subject of this artwork? Does image **A** make you think of a slow song or a song with a fast rhythm? Why? What kind of music does image **B** remind you of?

DID YOU KNOW?

In the 1920s, many African Americans used art to express feelings about their culture. This period was called the Harlem Renaissance because most of these artists worked in Harlem, New York. Writers, musicians, and artists were part of the Harlem Renaissance. Romare Bearden was one of these artists.

THINK ABOUT ART

Think about the music you like best. What kinds of lines, shapes, and colors could you use to show it in an artwork?

Multimedia Biographies
Visit *The Learning Site*
www.harcourtschool.com

117

Performing Arts Connection

Jazz Tell students that one important aspect of jazz music is improvisation, in which the musician invents the melody as he or she plays it.

For additional cross-curricular suggestions, see Art Transparency 15.

TEKS 3.4B

View an Artist's Work

Portfolios and Exhibitions Arrange for students to visit a museum to view a major artist's work. Ask students to apply simple criteria they have learned from this unit to identify main ideas in the artist's original artworks, portfolio, and exhibit.

DID YOU KNOW?

Use the facts below to discuss the Harlem Renaissance with students.

- Harlem is a neighborhood in New York City with a large African American population.
- During the Harlem Renaissance, many African American writers, musicians, and artists encouraged each other to explore their life and culture through the arts.
- Other well-known visual artists from this movement include Lois Mailou Jones, William H. Johnson, and Jacob Lawrence.

THINK ABOUT ART

Think about the music you like best. What kinds of lines, shapes, and colors could you use to show it in an artwork? (Responses will vary.)

PERSONAL RESPONSE TEKS 3.1A

ARTIST'S EYE ACTIVITY

Painting Music Ask students to think of an instrument they play or one they enjoy listening to. Have them produce a painting of a musician playing the instrument, using a variety of art materials appropriately. Tell students to include lines, shapes, and colors that stand for the sounds of the instrument. Have students share their completed paintings with the class and identify the expressive qualities of their painting and the kind of music they chose to show. TEKS 3.1A, TEKS 3.2A, TEKS 3.2C, TEKS 3.4A

Multimedia Biographies
Visit *The Learning Site*
www.harcourtschool.com

Lesson 25

PDAS Domains I, II

Collage

OBJECTIVES
- Identify unity and texture in artworks
- Produce collages
- Identify facts and opinions

RESOURCES
- Discussion Card 3, p. R35
- Electronic Art Gallery CD-ROM, Primary

5 Minutes

Warm-Up

Build Background Tell students that some artists use cutout shapes from magazines, newspapers, and photographs as the materials for their artwork. Have students discuss how an artist might plan this kind of artwork. (Possible response: sketch; gather and arrange materials)

10-15 Minutes

Teach

Discuss Art Concepts Have students read pages 118–119. Have them identify how the artist of image A created unity by repeating objects. Have students think of an object that would look out of place in this scene. Students should point out that image B is an abstract collage. Have students describe the tactile texture of the different materials. TEKS 3.1B

Think Critically

1.  READING SKILL **What are two facts about image B?** (Responses will vary.) FACT AND OPINION
2. **What advertisements would you include in a collage? Compare your idea to image A.** (Responses will vary.) ART HISTORY AND CULTURE TEKS 3.3A
3. WRITE **Write a funny story about the scene in image A.** NARRATIVE TAKS Writing Objective 1

Lesson 25

Vocabulary

collage

Collage

A **collage** is an artwork made by gluing pieces of paper and other material to a flat surface. A collage artist may use cut paper, photographs, fabric, or other kinds of scraps.

The artist of image **A** made collages of indoor scenes. He often cut pictures from popular advertisements. Look at the different objects in image **A**. Why does everything seem to belong in this scene? How did this artist create a feeling of unity?

A Tom Wesselmann, *Still Life #25*

118

Background Information

Art History

Pop artists used popular culture as inspiration for their artworks. By incorporating images from the media into their artworks, these artists hoped to make their art meaningful to everyday people.

For additional information about Pop Art, see pp. R44–R59.

RECOMMENDED READING

Me and Uncle Romie: A Story Inspired by the Life and Art of Romare Bearden by Claire Hartfield. Dial Books, 2000. CHALLENGING

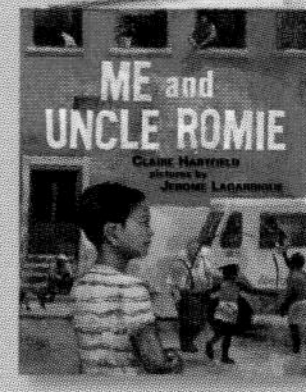

★ TEKS 3.1B identify elements and principles; TEKS 3.2C produce various artworks; TEKS 3.3A compare artworks from the past and present; PDAS Domain I active participation; PDAS Domain II learner-centered instruction; PDAS Domain III evaluation and feedback; *(continued)*

Now look at image B. This abstract collage is made of wood, fabric, metal, and paper. Why do you think the artist of image B used different textures in his collage? How is the collage in image B different from the collage in image A?

Kurt Schwitters,
Merz Picture 32A. (The Cherry Picture)

Artist's Workshop

Multi-Texture Collage

1. **Find a picture of an interesting scene in a magazine or book. Think about materials and textures you can use to show the scene as a collage.**
2. **Draw the shapes for your collage on the materials you have chosen. Use repeated colors, shapes, and textures to create unity. Cut out the shapes.**
3. **Arrange the shapes on a background. Then glue down the shapes.**

119

Science Connection

Recycling Point out that using scraps and other found materials to create artworks is a form of recycling. Tell students that recycling saves natural resources, reduces trash, and conserves energy. Have students research recyclable materials in your school or community.

PDAS Domain IV

ESL Help students **identify cognates** for shapes and objects in their scenes. You may use these examples as a starting point: *flor* (flower), *círculo* (circle), and *montaña* (mountain).

Challenge Have students incorporate images from advertisements into their design.

30-40 Minutes Artist's Workshop

Multi-Texture Collage

MATERIALS: sketchbook, pencil, scraps with different textures, scissors, glue, tagboard

Quick Tip: Students may add buttons or other small objects to their collage.

PLAN Tell students to use expected and unexpected textures for objects in their collage.

CREATE Have students produce their fiberart collages, using a variety of materials appropriately. Tell students to first glue down objects and shapes in the background. TEKS 3.2C

REFLECT Ask students to describe how they created unity in their collages.

Activity Options PDAS Domain IV

Quick Activity Have students use magazine pictures to make a collage.

Early Finishers Have students use Discussion Card 3 to talk about their collage with a partner.

Challenge See *Teacher Resource Book*, p. 75.

5-10 Minutes Wrap-Up

Informal Assessment PDAS Domain III

- **Is your collage abstract or realistic? Explain.** (Responses will vary.) PERCEPTION/AESTHETICS
- **What is your opinion of collage as an art form?** (Responses will vary.) FACT AND OPINION

Extend Through Writing

TAKS Writing Objective 1

Letter Have students write a letter to a fabric store, requesting material for making collages.

PDAS Domain IV classroom management; TAKS Writing Objective 1 composition

PDAS Domains I, III

Review and Reflect

Have students reflect on what they have learned about the ways artists use balance and unity in their artworks. Display **Art Prints 13, 14, 15, 16,** and **17.** Have students identify art elements and design principles in the images. Encourage small groups of students to use Discussion Cards 3 and 4, page R35, and their completed Word Knowledge Charts to discuss what they learned about balance, unity, and other vocabulary and concepts in this unit. TEKS 3.1B

Vocabulary and Concepts

Have students read each sentence and choose the letter of the word or phrase that best completes it. (1. C; 2. A; 3. C; 4. B; 5. B)

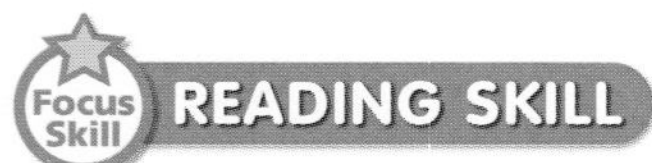

Fact and Opinion

Remind students that a fact can be proved and that an opinion is a person's own belief or feeling. Tell students to list facts about Romare Bearden in the diagram. Then have them write an opinion about each of Bearden's artworks. Tell them to use signal words such as *like* and *believe* to indicate opinions. TAKS Reading Objectives 3, 4

Facts	Opinions
Bearden grew up listening to jazz music. He lived in Harlem, New York.	I believe that *Gospel Song* is interesting because the artist used distortion.

Unit 5 Review and Reflect

Vocabulary and Concepts

Choose the letter of the word or phrase that best completes each sentence.

1 Artworks that match on two sides have ___.

A asymmetrical balance **C** symmetrical balance

B unity **D** distortion

2 ___ colors are opposite each other on the color wheel.

A Complementary **C** Primary

B Secondary **D** Neutral

3 A ___ is made by gluing different materials to a flat surface.

A mural **C** collage

B weaving **D** cityscape

4 Artworks that do not match on both sides have ___.

A emphasis **C** depth

B asymmetrical balance **D** symmetrical balance

5 When the parts of an artwork seem to belong together, the artwork has ___.

A movement **C** distortion

B unity **D** balance

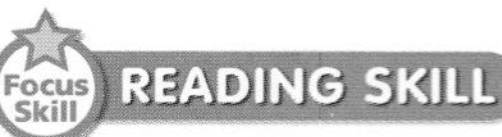

Fact and Opinion

Facts	Opinions

Reread the information about Romare Bearden on pages 116–117. Write facts from the text in a chart like the one shown here. Then write your opinions about Romare Bearden and his artworks.

120

TEKS 3.2A, TEKS 3.2C

Home and Community Connection

School-Home Connection

Have students work with parents or other family members to create a family collage based on experiences. Students may choose to include family pictures in their artwork. Copy and distribute *Teacher Resource Book* pp. 93–94 to inform parents about upcoming art projects.

Community Connection

Have students contribute to a seasonal exhibit to be displayed at a local library or another public building. Encourage students to work in the medium they most enjoy and use a variety of art materials appropriately.

★ **TEKS 3.1B** identify elements and principles; **TEKS 3.2A** create artworks; **TEKS 3.2C** produce various artworks; **TEKS 3.4B** identify main ideas in artworks by peers and others; **PDAS Domain I** active participation; **PDAS Domain III** evaluation and feedback; *(continued)*

Write About Art

Write a paragraph about one of the artworks in this unit. Include facts and your own opinions about the artwork. Use a chart to plan your writing.

REMEMBER—YOU SHOULD

- write information that can be proved.
- write your opinions about the artwork.
- use correct grammar, spelling, and punctuation.

Critic's Corner

Look at *Morning in the Village after Snowstorm* by Kasimir Malevich to answer the questions below.

DESCRIBE What is the subject of the painting?

ANALYZE Is the painting abstract or realistic? Where did the artist use complementary colors? How did the artist create unity?

INTERPRET What do you think the artist was trying to say about the village in the painting?

EVALUATE Do you think the artist got his message across? Why or why not?

Kasimir Malevich, *Morning in the Village after Snowstorm*

PDAS Domain III

Assessment

Portfolio Assessment

Work with students to choose a piece of their artwork to include in their portfolios. Suggest that they decide which piece best fulfilled the assignment or which piece they liked best for another reason. You may want to provide specific feedback that targets students' use of principles of design and techniques. See also Portfolio Recording Form, page R32.

Additional Assessment Options

- Progress Recording Form, p. R33
- Artist's Workshop Rubrics (Self/Teacher and Peer), pp. R30–R31
- Unit 5 Test, *Teacher Resource Book,* p. 103

Write About Art

Fact-and-Opinion Paragraph Read aloud the prompt with students. Tell them to use the fact-and-opinion diagram on page 120 to help them plan their paragraphs. Encourage students to choose an artwork that they have a strong opinion about. Remind students to use unit vocabulary words as they write. TAKS Writing Objectives 1, 2, 3, 5

Critic's Corner

RESPONSE/EVALUATION Use Discussion Card 2, page R34, and the steps below to guide students in analyzing *Morning in the Village after Snowstorm* by Kasimir Malevich.

DESCRIBE Have students describe the subject of the artwork. If they have difficulty, discuss how the title gives a clue about the season and time of day.

ANALYZE Students should describe the painting as abstract and identify the complementary colors blue and orange. Discuss how repeated shapes and colors create unity in the artwork. TEKS 3.1B

INTERPRET Have students share their ideas about the artist's message. Students may describe the village as cold or lonely. TEKS 3.4B

EVALUATE Students should share their opinion of whether or not the artist effectively conveyed his message. Students may also share ideas about how the artwork could be changed to improve the message.

TAKS Test Preparation: Reading and Writing Through Art, pp. 53–57

TAKS Reading Objective 3 use a variety of strategies; **TAKS Reading Objective 4** apply critical-thinking skills; **TAKS Writing Objective 1** composition; **TAKS Writing Objective 2** conventions; **TAKS Writing Objective 3** organization; **TAKS Writing Objective 5** usage

Unit 6

Variety and Rhythm

Old and New Ideas

Throughout history, artists have adapted ideas from the past and from different cultures. In this unit students will see how variety and rhythm have been used in artworks for thousands of years.

Resources

- Unit 6 Art Prints (16–18)
- Additional Art Prints (10, 15)
- Art Transparencies 16–18
- Test Preparation: Reading and Writing Through Art, pp. 58–78
- Artist's Workshop Activities: English and Spanish, pp. 51–60
- Encyclopedia of Artists and Art History, pp. R44–R59
- Picture Cards Collection, cards 8, 90, 94

Using the Art Prints

- Discussion Cards, pp. R34–R38
- Teaching suggestions, backs of Art Prints
- Art Print Teaching Suggestions: Spanish

Teacher Resource Book

- Vocabulary Cards in English and Spanish, pp. 27–30
- Reading Skill Card 6, p. 36
- Copying Master, p. 39
- Challenge Activities, pp. 76–80
- School-Home Connection: English/Spanish, pp. 95–96
- Unit 6 Test, p. 104

Technology Resources

Electronic Art Gallery CD-ROM, Primary
Picture Card Bank CD-ROM

Visit *The Learning Site*
www.harcourtschool.com

- Multimedia Art Glossary
- Multimedia Biographies
- Reading Skills and Activities

Art Prints for This Unit

ART PRINT 18

Lizard Alebrije
by Pepe Santiago

ART PRINT 17

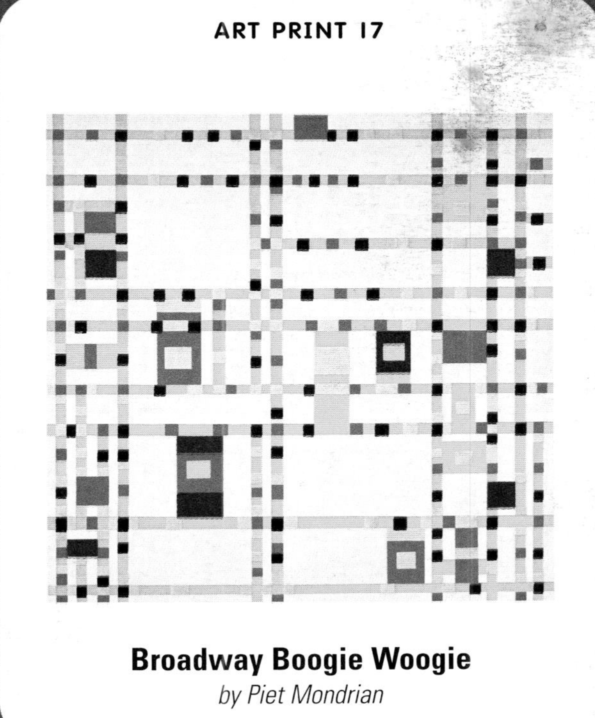

Broadway Boogie Woogie
by Piet Mondrian

ART PRINT 16

Unveiling of the Statue of Liberty
by Katherine Westphal

ART PRINT 10

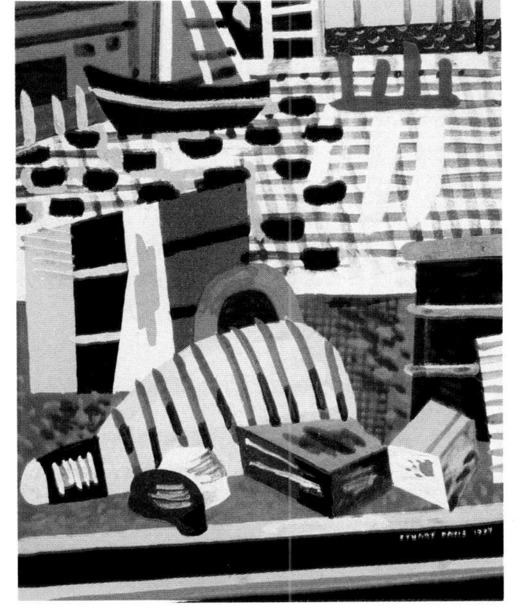

Marine Landscape
by Stuart Davis

ART PRINT 15

Brass Section (Jamming at Minton's)
by Romare Bearden

Unit 6 Old and New Ideas Variety and Rhythm

Planning Guide

PDAS Domain IV

Lesson	Objectives and Vocabulary	Art Images	Production/ Materials
Focus Skill Summarize, pp. 124–125			
26 SHAPES AND SYMBOLS pp. 126–127 30–60 minutes	• Identify variety and shape in artworks • Produce ceramics Focus Skill Summarize ideas in artworks **Vocabulary: symbol, variety**	• **Egyptian hieroglyphics** by Unknown artist • **'Sun Ray' Double-Handled Lotus Jug** by Clarice Cliff	**Clay Pinch Pot** ❑ sketchbook ❑ pencil ❑ clay ❑ paper bag ❑ carving tools
27 PRINTMAKING pp. 128–129 30–60 minutes	• Identify rhythm in artworks • Produce prints Focus Skill Summarize ideas in artworks **Vocabulary: prints, rhythm**	• **Sun Shines** by Beatricia Sagar • **Untitled** by Tanaya, grade 4	**Kaleidoscope Print** ❑ paper plate ❑ white paper ❑ ruler ❑ pencil ❑ scissors ❑ small objects ❑ tempera paints
Art ↔ Social Studies Connection: Styles of Architecture, pp. 130–131			
28 RHYTHM IN PHOTO-MONTAGE pp. 132–133 30–60 minutes	• Identify rhythm and pattern in artworks • Produce photomontages Focus Skill Summarize ideas in artworks **Vocabulary: photomontage**	• **Interior with Red Apples** by Louise Freshman-Brown	**Photomontage** ❑ magazines ❑ scissors ❑ construction paper ❑ glue
29 ASSEMBLAGE pp. 134–135 30–60 minutes	• Identify variety and texture in artworks • Produce constructions with found objects Focus Skill Summarize ideas in artworks **Vocabulary: assemblage, found objects**	• **World Series** by David Stewart • **Abstract Sculpture** by Louise Nevelson	**Found-Object Assemblage** ❑ found objects ❑ shoe box ❑ construction paper ❑ glue ❑ tempera paints ❑ paintbrush
Art ↔ Social Studies Connection: Nicario Jimenez, pp. 136–137			
30 GRAPHIC ARTS pp. 138–139 30–60 minutes	• Identify variety and color in artworks • Produce graphic designs Focus Skill Summarize ideas in artworks **Vocabulary: graphic arts**	• **Cactus Brand Oranges—Highland Fruit Growers Association, Promotional literature posters** • **"We're Waiting Just for You at the Zoo" Panda Print** by Johanna Kriesel	**Graphic Design** ❑ sketchbook ❑ colored pencils ❑ white paper
Review and Reflect, pp. 140–141			

★ TEKS 3.2C produce various artworks; PDAS Domain IV classroom management

Summarize, pp. 124–125

Opportunities for application of the skill are provided on pp. 126, 128, 129, 132, 134, 138, 140, and 141.

Resources and Technology	Suggested Literature	Across the Curriculum
• Art Print 16 • Reading Skill Card 6 Electronic Art Gallery CD-ROM, Primary	*The Seeker of Knowledge: The Man Who Deciphered Egyptian Hieroglyphs* by James Rumford 	**Social Studies** Rosetta Stone, p. 127 **Reading** Summarize, p. 126 **Writing** Narrative Paragraph, p. 127
• Art Prints 15 and 17 • Reading Skill Card 6 Electronic Art Gallery CD-ROM, Primary	*The Art Room* by Susan Vande Griek 	**Performing Arts** Rhythm in Music, p. 129 **Reading** Summarize, p. 128 **Writing** How-To Paragraph, p. 129
• Art Print 10 • Reading Skill Card 6 Electronic Art Gallery CD-ROM, Primary	*Photographers* by Fran Hodgkins 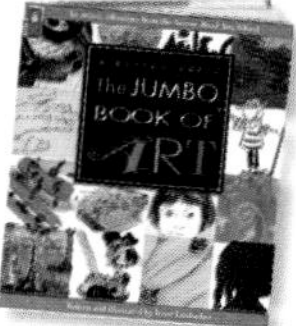	**Science** Camera Obscura, p. 133 **Reading** Summarize, p. 132 **Writing** Poem, p. 133
• Discussion Card 4, p. R35 • Reading Skill Card 6 Electronic Art Gallery CD-ROM, Primary	*The Jumbo Book of Art* by Irene Luxbacher	**Social Studies** The All-American Game, p. 135 **Reading** Summarize, p. 134 **Writing** Song, p. 135
• Discussion Card 3, p. R35 • Reading Skill Card 6 Electronic Art Gallery CD-ROM, Primary	*The Hatmaker's Sign: A Story by Benjamin Franklin* by Candace Fleming 	**Language Arts** Word Origin, p. 139 **Reading** Summarize, p. 138 **Writing** Commercial, p. 139

Art Puzzlers

Present these art puzzlers to students at the beginning or end of a class or when students finish an assignment early.

- Invent several **symbols** that look like Egyptian hieroglyphics. Tell what each one stands for.
- Make a **print** with **rhythm**. Paint repeated lines and shapes on one side of a piece of paper. Then fold the paper in half and press on it. TEKS 3.2C
- Draw the letters of your name on different pictures in magazines. Cut out the letters, and glue them to construction paper. Add pictures to your **photomontage**.
- Make an **assemblage** construction with objects that can be recycled. TEKS 3.2C
- Think of a kind of food you like. Then create an **advertisement** for that food.

School-Home Connection
The activities above are included in the School-Home Connection for this unit. See *Teacher Resource Book,* pp. 95–96.

Assessment Options

- Rubrics and Recording Forms, pp. R30–R33
- Unit 6 Test, *Teacher Resource Book,* p. 104

Visit *The Learning Site:* **www.harcourtschool.com**

Artist's Workshops PREVIEW

PDAS Domain IV

Use these pages to help you gather and organize materials for the production activity in each lesson.

LESSON	MATERIALS
26 Clay Pinch Pot p. 127 **Objective:** Produce ceramics that incorporate symbols and show variety  **30–40 minutes** **Challenge Activity:** See *Teacher Resource Book,* page 76.	• sketchbook • pencil • clay • paper bag • carving tools 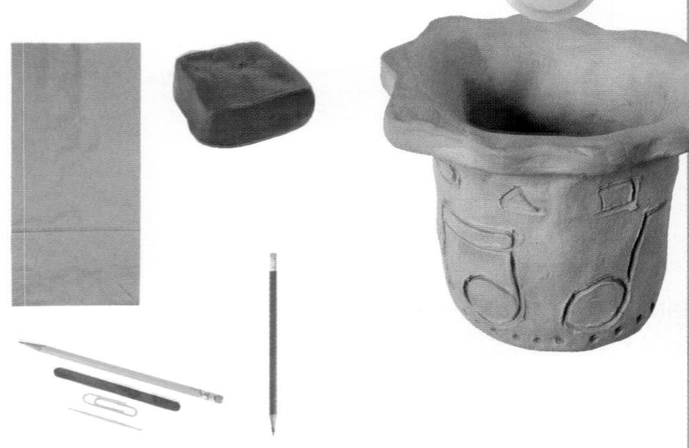
LESSON **27 Kaleidoscope Print** p. 129 **Objective:** Produce prints that use repeated shapes to create rhythm  **30–40 minutes** **Challenge Activity:** See *Teacher Resource Book,* page 77.	• paper plate • white paper • ruler • pencil • scissors • various small objects • tempera paints 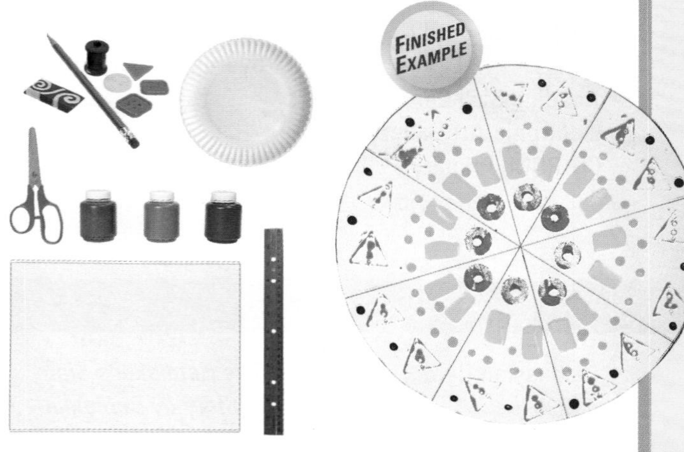

For safety information, see Art Safety, page R4; or the Art Safety Poster.

For information on media and techniques, see pp. R15–R23.

LESSON	MATERIALS

28 Photomontage
p. 133

Objective: Produce photomontages with effective compositions

 **30–40 minutes**

Challenge Activity: See *Teacher Resource Book,* page 78.

- magazines
- scissors
- construction paper
- glue

FINISHED EXAMPLE

LESSON

29 Found-Object Assemblage p. 135

Objective: Produce constructions with found objects

 **30–40 minutes**

Challenge Activity: See *Teacher Resource Book,* page 79.

- found objects
- shoe box
- construction paper
- glue
- tempera paints
- paintbrush
- water bowl

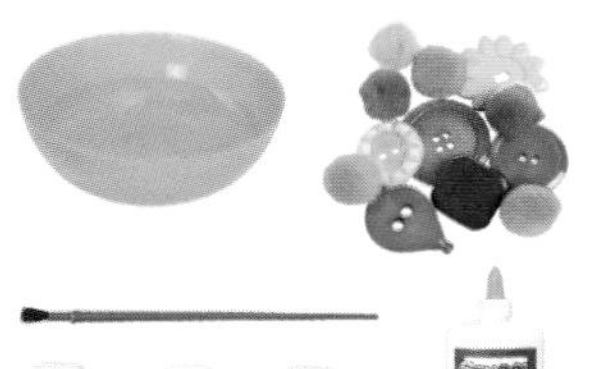

FINISHED EXAMPLE

LESSON

30 Graphic Design p. 139

Objective: Produce graphic designs that use variety to create an appealing composition

 **30–40 minutes**

Challenge Activity: See *Teacher Resource Book,* page 80.

- sketchbook
- colored pencils
- white paper

FINISHED EXAMPLE

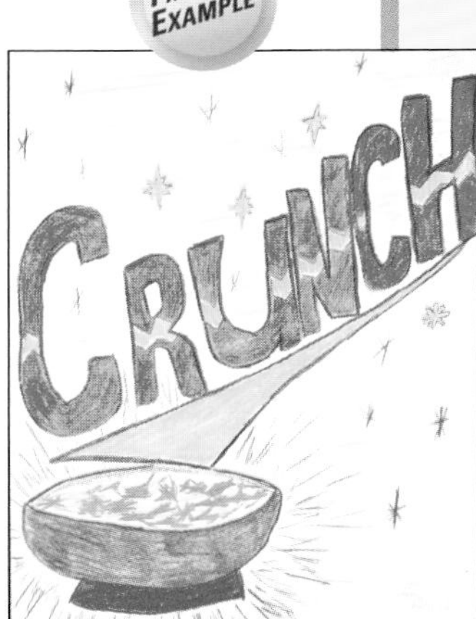

PDAS Domains I, II

Old and New Ideas

PREVIEW THE UNIT

Tell students that in this unit they will learn how artists are often inspired by artworks and traditions from the past. Have students page through the unit and identify two artworks that seem to be from the past and two artworks that seem to be from the present. Students should compare how the content in the chosen artworks tells a story or documents history and traditions. TEKS 3.3A

SHARE THE POEM

Have students discuss whether the artwork is old or new. Then have them read the poem on page 123 together.

How are the subjects of the poem and the artwork alike? (Possible response: The poem is about the sun, and the artwork shows the sun being pulled by a horse.) COMPARE AND CONTRAST

STEP INTO THE ART

Have students look carefully at the artwork and describe what they see.

How old do you think this sculpture is? Why do you think the horse is pulling the sun? (Responses will vary.) DRAW CONCLUSIONS

SHARE BACKGROUND INFORMATION

Tell students that Chariot of the Sun is a cast-bronze sculpture. Some historians believe the object represents a horse pulling the light of day across the sky. Point out that parts of the wheels have disintegrated or have been lost over thousands of years.

LOCATE IT See **Using the Maps of Museums and Art Sites**, p. R2.

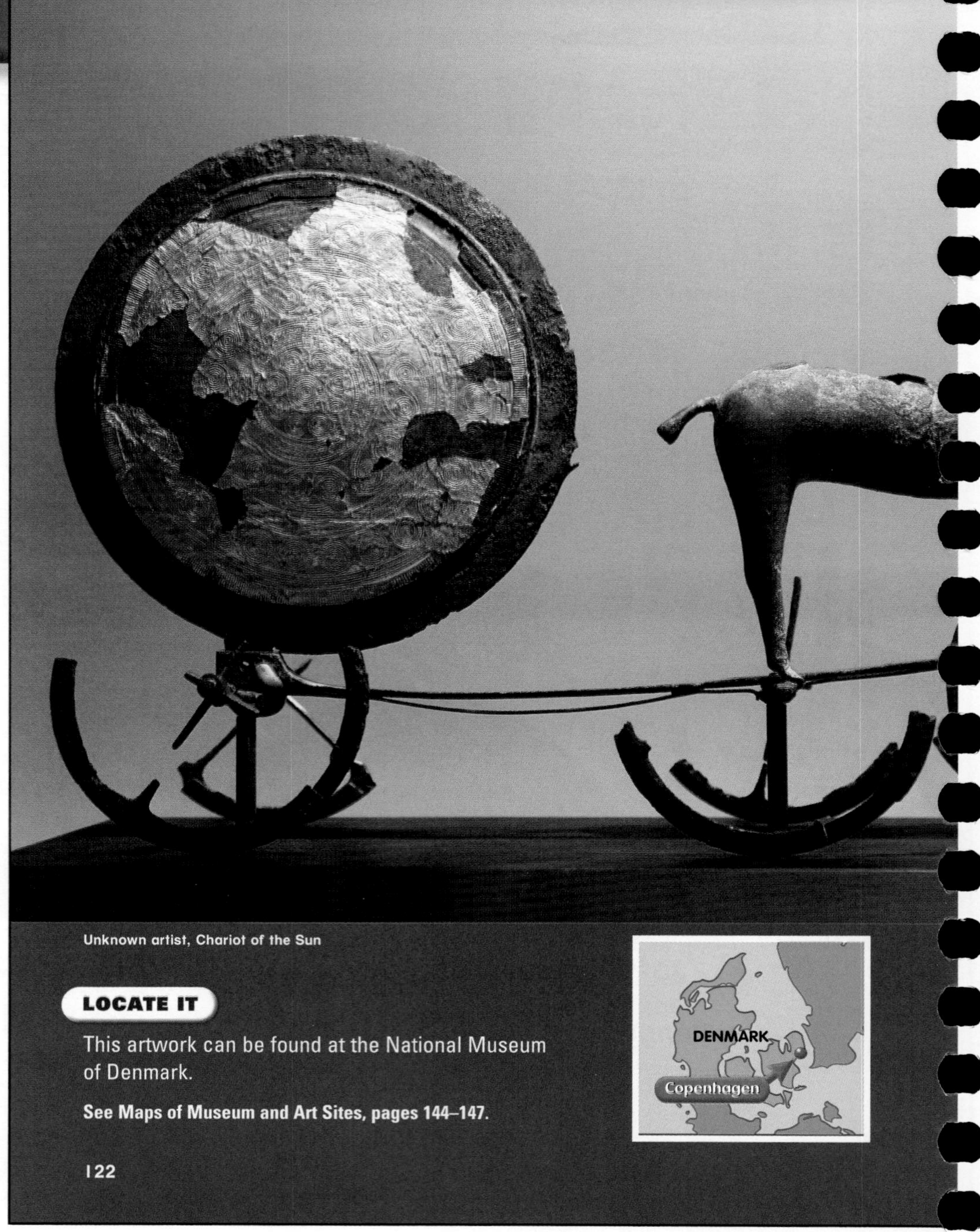

Unknown artist, Chariot of the Sun

LOCATE IT

This artwork can be found at the National Museum of Denmark.

See Maps of Museum and Art Sites, pages 144–147.

122

Background Information

Art History

Chariot of the Sun is one of the most important **Bronze Age** artifacts ever found. It was discovered in an ancient bog in Trundholm, Denmark. Historians believe the object was used around 1300 B.C. and that it might symbolize the power of the sun. Discs similar to the one on the carriage have been found on clothing from the same era.

For additional information about the Bronze Age, see the Encyclopedia of Artists and Art History, pp. R44–R59.

For related artworks, see **Electronic Art Gallery CD-ROM, Primary.**

★ TEKS 3.3A compare artworks from the past and present; **PDAS Domain I** active participation; **PDAS Domain II** learner-centered instruction

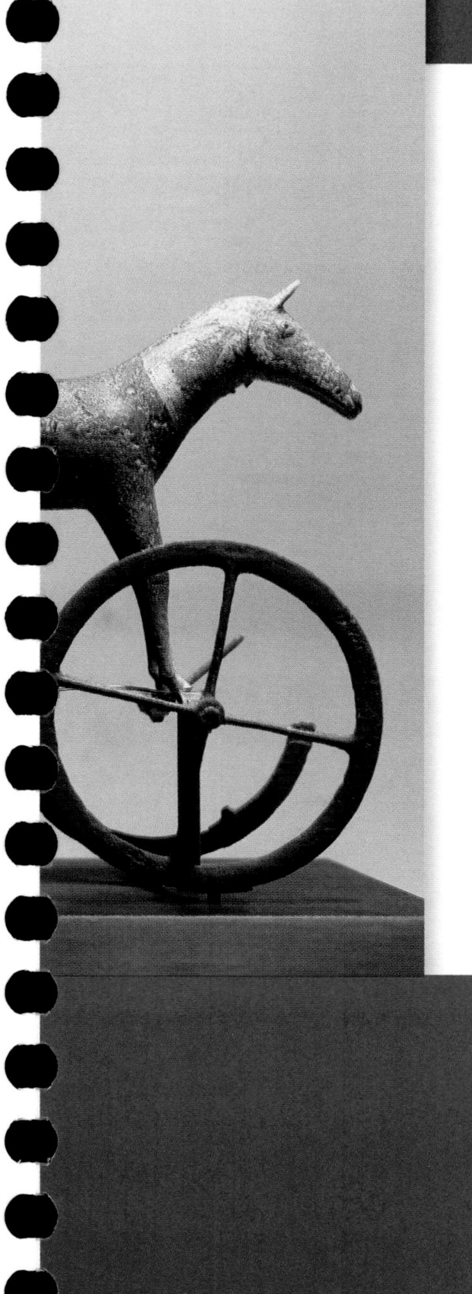

Unit 6 Variety and Rhythm

Old and New Ideas

The Sun

I told the Sun that I was glad,
I'm sure I don't know why;
Somehow the pleasant way he had
Of shining in the sky,
Just put a notion in my head
That wouldn't it be fun
If, walking on the hill, I said
"I'm happy" to the Sun.

John Drinkwater

Unit Vocabulary

symbol	photomontage
variety	assemblage
prints	found objects
rhythm	graphic arts

Multimedia Art Glossary
Visit *The Learning Site*
www.harcourtschool.com

123

Unit Vocabulary

Read aloud the terms with students, and use the Word Knowledge Chart below to assess and discuss their prior knowledge.

symbol a picture or object that stands for an idea

variety a design principle used to add interest to an artwork by including different objects and art elements

prints artworks made by pressing an object or printing block covered with wet color against a flat surface

rhythm the visual beat created by repeated lines, shapes, colors, or patterns in an artwork

photomontage an artwork made of cut or torn photographs

assemblage a sculpture made of different kinds of materials

found objects everyday objects used as part of an artwork

graphic arts a kind of artwork that can be used over and over in advertisements and signs

Vocabulary Resources

- Vocabulary Cards in English and Spanish: *Teacher Resource Book*, pp. 27–30
- Student Edition Glossary, pp. 189–197

Multimedia Art Glossary
Visit *The Learning Site*
www.harcourtschool.com

Language Arts Connection

Students may create a chart like the one below to identify familiar and unfamiliar vocabulary terms. Encourage them to add information to their charts as they work through this unit.

WORD KNOWLEDGE CHART		
I know this term.	I have seen this term before.	I have never seen this term.

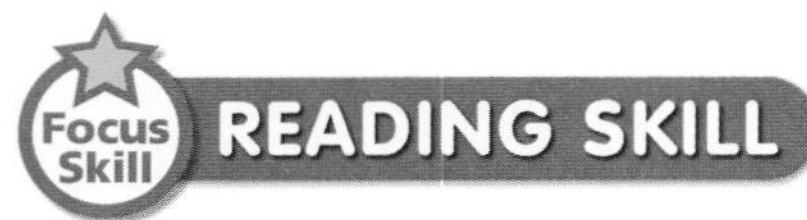

PDAS Domains I, II

Summarize

SKILL TRACE	
SUMMARIZE	
Introduce	pp. 124–125
Review	pp. 126, 128, 129, 132, 134, 138, 140, 141

DISCUSS THE SKILL

Access Prior Knowledge Name a game, such as baseball or kickball, that many students are familiar with. Tell students they will describe the game for someone who has never played it. Have students tell the main goal of the game as you record their ideas on the board. (to score more points than the other team) Then have students tell how players score points. Help students combine the most important ideas about the game in a few sentences.

APPLY TO ART

Summarize Ideas in Artworks Have students read page 124. Explain that summarizing will help them tell the most important ideas about an artwork. Have students reread the important ideas on page 124. Ask them to describe details in the painting—such as the name of the game in each scene—that were not included in the important idea statements. Then have students compare the summary statement with the title of the painting. Discuss with students whether the title is a good summary of the painting. TEKS 3.4B

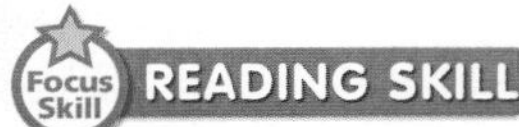

Summarize

When you *summarize*, you tell the most important ideas in one or two sentences.

Look at the scenes in the painting below. You can summarize what is happening in the painting by looking for the most important ideas.

- **Important Idea** Each scene shows children playing a different game.
- **Important Idea** The children are playing outdoors.
- **Summary** Children are playing different games outdoors.

Anna Belle Lee Washington, *Games We Played*

124

Background Information

About the Artist

Anna Belle Lee Washington (1924–2000) worked for 38 years in Detroit, Michigan, before she retired to St. Simons Island, Georgia. There she began painting images of African American life in the rural South. To help people relate to her paintings, Washington never put detailed faces on the people in her artworks. She wanted viewers to imagine the details or to even see themselves in the scenes.

For additional information about Washington, see pp. R44–R59.

For related artworks, see **Electronic Art Gallery CD-ROM, Primary.**

★ **TEKS 3.4B** identify main ideas in artworks by peers and others; **PDAS Domain I** active participation; **PDAS Domain II** learner-centered instruction; **PDAS Domain IV** classroom management; **TAKS Reading Objective 1** demonstrate understanding of texts; *(continued)*

You can also summarize information in text to help you understand what you read. When you summarize text, you retell the most important ideas in your own words. Read the passage below, looking for the most important ideas.

> When Anna Belle Lee Washington was a child, she never thought she would become a well-known artist. As an adult, Washington began painting as a hobby. Her paintings first became popular with her neighbors in St. Simons Island, Georgia. Now Washington's paintings can be seen on book covers and in museums around the world.

What are the important ideas in this passage? How can you combine them into a summary? Use a diagram like this to help you.

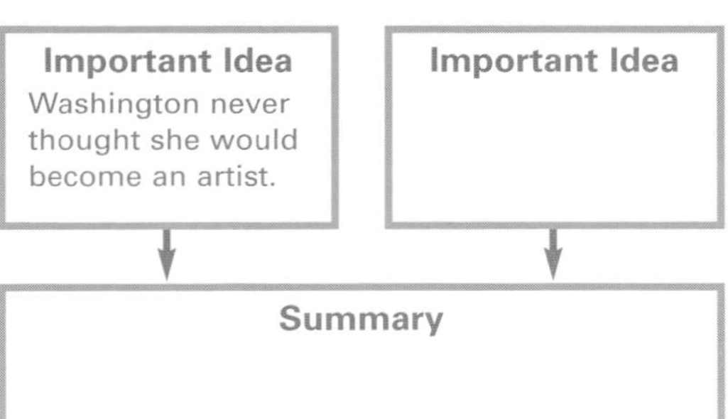

On Your Own

As you read the lessons in this unit, use diagrams like the one above to summarize the text and the ideas in the artworks.

APPLY TO READING

Summarize Text Tell students that being able to summarize information in a passage will help them check their understanding of the text. Explain that combining the most important ideas in one or two sentences is a good way to write a summary.

Have students read the passage about Anna Belle Lee Washington on page 125. Discuss the important idea in the diagram, and help students identify another important idea in the passage. Have students complete the diagram by writing a summary sentence about the passage.
TAKS Reading Objectives 1, 3, 4

ON YOUR OWN

As students read the lessons in this unit, have them use diagrams like the one on page 125 to summarize important ideas in the text and in the artworks. TAKS Reading Objectives 1, 3, 4

TAKS Reading Objectives 1, 3, 4

Reading Skill Card

Distribute Reading Skill Card 6, *Teacher Resource Book* page 36. Have students summarize important ideas in this unit.

Extend the Skill
For additional teaching suggestions, see **Art Transparency 16**.

PDAS Domain IV

ESL Read aloud the passage on page 125, sentence by sentence. Have students **paraphrase** each sentence to be sure they understand its meaning. Then ask students to identify the two most important sentences in the passage. Help students combine the sentences using the conjunction *and* or *but*.

TAKS Reading Objective 3 use a variety of strategies; TAKS Reading Objective 4 apply critical-thinking skills

Lesson 26

PDAS Domains I, II

Shapes and Symbols

OBJECTIVES
- Identify variety and shape in artworks
- Produce ceramics
- Summarize ideas in artworks

RESOURCES
- Art Print 16
- Electronic Art Gallery CD-ROM, Primary

5 Minutes

Warm-Up

Build Background Display **Art Print 16,** and ask students to describe what the Statue of Liberty stands for. (freedom) Discuss other state or national symbols, such as a state flower.

10-15 Minutes

Teach

Discuss Art Concepts Have students read page 126. Ask students to point out one symbol in image A and tell what they think it stands for. Then have students identify how the artist of image B created variety. (The complementary colors yellow and violet show contrast.) TEKS 3.1B

Think Critically

1. READING SKILL **Why do artists use symbols?** (to communicate ideas) SUMMARIZE
2. **Compare image A with other ancient artworks you have seen.** (Possible response: They show history and traditions of people in ancient cultures.) ART HISTORY AND CULTURE TEKS 3.3A
3. WRITE **Write a story about the message you think image A tells.** NARRATIVE TAKS Writing Objective 1

Lesson 26

Vocabulary

symbol

variety

Shapes and Symbols

A **symbol** is a shape that stands for an idea. In ancient times, people used symbols instead of words to send messages to one another. Look at the symbols on the ancient artwork in image A. What do you think they might stand for? Artists today may also use symbols in their artworks. The painted sun on the jug in image B might be a symbol for warmth or light.

Artists create **variety** in artworks by using contrasting lines, shapes, and colors. Variety can make an artwork more interesting. What contrasting colors and lines did the artist of image B use to show variety?

Unknown artist, Egyptian hieroglyphics

Clarice Cliff, *'Sun Ray' Double-Handled Lotus Jug*

126

FYI Background Information

Art History

Hieroglyphics (hy•ruh•GLIF•iks) is a form of writing used in ancient Egypt in which pictures symbolize ideas and sounds. The writing was used to record messages on temples and stone monuments. The Egyptians used hieroglyphic writing for more than 3,000 years.

For additional information about Egyptian art, see pp. R44–R59.

RECOMMENDED READING

The Seeker of Knowledge: The Man Who Deciphered Egyptian Hieroglyphs by James Rumford. Houghton Mifflin, 2000. CHALLENGING

★ **TEKS 3.1A** identify sources for ideas; **TEKS 3.1B** identify elements and principles; **TEKS 3.2A** create artworks; **TEKS 3.2C** produce various artworks; **TEKS 3.3A** compare artworks from the past and present; **TEKS 3.4A** identify intent in personal artworks; **PDAS Domain I** active participation; *(continued)*

Artist's Workshop

Clay Pinch Pot

PLAN

Think of some symbols that tell about you or about something that is important to you. Sketch these symbols.

CREATE

1. **Make a clay ball about the size of an orange.**
2. **Press your thumbs into the ball to make a dent. Keep pressing your thumbs out from the center to make the sides of your pot. Pinch the sides of your pot evenly all the way around.**
3. **Carve symbols and lines onto the sides of your pot. Use different symbols and lines to create variety.**

REFLECT

What do the symbols on your pinch pot stand for? How did you create variety?

Quick Tip

As you carve, press lightly so that you do not make a hole through your pot.

127

Clay Pinch Pot

MATERIALS: sketchbook, pencil, clay, paper bag, carving tools

PLAN Tell students to identify life experiences and sensory knowledge to invent visual symbols about self and life events. TEKS 3.1A

CREATE Have students produce their ceramic pots, using a variety of art materials appropriately. Tell them to turn their pots as they pinch the sides and to make sure the sides are not too thin. Pots will dry overnight. TEKS 3.2A, TEKS 3.2C

REFLECT Students should describe how they used different lines and shapes to create variety. TEKS 3.4A

Activity Options PDAS Domain IV

Quick Activity Have students sketch some symbols that are important to them.

Early Finishers Have students complete a museum card to display with their work. See *Teacher Resource Book*, p. 39.

Challenge See *Teacher Resource Book*, p. 76.

Wrap-Up

Informal Assessment PDAS Domain III

- **How do the symbols on your pot express something about you?** (Responses will vary.) EVALUATION/CRITICISM TEKS 3.4A
- **Compare the symbols on your pot with the symbols in image A.** (Responses will vary.) ART HISTORY AND CULTURE TEKS 3.3A

Extend Through Writing

TAKS Writing Objective 1

Narrative Paragraph Ask students to write about the discovery of an ancient pot.

Social Studies Connection

Rosetta Stone Tell students that the secret to understanding hieroglyphics was lost for centuries until the discovery of the Rosetta Stone in 1799. Have students research the Rosetta Stone and describe how it helped historians translate an ancient language.

PDAS Domain IV

ESL Have students **build vocabulary** by working with an English-fluent peer to make a two-column chart that lists the symbols on their pots. Students should draw the symbols in the first column and describe what they stand for in the second column. Encourage students to add other symbols that describe their interests or hobbies.

PDAS Domain II learner-centered instruction; **PDAS Domain III** evaluation and feedback; **PDAS Domain IV** classroom management; **TAKS Writing Objective 1** composition

Lesson 27

PDAS Domains I, II

Printmaking

OBJECTIVES
- Identify rhythm in artworks
- Produce prints
- Summarize ideas in artworks

RESOURCES
- Art Prints 15, 17
- Electronic Art Gallery CD-ROM, Primary

5 Minutes

Warm-Up

Build Background Display **Art Print 15,** and point out the repeated shapes of the musicians and their trombones. Explain that repetition in artworks creates a visual beat, like the rhythm of a drumbeat in a song.

10-15 Minutes

Teach

Discuss Art Concepts Have students read pages 128–129. Students should identify rhythm by pointing out that the shapes and colors repeat. Students may also note that the colors remind them of a blue sky and a bright sun. In image B, discuss the circular arrangement and the different colors that create variety. Then display **Art Print 17.** Have students discuss how the artist created irregular rhythm in the artwork. TEKS 3.1B

Think Critically

1. READING SKILL **How do artists create rhythm?** (by repeating lines, shapes, colors, or patterns) SUMMARIZE
2. **What shapes would you like to show in a print?** (Responses will vary.) PERSONAL RESPONSE
3. WRITE **Describe how rhythm in music and in art are alike.** DESCRIPTIVE TAKS Writing Objective 1

Lesson 27

Vocabulary

prints

rhythm

Printmaking

Images A and B show examples of prints. To make **prints**, artists paint a design on a flat object or printing block. While the paint is still wet, they press the block onto a piece of paper. Artists can create many prints by using the same printing block.

Look at the print in image A. What shapes are repeated? Artists can create **rhythm** in an artwork by repeating lines, shapes, colors, or patterns. Rhythm guides your eyes around the artwork. It can also make you feel a certain way. Does the print in image A remind you of a summer day or a winter day? Why?

A Beatricia Sagar, *Sun Shines*

128

Background Information

About the Artist

Beatricia Sagar grew up in New York City and lived there most of her life. The busy billboards, buildings, rooftops, and people in that environment influenced her artworks. She currently lives and works in Miami, Florida.

For additional information about Sagar, see pp. R44–R59.

RECOMMENDED READING

The Art Room by Susan Vande Griek. Groundwood, 2002. AVERAGE

★ **TEKS 3.1B** identify elements and principles; **TEKS 3.2C** produce various artworks; **TEKS 3.4A** identify intent in personal artworks; **PDAS Domain I** active participation; **PDAS Domain II** learner-centered instruction; **PDAS Domain III** evaluation and feedback; **PDAS Domain IV** classroom management; *(continued)*

B Tanaya, grade 4, Untitled

The artist of image B created rhythm by printing the same design four times. How do your eyes move around image B? How did the artist create variety?

Artist's Workshop

Kaleidoscope Print

1. **Use a large paper plate to trace the shape of a circle onto white paper. Use a ruler and a pencil to divide your circle into eight pie-shaped pieces. Cut out the circle.**
2. **Pour small amounts of different paint colors onto your plate. Dip different small objects into the paint. Press them onto a section of your cutout circle.**
3. **Repeat the same design in each section of your circle to create rhythm.**

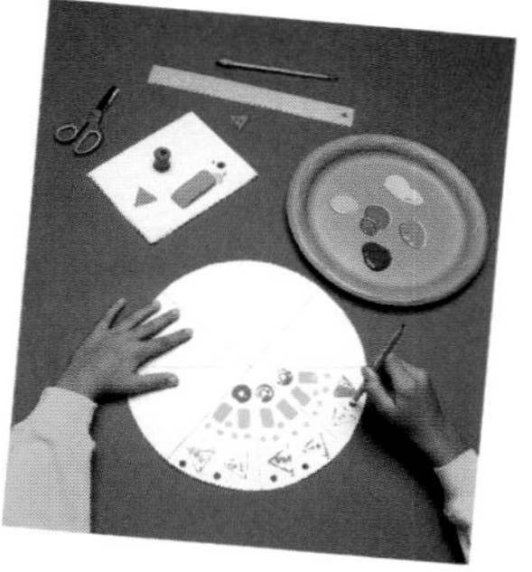

129

30-40 Minutes

Artist's Workshop

Kaleidoscope Print

MATERIALS: paper plate, white paper, ruler, pencil, scissors, various small objects, tempera paints

Quick Tip Tell students to use objects with a variety of shapes.

PLAN Have students collect objects such as thimbles and buttons for their print.

CREATE Tell students to mark the center of their circle. Model how to create eight equal shapes by drawing a vertical line and a horizontal line through the center of an X. Then have students produce their prints, using paints and other materials appropriately. TEKS 3.2C

REFLECT Have students describe how they used repetition to create rhythm. TEKS 3.4A

Activity Options PDAS Domain IV

Quick Activity Have students draw a design that is repeated in each segment of their circle.

Early Finishers Have students glue their print to construction paper and add a decorative border.

Challenge See *Teacher Resource Book*, p. 77.

Performing Arts Connection

Rhythm in Music Play several short recordings of songs, and have students tap the rhythm as they listen. Then encourage students to create an original rhythm based on their prints or another artwork.

PDAS Domain IV

ESL Encourage **peer interaction** and **oral language development** by having partners describe what they like about each other's print.

Extra Support Demonstrate how to use the objects as stamps for printing. Show students how to blot excess paint on a paper towel before printing.

5-10 Minutes

Wrap-Up

Informal Assessment PDAS Domain III

- **What title would you use to summarize image A?** (Responses will vary.) SUMMARIZE
- **What do you like about making prints?** (Responses will vary.) PERSONAL RESPONSE

Extend Through Writing

TAKS Writing Objective 1

How-To Paragraph Have students write instructions for making a kaleidoscope print.

TAKS Writing Objective 1 composition

PDAS Domains I, II

Styles of Architecture

CAREERS IN ART

DISCUSS THE IMAGES

Have students read pages 130–131.

- Tell students that the building in image A was designed by architect John Gaw Meem. Point out the rough texture of the adobe walls, the round corners, and the projecting roof timbers, called *vigas*. Explain that these are all characteristics of the Spanish-Pueblo style.
- Tell students that when Meem first saw Santa Fe, New Mexico, he was attracted to the mix of Spanish and Native American architectural styles. Meem wanted to preserve the look of old Santa Fe, so he helped develop the Spanish-Pueblo style of architecture.
- Have students compare artworks from the past and artworks from the present for various purposes, such as documenting history and traditions or serving a functional purpose. Have them compare the traditional building in image A with a photograph of another adobe building. Then provide photographs of unusual modern buildings for students to compare with image B. Have students discuss how the architects may have been influenced by the location of the building sites and when the buildings were designed. Then have students relate art to different kinds of jobs in everyday life by discussing reasons why an architect's job is important. TEKS 3.3A, TEKS 3.3C

ART ⟷ SOCIAL STUDIES CONNECTION

Styles of Architecture

What do architects do?

Architects are people who design schools, houses, airports, hospitals, and other buildings. The museums in images A and B were also designed by architects.

The museum in image A was built in 1917. It is located in an old Spanish plaza in Santa Fe, New Mexico, one of the oldest cities in North America. The museum was designed in the Spanish-Pueblo style. In this style, buildings are made of adobe, a mixture of clay, mud, and straw. Many of the buildings in the Santa Fe plaza are made in the Spanish-Pueblo style in order to keep alive the history and traditions of the city.

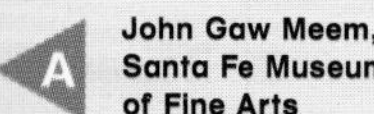

A John Gaw Meem, Santa Fe Museum of Fine Arts

Background Information

About the Architects

A John Gaw Meem (1894–1983) designed more than 650 buildings, including houses, churches, museums, and schools.

B Frank O. Gehry (1929–) gained a reputation for creating unusual buildings when he remodeled his own house with inexpensive everyday materials: chain link fencing, tin walls, plywood, and pipes.

For additional information about the architects and Spanish-Pueblo architecture, see pp. R44–R59.

For related artworks, see **Electronic Art Gallery CD-ROM, Primary.**

★ **TEKS 3.2C** produce various artworks; **TEKS 3.3A** compare artworks from the past and present; **TEKS 3.3C** relate art to different jobs; **TEKS 3.4B** identify main ideas in artworks by peers and others; **PDAS Domain I** active participation; **PDAS Domain II** learner-centered instruction

The building in image B was built in Bilbao, Spain, in 1997. The architect designed the glass walls to protect the artworks inside from heat. How would you describe this building?

B Frank O. Gehry, Guggenheim Bilbao

DID YOU KNOW?

Architects make drawings and build models of their designs. Models show what a building will look like when it is finished. The model below was created for a house in California.

Frank O. Gehry, Architect's model

Think About Art

Describe the style of the buildings in your community. What do you think they are made of?

131

DID YOU KNOW?

Use the facts below to discuss how Frank O. Gehry plans his major buildings.

- Gehry begins by making quick sketches that look more like scribbles.
- Then Gehry and his team make the first of many models. For the Bilbao museum, the first model was made of sheets of paper that were rolled up and taped together. The next models were made of wood, paper, and cloth.
- Once Gehry is satisfied with the design, a special pen is used to trace the shape of the model so a computer program can turn it into a drawing. It took two years, hundreds of models, and 565 drawings before the Guggenheim Bilbao plan was complete.

Think About Art

Describe the style of the buildings in your community. What do you think they are made of?

(Responses will vary.) PERSONAL RESPONSE

ARTIST'S EYE ACTIVITY

Building a Model Have small groups of students build an architectural model for a building of their own design. As students produce their constructions, tell them to use a variety of art materials appropriately. Supply students with materials such as cardboard tubes, boxes, poster board, shoe boxes, scissors, and tape. Tell students to think about how people would use the building and to include cutouts for windows and doors. TEKS 3.2C

Social Studies Connection

Ancient Pueblos Tell students that the Spanish-Pueblo style was partly inspired by the adobe buildings built by Native Americans in what is now New Mexico and Arizona.

For additional cross-curricular suggestions, see Art Transparency 17.

TEKS 3.4B

Student Art Show

Portfolios and Exhibitions Have students create an exhibition of their portfolios or other finished artworks. Students should apply simple criteria related to symbols, rhythm, and variety to identify main ideas in peers' artworks. See page 142 for information on planning and preparing a student art show.

Lesson 28

PDAS Domains I, II

Rhythm in Photomontage

OBJECTIVES
- Identify rhythm and pattern in artworks
- Produce photomontages
- Summarize ideas in artworks

RESOURCES
- Art Print 10
- Electronic Art Gallery CD-ROM, Primary

Warm-Up

Build Background Display **Art Print 10,** and point out the pattern on the water in the background. Explain to students that repeated lines in the pattern create a visual beat.

Teach

Discuss Art Concepts Have students read page 132. Ask students to identify patterns with regular rhythm, such as the pattern on the table. Students should recognize that contrasting patterns give the artwork a restless feeling. Then have them describe how patterns with irregular rhythm would look. (space between elements would not be the same) TEKS 3.1B

Think Critically

1. READING SKILL **What is a photomontage?** (an artwork made with photographs) SUMMARIZE

2. **How could the artist have given the artwork a peaceful feeling?** (by using simple patterns and colors that are similar) PERCEPTION/AESTHETICS
3. WRITE **Describe the view from the chair in the photomontage.** DESCRIPTIVE TAKS Writing Objective 1

Lesson 28

Vocabulary

photomontage

Rhythm in Photomontage

Louise Freshman-Brown, *Interior with Red Apples*

The image above is a photomontage. A **photomontage** is made by cutting out parts of different photographs and arranging them in an interesting way. Look carefully at the artwork above. What kinds of objects do you see?

The artist of this photomontage used photographs with many different patterns. The repeating lines, colors, and shapes in the patterns give the artwork rhythm. How do your eyes move around the artwork? Do the contrasting patterns in this artwork give you a peaceful feeling or a restless feeling?

132

FYI Background Information

About the Artist

Louise Freshman-Brown is a painter, printmaker, and teacher who uses many different media to create her artworks. She is known for her imaginative drawings of exotic birds. Freshman-Brown's still lifes and interiors are filled with colorful abstract and realistic images, inspired by Henri Matisse.

For additional information about Freshman-Brown, see pp. R44–R59.

RECOMMENDED READING

Photographers by Fran Hodgkins. Bridgestone, 2001. EASY

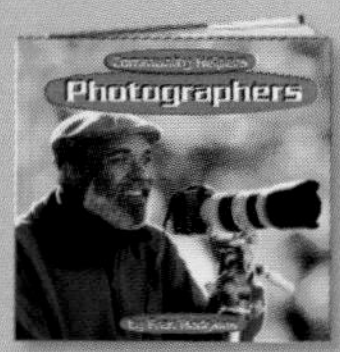

★ TEKS 3.1B identify elements and principles; TEKS 3.2B develop effective compositions; PDAS Domain I active participation; PDAS Domain II learner-centered instruction; PDAS Domain III evaluation and feedback; PDAS Domain IV classroom management; TAKS Writing Objective 1 composition

Artist's Workshop

Photomontage

PLAN

Think about a scene or idea you want to show in a photomontage. Look for magazine pictures to use in your artwork.

CREATE

1. Cut out pictures with similar shapes, colors, or patterns.
2. Arrange your pictures on a sheet of construction paper.
3. Create rhythm by using pictures with similar shapes, colors, or patterns.
4. Glue your pictures to the construction paper.

REFLECT

Look at your finished photomontage. How did you create rhythm?

Quick Tip

Create depth in your photomontage by overlapping pictures. Use larger pictures in the background.

133

30-40 Minutes

Artist's Workshop

Photomontage

MATERIALS: magazines, scissors, construction paper, glue

PLAN Tell students to look for different pictures of a similar scene, such as a landscape or a room.

CREATE Have students think about rhythm to develop an effective composition, using design skills. Tell them to overlap pictures to add interest. TEKS 3.2B

REFLECT Have students point out repeated elements to describe rhythm in their artwork. TEKS 3.1B

Activity Options PDAS Domain IV

Quick Activity Have students cut one large magazine picture into small pieces and rearrange the pieces to show rhythm.

Early Finishers Have students use magazine pictures to design the front of a greeting card.

Challenge See *Teacher Resource Book*, p. 78.

5-10 Minutes

Wrap-Up

Informal Assessment PDAS Domain III

- **Do the patterns in your photomontage have regular rhythm or irregular rhythm? Explain.** (Responses will vary.) PERCEPTION/AESTHETICS
- **How did your classmates show rhythm in their photomontages?** (Responses will vary.) EVALUATION/CRITICISM

Extend Through Writing

TAKS Writing Objective 1

Poem Have students write a poem reflecting the rhythm they created in their photomontage.

Science Connection

Camera Obscura Have small groups of students research the first kind of camera, called camera obscura. Tell students to write a description of what the camera looks like and how it was used. Encourage students to sketch a diagram of the camera.

PDAS Domain IV

ESL Use the Artist's Workshop activity as an opportunity for **oral language development**. Have students work in groups to page through the magazines. Tell them to name or describe the objects they want to use in their artwork and help each other find pictures.

Lesson 29

PDAS Domains I, II

Assemblage

OBJECTIVES
- Identify variety and texture in artworks
- Produce constructions with found objects
- Summarize ideas in artworks

RESOURCES
- Discussion Card 4, p. R35
- Electronic Art Gallery CD-ROM, Primary

5 Minutes

Warm-Up

Build Background Display a group of found objects. Have students brainstorm ways an artist might put the objects together in an artwork and explain their ideas by arranging the objects.

10-15 Minutes

Teach

Discuss Art Concepts Have students read page 134. Students should recognize that the baseballs in image A are spheres and that they have been painted to look like the American flag. Discuss how the lines, shapes, and colors in the flag design create variety. In image B, have students identify forms with textures that are rough and smooth. TEKS 3.1B

Lesson 29

Vocabulary

assemblage

found objects

Assemblage

An **assemblage** is a sculpture made of different objects and materials. Artists who make assemblages often use **found objects**, or everyday objects they find, in their artworks. Look at the assemblage shown in image **A**. What found objects did the artist use in his artwork? What lines, shapes, colors, and forms did he use to create variety?

Image **B** shows an assemblage made of found pieces of wood. What forms did this artist include in her artwork? What textures did she use?

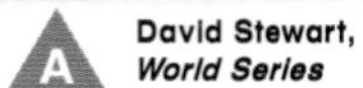

A David Stewart, *World Series*

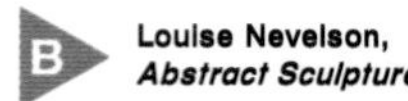

B Louise Nevelson, *Abstract Sculpture*

134

Think Critically

1. READING SKILL **How do artists make assemblages?** (They use found objects as the materials for a sculpture.) SUMMARIZE

2. **Why do you think image A is painted to look like a flag?** (because baseball is a popular American sport) PERCEPTION/AESTHETICS

3. WRITE **Write a story about where the baseballs in image A were found.** NARRATIVE
TAKS Writing Objective 1

FYI

Background Information

About the Artists

A David Stewart (1939–) was a plumber working at a college when he first tried an assignment written on the board in the art department.

B Louise Nevelson (1900–1988) created her artworks by filling boxes with found wooden objects.

For additional information about the artists, see pp. R44–R59.

RECOMMENDED READING

The Jumbo Book of Art by Irene Luxbacher. Kids Can Press, 2003.
CHALLENGING

★ **TEKS 3.1B** identify elements and principles; **TEKS 3.2C** produce various artworks; **PDAS Domain I** active participation; **PDAS Domain II** learner-centered instruction; **PDAS Domain III** evaluation and feedback; **PDAS Domain IV** classroom management; **TAKS Writing Objective 1** composition

Artist's Workshop

Found-Object Assemblage

PLAN

Gather some found objects to use in your assemblage. Practice arranging them in different ways.

CREATE

1. Paint the objects in your assemblage. Use different colors to create variety.
2. Arrange your objects inside a shoe box. Make sure to put objects in each corner of your box.
3. Glue your objects into place.

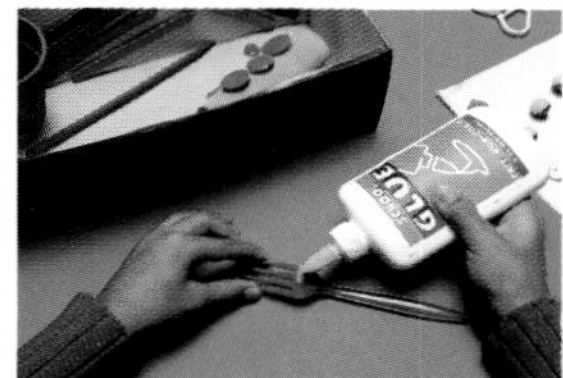

REFLECT

Look at your finished assemblage. What found objects did you use? How did you create variety?

Quick Tip: Glue smaller objects onto larger objects to add interest to your assemblage.

135

Social Studies Connection

The All-American Game Tell students that the assemblage in image A is meaningful because the game of baseball is often called America's national pastime. Have students research popular sports in other countries around the world.

Meeting Individual Needs

PDAS Domain IV

ESL Use **visuals** to support **comprehensible input** for names of found objects. Display ***Picture Cards Collection,*** cards 8, 90, and 94, for students to use as reference.

See also ***Picture Card Bank* CD-ROM,** Category: At School.

Artist's Workshop

30–40 Minutes

Found-Object Assemblage

MATERIALS: found objects, shoe box, construction paper, glue, tempera paints, paintbrush, water bowl

Quick Tip: Tell students to glue construction paper to the inside of the box as a background.

PLAN Provide objects such as cardboard tubes, craft sticks, old pencils, and buttons.

CREATE Have students produce their constructions, using found objects and art materials appropriately. TEKS 3.2C

REFLECT Have students describe forms and colors they used to create variety.

Activity Options PDAS Domain IV

Quick Activity Have partners work together to create one assemblage.

Early Finishers Students may use Discussion Card 4 to describe variety in their artworks.

Challenge See *Teacher Resource Book*, p. 79.

5–10 Minutes

Wrap-Up

Informal Assessment PDAS Domain III

- **How did looking at images A and B help you decide how to place your objects?** (Responses will vary.) PERCEPTION/AESTHETICS
- **What found objects would you include in an assemblage about your school?** (Responses will vary.) PERSONAL RESPONSE

Extend Through Writing

TAKS Writing Objective 1

Song Have students write a patriotic song inspired by image A.

PDAS Domains I, II

Nicario Jimenez

ARTIST BIOGRAPHY

DISCUSS THE IMAGES

Have students read pages 136–137.

- Tell students that retablos are a kind of folk art that have been made in Peru for more than 500 years. Families have passed down the craft from one generation to the next.
- Have students discuss what they see in image A. Tell them to point out the booths under the tents and the crowds of buyers and sellers at the art festival. Point out that the two opened doors on the retablo are painted with flowers.
- Have students point out the detailed weavings hanging above the weavers in image B. Explain to students that this retablo shows the traditional clothes and textiles of native Peruvians. Have students compare patterns and details on these textiles from the past to the traditional clothing in the photographs on pages 56–57. TEKS 3.3A
- Explain to students that folk artists like Jimenez preserve traditions of their culture. Display **Art Print 18**, and tell students that the image shows a Oaxacan woodcarving, a folk art from Oaxaca, Mexico. Have students discuss the retablos and the woodcarving and compare these selected artworks from different cultures. Students should point out the differences between the art forms, including the materials and the process used to create the artworks. They should also discuss how the subject of each artwork reflects the culture in which it was created. TEKS 3.3B

ART ⟷ SOCIAL STUDIES CONNECTION

Nicario Jimenez

Nicario Jimenez, ***Art Festival***

What are retablos?

Nicario Jimenez is an artist from Peru known for making retablos. A retablo is a wooden box filled with figures that show a scene from daily life. What scene does the retablo in image **A** show?

The tiny figures that Jimenez creates are made from a mixture of boiled potatoes and a special powder. To carve details, he uses a small wooden tool that looks like a toothpick. Then he paints the figures. The boxes themselves are also painted as part of the artwork.

The retablo in image **B** shows a weaver's workshop. Notice the tiny workers and the finished weavings. What other details do you see in this retablo?

136

Background Information

About the Artist

Nicario Jimenez was born in the Andes Mountains in Peru. He and his two brothers make retablos that portray the traditions of the Ayacucho region where their family has lived for many generations.

Jimenez has exhibited his retablos all over the United States.

For additional information about Jimenez, see pp. R44–R59.

For related artworks, see **Electronic Art Gallery CD-ROM, Primary.**

★ **TEKS 3.1A** identify sources for ideas; **TEKS 3.2A** create artworks; **TEKS 3.2C** produce various artworks; **TEKS 3.3A** compare artworks from the past and present; **TEKS 3.3B** compare artworks from different cultures; **TEKS 3.4B** identify main ideas in artworks by peers and others; **PDAS Domain I** active participation; *(continued)*

DID YOU KNOW?

Art festivals began as a way to show art to people who did not usually visit museums. Art festivals may take place outdoors once or twice a year. Artists set up their own booths along a street or sidewalk to show and sell their artworks.

Think About Art

What scene would you show in your own retablo?

Multimedia Biographies
Visit *The Learning Site*
www.harcourtschool.com

B Nicario Jimenez, *Weaver's Workshop*

137

DID YOU KNOW?

Use the facts below to discuss art festivals with students.

- Art festivals are important to artists and craftspeople who don't usually show their artwork in museums or galleries. Selling their work at festivals and fairs helps them make a living.
- Art festivals are annual events in some towns and neighborhoods. Local artists often display their work. Some festivals include live entertainment and booths selling festive and traditional foods.

Think About Art

What scene would you show in your own retablo? (Responses will vary. Ask students to identify sensory knowledge and life experiences as sources for ideas about life events to show in the retablo.) PERSONAL RESPONSE TEKS 3.1A

ARTIST'S EYE ACTIVITY

Make a Retablo Have students plan a retablo showing a scene based on personal experiences from a family-oriented holiday or a cultural event. Then have them use modeling clay to create miniature ceramics to include in their retablos. Students may produce their constructions by arranging the objects in a shoe box or tissue box.
TEKS 3.1A, TEKS 3.2A, TEKS 3.2C

Social Studies Connection

Elevation Tell students that the place where Nicario Jimenez was born is 9,007 feet high in the Andes Mountains. Have students use an elevation map to find the highest elevation in your state.

For additional cross-curricular suggestions, see Art Transparency 18.

TEKS 3.4B

View an Artist's Work

Portfolios and Exhibitions
Arrange for students to visit a museum or gallery to view original artworks in a major artist's portfolio or exhibition. Students should apply simple criteria such as identifying the subject and how the artist used art elements and principles to identify main ideas in what they see.

Multimedia Biographies
Visit *The Learning Site*
www.harcourtschool.com

Lesson 30

PDAS Domains I, II

Graphic Arts

OBJECTIVES
- Identify variety and color in artworks
- Produce graphic designs
- Summarize ideas in artworks

RESOURCES
- Discussion Card 3, p. R35
- Electronic Art Gallery CD-ROM, Primary

Warm-Up

Build Background Display several illustrated advertisements from a magazine. Explain that artists who create these images have important roles in selling a product. Have students tell what catches their attention in each advertisement. TEKS 3.3C

Teach

Discuss Art Concepts Have students read pages 138–139. Point out that the artist of image A placed a cactus next to the oranges to help people remember the name of the product. Have students identify shapes and colors that create variety. Then discuss how the artist of image B used white on a dark background to make objects stand out. TEKS 3.1B

Think Critically

1. READING SKILL **Summarize the important ideas in image B.** (Visitors will see pandas at the zoo.) SUMMARIZE
2. **Describe an advertisement that you would like to design.** (Responses will vary.) PERSONAL RESPONSE
3. WRITE **Write your opinion about the advertisement in image A.** EXPOSITORY
TAKS Writing Objective 1

Lesson 30

Vocabulary
graphic arts

Graphic Arts

Most paintings and sculptures must be viewed in museums or art galleries. **Graphic arts**, such as advertisements, can be viewed almost anywhere. Artists create images that can be printed over and over in magazines, on posters and billboards, and on television.

Image A is an advertisement for oranges. The artist has included details to help people remember the product. What would you remember about this advertisement? How did the artist create variety?

A Cactus Brand Oranges—Highland Fruit Growers Association, Promotional literature posters

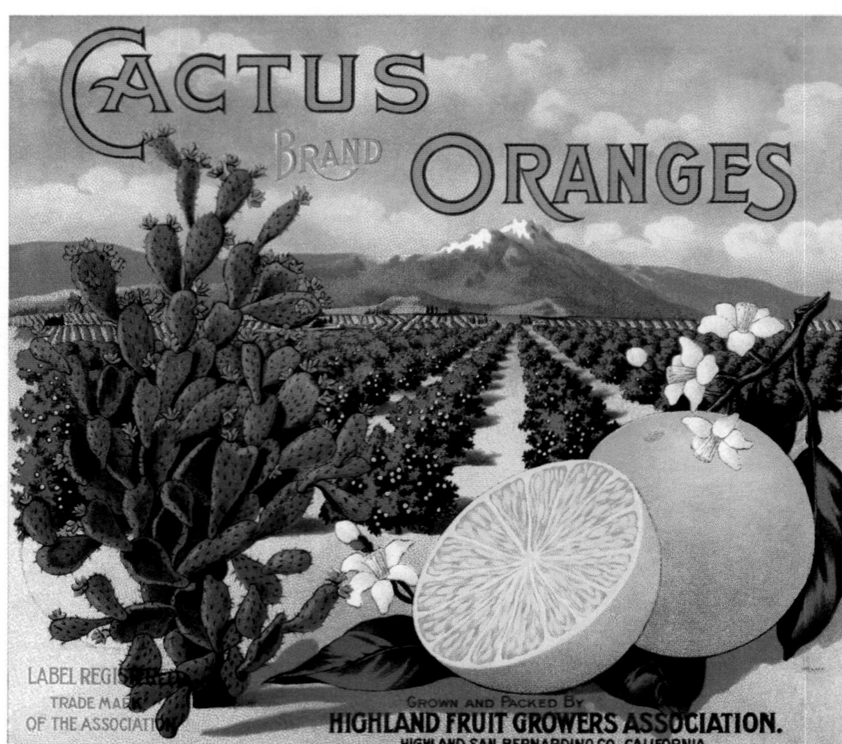

138

FYI Background Information

Art History

Fruit crate labels began in the United States in the 1800s when farmers shipped fruit in wooden crates. Graphic artists designed and printed the labels to compete with other fruit companies. Today many people collect rare fruit crate labels from as far back as the 1880s.

For additional information about Kriesel, see pp. R44–R59.

RECOMMENDED READING

The Hatmaker's Sign: A Story by Benjamin Franklin by Candace Fleming. Orchard, 1998. AVERAGE

★ **TEKS 3.1B** identify elements and principles; **TEKS 3.2C** produce various artworks; **TEKS 3.3C** relate art to different jobs; **TEKS 3.4A** identify intent in personal artworks; **PDAS Domain I** active participation; **PDAS Domain II** learner-centered instruction; **PDAS Domain III** evaluation and feedback; *(continued)*

Now look at image **B**. What does this poster advertise? This graphic artist used a computer drawing program to draw and color her artwork. What lines, shapes, and colors did she use to create variety?

Johanna Kriesel, *"We're Waiting Just for You at the Zoo" Panda Print*

Artist's Workshop

Graphic Design

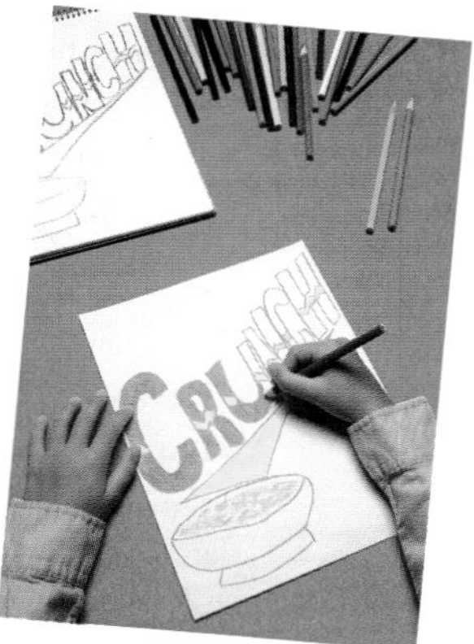

1. **Design the front of a cereal box. Think of a name for your cereal, and sketch some ideas.**
2. **Use colored pencils and paper to create your design. Include letters and details to help people remember your product.**
3. **Use different lines, shapes, and colors to create variety.**

139

Language Arts Connection

Word Origin Explain to students that the word *graphic* can be traced to an ancient Greek word that meant "write or scratch on clay tablets." Have students create webs that show other words with the root *graph.*

graph
autograph
graphite
telegraph

PDAS Domain IV

ESL Support **language acquisition** by using questions or cues to discuss students' finished designs. Have students answer by pointing to a part of their design or by answering orally.

Challenge Have students create their cereal box designs by using a computer drawing program.

30-40 Minutes

Artist's Workshop

Graphic Design

MATERIALS: sketchbook, colored pencils, white paper

PLAN Have students first decide the name of their cereal and its ingredients.

CREATE Tell students to use bold colors and large letters in their design. As students produce their drawings, remind them to create variety to make the design stand out on a shelf or in a magazine advertisement. TEKS 3.2C

REFLECT Have students identify their general intent for using certain shapes and colors in their design. TEKS 3.4A

Activity Options PDAS Domain IV

Quick Activity Have students sketch a cereal box design.

Early Finishers Have students use Discussion Card 3 to talk about lines, shapes, and colors in their designs.

Challenge See *Teacher Resource Book*, p. 80.

5-10 Minutes

Wrap-Up

Informal Assessment PDAS Domain III

- **What graphic design would you create to advertise a park in your community?** (Responses will vary.) PERSONAL RESPONSE
- **How is the job of a graphic artist similar to other art careers?** (Responses will vary.) ART HISTORY AND CULTURE TEKS 3.3C

Extend Through Writing

TAKS Writing Objective 1

Commercial Have students write the text for a television commercial to sell their cereal.

PDAS Domain IV classroom management; TAKS Writing Objective 1 composition

PDAS Domains I, III

Review and Reflect

Have students reflect on what they have learned about the ways artists over time have used variety and rhythm in their artworks. Display **Art Prints 10, 15, 16, 17,** and **18**. Encourage small groups of students to use Discussion Cards 3 and 4, page R35, and their completed Word Knowledge Charts to discuss what they learned about the vocabulary and concepts in this unit. Students should identify art elements and art principles in the images. TEKS 3.1B

Vocabulary and Concepts

Have students read each sentence and choose the letter of the word or phrase that best completes it. (1. C; 2. A; 3. B; 4. B; 5. A)

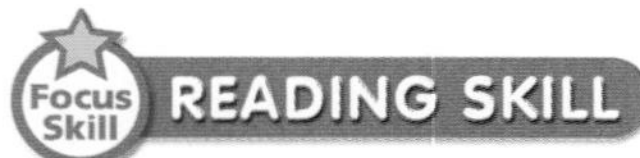

Summarize

Remind students that when you summarize, you tell the most important ideas in one or two sentences. Then have students reread the information about printmaking on page 128 and summarize it in one sentence. Have students use the diagram to help them organize their ideas. TAKS Reading Objectives 1, 3

Important Idea	Important Idea
Prints are made by painting a design on a flat object and pressing it onto paper.	Artists create many prints with the same block.

Summary
Artists use printing blocks to create many prints of the same image.

Unit 6 Review and Reflect

Vocabulary and Concepts

Choose the letter of the word or phrase that best completes each sentence.

1 A ___ is a shape that stands for an idea.

A print **B** found object **C** symbol **D** pattern

2 Artists can use contrasting lines, shapes, and colors to create ___.

A variety **B** movement **C** rhythm **D** unity

3 Artists can create ___ by repeating lines, shapes, colors, and patterns.

A variety **B** rhythm **C** emphasis **D** distortion

4 Artists use cut photographs to create ___.

A graphic arts **B** photomontages **C** murals **D** prints

5 ___ are sculptures made of found objects and other materials.

A Assemblages **B** Weavings **C** Prints **D** Symbols

READING SKILL

Summarize

Reread the first paragraph on page 128. Look for the most important ideas. Then summarize the paragraph. Use a diagram like the one shown here to help you.

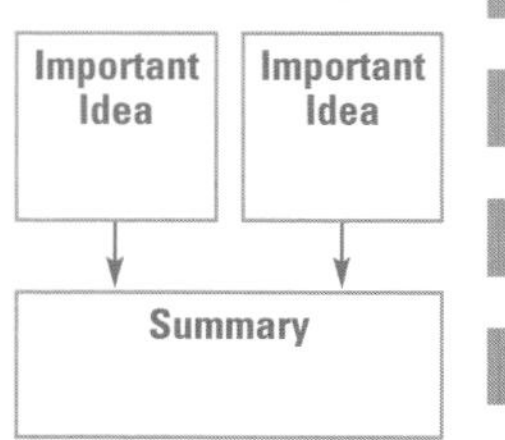

TEKS 3.2C, TEKS 3.3C

Home and Community Connection

School-Home Connection

Copy and distribute *Teacher Resource Book* pp. 95–96 to inform parents about upcoming art projects. After completing the unit, ask students to work at home with a parent or another adult to produce potato prints, demonstrating the appropriate use of art materials.

Community Connection

You may want to arrange a visit to a local printer so that students can see the process of manufacturing multiple pieces of art or graphic designs. Invite one of the printers to speak to the group.

★ **TEKS 3.1B** identify elements and principles; **TEKS 3.2C** produce various artworks; **TEKS 3.3C** relate art to different jobs; **PDAS Domain I** active participation; **PDAS Domain III** evaluation and feedback; **TAKS Reading Objective 1** demonstrate understanding of texts; *(continued)*

Write About Art

Reread the information about Nicario Jimenez on page 136. Then write a summary of the text. Use a diagram to organize your ideas.

REMEMBER—YOU SHOULD

- tell the most important ideas in your own words.
- use correct grammar, spelling, and punctuation.

Critic's Corner

Look at *Mercedes-Benz Type C111 prototype* by Andy Warhol to answer the questions below.

DESCRIBE What is the subject of the painting?

ANALYZE How did the artist create rhythm in his painting? How did he create variety?

INTERPRET Does the painting seem old, or does it seem modern? Why do you think so?

EVALUATE Is this a painting you will remember? Why or why not?

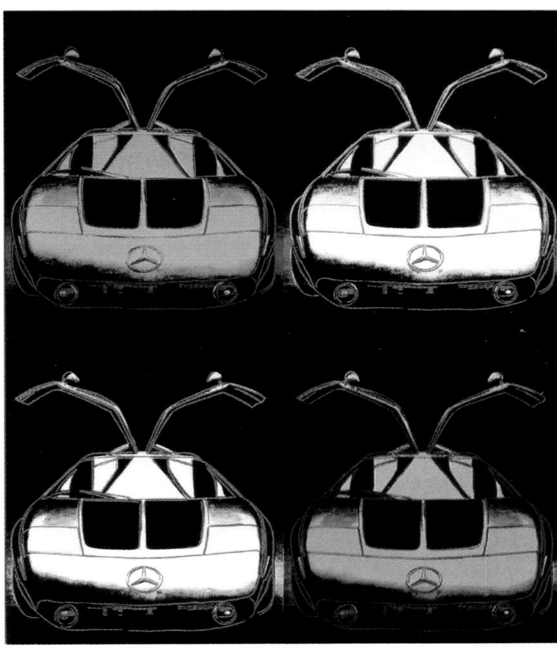

Andy Warhol,
Mercedes-Benz Type C111 prototype

141

PDAS Domain III

Assessment

Portfolio Assessment

Work with students to choose a piece of their artwork to include in their portfolios. Suggest that they decide which piece best fulfilled the assignment or which piece they liked best for another reason. You may want to provide specific feedback that targets students' use of the principles of design. See also Portfolio Recording Form, page R32.

Additional Assessment Options

- Progress Recording Form, p. R33
- Artist's Workshop Rubrics (Self/Teacher and Peer), pp. R30–R31
- Unit 6 Test, *Teacher Resource Book,* p. 104

Write About Art

Summary Read aloud the directions with students and remind them that details should not be included in a summary. Tell students to use conjunctions to connect related ideas. Remind them to proofread their sentences. TAKS Writing Objectives 1, 2, 4, 6

Critic's Corner

RESPONSE/EVALUATION Use Discussion Card 2, page R34, and the steps below to guide students in analyzing *Mercedes-Benz Type C111 prototype* by Andy Warhol.

DESCRIBE Students should recognize that the subject of the painting is four cars.

ANALYZE Discuss how the repeated shapes of the cars and the details on the cars create rhythm. Students should point out that the artist used different colors on each car to create variety. TEKS 3.1B

INTERPRET Students might point out that the painting seems modern because the cars look like they are from the future. Explain that this automobile design is a prototype for a car that might be made in the future.

EVALUATE Students may explain that the painting is memorable because the cars are like nothing they have seen before.

TAKS Test Preparation: Reading and Writing Through Art, pp. 58–78

TAKS Reading Objective 3 use a variety of strategies; TAKS Writing Objective 1 composition; TAKS Writing Objective 2 conventions; TAKS Writing Objective 4 sentence construction; TAKS Writing Objective 6 proofreading

Student Art Exhibitions

When students display their work in art exhibitions, they gain confidence in their abilities to create and evaluate artworks.

PREPARATION

- Decide whether to hold the exhibition at the end of the school year as a culminating activity or at intervals throughout the year.
- Decide whether to include the work of several grade levels or groups or just one at a time.
- Ask students to create and distribute invitations to family members, friends, and classmates.
- Have students use the ideas on *Student Edition* pages 164–165 to mount, frame, and label their artworks to prepare them for display. See *Teacher Resource Book*, page 39, for an example of a museum card.

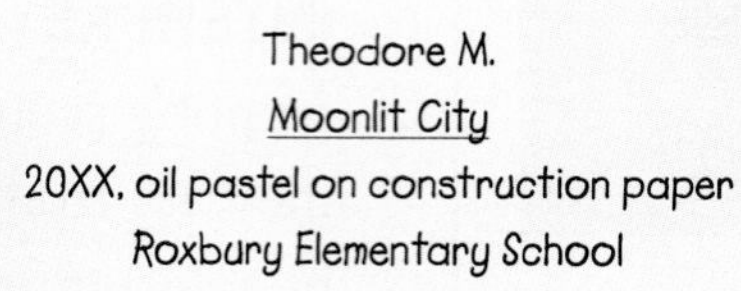

▲ **museum card**

DISPLAYS

Two-Dimensional Artworks

- Tack to bulletin boards in the classroom or hallway.
- Clip with clothespins to drying racks or a clothesline.
- Line up along chalk trays.
- Prop up on makeshift easels.

Three-Dimensional Artworks

- Place on a large table, bookcase, or a group of desks.
- Cover surfaces with cloth or colored paper.
- Place boxes of varying heights under the cloth.
- Arrange larger artworks behind smaller ones.

RECORDING THE EVENT

- Videotape the art show in progress.
- Take digital photographs before and during the art show. You can use these images to create a slide show or a digital portfolio.

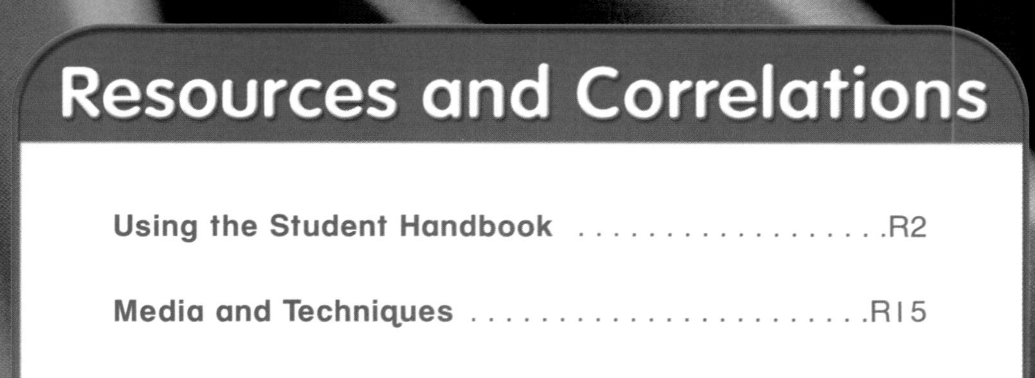

Resources and Correlations

Using the Student Handbook

Introduce the Student Handbook by having students turn to page 143. Do a walk-through with students, explaining how they can use the sections throughout the year.

USING THE MAPS OF MUSEUMS AND ART SITES

Guide students in looking at the maps on pages 144–147.

- Explain that art comes from all over the United States and the world and that these maps show only a small number of the world's art museums and art sites.
- Model how to select one site on the map and locate the corresponding artwork in the *Student Edition*.
- Have volunteers follow the same process to locate several art sites.

Use the following optional map activities to extend the learning.

MAP CONCENTRATION

MATERIALS: paper, pencils, scissors

DIRECTIONS:

- Distribute to pairs of students 30 self-stick notes or small paper squares.
- Using the United States map or the world map, have one partner write on the squares the names of the museums and art sites in the LOCATE IT key.
- Ask the other partner to write on the squares the names of the locations on the map.
- Have students place all the squares face down on a desk or table.
- Have partners take turns choosing two squares at a time and using the map to look for a match between the name of the art site and its location. The partner with the most matches wins.

VOCABULARY CHALLENGE

MATERIALS: cube pattern (*Teacher Resource Book*, p. 44), Vocabulary Cards in English and Spanish (*Teacher Resource Book*, pp. 7–30), scissors, glue

DIRECTIONS:

- Provide small groups with one cube pattern and copies of the Vocabulary Cards.
- Have groups select any six numbers from the LOCATE IT key, write one number on each square of the cube pattern, and assemble the cube.
- Have students take turns rolling the number cube and using the LOCATE IT key to find the corresponding artwork in the *Student Edition*.
- Then have students select one or more Vocabulary Cards to help them describe the image.

TOUR GUIDE

MATERIALS: index cards; pencils

DIRECTIONS:

- Have students imagine they are tour guides for one of the art sites on the map. Ask small groups to select one museum or art site from the LOCATE IT key.
- Have groups work together to write an introduction for their tour by naming the museum or art site, describing its location, and telling about the image on the corresponding *Student Edition* page.
- Groups should write their introduction on an index card and select a spokesperson to share it with the class.

Use the **Electronic Art Gallery CD-ROM, Primary,** for additional images in the United States.

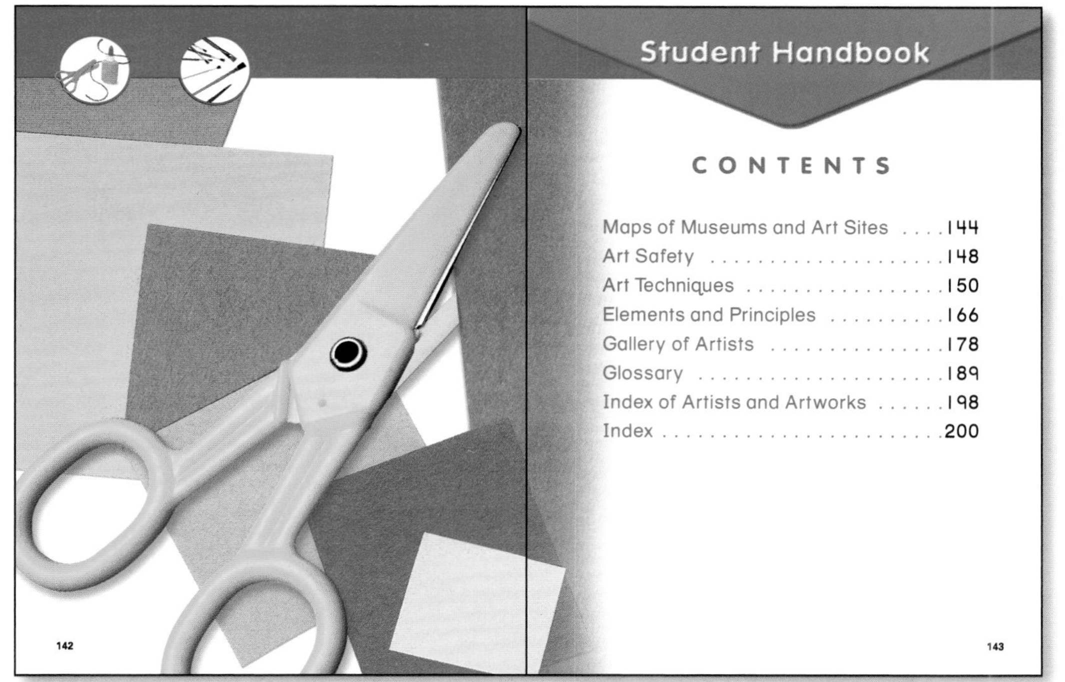

Student Handbook
CONTENTS
Maps of Museums and Art Sites 144
Art Safety 148
Art Techniques 150
Elements and Principles 166
Gallery of Artists 178
Glossary 189
Index of Artists and Artworks 198
Index 200
142
143

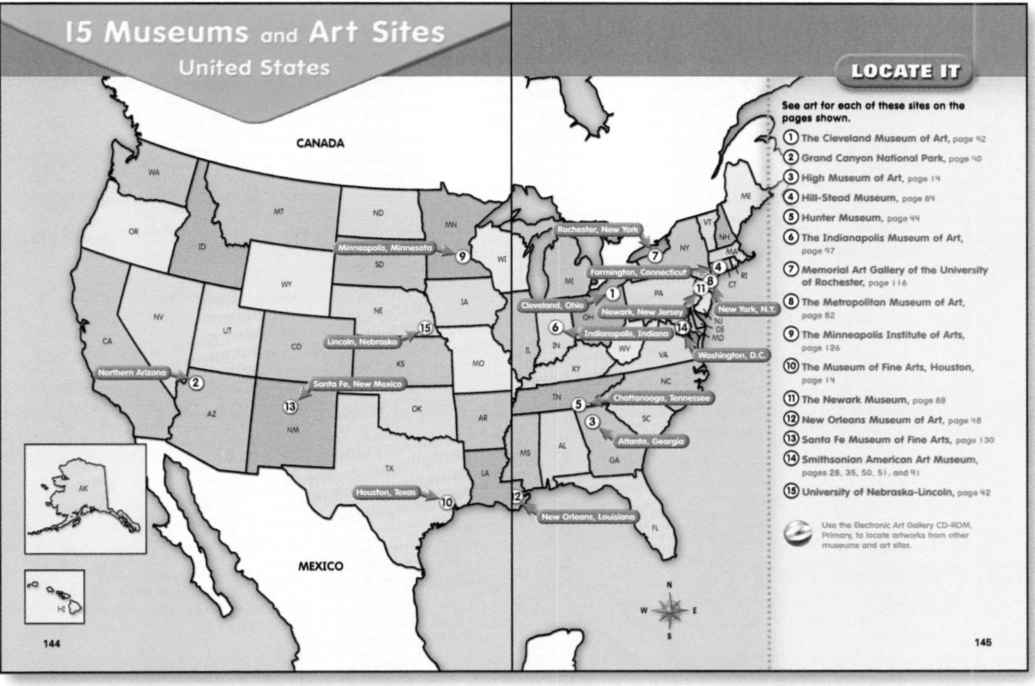

15 Museums and Art Sites
United States
CANADA
MEXICO
Minneapolis, Minnesota
Rochester, New York
Farmington, Connecticut
Cleveland, Ohio
Newark, New Jersey
New York, N.Y.
Indianapolis, Indiana
Washington, D.C.
Lincoln, Nebraska
Northern Arizona
Santa Fe, New Mexico
Chattanooga, Tennessee
Atlanta, Georgia
Houston, Texas
New Orleans, Louisiana
LOCATE IT
See art for each of these sites on the pages shown.
1 The Cleveland Museum of Art, page 92
2 Grand Canyon National Park, page 90
3 High Museum of Art, page 14
4 Hill-Stead Museum, page 84
5 Hunter Museum, page 44
6 The Indianapolis Museum of Art, page 97
7 Memorial Art Gallery of the University of Rochester, page 116
8 The Metropolitan Museum of Art, page 82
9 The Minneapolis Institute of Arts, page 126
10 The Museum of Fine Arts, Houston, page 14
11 The Newark Museum, page 88
12 New Orleans Museum of Art, page 48
13 Santa Fe Museum of Fine Arts, page 130
14 Smithsonian American Art Museum, pages 28, 35, 50, 51, and 91
15 University of Nebraska-Lincoln, page 42
Use the Electronic Art Gallery CD-ROM, Primary, to locate artworks from other museums and art sites.
144
145

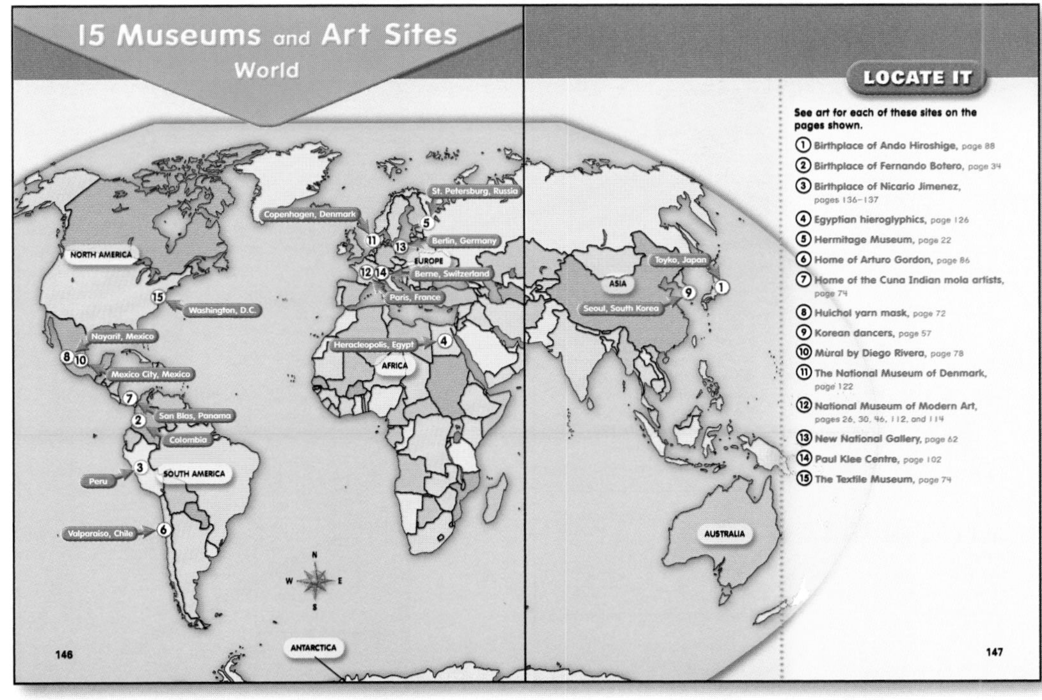

15 Museums and Art Sites
World
NORTH AMERICA
SOUTH AMERICA
EUROPE
AFRICA
ASIA
AUSTRALIA
ANTARCTICA
St. Petersburg, Russia
Copenhagen, Denmark
Berlin, Germany
Berne, Switzerland
Paris, France
Toyko, Japan
Seoul, South Korea
Washington, D.C.
Heracleopolis, Egypt
Nayarit, Mexico
Mexico City, Mexico
San Blas, Panama
Colombia
Peru
Valparaiso, Chile
LOCATE IT
See art for each of these sites on the pages shown.
1 Birthplace of Ando Hiroshige, page 88
2 Birthplace of Fernando Botero, page 34
3 Birthplace of Nicario Jimenez, pages 136–137
4 Egyptian hieroglyphics, page 126
5 Hermitage Museum, page 22
6 Home of Arturo Gordon, page 86
7 Home of the Cuna Indian mola artists, page 74
8 Huichol yarn mask, page 72
9 Korean dancers, page 57
10 Mural by Diego Rivera, page 78
11 The National Museum of Denmark, page 122
12 National Museum of Modern Art, pages 26, 30, 46, 112, and 114
13 New National Gallery, page 62
14 Paul Klee Centre, page 102
15 The Textile Museum, page 74
146
147

Art Safety

Art Safety

Listen carefully when your teacher explains how to use art materials.

Wear a smock or apron to keep your clothes clean.

Read the labels on materials before you use them.

Use tools carefully. Hold sharp objects so that they cannot hurt you or others. Wear safety glasses to protect your eyes.

Tell your teacher if you have allergies.

148

Use the kind of markers and inks that will not stain your clothes.

Show respect for other students. Walk carefully around their work. Never touch classmates' work without asking first.

Clean up spills right away so no one will slip and fall.

Always wash your hands after using art materials.

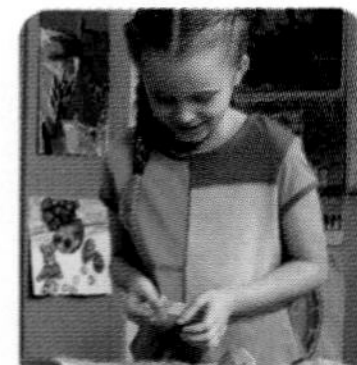
Cover your skin if you have a cut or scratch.

149

Art Techniques

Art Techniques

Trying Ways to Draw

There are lots of ways to draw. You can sketch quickly to show a rough idea of your subject, or you can draw carefully to show just how it looks to you. Try to draw every day. Keep your drawings in your sketchbook so you can see how your drawing skills improve.

Here are some ideas for drawing. To start, get out some pencils and either your sketchbook or a sheet of paper.

GESTURE DRAWING

Gesture drawings are quick sketches that are made with loose arm movements. The gesture drawing on the left shows a rough idea of what a baseball player looks like. The more careful drawing on the right shows details of the player's uniform and face. ▶

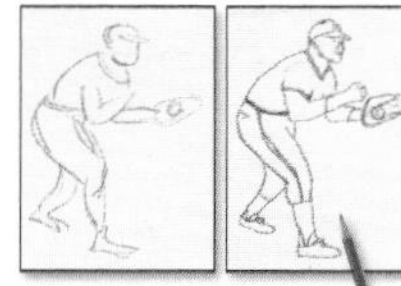

◀ Find some photographs of people or animals. Make gesture drawings of them. Draw quickly. Don't try to show details.

◀ Ask a friend to pose for a gesture drawing. Take no more than two or three minutes to finish your sketch.

150

CONTOUR DRAWING

Contour drawings show only the outlines of the shapes that make up objects. They do not show the objects' color or shading. The lines that go around shapes are called **contour lines.** Use your finger to trace around the contour lines of the truck in this picture. Trace the lines around each of the shapes that make up the truck.

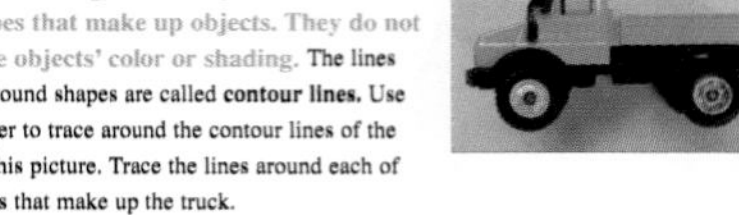

◀ A blind contour drawing is made without looking at your paper as you draw. Choose a simple object to draw, like a leaf. Pick a point on the object where you will begin drawing. Move your eyes slowly around the edge of the object. Without looking at your paper, move your pencil in the same way that your eyes move. Your first drawings may not look like the object you are looking at. Practice with different objects to improve your skill.

Continuous contour drawings are made without lifting your pencil off the paper. Draw something simple, like a chair. Look back and forth between the object and your paper. You will have to go over some lines more than once to keep from lifting your pencil off the paper. ▶

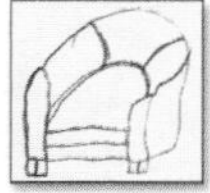

◀ Now try making a contour drawing of another object, such as a shoe. Look at your paper and lift your pencil whenever you want to. Then add details.

151

Art Techniques

TONAL DRAWING

Tonal drawings show the dark and light areas of objects using tones, or shades, of one color. They do not include contour lines. Look at the photograph at the right. Notice which areas are dark and which are light. Now look at the tonal drawing. Even without contour lines, you can tell what the drawing shows. ▶

◀ Experiment with your pencils. You can use **cross-hatching,** or a pattern of crossed lines, to show dark areas in a tonal drawing. Try smudging some of the lines together with your fingers. To darken large areas, use the flat edge of a dull pencil point. Use an eraser to lighten some of your marks.

Try a tonal drawing of a simple object like a spoon. Look at the object closely. Do not draw contour lines. Notice the shapes of the dark and light areas on the object. Use the edge of your pencil point to copy the dark shapes. Use cross-hatching in some areas. Use an eraser to lighten marks where needed. ▶

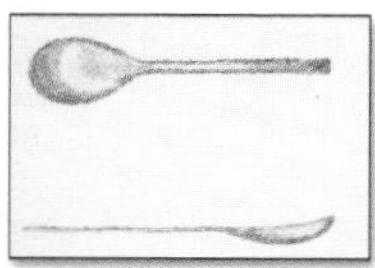

152

CONTOURS AND TONES

Try combining tonal drawing with contour drawing. Start by making a tonal drawing of something with an interesting shape, like a backpack. Look at it carefully to see the tones of dark and light. ▶

Then look at the object again to see its contours. Draw contour lines around the shapes that make up the object. ▶

You might prefer to start with a contour drawing. Be sure you draw the outline of each shape in the object. Then add tones with shading or cross-hatching. ▼

Did you prefer to start with shading or with contours?

153

Experimenting with Paint

Working with colors is always fun. Experimenting with paint will help you learn about color and how you can use it in your artwork.

These are some things you should have when you paint: old newspapers to cover your work area, an old shirt to cover your clothes, tempera paints or watercolors, plastic plates or plastic egg cartons for mixing paint, paper, paintbrushes, a jar or bowl of water, and paper towels.

TEMPERA PAINTS

Tempera paints are water-based, so they are easy to clean up. The colors are bright and easy to mix.

GETTING STARTED

Start experimenting with different kinds of brushstrokes. Try painting with lots of paint on the brush and then with the brush almost dry. (You can dry the paintbrush by wiping it across a paper towel.) Make a brushstroke by twisting the paintbrush on your paper. See how many different brushstrokes you can make by rolling, pressing, or dabbing the brush on the paper.

Now load your brush with as much paint as it will hold, and make a heavy brushstroke. Use a craft stick or another tool to draw a pattern in it. ▶

Use what you've learned to paint a picture. Use as many different brushstrokes as you can. ▶

154

MIXING COLORS

Even if you have only a few colors of tempera paint, you can mix them to make almost any color you want. Use the **primary colors** red, yellow, and blue to create the **secondary colors** orange, green, and violet.

◀ Mix dark and light colors. To make darker colors (**shades**), add black. To make lighter colors (**tints**), add white. See how many shades and tints of a single color you can make.

TECHNIQUES TO TRY

Pointillism is a technique that makes the viewer's eyes mix the colors. Use colors, such as blue and yellow, that make a third color when mixed. Make small dots of color close together without letting the dots touch. In some areas, place the two different colors very close together. Stand back from your paper. What happens to the colors as your eyes "mix" them? ▶

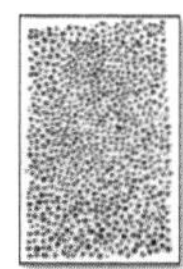

◀ Impasto is a technique that creates a thick or bumpy surface on a painting. You can create an impasto painting by building up layers of paint, or by thickening your paint with a material such as wheat paste. Mix some paint and wheat paste in a small bowl. Spread some of the mixture on a piece of cardboard. Experiment with tools such as a toothpick, a plastic fork, or a comb to make textures in the impasto. Mix more colors and use them to make an impasto picture or design.

155

Art Techniques

WATERCOLORS

Watercolors usually come in little dry cakes. You have to add the water! So keep a jar of clean water and some paper towels nearby as you paint. Use paper that is made for watercolors.

GETTING STARTED

Dip your paintbrush in water and then dab it on one of the watercolors. Try a brushstroke. Watercolors are transparent. Since you can see through them, the color on your paper will never be as dark as the color of the cake. Use different amounts of water. What happens to the color when you use a lot of water?

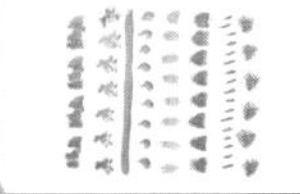

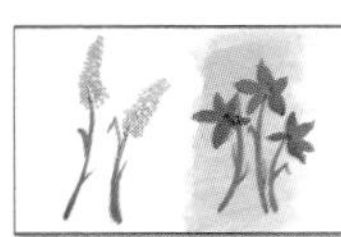

Now rinse your brush in water and use another color. Try different kinds of brushstrokes—thick and thin, squiggles and waves, dots and blobs. Change colors often.

Try using one color on top of a different color that is already dry. Work quickly. If your brushstrokes are too slow, the dry color underneath can become dull. If you want part of your painting to be white, don't paint that part. The white comes from the color of the paper.

156

MIXING COLORS

Experiment with mixing watercolors right on your paper. Try painting with a very wet brush. Add a wet color on top of, or just touching, another wet color. Try three colors together. ▶

You can also mix colors on your paintbrush. Dip your brush into one color and then another before you paint. Try it with green and yellow. Clean your paintbrush and try some other combinations. To clean any paint cakes that you have used for mixing, just wipe them with a paper towel. ▶

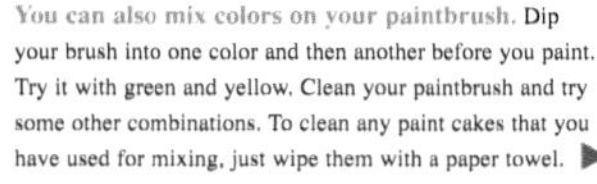

TECHNIQUES TO TRY

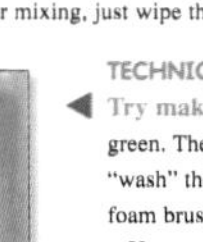

◀ Try making a watercolor wash. Start with a patch of dark green. Then clean your paintbrush and get it very wet. Use it to "wash" the color down the page. (You can also do this with a foam brush or a sponge.)

You can wet all of one side of the paper, brush a stroke of color across it, and let the color spread. Try two or three color washes together. For a special effect, sprinkle salt onto the wet paper.

Try using tempera paints and watercolors together. ▶ Start with a two-color watercolor wash. Let it dry. Then use several kinds of brushstrokes to paint a design on top of the wash with tempera paint.

Remember these techniques when you paint designs or pictures. Be sure to clean your paintbrushes and work area when you have finished.

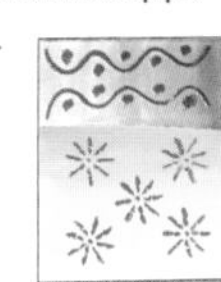

157

Art Techniques

Working with Clay

Clay is a special kind of mud or earth that holds together and is easy to shape when it is mixed with water. Clay objects can be fired, or heated at a high temperature, to make them harden. They can also be left in the air to dry until hard.

To make an object with clay, work on a clean, dry surface. (A brown paper bag makes a good work surface.) Have some water handy. If the clay starts to dry out, add a few drops of water at a time. When you are not working with the clay, store it in a plastic bag to keep it moist.

▲ You can use an assortment of tools. Use a rolling pin to make flat slabs of clay. Use a plastic knife or fork, keys, a comb, or a pencil to add texture or designs to the objects you make out of clay.

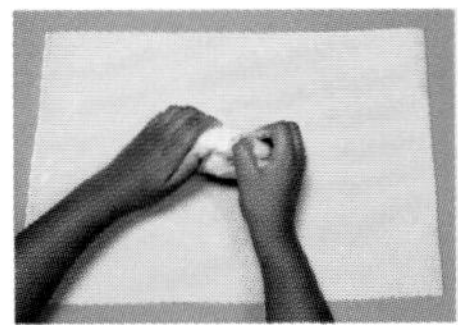

▲ Start working with a piece of clay by making sure it has no air bubbles in it. Press it down, fold it over, and press it down again. This process is called **kneading**.

158

MODELING

Try making different forms with your clay. If one of your forms reminds you of an animal or a person, continue to mold the form by pinching and pulling the clay. ▶

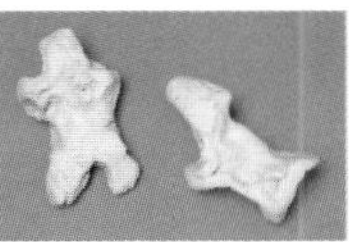

◀ You can join two pieces of clay together. Carve small lines on the edges that will be joined. This is called **scoring**. Then use **slip**, or clay dissolved in water, to wet the surfaces. Press the pieces together and smooth the seams.

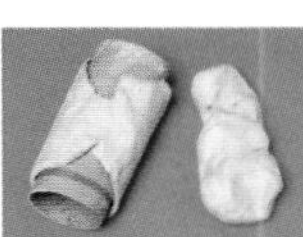

To make a bigger form, wrap a slab of clay around a tube or crumpled newspaper.

Try adding patterns, textures, or details to your form. Experiment with your tools. Press textured objects into the clay and lift them off. Brush a key across the clay. Press textured material like burlap into your clay, lift it off, and add designs. If you change your mind, smooth the clay with your fingers and try something else.

159

Art Techniques

USING SLABS
Roll your clay out flat, to between $\frac{1}{4}$ inch and $\frac{1}{2}$ inch thick. Shape the clay by molding it over something like a bowl or crumpled paper.

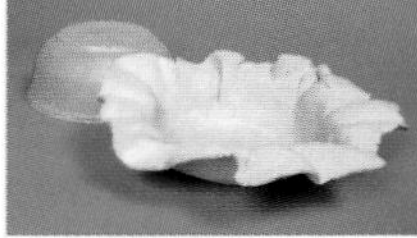

To make a slab box, roll your clay out flat. Use a plastic knife to cut six equal-sized squares or rectangles for the bottom, top, and sides of your box. Score the edges, and then let the pieces dry until they feel like leather.

Join the pieces together with slip. Then smooth the seams with your fingers.

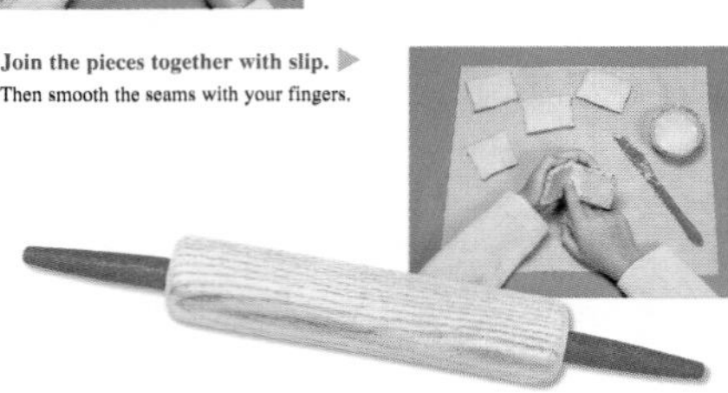

160

USING COILS
To make a coil pot, roll pieces of clay against a hard surface. Use your whole hand to make long clay ropes.

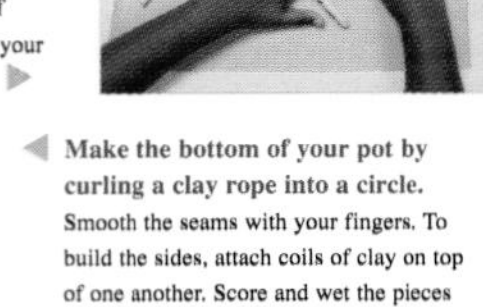

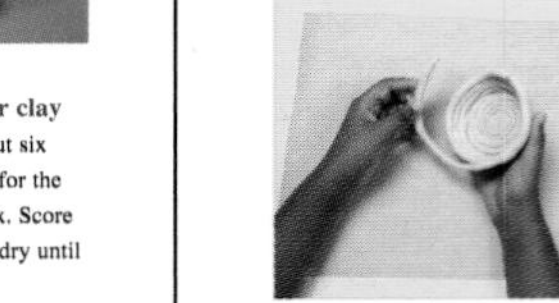

Make the bottom of your pot by curling a clay rope into a circle. Smooth the seams with your fingers. To build the sides, attach coils of clay on top of one another. Score and wet the pieces with slip as you attach them. Smooth the inside as you work. You may smooth the outside or let the coils show.

MAKING A CLAY RELIEF
A relief is a sculpture raised from a surface. To make a relief, draw a simple design on a slab of clay. Roll some very thin ropes and attach them to the lines of the design. This is called the **additive method** because you are adding clay to the slab.

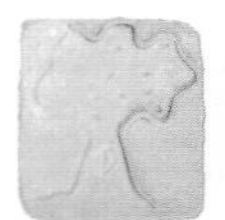

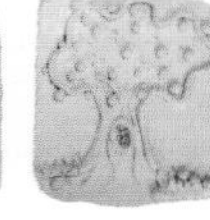

You can also make a relief sculpture by carving a design out of your clay slab. This is called the **subtractive method** because you are taking away, or subtracting, clay from the slab.

161

Art Techniques

Exploring Printmaking
When you make a print, you transfer color from one object to another. If you have ever left a muddy footprint on a clean floor, you know what a print is. Here are some printmaking ideas to try.

COLLOGRAPH PRINTS
A **collograph** is a combination of a **collage** and a **print**. To make a collograph, you will need cardboard, glue, paper, newspapers, a brayer (a roller for printing), printing ink or paint, a flat tray such as a foam food tray, and some paper towels or sponges. You will also need some flat objects to include in the collage. Try things like old keys, string, lace, paper clips, buttons, small shells, or burlap.

Arrange objects on the cardboard in a pleasing design. Glue the objects to the surface, and let the glue dry.

Prepare your ink while the collage is drying. Place a small amount of ink or paint on your foam tray. Roll the brayer through the ink until it is evenly coated. Gently run the brayer over the collage. Most of the ink should be on the objects.

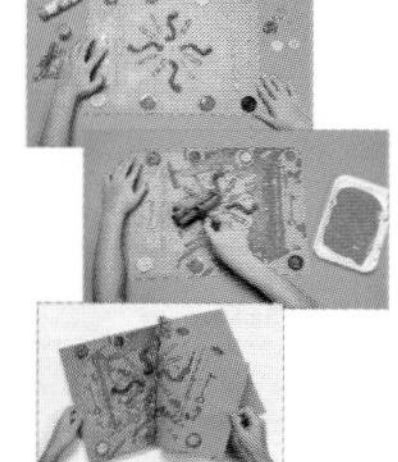

Now press a piece of paper onto the inked collage. Gently rub the paper. Peel off the paper and let the ink dry. You've made a collograph!

162

MULTICOLOR PRINTS
You can use different colors of tempera paint to make a multicolor print with repeated shapes. You will need poster board or a foam tray (such as a food tray), cardboard, scissors, glue, paper, water, tempera paint, and a paintbrush.

First cut out some interesting shapes from the poster board or foam tray. Carve or poke holes and lines into the shapes.

Arrange the shapes on the cardboard to make an interesting design. Glue down the pieces. When the glue is dry, paint the shapes with different colors of tempera paint. Try not to get paint on the cardboard.

While the paint is wet, place a sheet of paper on top of your design. Gently rub the paper, and peel it off carefully. Let the paint dry.

After the shapes dry, paint them again with different colors. Print the same paper again, but turn it so that the designs and colors overlap.

Try using different colors, paper, and objects to make prints.

163

Art Techniques

Displaying Your Artwork
Displaying your artwork is a good way to share it. Here are some ways to make your artwork look its best.

DISPLAYING ART PRINTS
Select several pictures that go together well. Line them up along a wall or on the floor. Try grouping the pictures in different ways. Choose an arrangement that you like. Attach a strong string across a wall. Use clothespins or paper clips to hang your pictures on the string.

Make a frame. Use a piece of cardboard that is longer and wider than the art. In the center of the cardboard, draw a rectangle that is slightly smaller than your picture. Have an adult help you cut out the rectangle. Then decorate your frame. Choose colors and textures that look good with your picture. You can paint the frame or use a stamp to print a design on it. You can add texture by gluing strips of cardboard or rows of buttons onto your frame.

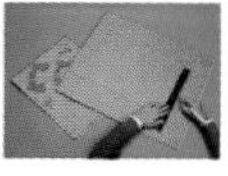

Mount your picture. Tape the corners of your artwork to the back of the frame. Cut a solid piece of cardboard the same size as the frame. Then glue the framed artwork to the cardboard. Tape a loop of thread on the back. Hang up your framed work.

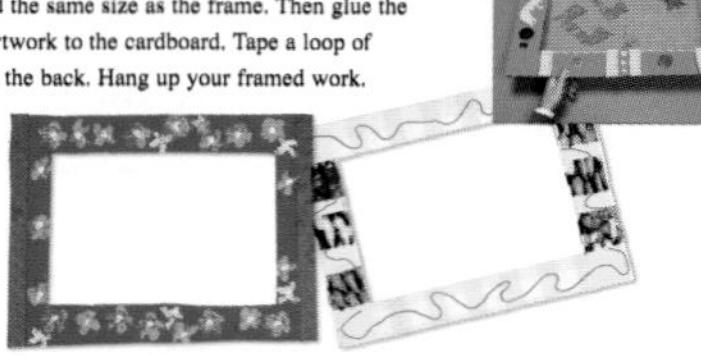

164

DISPLAYING SCULPTURES
To display your clay objects or sculptures, find a location where your work will be safe from harm. Look for a display area where people won't bump into your exhibit or damage your work.

Select several clay objects or sculptures that go together well. Try grouping them in different ways. Place some of the smaller objects on boxes. When you find an arrangement that you like, remove your artworks, tape the boxes to the table, and drape a piece of cloth over the boxes. Pick a plain cloth that will look good under your artworks, try adding a few interesting folds in the cloth, and place your artworks back on the table.

Now invite your friends and family over to see your work!

165

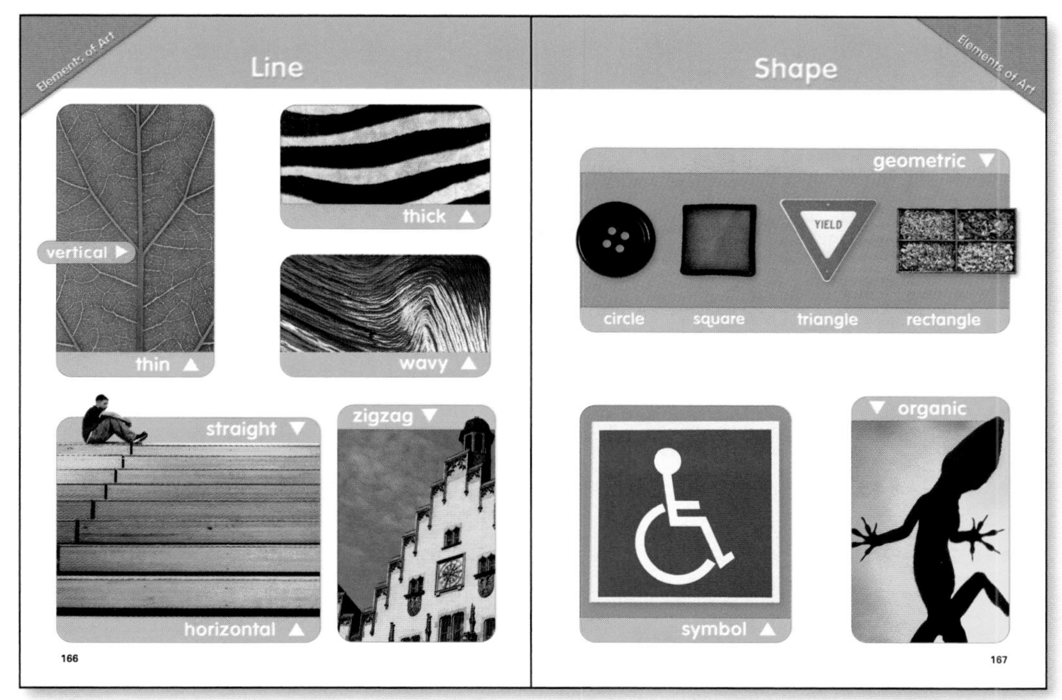

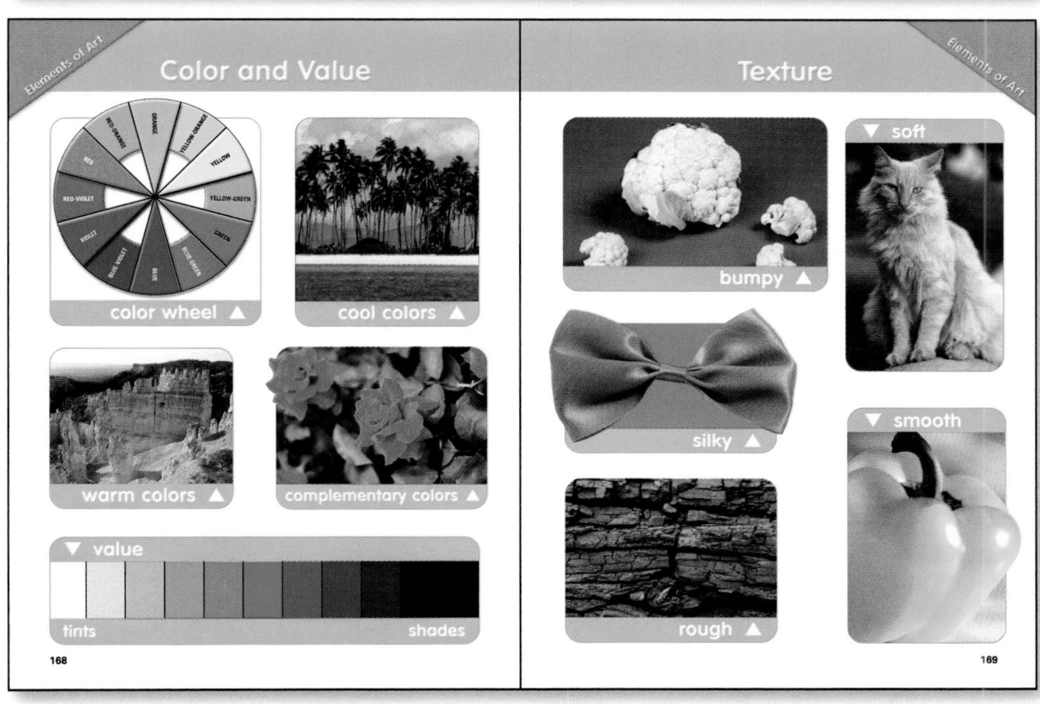

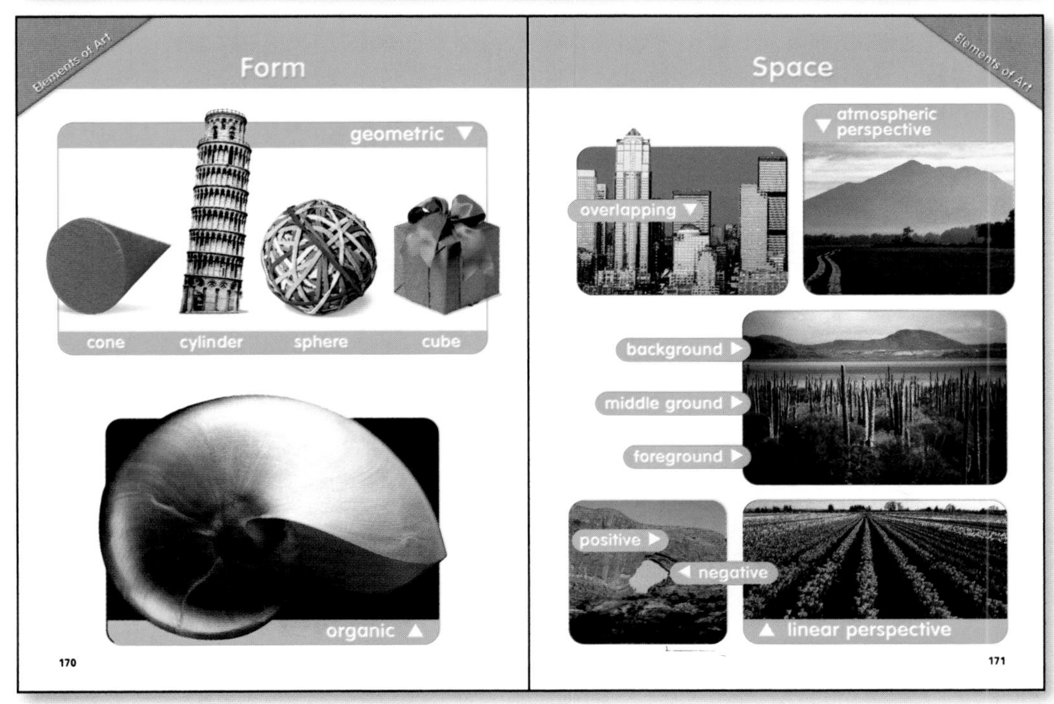

Elements and Principles

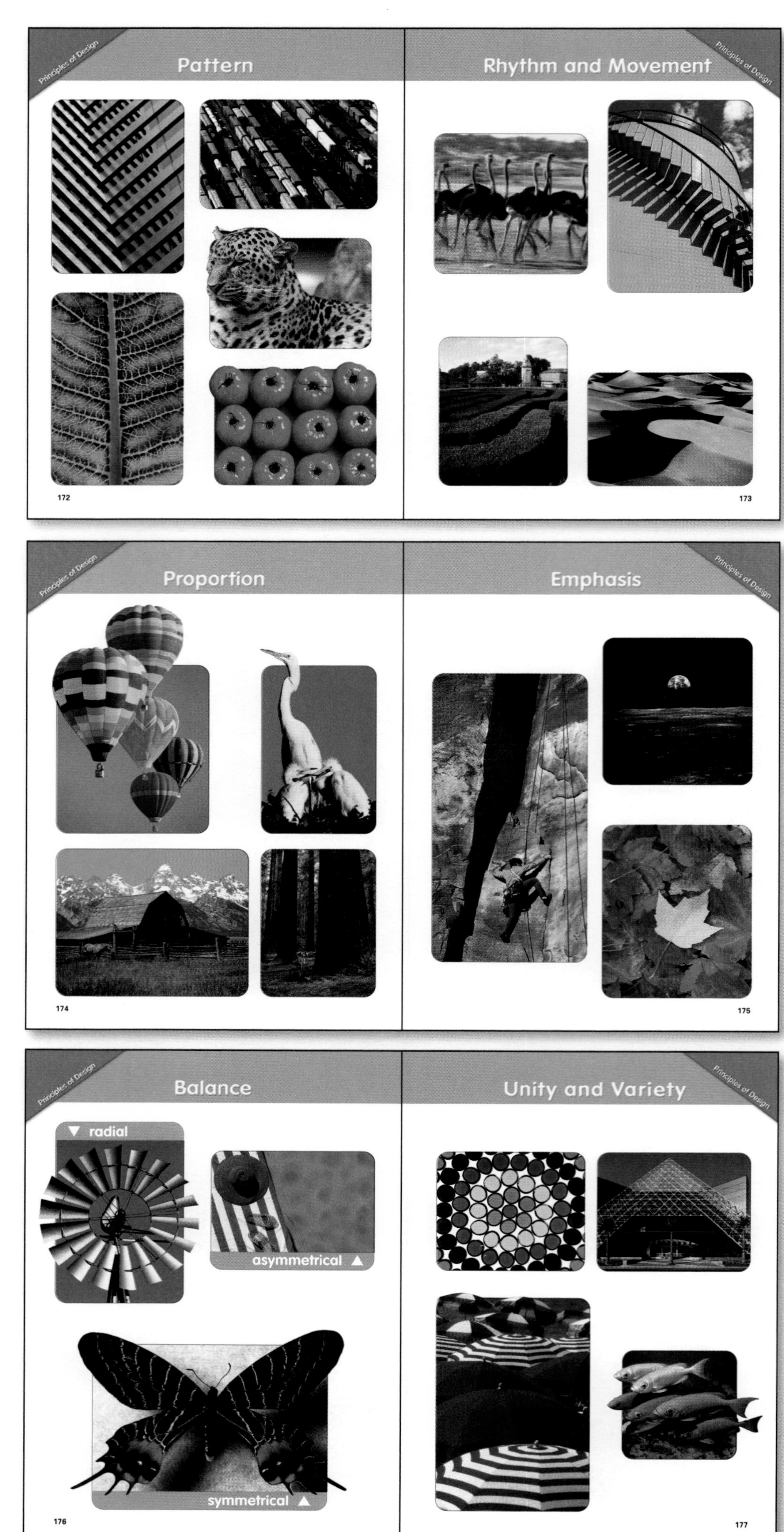

Principles of Design
Pattern
172
Principles of Design
Rhythm and Movement
173
Principles of Design
Proportion
174
Principles of Design
Emphasis
175
Principles of Design
Balance
radial
asymmetrical
symmetrical
176
Principles of Design
Unity and Variety
177

Gallery of Artists

Alexander Archipenko
(1887–1964) page 38

Romare Bearden
(1911–1988) pages 116 and 117

Emil Armin
(1883–1971) page 28

Charles Bell
(1935–1995) page 58

Jennifer Bartlett
(1941–) page 106

Thomas Hart Benton
(1889–1975) page 44

178

Carl Oscar Borg
(1879–1947) page 91

Dale Chihuly
(1941–) page 38

Fernando Botero
(1932–) page 34

Christo
(1935–) page 99

Alexander Calder
(1898–1976) page 104

Clarice Cliff
(1899–1972) page 126

179

Gallery of Artists

Robert Delaunay
(1885–1941) page 46

Robert S. Duncanson
(1821–1872) page 87

Sonia Delaunay
(1885–1979) page 114

Louise Freshman-Brown
page 132

Arthur G. Dove
(1880–1946) page 61

Frank O. Gehry
(1929–) page 131

180

Arturo Gordon
(1883–1944) page 86

Jack Gunter
page 59

Juan Gris
(1887–1927) page 112

Barbara Hepworth
(1903–1975) page 37

Red Grooms
(1937–) page 92

Ando Hiroshige
(1797–1858) page 88

181

Gallery of Artists

Winslow Homer
(1836–1910) pages 96 and 97

Nicario Jimenez
pages 136 and 137

Edward Hopper
(1882–1967) page 82

William H. Johnson
(1901–1970) page 35

Jeanne-Claude
(1935–) page 99

Frida Kahlo
(1907–1954) page 66

182

Wassily Kandinsky
(1866–1944) pages 30 and 31

Kasimir Malevich
(1878–1935) page 121

Paul Klee
(1879–1940) page 102

Henri Matisse
(1869–1954) pages 22 and 26

Johanna Kriesel
page 139

John Gaw Meem
(1894–1983) page 130

183

Gallery of Artists

Reynard Milici
(1942–) page 94

Henry Moore
(1898–1986) pages 70 and 71

Joan Miró
(1893–1983) page 41

Bartolomé E. Murillo
(1618–1682) page 24

Claude Monet
(1840–1926) page 84

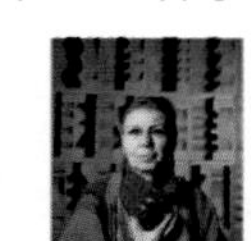
Louise Nevelson
(1899–1988) page 134

Georgia O'Keeffe
(1887–1986) page 48

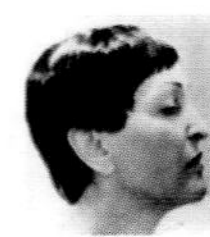
Meret Oppenheim
(1913–1985) page 54

Claes Oldenburg
(1929–) page 42

Pablo Picasso
(1881–1973) page 108

Diana Ong
(1940–) page 36

Patricia Polacco
(1944–) page 111

Gallery of Artists

Edward Potthast
(1857–1927) page 68

Henri Rousseau
(1844–1910) page 66

Pierre-Auguste Renoir
(1841–1919) page 62

Beatricia Sagar
page 128

Diego Rivera
(1886–1957) pages 52 and 78

Kurt Schwitters
(1887–1948) page 119

David Stewart
(1939–) page 134

Josephine Trotter
page 49

Harriet Peck Taylor
(1954–) page 64

Patssi Valdez
page 107

Alma Woodsey Thomas
(1891–1978) pages 50 and 51

Coosje van Bruggen
(1942–) page 42

Gallery of Artists

Vincent van Gogh
(1853–1890) page 101

Anna Belle Lee Washington
(1924–2000) page 124

Andy Warhol
(1928–1987) page 141

Tom Wesselmann
(1931–) page 118

Glossary

The Glossary contains important art terms and their definitions. Each word is respelled as it would be in a dictionary. When you see this mark ʹ after a syllable, pronounce that syllable with more force than the other syllables.

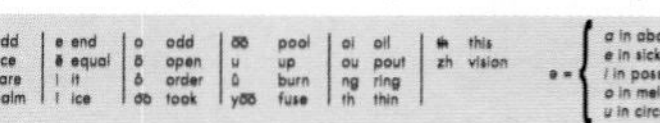

abstract art [abʹstrakt ärt] Art that does not look realistic. Abstract art may show either distorted objects or no real objects at all. (page 112)

artist [ärʹtist] A person who makes art. (page 12)

artwork [ärtʹwûrk] A work of art, such as a drawing, painting, or sculpture. (page 14)

assemblage [ə•semʹblij] A sculpture made of different kinds of materials. (page 134)

asymmetrical balance [ā•sə•meʹtri•kəl baʹləns] A kind of balance in which different lines, shapes, and colors are used on each side of an artwork to make both sides seem equal. (page 108) (*See also* symmetrical balance.)

background [bakʹground] The part of an artwork that seems to be farthest away from the viewer. (page 88)

Glossary

C

center of interest [sen′tər əv in′trəst] The part of an artwork that the viewer notices first. (page 94)

cityscape [si′tē•skāp] An artwork that shows a view of a city. (page 92)

collage [kə•läzh′] An artwork made by gluing bits of paper, fabric, scraps, photographs, or other materials to a flat surface. (page 118)

complementary colors [kom•plə•men′tər•ē kul′ərz] Pairs of colors that are opposite each other on the color wheel. (page 114)

complementary colors

composition [kom•pə•zish′ən] The way the parts of an artwork are put together. (page 34)

contour line [kon′to͝or līn] An outline drawn around a shape or an object. (page 27)

contrast [kän′trast] A difference between two parts of an artwork that makes one or both stand out. (page 94)

cool colors [ko͞ol kul′ərz] The colors green, blue, and violet. These colors appear on one half of the color wheel. (page 49) (*See also* warm colors.)

cool colors

D

depth [depth] The appearance of space or distance in a two-dimensional artwork. (page 86)

distortion [dis•tôr′shən] The changing of the way an object looks by bending or stretching its shape. (page 112)

E

earthwork [ûrth•wûrk] A kind of art that is made of natural materials and placed in a natural setting. Also called *land art* or *environmental art*. (page 98)

emphasis [em′fə•sis] A design principle used to show which part of an artwork is most important. (page 94)

F

foreground [fôr′ground] The part of an artwork that seems to be closest to the viewer. (page 88)

foreground

form [fôrm] An object that has height, width, and depth. Forms can be geometric or organic. (page 38)

forms

found object [found ob′jikt] An everyday object used as part of an artwork. (page 134)

G

geometric shape [jē•ə•met′rik shāp] A shape, such as an oval, circle, square, triangle, or rectangle, that has a regular outline. (page 32) (*See also* organic shape.)

rectangle circle oval square triangle

graphic arts [graf′ik ärts] A kind of artwork that can be used over and over in advertisements and signs. (page 138)

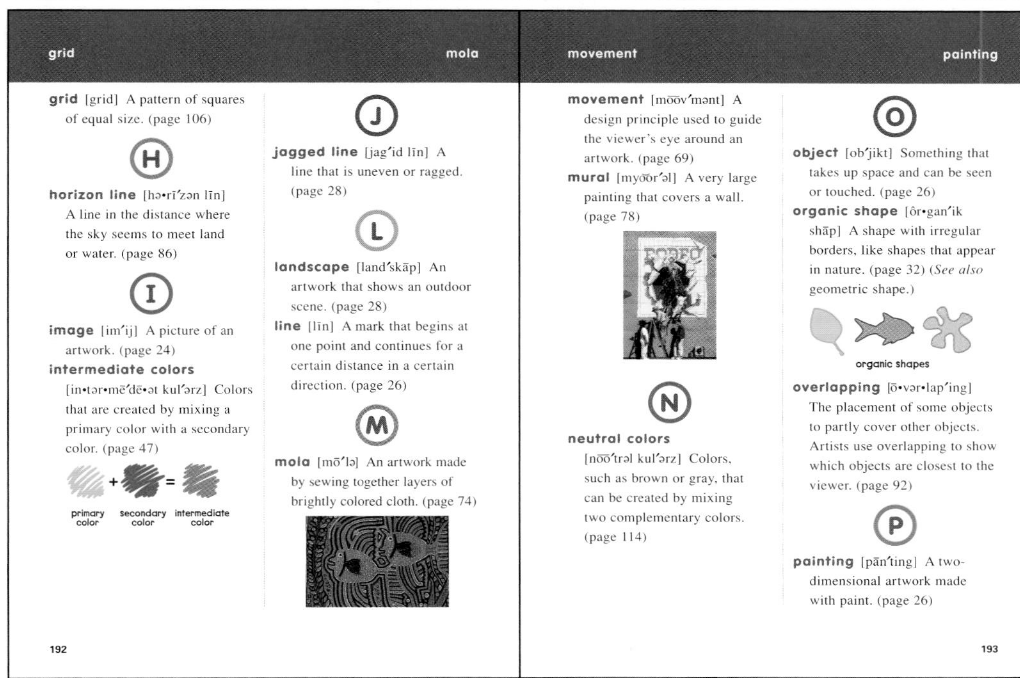

grid [grid] A pattern of squares of equal size. (page 106)

H

horizon line [hə•rī′zən līn] A line in the distance where the sky seems to meet land or water. (page 86)

I

image [im′ij] A picture of an artwork. (page 24)

intermediate colors [in•tər•mē′dē•ət kul′ərz] Colors that are created by mixing a primary color with a secondary color. (page 47)

primary color + secondary color = intermediate color

J

jagged line [jag′id līn] A line that is uneven or ragged. (page 28)

L

landscape [land′skāp] An artwork that shows an outdoor scene. (page 28)

line [līn] A mark that begins at one point and continues for a certain distance in a certain direction. (page 26)

M

mola [mō′lə] An artwork made by sewing together layers of brightly colored cloth. (page 74)

movement [mo͞ov′mənt] A design principle used to guide the viewer's eye around an artwork. (page 69)

mural [myo͝or′əl] A very large painting that covers a wall. (page 78)

N

neutral colors [no͞o′trəl kul′ərz] Colors, such as brown or gray, that can be created by mixing two complementary colors. (page 114)

O

object [ob′jikt] Something that takes up space and can be seen or touched. (page 26)

organic shape [ôr•gan′ik shāp] A shape with irregular borders, like shapes that appear in nature. (page 32) (*See also* geometric shape.)

organic shapes

overlapping [ō•vər•lap′ing] The placement of some objects to partly cover other objects. Artists use overlapping to show which objects are closest to the viewer. (page 92)

P

painting [pān′ting] A two-dimensional artwork made with paint. (page 26)

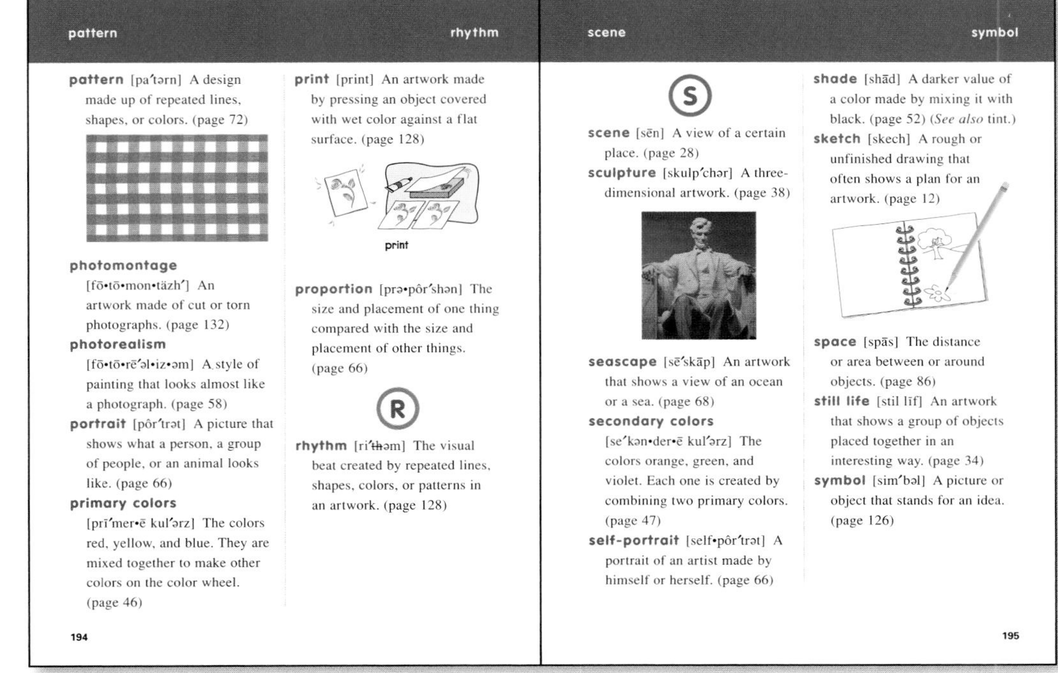

pattern [pa′tərn] A design made up of repeated lines, shapes, or colors. (page 72)

photomontage [fō•tō•mon•täzh′] An artwork made of cut or torn photographs. (page 132)

photorealism [fō•tō•rē′əl•iz•əm] A style of painting that looks almost like a photograph. (page 58)

portrait [pôr′trət] A picture that shows what a person, a group of people, or an animal looks like. (page 66)

primary colors [prī′mer•ē kul′ərz] The colors red, yellow, and blue. They are mixed together to make other colors on the color wheel. (page 46)

print [print] An artwork made by pressing an object covered with wet color against a flat surface. (page 128)

print

proportion [prə•pôr′shən] The size and placement of one thing compared with the size and placement of other things. (page 66)

R

rhythm [ri′thəm] The visual beat created by repeated lines, shapes, colors, or patterns in an artwork. (page 128)

S

scene [sēn] A view of a certain place. (page 28)

sculpture [skulp′chər] A three-dimensional artwork. (page 38)

seascape [sē′skāp] An artwork that shows a view of an ocean or a sea. (page 68)

secondary colors [se′kən•der•ē kul′ərz] The colors orange, green, and violet. Each one is created by combining two primary colors. (page 47)

self-portrait [self•pôr′trət] A portrait of an artist made by himself or herself. (page 66)

shade [shād] A darker value of a color made by mixing it with black. (page 52) (*See also* tint.)

sketch [skech] A rough or unfinished drawing that often shows a plan for an artwork. (page 12)

space [spās] The distance or area between or around objects. (page 86)

still life [stil līf] An artwork that shows a group of objects placed together in an interesting way. (page 34)

symbol [sim′bəl] A picture or object that stands for an idea. (page 126)

symmetrical balance [sə•me′tri•kəl ba′ləns] A kind of balance in which the same lines, shapes, and colors are placed on both sides of an artwork. (page 106) (*See also* asymmetrical balance.)

symmetry [sim′ə•trē] An arrangement in which one half of an artwork is a mirror image of the other half. (page 72)

T

tactile texture [tak′təl teks′chər] The way a surface of a real object feels when you touch it. *Smooth, rough,* and *furry* are words that describe tactile textures. (page 54)

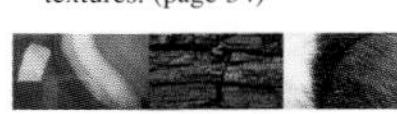

three-dimensional [thrē•də•men′shə•nəl] Having height, width, and depth. (page 38) (*See also* two-dimensional.)

tint [tint] A lighter value of a color made by mixing it with white. (page 52) (*See also* shade.)

two-dimensional [tōō•də•men′shə•nəl] Having height and width; flat. (page 32) (*See also* three-dimensional.)

unity [yōō′nə•tē] The sense that an artwork looks whole or complete. (page 114)

value [val′yōō] The lightness or darkness of a color. (page 52)

variety [və•rī′ə•tē] A design principle used to add interest to an artwork by including different objects and art elements. (page 126)

visual texture [vizh′ōō•əl teks′chər] Drawn or painted texture that looks like real textures. (page 58)

warm colors [wärm kul′ərz] The colors red, orange, and yellow. These colors appear on one half of the color wheel. (page 48) (*See also* cool colors.)

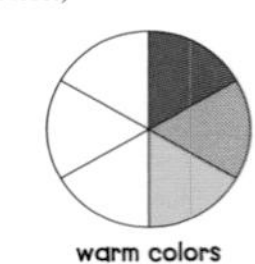

warm colors

weaving [wēv′ing] An artwork made by lacing together fibers such as yarn, thread, or strips of fabric. Rugs and baskets are kinds of weavings. (page 54)

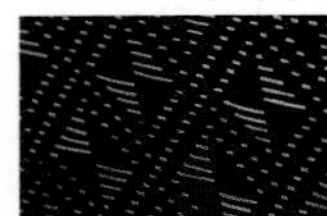

Index of Artists and Artworks

Index

Acknowledgments

Photo Credits:

Page Placement Key: (t)-top (c)-center (b)-bottom (l)-left (r)-right (fg)-foreground (bg)-background.

All photos property of Harcourt except for the following:

Frontmatter:

5 (tl) Erich Lessing/Art Resource, NY; (tc) Louis K. Meisel Gallery/Corbis; 6 (tl) Indigo Arts Gallery; (tr) Superstock; (tc) Reprinted with the permission of Simon & Shuster Books for Young Readers, an imprint of Simon & Schuster Children's Publishing Division from COYOTE PLACES THE STARS by Harriet Peck Taylor; 7 (tr) Laura Atkins; (tc) Michael Boys/Corbis; 8 (tc) Artist Rights Society (ARS), New York, NY/National Museum of Modern Art, Paris, France/Lauros-Giraudon, Paris/Superstock ; 9 (tl) Tanaya2/May Lee Clark Elementary School ; 14 (tr) Bob Kirst/Corbis; (bl) F. Carter Smith/Corbis Sygma; 15 (bl) Royalty-Free/Corbis; 16 (b) Josephine Trotter/Superstock; 17 (b) Artist Rights Society (ARS), New York, NY/Los Angeles County Museum of Art, Gift of Mr. and Mrs. Milton W. Lipper from the Milton W. Lipper Fund; 21 (tl) Alamy Images; (tr) Alamy Images.

Unit 1:

22 (t) Artist Rights Society (ARS), New York, NY/Erich Lessing/Art Resource, NY; 23 (bl) AKG Images; 24 (b) National Gallery of Art, Washington D.C.; 26 (c) Artist Rights Society (ARS), New York, NY/CNAC/MNAM/Dist. Reunion des Musees Nationaux/Art Resource, NY; 28 (c) Smithsonian American Art Museum, Washington, DC/Art Resource, NY; 30 (t) Artist Rights Society (ARS), New York, NY/CNAC/NMAM/Dist. Reunion des Musees Nationaux/Art Resource, NY; (b) Bettmann/Corbis; 31 (b) Erich Lessing/Art Resource, NY; (t) Artist Rights Society (ARS), New York, NY/Christie's Images/Superstock; 32 (cl) Joseph Barnell/Superstock; 34 (b) Christie's Images/Corbis; 35 (tl) Smithsonian American Art Museum, Washington, DC/Art Resource, NY; (tr) Lauren/Smiley Elementary School; 36 (b) Artist Rights Society (ARS), New York, NY/Diana Ong/Superstock; 37 (b) Licensed by VAGA, New York, NY/Alan Bowness, Hepworth Estate/Tate; 38 (br) Dale Chihuly; (bl) Artist Rights Society (ARS), New York/Solomon R. Guggenheim Museum; 41 (cr) Solomon R. Guggenheim Museum.

Unit 2:

42 (t) University of Nebraska-Lincoln, Olga N. Sheldon Acquisition Trust and friends of Sheldon Memorial Art Gallery; 43 (bl) AP/Wide World Photos; (bl) Thomas Hoepker/Magnum Photos; 44 (b) (copyright) T.H. Benton and R.P. Benton Testamentary Trusts/Licensed by VAGA, New York, NY/Hunter Museum of American Art, Chattanooga, Tennessee, Gift of the Benwood Foundation; 46 (b) Giraudon/Art Resource, NY; 48 (b) Artist Rights Society (ARS), New York, NY/New Orleans Museum of Art: Museum purchase, City of New Orleans Capital Funds; 49 (tr) Josephine Trotter/Superstock; 50 (br) Licensed by VAGA, New York, NY/Smithsonian American Art Museum, Washington, DC/Art Resource, NY; (t) Smithsonian American Art Museum, Washington, DC/Art Resource, NY; 51 (t) Licensed by VAGA, New York,NY/Smithsonian American Art Museum, Washington, DC/Art Resource, NY; 52 (b) Los Angeles County Museum of Art, Gift of Mr. and Mrs. Milton W. Lipper from the Milton W. Lipper Fund; 54 (b) Artist Rights Society (ARS), New York, NY/Digital Image (c) The Museum of Modern Art/Licensed by SCALA/Art Resource, NY; 56 (b) Swift/Vanuga Images/Corbis; 57 (b) Kelly-Mooney Photography/Corbis; (t) Massimo Mastrorillo/Corbis; 58 (b) Louis K. Meisel Gallery/Corbis ; 59 (t) Jack Gunter/Corbis; 61 (bl) Butler Institute of American Art.

Unit 3:

62 (t) National Gallery, Berlin/Superstock; 63 (bl) Francis G. Mayer/Corbis; 64 (t, b) Artist Rights Society (ARS), New York, NY/Simon & Schuster Publishing; 66 (bl) Schalkwijk/Art Resource, NY; (br) Art Resource, NY; 68 (c) Superstock; 70 (b) Francis G. Mayer/Corbis; 71 (cr) John Swope Collection/Corbis; (t) Henry Moore Foundation/Scala/Art Resource, NY; 72 (bl) Peabody Museum of Archeology and Ethnology; (br) Indigo Arts Gallery; 74 (b) Gift of Mrs. H. Lester Cooke/Textile Museum; 76 (b) National Archives and Records Administration; 77 (t) Richard Cummins/Corbis; (b) Hannah Goodwin/Harcourt; (c) Danny Lehman/Corbis; 78 (b) Schalkwijk/Art Resource, NY; 79 (t) Ms. Filis; 81 (c) Royalty-Free/Corbis.

Unit 4:

82(t) Francis G. Mayer/Corbis; 83 (bl) Copyright National Portrait Gallery, Smithsonian Institution/Art Resource, NY; 84 (b) Alfred Atmore Pope Collection, Hill-Stead Museum, Farmington CT; (tl) The Shelburne Museum; 86 (b) Kactus Foto/Superstock; 87 (tl) Smithsonian American Art Museum, Washington, DC/Art Resource, NY; 88 (bl) The Newark Museum/Art Resource, NY; 90 (l) Royalty-Free/Corbis; 91 (l) Smithsonian American Art Museum, Washington, DC/Art Resource, NY; 92 (l) Artist Rights Society (ARS), New York, NY/Red Grooms, b. 1937. *Looking Along Broadway Towards Grace Church, 1981. Mixed media, H. 180.3 cm. Image (copyright)* The Cleveland Museum of Art, gift of Agnes Gund in honor of Edward Henning, 1991.27; 93 (t) Laura Atkins; 94 (bl) Louis K. Meisel Gallery/Corbis; 96 (b) Burstein Collection/Corbis; (tl) Bettmann/Corbis; 97 (t) Indianapolis Museum of Art, Martha Delzell Memorial Fund; 98 (b) Michael Boys/Corbis; 99 (tl) Christo and Jeanne Claude; 101 (br) Art Resource, NY.

Unit 5:

102 (t) Artist Rights Society (ARS), New York, NY/Francis G. Mayer/Corbis; 103 (bl) Hulton Archive/Getty Images; 104 (b) Art Resource, NY; 106 (b) Geoffrey Clements/Corbis; 107 (t) Patssi Valdez/Patricia Correia Gallery; 108 (bl) Artist Rights Society (ARS), New York, NY/Giraudon/Art Resource, NY; 110 (t) From APPELEMANDO'S DREAM by Patricia Polacco, copyright (c) 1991 by Patricia Polacco. Used by permission of Philomel Books, A Division of Penguin Young Readers Group, A Member of Penguin Group (USA) Inc., 345 Hudson Street, New York, NY 10014. All rights reserved.; 110-111 (b) Patricia Polacco ; 111 (t) From APPELEMANDO'S DREAM by Patricia Polacco, copyright (c) 1991 by Patricia Polacco. Used by permission of Philomel Books, A Division of Penguin Young Readers Group, A Member of Penguin Group (USA) Inc., 345 Hudson Street, New York, NY 10014. All

204

rights reserved.; 112 (t) Artist Rights Society (ARS), New York, NY/National Museum of Modern Art, Paris, France/Lauros-Giraudon, Paris/Superstock; 114(b) CNAC/MNAM/Dist. Reunion des Musees Nationaux/Art Resource, NY;116 (b) (copyright) Romare Bearden Foundation/Licensed by VAGA, New York, NY/Memorial Art Gallery of the University of Rochester: Marion Stratton Gould Fund; (t) Chester Higgins, Jr.; 117 (t) (copyright) Romare Bearden Foundation/Licensed by VAGA, New York, NY/The Pennsylvania Academy of Fine Arts, The Harold A. and Ann R. Sorgent Collection of Contemporary African-American Art; 118 (b) (copyright) Tom Wesselmann/Licensed by VAGA, New York, NY/Burstein Collection/Corbis; 119 (t) Artist Rights Society (ARS), New York, NY/The Museum of Modern Art/Licensed by SCALA/Art Resource, NY; 121 (b) David Heald/Solomon R. Guggenheim Foundation, New York.

Unit 6:

122(t) Archivo Iconografico, S.A./Corbis; 124 (b) Anna Belle Lee Washington/Superstock; 126 (cl) Kurt Scholz/Superstock; (br) The Modernism Collection, gift of Norwest Bank Minnesota/The Minneapolis Institute of the Arts; 128 (c) Artist Rights Society (ARS), New York, NY/Beatricia Sagar/Superstock; 129 (t) Tanaya2/May Lee Clark Elementary School; 130 (b) Jan Butchofsky-Houser/Corbis; 131 (cl) Licensed by VAGA, New York, NY/Jose Fuste Raga/Corbis; (cr) Roger Ressmeyer/Corbis; 132 (t) Louise Freshman Brown/Superstock; 134 (cl) Museum Purchase - Nebraska Art Collection, Olga N. Sheldon Acquisition Trust and Friends of Sheldon Memorial Art Gallery; (br) Geoffrey Clements/Corbis; 136 (b) Artist of the Andes; (t) Nicario Jimenez; 137 (b) Nicario Jimenez; 138 (b) Huntington Library/Superstock; 139 (t) Linnea Design/Corbis; 141 (b) Artist Rights Society (ARS), New York, NY/The Andy Warhol Foundation/Art Resource, NY.

Backmatter:

Gallery of Artists:

178 (tl) The Granger Collection; (cl) Courtesy Illinois State Museum, photographer: Ernest Martin; (bl) Christopher Felver/Corbis; (tr) Chester Higgins, Jr.; (cr) Photograph by Steven Lopez/Courtesy Louis K. Meisel Gallery, New York; (br) Bettmann/Corbis; 179 (tl) Santa Barbara Historical Society Museum; (cl) Arnaldo Magnani/Liaison/Getty Images; (bl) Jean Gaumy/Magnum Photos; (tr) AP/Wide World Photos; (cr) Bettmann/Corbis; 180 (tl) Painting by Metzinger/Artists Rights Society (ARS), NY/Bettmann/Corbis; (cl) Painting by Metzinger/Artists Rights Society (ARS), NY/Bettmann/Corbis; (bl) The Alfred Stieglitz Collection/The Art Institute of Chicago; (tr) Artist Rights Society (ARS), New York, NT/Notman Photographic Archives/McCord Museum of Canadian History; (cr) Superstock; 181 (tl) Library of the National Museum of Fine Arts of Chile/Museo Nacional de Bellas Artes; (cl) Getty Images; (bl) Richard Schulman/Corbis; (tr) Karla Matzke/Jack Gunter; (cr) Peter Kinnear/Bridgeman Art Library; (br) Peter Harholdt/Corbis; 182 (tl) Bettmann/Corbis; (cl) National Portrait Gallery, Smithsonian Institution/Art Resource, NY; (tr) Artist of the Andes; (cr) Indiana University South Bend/Art Resource, NY; (br) Bettmann/Corbis; 183 (tl) Roger Viollet/Getty Images; (cl) Hulton Archive/Getty Images; (bl) Johanna Kriesel/Linnea Design; (tr) AKG Images; (cr) Succession, H. Matisse, Paris/Artists Rights Society (ARS), NY/AKG Images; 184 (tl) Richard Milici/Reynard Milici; (cl) James A. Sugar/Corbis; (bl) Reunion des Musees Nationaux/Art Resource, NY; (tr) AP/Wide World Photos; (cr) The Granger Collection; (br) Charles Moore/Stockphoto.com/Stock Photo; 185 (tl) National Portrait Gallery, Smithsonian Institution/Art Resource, NY; (cl) AP/Wide World Photos; (bl) Diana Ong/Superstock; (tr) AKG Images; (cr) Philadelphia Museum of Art/Corbis; (br) Patricia Polacco; 186 (tl) National Academy of Design, New York (1020-P)/Frick Art Reference Library; (cl) Francis G. Mayer/Corbis; (bl) Bettmann/Corbis; (tr) Erich Lessing/Art Resource, NY; (br) Many Ray/Artists Rights Society (ARS), NY/AKG Images; 187 Ann Mays/David Stewart; (bl) Smithsonian American Art Museum, Washington, DC/Art Resource, NY; (tr) Josephine Trotter/Connaught Brown Gallery; (cr) Michel Boutefeu/Getty Images; (br) Thomas Hoepker/Magnum Photos; 188 (tl) Reunion des Musees Nationaux/Art Resource, NY; (cl) Corbis; (tr) Artist Rights Society (ARS), New York, NY/Florence/Art Resource; (br) Artist Rights Society (ARS), New York, NY/Christopher Felver/Corbis.

For permission to reprint copyrighted material, grateful acknowledgement is made to the following sources:

Flint Public Library, 0126 East Kearsley, Flint, MI 48502-1994: "Wind Tricks" from *Ring a Ring o' Roses: Finger Plas for Pre-school Children,* Tenth Edition. Text copyright 1996 by Flint Public Library.

Houghton Mifflin Company: "The Sun" from *All About Me* by John Drinkwater.

Marian Reiner: "A Book" from *My Head Is Red and Other Riddle Rhymes* by Myra Cohn Livingston. Text copyright © 1990 by Myra Cohn Livingston. Published by Holiday House, Inc.

Marian Reiner on behalf of the Boulder Public Library Foundation, Inc.: "Waves of the Sea" from *Out in the Dark and Daylight* by Aileen Fisher. Text copyright © 1980 by Aileen Fisher.

205

Media & Techniques

Creating art is an exhilarating process of self-expression.

Children who are experienced in basic art techniques have the confidence to take risks and try new approaches, with surprisingly original pieces of artwork often resulting. Here are some brief descriptions of media and techniques suitable for students in elementary school.

• TYPES OF PAPER

BUTCHER PAPER

Available in wide rolls and several colors, this hard-surfaced paper is useful for murals and other large art projects.

CONSTRUCTION PAPER

Available in different colors, this paper is useful for crayon and tempera projects. It is easy to cut or tear, and can be used in collages and paper sculptures.

DRAWING AND PAINTING PAPER

This slightly rough paper is useful for drawing and watercolor painting projects, especially at the elementary level.

NEWSPRINT

This thin, inexpensive paper is good for sketching, printmaking, and making papier-mâché.

TISSUE PAPER

Available in bright colors, tissue paper is especially useful for making collages and for projects that require transparent color.

OTHER KINDS OF PAPER

Wallpaper and gift-wrapping paper can be cut into shapes and used in collages. Photographs in old magazines can be cut out and arranged into photomontages.

• ART BOARDS

POSTER BOARD

This lightweight, flexible art board comes in a variety of colors. It has a smooth, hard surface and is easily cut with dull scissors. It can be used for tempera painting projects, collages, and for mounting paper artworks.

CARDBOARD

Used boxes are a good source of cardboard. Pieces of cardboard can be used to back a framed artwork or to build three-dimensional forms. They can also be used as bases for sculptures. Teachers should use sharp scissors to cut boxes ahead of time.

FOAMCORE BOARD

This lightweight board is made by laminating a layer of foam between two pieces of poster board. Foam boards come in various thicknesses and are easy to cut. They are useful for mounting artwork and building three-dimensional forms.

MATBOARD

Matboard is a stiff, heavy, professional-quality board used for framing photographs and paper artworks. Matboards are cut with a razor-edge mat knife.

Closely supervise students when they are using hard or pointed instruments.

GLUE, STARCH, AND PASTE

WHITE GLUE

This nontoxic, creamy liquid comes in plastic squeeze bottles and in larger containers. It is recommended for use with cardboard, wood, cloth, plastic foam, and pottery. White glue causes wrinkling when used with paper, especially when too much is used.

POWDERED ART PASTE OR STARCH

Mixed to a thin, watery consistency, this material is recommended for use in making tissue-paper collages.

SCHOOL PASTE (LIBRARY PASTE)

Although this substance is nontoxic, young children like its smell and may be tempted to eat it. It should be used by the teacher for pasting pieces of paper onto other pieces of paper or onto cardboard. School paste and glue sticks are not recommended for more elaborate projects because they may not hold the materials together.

USING GLUE OR PASTE

1. Spread out sheets of newspaper.
2. Place the artwork to be glued facedown. Spread the glue or paste evenly from the center, using a finger or a piece of cardboard. Be sure the edges and corners of the paper are covered.
3. Lift the paper and carefully lay it in the desired position on the surface to which it will be affixed. Place a sheet of clean paper over the artwork and smooth it with the palm of the hand.

Starch and powdered art paste should be mixed by the teacher without students present.

DRAWING TOOLS AND TECHNIQUES

PENCILS

Many different effects can be created with an art pencil, depending on how it is held and how much pressure is applied. Art pencil leads vary from 6B, which makes the darkest, softest mark, to 9H, which makes the lightest, hardest mark.

Students can also achieve a variety of effects with regular number 2 or $2\frac{1}{2}$ pencils. Shading or making light and dark values can be made by using the flat side of the lead.

Colored pencils are most effectively used by first making light strokes and then building up the color to develop darker areas.

CRAYONS

When applied with heavy pressure, crayons produce rich, vivid colors. Always save crayon stubs. Allow students to unwrap them so they can experiment with using the side of the crayon rather than the tip.

Crayon etching is a technique in which layers of light-colored crayon are built up on shiny, nonabsorbent paper. The colors are covered with black crayon or black tempera paint that has been mixed with a small amount of liquid soap. Students must press hard with all the crayons to apply enough wax to the paper. With a toothpick, fingernail, or other pointed tool, students etch, or scratch away, the black layer to expose the colors or the white paper underneath **(Figure 1)**.

Figure 1. Crayon etching

OIL PASTELS

Softer than wax crayons, oil pastels produce bright, glowing color effects. Pressing an oil pastel hard on the paper creates rich, vibrant color; less pressure produces a softer color. Oil pastels smudge more easily than crayons. As with crayons, drawing can be done with the points or with the unwrapped sides, and students may wish to break their oil pastels in half.

Colors can be mixed by adding one over another or by placing dots of different colors side by side and blending them by rubbing.

COLORED MARKERS

Nonpermanent felt- or plastic-tipped markers are safe and easy to use, and they are available in a wide range of colors and sizes. They are useful for outdoor sketching, for making contour drawings, and for other art assignments. Dried-out markers can be renewed by running warm water on the tip.

PAINTING TOOLS AND TECHNIQUES

TEMPERA

Tempera paint works best when it has the consistency of thick cream. It is available in powder or, more commonly, liquid form. Tempera is opaque—the paper beneath cannot be seen through paint of normal consistency.

Tempera powder is available in cans or boxes, and it should be mixed in small amounts. Mix water and powder to the desired consistency. Tempera may be mixed with wheat paste to make a very thick paint for impasto painting. Dried-out tempera paint should not be used again.

Powdered tempera can irritate eyes and nasal passages during mixing. If you use powdered tempera, wear a mask and mix it ahead of time.

Liquid tempera is available in jars or plastic containers and is ready to use. Shake the container well before using. Keep a lid on the paint when it is not being used, and keep paint cleaned out of the cap to prevent sticking.

Some manufacturers supply helpful pouring spouts. If you use them, put a galvanized nail in the spout openings when not in use to keep them from stopping up.

WATERCOLORS

Watercolors should be softened ahead of time by placing a drop of water on each color cake. Paintings can be done with a dry or wet brush for different effects. Students may use the top of the open box to mix colors. Small, soft-bristle brushes are used with watercolors to achieve the transparent, fluid quality of the medium.

Interesting effects with watercolors include

- making a watercolor wash by painting a line and then smudging the line with a wet brush.
- blotting watercolors with crumpled paper.
- sprinkling salt on a wet watercolor picture.
- painting on wet paper.

BRUSHES

Choose well-made brushes with metal ferrules (the ring around the paintbrush shaft near the bristles). Ferrules should be tightly bonded to the handles so the bristles will not come off onto students' paintings.

Dozens of sizes and varieties of brushes are available, from nylon-bristle brushes to fairly expensive sable brushes. Students should have access to a wide variety of brushes—round and flat, thick and thin, square-ended and oval-tipped. After each art session, brushes should be cleaned in a warm solution of mild detergent and water. Students can experiment with other painting tools, such as toothbrushes, eye-makeup brushes, sponges, and cotton swabs.

PAINT CONTAINERS

Mixing trays or paint palettes can be made from many free or inexpensive materials, such as pie pans, muffin tins, plastic food trays, and paper plates. Egg cartons make good mixing trays because they can be closed, labeled with the student's name, and stored for later use.

When storing tempera paint in a mixing tray for later use, add a little water to keep the paint from drying out overnight. You can use a spray bottle to wet the paints before storing.

Always provide students with containers of water for cleaning their brushes while painting. Use plastic margarine containers or other small plastic tubs. Demonstrate for students how to rinse the brush in water before dipping it into a new color. Students can dry the brush as needed by stroking it across a folded paper towel.

Make your own portable paint holder by cutting holes in the lid of a shoe box. Place babyfood jars filled with paint into the openings.

COLOR-MIXING TECHNIQUES

When mixing **tints**, start with white and gradually add small amounts of a color to make the desired tint. When mixing **shades**, gradually add small amounts of black to a color.

Mix the **primary colors** (red, yellow, and blue) to create the **secondary colors** (green, orange, and violet).

- To make green, add small amounts of blue to yellow.
- To make orange, add small amounts of red to yellow.
- To make violet, add small amounts of blue to red.

To make **neutral colors**, such as brown, combine **complementary color pairs** (red plus green, yellow plus violet, blue plus orange).

PRINTMAKING TOOLS AND TECHNIQUES

Prints can be made from a wide variety of materials, including plastic foam meat trays with indented designs, dried glue lines on cardboard, and flat shapes or objects glued to cardboard.

The following technique may be used for printmaking:

1. Pour water-based printing ink on a plastic tray or a cookie sheet.
2. Roll a brayer or roller over the ink.
3. Roll the coated brayer over the printing surface until it is evenly covered. Roll first in one direction and then at right angles.
4. Place a piece of paper on top of the inked surface. Rub the back of the paper with the fingertips or the back of a spoon, being careful not to move it.
5. Pull the paper away from the surface. This is called "pulling the print." The print is ready to dry.

Even water-based ink stains clothing. Have students wear smocks or old shirts when they are making prints.

PRINTMAKING PAPER

Recommended paper for printing includes newsprint, construction paper, and tissue paper. Avoid using paper with a hard, slick finish because it absorbs ink and paint poorly.

To use paint instead of ink for a relief print, mix several drops of glycerine (available in drugstores) with one tablespoon of thick tempera paint. If brayers are not available, have students apply the ink or the paint with a foam brush.

CLEANUP

Drop a folded piece of newspaper into the pan filled with printmaking ink. Roll the brayer on the newspaper. This removes most of the ink from both the pan and the brayer. Lift the newspaper, refold it with the ink inside, and throw it away. Repeat until most of the ink is out of the pan, and then rinse the pan and the brayer at the sink.

ASSEMBLAGE

An assemblage is an artwork made by joining three-dimensional objects. It can be either free-standing or mounted on a panel, and it is usually made from "found" materials—scraps, junk, and objects from nature. Students can help you collect and sort objects such as

- carpet, fabric, foil, leather, paper, and wallpaper scraps.
- boxes in all sizes, film cans, spools, corks, jar lids.
- packing materials such as foam peanuts and cardboard.
- wire, rope, twine, string, yarn, ribbon.

SCULPTING TOOLS AND TECHNIQUES

Sculpture is three-dimensional art. It is usually made by carving, modeling, casting, or assembling. Sculptures can be created by adding to a block of material (**additive**) or taking away from a block of material (**subtractive**).

Materials recommended for additive sculpture include clay, papier-mâché, wood, and other materials that can be joined together.

Materials appropriate for subtractive sculpture in school include child-safe clay, wax, soft salt blocks, and artificial sandstone. Synthetic modeling materials are also available.

In the primary grades, salt dough may be substituted for clay in some art activities. Combine 2 cups of flour with 1 cup of salt. Add 1 cup of water and mix thoroughly. Press the mixture into a ball and then knead for several minutes on a board.

Foil offers interesting possibilities for sculpture and embossing. Heavy aluminum foil works best. In addition to making three-dimensional forms with foil, students can smooth it over textured objects to make relief sculptures or jewelry.

Wire, including pipe cleaners, telephone wire, and floral wire, is easily shaped and reshaped. Teachers should cut wire into pieces ahead of time. When using long wires, tape the ends to prevent injury. Students should wear safety goggles and sit a safe distance from each other.

PAPER SCULPTURE

Stiff paper or poster board, cut in a variety of shapes and sizes, yields colorful and inventive three-dimensional forms. For best results, students should always use glue, not paste, when assembling a paper sculpture. They can use a paper clip or tape to hold parts together while the glue is drying.

CLAY

Clay comes from the ground and usually has a gray or reddish hue. It is mixed with other materials so that it is flexible, yet able to hold a shape.

Oil-based clay is mixed with oil, usually linseed, and cannot be fired or glazed. It softens when it is molded with warm hands. When the clay becomes old and loses oil, it becomes difficult to mold and will eventually break apart. Oil-based clay is available in a variety of colors.

Water-based or wet clay comes in a variety of textures and can be fired to become permanent. It should be stored in a plastic sack to keep it moist until it is used. If the clay begins to dry out, dampen it with a fine spray of water. If it has not been fired, dried water-based clay can be recycled by soaking it in water.

Before firing, or baking clay in a kiln, there are two important considerations:

- Read and carefully follow the instructions for operating the kiln.
- Be certain that the clay has been kneaded before being molded to prevent air pockets that can explode during firing.

PREPARING CLAY

If clay is reused or made from a powder mix, knead thoroughly to remove air pockets.

- Take a chunk of soft clay and form it into a ball. Then use a wire cutting tool to cut the ball in half. From a standing position, throw the clay onto a tabletop to flatten it.
- Press down on the clay with the palms of both hands against a hard surface. Fold the clay, and press hard again. Keep folding and pressing in this manner until the air pockets have been removed.

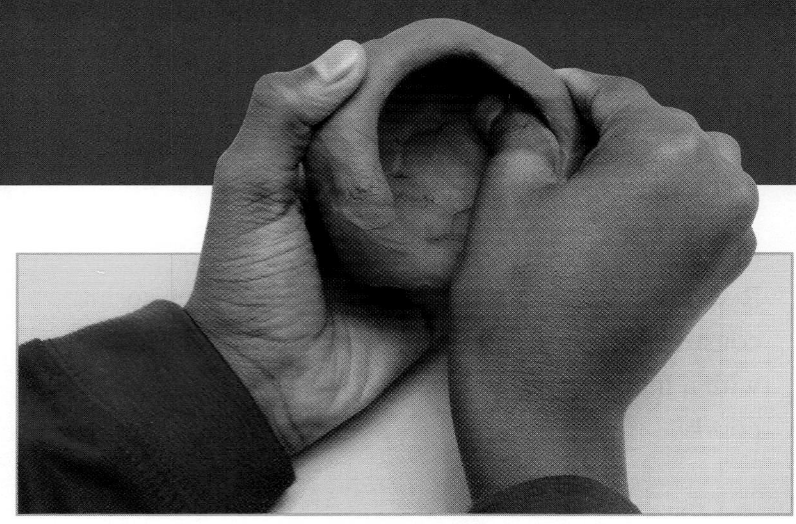

Figure 2. Pinch method

METHODS FOR MOLDING CLAY

Clay can be molded and formed using the pinch, slab, and coil methods.

- To make a pot using the **pinch method (Figure 2)**, mold a chunk of clay into a ball. Holding the ball in one hand, press the thumb in and carefully squeeze the clay between thumb and forefinger. Begin at the bottom, and gradually work upward and out. Continually turn the ball of clay while pinching it.
- To make a **slab**, use a rolling pin to flatten a chunk of clay between a quarter of an inch and half an inch thick. Shapes cut from the slab **(Figure 3)** can be draped over bowls or crumpled newspapers and left to dry. Clay shapes can also be joined together to form containers or sculptures.

Figure 3. Slab method

Textures can be added by pressing found objects, such as combs, coins, buttons, bottle caps, and other interesting objects, into the clay. Designs can also be etched with tools such as pencil points, paper clips, and toothpicks.

To create a **coil**, use the whole hand to roll a chunk of clay against a hard surface until it forms a rope of even thickness **(Figure 4)**. Ropes can be attached to each other and coiled into a shape, or they can be added to a slab base and smoothed out.

Figure 4. Coil method

Plastic spray bottles provide an easy way to keep clay pieces moist.

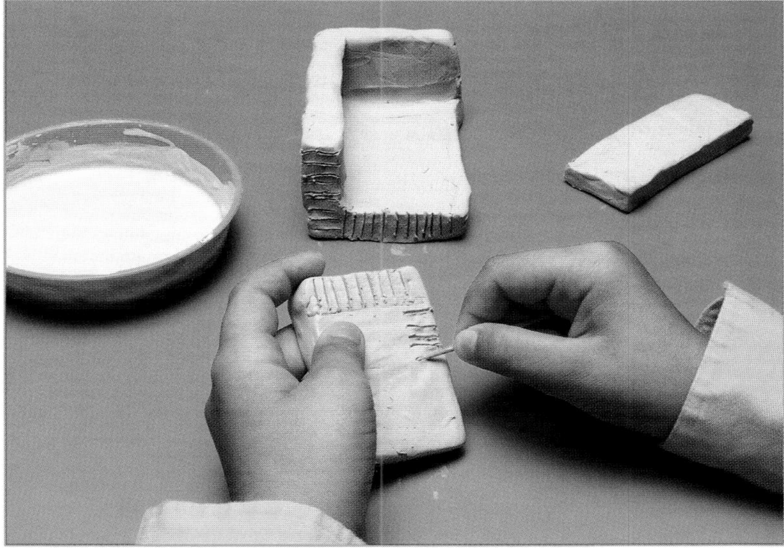

Figure 5. Joining clay pieces

JOINING CLAY TOGETHER

Oil-based clay pieces can be pressed together and blended with the fingertips.

Water-based clay pieces should be joined by **scoring**, or scratching the surface, of the adjoining pieces with the tip of a toothpick. Adding **slip**, or water-thinned clay, will make the two pieces adhere **(Figure 5)**.

Clean up dry clay with a wet cloth or a wet mop to keep silica dust from dispersing into the air.

PAPIER-MÂCHÉ

This art material is made by mixing paper pulp or strips with art paste or glue. It can be molded into three-dimensional forms or applied to a foundation form, or **armature**, then painted when dry.

Good forms that can be used as foundations for papier-mâché include inflated balloons, plastic bottles, paper sacks stuffed with newspapers, and wire armatures shaped into skeletal forms.

PREPARING PULP

Shred pieces of soft paper, such as newsprint, paper towels, or facial tissue, into small bits or thin strips. Soak them for several hours in water, then drain them, squeeze out the extra water, and mix the pulp with prepared paste until it reaches the consistency of soft clay. Let the mixture stand for an hour before beginning to work with it.

PREPARING STRIPS

Tear newsprint into long strips about one-half inch wide. Dip the strips into art paste or a white-glue mixture, and put down a layer of wet strips over the foundation form. Allow the piece to dry after every two layers of application. Continue putting strips on the form until there are five or six layers. This thickness is strong enough to support most papier-mâché projects.

Do not use pages from a printed newspaper to make papier-mâché. The printing inks may contain toxic pigments.

MAKING PAPER

Help children rip up scrap paper and put in a blender with water to make pulp. Pour it into a basin. Children can add things from nature like seeds, flower petals, or leaves. Dip a section of screen into the pulp and raise it up, covering it with a thin, even layer. Place a towel over the pulp, push on it to drain out the water, and flip it over carefully so that the layer of pulp is lying on the towel. Place another towel over the pulp and iron until it is dry. Spray on starch to make the paper easier to write on.

FABRIC ARTS

BATIK

The traditional batik method of dyeing fabric is a **wax-resist** technique. First, patterns are drawn on the fabric with wax. When the fabric is dyed, waxed areas resist the dye. When the wax is removed, the pattern emerges. To make an acrylic batik, draw patterns on the fabric with acrylic white paint, rather than wax. Then dye the fabric or brush it with a water-based paint. After it has dried, scratch the white paint off to reveal the pattern **(Figure 6)**.

Figure 6. Simple batik

WEAVING

A weaving is an artwork created on a **loom** by lacing together or interlocking strands of thread, yarn, or other materials. Simple square looms can be made by stretching thick rubber bands across stiff cardboard. Circular weavings can be made on looms formed from wire hangers bent into a circle. Students can weave a variety of materials through the loom, including ribbon, yarn, strands of beads, twine, and fabric strips **(Figure 7)**.

Figure 7. Weaving

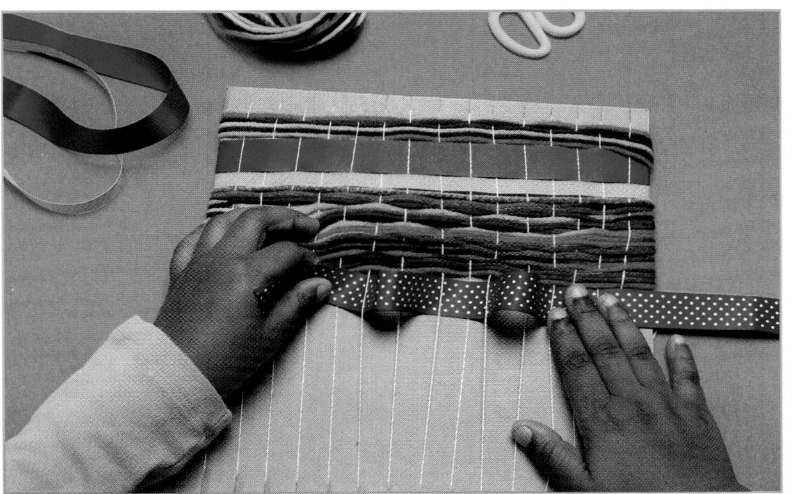

DISPLAYING ARTWORK

Frames usually improve the appearance of artwork, and they make attractive displays.

MOUNTING

The simplest kind of frame is a **mount**, or a solid sheet of paper or cardboard attached to the back of an artwork. It should be at least an inch larger than the work on all sides.

MATTING

A **mat** is a piece of paper or cardboard with a cut-out center. A picture is taped in place behind it, with the mat forming a border. Professional-style mats made from matboard should be cut only by the teacher.

To make a mat, use a piece of cardboard that extends two or three inches beyond the picture on all sides. On the back of the board, mark the position where the art is to be placed. Then measure one-fourth inch in from the outer edge of the artwork. This will make the picture overlap the cutout window on all sides.

FRAMING

Students can turn cardboard mats into finished frames. Have them paint and decorate a mat, attach their artwork to the back of it, and then attach a solid piece of cardboard to the back of the mat.

Teachers should work carefully when using a mat knife. Keep the blade pointed away from you, and retract the blade or return the knife to its container when not in use.

Meeting Individual Needs

Art instruction can be particularly useful in helping to meet a wide spectrum of individual needs in the classroom. Knowing some of the characteristics of the developmental stages in art can help teachers make better decisions concerning individual needs.

▲ **Preschematic Stage**

▲ **Late Schematic Stage**

STAGES OF ARTISTIC DEVELOPMENT

Students' interests and skills in art develop at different rates, just as they do in other disciplines. The following information describes five basic stages of artistic development. Of course, at any age, individual students may show characteristics of various stages.

Scribbling (2–4 YEARS)

- Children begin drawing disorganized scribbles, progress to controlled scribbling, and then advance to named scribbling.
- Children work with art materials for the joy of manipulating them.

Preschematic (4–6 YEARS)

- Drawings are often direct, simple, and spontaneous, showing what children believe is most important about the subject.
- There is usually little concern about technical skill or physical appearance, and color is selected for emotional reasons.
- There is little understanding of space, and objects may be placed haphazardly throughout pictures. The self often appears in the center.

Schematic (7–9 YEARS)

- An understanding of space is demonstrated in most drawings, and objects have a relationship to what is up and down.
- In drawings, a horizon becomes apparent, and items are spatially related.
- Exaggeration between figures, such as humans taller than a house, is used to express strong feelings about subjects.

Beginning of Realism (9–11 YEARS)

- Children begin using perspective.
- Overlapping objects and three-dimensional effects are achieved, along with shading and use of subtle color combinations.
- Drawings may appear less spontaneous than in previous stages because of the students' attempts at achieving realism.

Increasing Realism (11–13 YEARS)

- Students may value the finished product over the process.
- Students strive to show things realistically and in three dimensions.
- Perspective and proportion are used.

ESL

Art instruction provides an exceptional opportunity for English-language learners to build both language ability and self-esteem because of the abundance of visual images, hands-on experiences, and peer interaction involved.

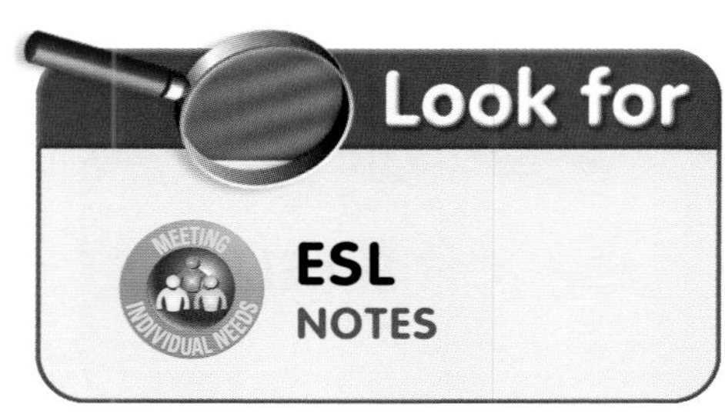

Strategies for Success

To help English-language learners:

Use physical movement and gestures, realia, and visuals to make language comprehensible and to encourage oral language development. You may want to use Harcourt's *Picture Card Collection* and *Picture Card Bank CD-ROM* to reinforce concepts visually.

Introduce concepts and words using rhymes and poetry. At Grades 1–3, you will find rhymes and poems in the unit openers.

Explain concepts, using the Grades 1–2 *Big Books* and Grades 1–5 *Art Prints*.

Encourage students to speak, but never force them to do so. All responses should be voluntary.

Display the *Posters of Elements, Principles, and Safety* in both English and Spanish. *Artist's Workshop Activities: English and Spanish* are also available.

EXTRA SUPPORT

Students may need extra support due to insufficient background experiences or home support or because of learning disabilities that affect the way they receive and process information. Some of the problems these students may have include difficulty in organizing work, expressing ideas through speech and language, following directions, or maintaining attention.

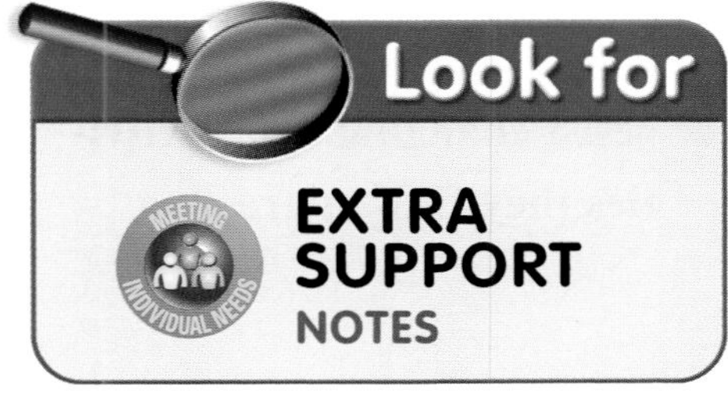

Strategies for Success

To help students who need extra support:

Involve students in setting goals and in determining rubrics.

Modify art instruction to meet students' learning styles.

Maintain a consistent art-program schedule.

Simplify complex directions or use fewer words to explain them.

Give students a desk copy of board work or directions.

Model directions for art activities.

Provide concrete examples of concepts and vocabulary to aid retention.

Review regularly what students have previously done or learned.

Allow student choice, and build on student interests.

KEEP IN MIND

Gifted children may

- **become bored with routine tasks.**
- **be overly critical of others or perfectionistic.**
- **dominate or withdraw in cooperative learning situations.**
- **resist changing from activities they find interesting.**

GIFTED AND TALENTED

Gifted and talented students are those who consistently perform at a high level in art.

Characteristics

When gifted and talented students produce art, they typically:

- show willingness to experiment and try new materials and techniques.
- appear keenly interested in the art of other artists.
- produce art frequently.
- show originality.
- display ease in using materials and tools.

Strategies for Success

Use these strategies with gifted and talented students:

Provide more challenging art assignments and projects. See the Challenge Activities in the *Teacher Resource Book*.

Enable students to participate in long-term projects in which they explore techniques or styles in depth.

Encourage and provide opportunities for individual exploration.

Challenge students with cross-disciplinary experiences in which they combine aspects of two disciplines, such as making a "sound collage."

Plan for additional outlets and audiences for students' work—in the community as well as at school.

Arrange for additional art opportunities, such as noon "drop-in" classes or after-school classes.

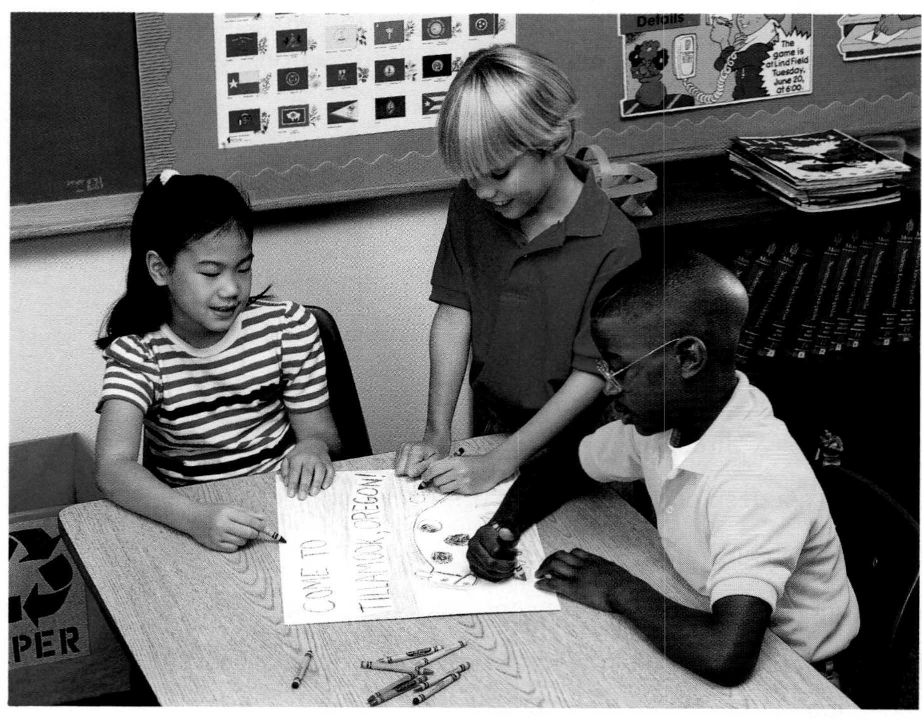

SPECIAL NEEDS

Special-needs students may have mobility, visual, or hearing impairments; be multiply disabled; or have behavioral or developmental disabilities. Art experiences can provide these students with unique opportunities to express their ideas and feelings and to improve their self-esteem and independence.

Strategies for Success

Here are a few of the many strategies you can use to help these students achieve success. Not all strategies work with all students or situations. Check individualized educational plans for each student's personal goals as well as the objectives of your curriculum.

Mobility Impairments

Consider whether a different medium might be easier to use, such as oil pastels instead of tempera paints.

Use assistive technology, or use or make adaptive devices. For example, for a student who has trouble gripping a crayon, place the crayon inside a foam curler.

Tape paper to the table to hold it in place while students draw.

Visual Impairments

Demonstrate for the child, allowing the student to touch your hands as you model.

Provide tactile materials in lieu of primarily visual ones, such as yarn for forming lines, clay for sculpting, and finger paints for painting.

Tape a shallow box lid or frame in the student's workspace, where the student's tools can be kept and easily located.

Hearing Impairments

Provide additional visual models.

Repeat demonstrations of skills, such as mixing colors.

Use signing, if known.

Behavioral Disabilities

Praise students for all tasks well done.

Provide opportunities for working with three-dimensional materials.

Make these students your helpers.

Developmental Disabilities

Explain each task separately, allowing it to be done before starting another.

Allow frequent opportunities for free drawing.

Repeat each direction, demonstrating it several times.

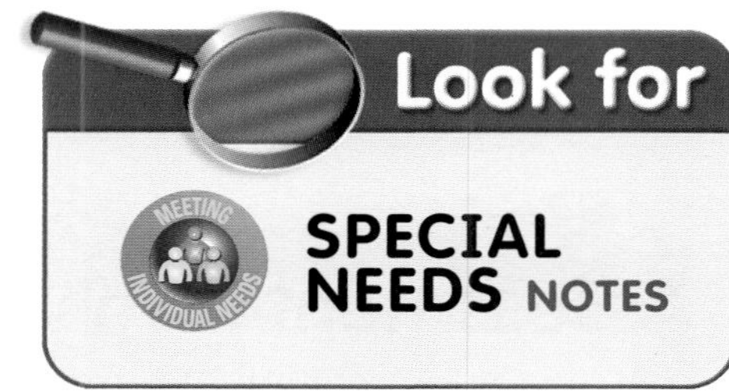

KEEP IN MIND

You may want to share the work of some artists with disabilities:

- **Chuck Close (mobility)**
- **Dale Chihuly (vision)**
- **Francisco Goya (hearing)**
- **Auguste Renoir (mobility)**
- **Frida Kahlo (mobility)**

For more information and resources:

- http://www.vsarts.org
- http://finearts.esc20.net/fa_forall.htm
- http://www.vsatx.org

Assessment Options

Assessment involves the selection, collection, and interpretation of information about student performance. The goal of assessment is to help students show what they know and what they can do. Effective assessment in an art program should include both creating and responding experiences that engage a variety of knowledge and skills in studio production, art criticism, art history, and aesthetics. Student learning may be demonstrated in products, paper-pencil format, and discussions or conferences.

Art Everywhere includes a variety of tools that teachers may use to construct a complete picture of a student's accomplishments.

TOOLS AND STRATEGIES

Student Edition Review and Reflect Pages

Use to determine whether the student

- Responds to questions of art and design using appropriate vocabulary through discussion, writing, and visual analysis
- Applies knowledge in art criticism, art history, and aesthetics

Two pages at the end of each instructional unit in the *Student Edition* provide exercises and activities for students to review and reflect upon the unit content. These activities encourage students to demonstrate their knowledge of visual art vocabulary, to apply reading and thinking skills to art, to write in response to art, and to describe, analyze, interpret, compare, and evaluate works of art.

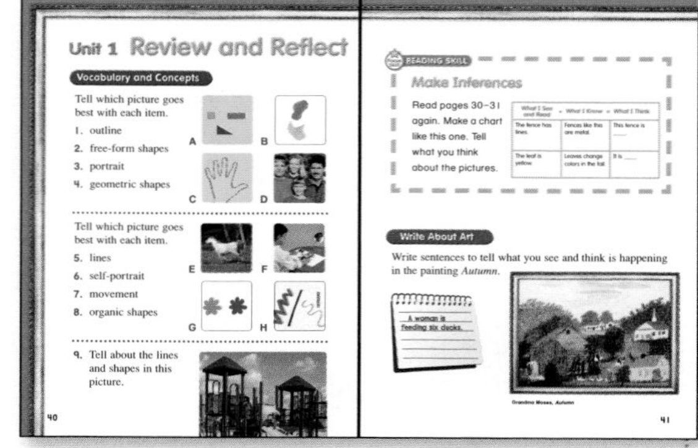

▲ Review and Reflect

Studio Production Activities

Use to determine whether the student

- Demonstrates and applies technical skills and control of media and tools in studio production
- Constructs and communicates meaning by using different media, techniques, and processes to communicate ideas and experiences and solve problems

The Artist's Workshop, a production activity in each lesson in the *Student Edition*, provides an opportunity for students to demonstrate technical skills and control of media and tools and to apply elements and principles taught in the lesson. The Artist's Workshop Rubrics on pages R30–R31 may be used to help students assess their own work and to discuss personal artworks with peers and the teacher. The completed forms may serve to guide a student-teacher conference or a student-student discussion.

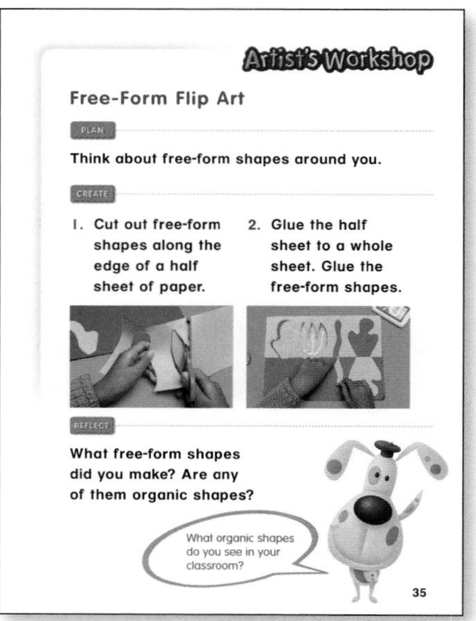

▲ Artist's Workshop

Unit Tests

Use to determine whether the student

- Uses appropriate vocabulary to respond to questions of art and design through discussion, writing, and visual analysis

The *Teacher Resource Book* includes a set of multiple-choice and short-answer questions, in blackline master format, which may be duplicated and used to assess students' knowledge of visual art vocabulary and concepts orally or in writing.

Portfolio

> Use to determine whether the student
> - Recognizes personal strengths and weaknesses and discusses own work
> - Constructs and communicates meaning by using different media, techniques, and processes

A portfolio, a purposeful collection of a student's work, provides a continuous record of a student's growth and learning. It is an effective strategy to be used to compare a student's current work to earlier work.

Organized chronologically, a portfolio benefits both the student and the teacher. Students reflect on their own growth and development as they self-assess and select materials to include in their portfolio. For the teacher, a portfolio provides a forum for a student-teacher discussion or conference. See page R32 for the Portfolio Recording Form.

Art Prints and Discussion Cards

> Use to determine whether the student
> - Responds to works of art and design, using appropriate vocabulary, through discussion and visual analysis
> - Identifies specific works of art as belonging to particular cultures, times, and places
> - Recognizes connecting patterns, shared concepts, and connections between and among works of art

The Discussion Cards, found on pages R34–R38, may be used to help students focus their thoughts as they view the program *Art Prints*. Each card provides a framework for students to respond to works of art and design using technical vocabulary appropriately and to demonstrate an understanding of the nature and meaning of artworks.

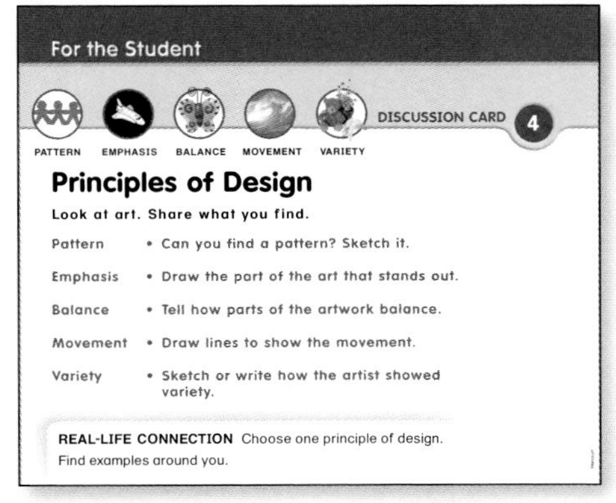

▲ Student Discussion Card

Observations

> Use to determine whether the student
> - Demonstrates and applies technical skills and control of media, tools, and processes
> - Applies art knowledge in art criticism, art history, and aesthetics

A checklist or inventory is one of the easiest tools for recording students' progress. Observe students at various times and in various circumstances, and record observations. The Progress Recording Form, found on page R33, is a checklist based on instructional objectives that may be used for monitoring students' acquisition of art skills and knowledge.

Self- and Peer Assessment

> Use to determine whether the student
> - Describes, analyzes, interprets, and judges or evaluates design or artwork done by self, peers, or other artists
> - Recognizes personal strengths and weaknesses and discusses own work
> - Responds to works of art and design, using technical vocabulary that describes visual experiences and supports assertions

Self-assessment helps students learn to reflect on their own artwork and on their strengths and weaknesses as artists. The Artist's Workshop Rubric for Self/Teacher Assessment, on page R30, provides a format for both the student and the teacher to assess student artwork and habits.

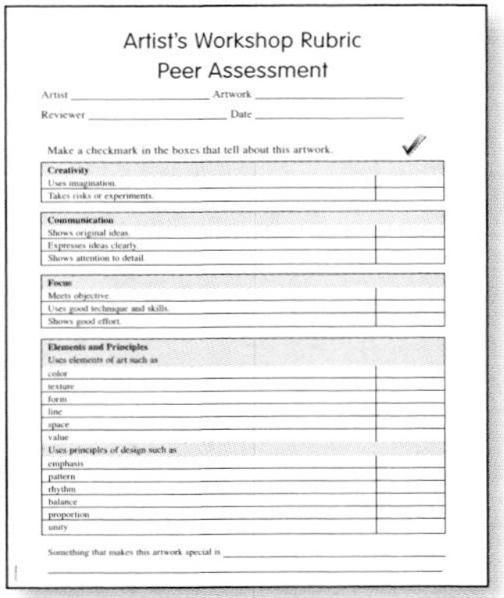

▲ Peer Assessment Rubric

Peer assessment provides students with a forum to share their ideas as artists and as viewers of art in a positive and constructive setting. In evaluating each other's work, students can use art-specific vocabulary and knowledge, exercise their art-response skills, and reflect on their own learning and development. Use the Artist's Workshop Rubric for Peer Assessment on page R31 to guide students' responses.

Artist's Workshop Rubric
Self/Teacher Assessment

Artist ______________________ Artwork ______________________

Teacher ______________________________ Date ______________

Knowledge and Skills	Rate your own work.	Teacher Rating
Creativity Work shows creativity. Work is imaginative and original.	☆ ☆ ☆ ☆	☆ ☆ ☆ ☆
Design Work shows application of art principles and elements.	☆ ☆ ☆ ☆	☆ ☆ ☆ ☆
Technique Shows skillful use of tools, techniques, and media.	☆ ☆ ☆ ☆	☆ ☆ ☆ ☆
Following Directions Stays on task. Completes activity as directed.	☆ ☆ ☆ ☆	☆ ☆ ☆ ☆
Work Habits Applies self to activity. Shows safe and proper use of tools.	☆ ☆ ☆ ☆	☆ ☆ ☆ ☆

Excellent	Above Average	Satisfactory	Unsatisfactory
☆ ☆ ☆ ☆	☆ ☆ ☆	☆ ☆	☆

Comments

Artist's Workshop Rubric
Peer Assessment

Artist ______________________ Artwork ______________________

Reviewer ______________________ Date ______________________

Make a checkmark in the boxes that tell about this artwork. ✔

Creativity	
Uses imagination.	
Takes risks or experiments.	

Communication	
Shows original ideas.	
Expresses ideas clearly.	
Shows attention to detail.	

Focus	
Meets objective.	
Uses good technique and skills.	
Shows good effort.	

Elements and Principles Uses elements of art such as	
color	
texture	
form	
line	
space	
value	
Uses principles of design such as	
emphasis	
pattern	
rhythm	
balance	
proportion	
unity	

Something that makes this artwork special is ______________________

____.

Portfolio Recording Form

Name ____

Artwork/Date Done	Notes

My portfolio includes

_______ plans or sketches.
_______ finished work.
_______ photos of finished work.
_______ writing about finished work.
_______ only my best work.
_______ some of my early artwork.
_______ artworks that show how I have improved.

My favorite artwork in my portfolio is ______________________________
because ____.

My least favorite artwork in my portfolio is ______________________________
because ____.

Progress Recording Form

Name ______________________ Teacher ______________________

Knowledge and Skills   Date

Perception						
Identifies sensory knowledge and life experiences as sources for ideas about visual symbols, self, and life events.						
Identifies art elements such as color, texture, form, line, space, and value and art principles such as emphasis, pattern, rhythm, balance, proportion, and unity in artworks.						
Creative Expression/Performance						
Creates artworks based on personal observations and experiences.						
Develops a variety of effective compositions, using design skills.						
Produces drawings, paintings, prints, constructions, ceramics, and fiberart, using a variety of art materials appropriately.						
Historical/Cultural Heritage						
Compares content in artworks from the past and present for various purposes such as telling stories and documenting history and traditions.						
Compares selected artworks from different cultures.						
Relates art to different kinds of jobs in everyday life.						
Response/Evaluation						
Identifies general intent and expressive qualities in personal artworks.						
Applies simple criteria to identify main ideas in original artworks, portfolios, and exhibitions by peers and major artists.						

Key: R = Rarely or never exhibits behavior
S = Sometimes exhibits behavior
C = Consistently exhibits behavior

Comments

TEACHER DISCUSSION CARD 1

Looking at Art

1. **Have students describe the subject and details in the artwork.**
   - What do you see? What is happening here?
2. **Use prompts such as these to encourage students to talk about the artwork's elements, principles, materials, and meaning.**

   ELEMENTS
   - What kinds of shapes do you see? **SHAPE**
   - Where do you see tints and shades? **VALUE**

   PRINCIPLES
   - What part of the artwork do you notice first? **EMPHASIS**
   - What is repeated in the artwork? **PATTERN**

   MATERIALS
   - What is the artwork made of? **MEDIA**
   - How was this artwork created? **TECHNIQUE**

   MEANING
   - What feeling does the artwork express? **IDEAS AND FEELINGS**
   - Why do you think the artist created the artwork? **PURPOSE**
3. **Present historical information about the artwork and artist, as appropriate.**

TEACHER DISCUSSION CARD 2

Art Criticism

DESCRIBE

1. **Have students describe the subject of the artwork and share facts about what they see. Ask:**
   - What is the subject of the artwork? Does the artwork show people, a place, an object, or something else?
   - What details do you see in the artwork?

ANALYZE

2. **Students should describe how the artist used the elements of art and the principles of design. Ask questions such as these:**
   - What kinds of lines, shapes, and colors do you see?
   - How did the artist create movement?

INTERPRET

3. **Have students discuss the artist's message or the mood of the artwork. Ask:**
   - Does the artwork tell a story? Does it show a mood? How?
   - What do you think the artist wanted to tell viewers about the subject?

EVALUATE

4. **Have students give reasons for their opinions about the artwork. Ask:**
   - Do you think the artist clearly expressed a mood or message? Explain.
   - What will you remember most about this artwork? Why?

STUDENT DISCUSSION CARD 3

Elements of Art

Line
- Name as many kinds of lines in the artwork as you can.

Shape
- What geometric shapes did the artist use? Do you see any organic shapes? Describe them.

Form
- What geometric forms or organic forms do you see?

Color
- Name the colors you see in the artwork. Where did the artist use warm or cool colors?

Value
- Where did the artist use shades and tints of a color?

Texture
- Does the artwork have tactile texture or visual texture? Describe the texture.

Space
- How did the artist show depth?

STUDENT DISCUSSION CARD 

Principles of Design

Proportion
- How did the artist show proportion?

Pattern
- What lines, shapes, or colors are repeated?

Movement
- How do your eyes move around the artwork?

Emphasis
- What part of the artwork do you notice first?

Balance
- How did the artist create balance?

Unity
- Explain how the parts of the artwork work together.

Rhythm
- What feeling do repeated lines, shapes, colors, or patterns create in the artwork?

Variety
- How did the artist use different lines, shapes, and colors to create variety?

STUDENT DISCUSSION CARD 5

Portraits

1. Describe Who is the subject of the portrait? What details do you notice?

2. Analyze How did the artist use line and color? Describe how the artist used proportion in the subject's face.

3. Interpret What do you think the subject of this portrait is thinking or feeling?

4. Evaluate Have you ever felt the way the subject seems to feel? Explain.

STUDENT DISCUSSION CARD 

Landscapes

1. Describe What objects are included in the landscape? What time of year do you think it shows?

2. Analyze How did the artist create a sense of depth? What part of the landscape seems closest to you? What part seems farthest away?

3. Interpret What mood or feeling does this landscape express?

4. Evaluate Would you like to visit the place shown in this artwork? Why or why not?

For the Student

STUDENT DISCUSSION CARD 7

Stories

1. **Describe** Describe the characters you see in this artwork. What are the characters doing? Where are they? What story does the artwork tell?
2. **Analyze** How do your eyes move around the artwork? What part of the artwork seems most important?
3. **Interpret** Does the scene in this artwork show the beginning, middle, or end of a story? Explain.
4. **Evaluate** What do you think of the way the artist told this story?

STUDENT DISCUSSION CARD 8

Abstract Art

1. **Describe** Describe what you see in this artwork. Is the artwork two-dimensional or three-dimensional? What is it made of?
2. **Analyze** What kind of balance did the artist use? How did the artist create a feeling of unity?
3. **Interpret** What ideas do you think the artist was trying to express?
4. **Evaluate** What do you think of the way the artist showed his or her subject? What part of this artwork do you think is most interesting?

STUDENT DISCUSSION CARD **9**

Art Criticism

1. Describe Describe what you see. What is happening in this artwork?

2. Analyze What kinds of lines, shapes, forms, or colors did the artist use? How did the artist organize them in the artwork?

3. Interpret Do you think the artwork has a message? Tell what you think it is.

4. Evaluate Would you tell a friend to visit a museum to see this artwork? Why or why not?

STUDENT DISCUSSION CARD **10**

Community Art

1. Describe What kind of artwork is this? What is its subject?

2. Analyze How did the artist use shapes, form, or space?

3. Interpret Does the artwork tell anything about the community? Explain.

4. Evaluate Do you think this artwork fits in with its community? Why or why not? Would you want this artwork displayed in your community? Explain.

Materials

	UNIT					
	1	2	3	4	5	6
PAPER						
butcher paper			●			
construction paper, assorted colors	●	●		●		●
graph paper					●	
paper, white	●	●	●	●	●	●
sketchbook	●	●	●	●	●	●
tagboard (or file folders)			●		●	
watercolor paper				●		
PAINTING, DRAWING, PRINTMAKING						
crayons	●	●		●		
markers	●	●	●	●		
oil pastels			●		●	
paintbrushes	●	●	●	●	●	●
pencils	●	●	●	●	●	●
pencils, colored	●	●	●	●	●	●
small containers to hold paints/water	●	●	●	●	●	●
tempera paints	●	●	●	●	●	●
watercolor paints		●		●		
CLAY						
carving tools (toothpicks, paper clips, craft sticks, etc.)	●		●			●
clay	●		●			●
paper bags	●					●

continued

OTHER MATERIALS	UNIT 1	2	3	4	5	6
audiocassette of instrumental music	•					
cardboard		•				
cotton swabs					•	
craft sticks			•			
fabric scraps and felt material			•		•	
found objects						•
glue or glue sticks	•	•	•		•	•
household sponges	•					
magazines and books			•	•		•
mirror			•			
objects (natural objects, classroom objects, textured objects, clothespins, paper clips, buttons, cardboard tubes, etc.)	•					•
paper bags	•					•
paper plates		•			•	•
ruler		•				•
scissors	•	•	•		•	•
shoe boxes and other small boxes						•
table salt				•		
tape		•				
weaving and fiberart materials (yarn, ribbons, string)		•	•			

FREE AND INEXPENSIVE MATERIALS

GENERAL CLASSROOM MATERIALS	WHERE TO FIND THEM
artificial flowers, leaves	fabric stores, department stores, craft stores
building materials (dowels, scrap lumber, wood shavings, bricks, screws, nuts, bolts)	contractors, builders, lumberyards
carpet scraps, foam	carpet manufacturers and retailers
fabric scraps, ribbon, yarn	fabric stores, craft stores
hangers	discount department stores, consignment shops, thrift stores
leaves, woodchips	local lawn services
magazines, catalogs, and newspapers	libraries, bookstores
packing supplies (Styrofoam™ noodles, cardboard scraps, bubble wrap, etc.)	storage and moving suppliers
shoe boxes	shoe stores, discount department stores
straws, napkins	fast food or restaurant chains
Styrofoam™	packing supply stores, hardware stores, retail stores
tile (damaged, samples, seconds)	hardware/paint stores, plumbers, tile manufacturers
wallpaper samples	home improvement stores, discount stores
watercolor paints, regular paints	art supply stores, school resources
wire	television repair shops, florists, hardware stores, plumbers, telephone/power companies
wood scraps	home improvement stores, lumberyards

TECHNOLOGY RESOURCES

Visit *The Learning Site*
www.harcourtschool.com

Link Bank for Teachers

- Links to museum sites
- Links to sites that offer free and inexpensive materials
- Links to key educational organizations

Alternative Planners

TEACHING BY MEDIA

The following chart shows the pages you can use if you wish to teach with the same media across different grades.*

MEDIA	PAGES GRADE 1	GRADE 2	GRADE 3	GRADE 4	GRADE 5
Clay	73, 89	87, 93	39, 127	105	71, 135
Colored Pencils/ Crayons/Markers	27, 35, 39, 75, 93, 109, 129	27, 29, 39, 59, 79, 109, 113, 135, 139	27, 29, 49, 67, 89, 95, 99, 107, 139	31, 91, 125, 131, 155, 161, 165	31, 35, 65, 91, 105, 121, 141, 171, 195
Computers	--	57	--	201	201
Drawing Pencils/ Charcoal	93	39, 115, 133	29, 67, 89, 95, 99, 107,	75	--
Fiber/Textiles	87, 129	75, 135	55, 73, 75, 119	121	185
Found Objects	79, 87, 95, 127	67, 75, 79, 95, 109, 119	135	191	111
Oil Pastels	49	55, 73, 109, 113, 115, 139	69, 109	81, 95, 151	151, 155
Paper/Foil/Tissue Paper	33, 59, 69, 93, 109, 127, 129, 135, 139	27, 29, 33, 35, 47, 67, 69, 75, 79, 107, 113, 127	33, 119, 133	51, 65, 125, 131, 195	121
Photographic Imagery	133	113	133	51, 161, 195	45
Tempera Paints	29, 47, 53, 55, 67, 107, 113, 115, 127	39, 47, 49, 53, 69, 99, 107, 119, 129, 133	35, 47, 53, 79, 93, 113, 115, 129, 135	35, 41, 45, 61, 71, 125, 135, 141, 171, 181, 185, 191	41, 131
Watercolors	99, 119, 135	59, 99, 107, 139	59, 87	71	51, 61, 81, 95, 101, 125, 161, 165

* See also **Challenge Activities**, *Teacher Resource Book*.

TEACHING BY ELEMENTS AND PRINCIPLES

The following chart shows the pages you can use if you wish to teach the same elements and principles across different grades.

ELEMENTS & PRINCIPLES	PAGES GRADE 1	GRADE 2	GRADE 3	GRADE 4	GRADE 5
Balance	106–107, 108–109, 110–111, 120	112–113, 114–115, 116–117, 118–119	106–107, 108–109, 112–113, 120–121	122–125, 128–131, 132–135, 138–141, 159, 162–165	148–151, 152–155, 158–161, 162–165
Color	42–43, 46–47, 48–49, 52–53, 54–55, 58–59, 60	46–47, 48–49, 50–51, 52–53, 54–55, 58–59	30–31, 46–47, 48–49, 50–51, 52–53, 60–61, 72–73, 94–95, 98–99, 106–107, 114–115	38–41, 42–45, 48–51, 58–61, 68–71, 152–155, 159, 183, 193–194, 198–199	38–41, 42–45, 48–51, 98–101, 148–151, 158–161, 162–165, 168–171, 178–181, 183–185, 188–191, 193, 200
Emphasis	102–103, 112–113, 114–115, 118–119, 120	106–107, 108–109, 110–111	94–95, 98–99, 100–101	78–81, 182–185	88–91, 158–161, 163–164, 169, 194
Form	82–83, 86–87, 88–89, 92–93, 94–95, 96–97, 100	86–87, 88–89, 90–91, 92–93, 94–95, 96–97	38–39, 40–41, 98–99, 134–135	102–105, 108–111	72–75, 78–81, 132–135
Line	26–27, 28–29, 30–31, 32–33, 36–37, 40	26–27, 28–29, 58–59	26–27, 28–29, 30–31, 40–41, 72–73, 92–93, 94–95, 106–107	28–31, 62, 149, 153–154, 183, 193–194, 198	28–31, 32–35, 58–59, 102–105, 130, 162
Movement	28–29, 68–69	28–29, 72–73	68–69, 78–79, 80–81	158–161, 168–171	93–94, 163, 192–195
Pattern	58–59, 62–63, 66–67, 68–69, 70–71, 76–77, 80	66–67, 68–69, 70–71, 72–73, 74–75, 78–79	72–73, 74–75, 77, 79, 80–81	118–121, 128–131	58–61, 68–71
Proportion	– –	98–99, 108–109	66–67, 80–81	88–91, 92–95	92–95, 103, 119, 124, 125
Rhythm	62–63, 66–67, 68–69, 76–77, 80	72–73	128–129, 132–133, 140–141	98–101	178–185, 189–191, 192–195
Shape	32–33, 34–35, 36–37, 38–39, 40, 86–87	32–33, 34–35, 36–37, 38–39, 86–87	30–31, 32–33, 34–35, 36–37, 40–41, 72–73, 74–75, 92–93, 94–95, 112–113, 126–127	32–35, 48–51, 79, 92–95, 99, 183, 198–199	28–31, 32–34, 58, 62–65, 148–151, 152–155
Space	94–95, 96–97, 98–99, 100	88–89, 92–93, 94–95, 96–97, 98–99	86–87, 88–89, 91, 92–93, 97, 100–101	102–105, 148–151, 152, 155	68–71, 89–91, 92–95, 98–101, 103, 164
Texture	62–63, 72–73, 74–75, 78–79, 80	74–75, 78–79	54–55, 58–59, 60–61, 94–95, 118–119	62–65, 72–75, 160, 198, 200	129–131, 135, 198
Unity	122–123, 132–133, 136–137, 138–139, 140	126–127, 128–129, 130–131, 132–133, 134–135, 138–139	114–115, 118–119, 120–121	158–161, 162–165, 168–171, 178–181, 188–190, 192	152–155
Value	42–43, 52–53, 54–55, 60	52–53, 58–59	52–53, 60–61, 115	58–61, 62–65, 68–71, 72–75, 78, 183, 200	38–41, 48–49, 129, 159, 168–171, 199
Variety	122–123, 126–127, 128–129, 130–131, 136–137, 140	132–133, 134–135, 138–139	126–127, 129, 132–133, 134–135, 138–139, 140–141	178–181, 182–185, 188–191, 192–195, 198–201	178–181, 182–185, 189–191

Encyclopedia of Artists and Art History

These pages provide additional information about the artists and art history terms in this grade level.

Abstract Expressionism Mid-twentieth-century extension of abstract art characterized by an emotional approach to artistic concepts. Abstract art consists of colors and forms for their own sake, rather than to depict reality. Abstract Expressionism flourished in New York City from the mid-1940s to the mid-1950s and influenced the development of art in Europe. Painters practice Abstract Expressionism to express personal emotions and to implement unstructured techniques rather than conventional structured composition. They use different techniques to emphasize color and the physical quality of paint to express emotion in an abstract composition. Painting techniques include making sweeping, slashing brushstrokes, dripping or spilling paint directly onto the canvas, and spreading large areas of flat, thin paint over the typically large canvas. The most prominent Abstract Expressionists include Jackson Pollock and Willem de Kooning.

American Scene Painting Twentieth-century movement in American painting that concentrated on realistic art with social content. *American Scene Painting* is a term used to describe art that included scenes of everyday American life. It developed between 1920 and 1942 as a reaction against the influence of European modern styles and rejected radical abstract styles. The American Scene Painting style can be found in the works of Edward Hopper and Charles Burchfield.

Archipenko, Alexander [ar•kih•PENG•koh] (1887–1964) Russian-born American sculptor known for his innovative three-dimensional works. Archipenko was born in Kiev, Ukraine, which was then part of the Russian Empire. He studied in Kiev, Moscow, and briefly in Paris, before he rejected traditional training and began teaching himself by studying sculptures in the Louvre. Archipenko created collage sculptures using wood, glass, and other materials. He also invented "sculpto-painting," in which three-dimensional forms project from a painted background. Archipenko immigrated to the United States in 1923 and became a citizen in 1928. He founded art schools in New York, Los Angeles, and Chicago. *Images by this artist: Student Edition p. 38.*

Armin, Emil [AR•min, ay•MEEL] (1883–1971) Romanian-born American artist best known for his Post-Impressionist paintings of life in urban Chicago. As a child, Armin carved wooden canes and ornaments, and he liked to draw. He left Romania at the age of twenty-one and immigrated to the United States, attending night classes at the Art Institute of Chicago. During the Depression, Armin worked as an easel painter for the Works Progress Administration. His painting *The Open Bridge* shows his style of using strong brushstrokes. Armin's modern style reflected the influence of French Post-Expressionist and German Expressionist painters. *Images by this artist: Student Edition p. 28.*

Art Deco Twentieth-century French design movement that originated in mass-produced pieces of decorative art such as furniture, jewelry, pottery, textiles, and graphics, as well as in architecture. First exhibited in Paris in 1925, Art Deco developed into a major style and became popular in the United States and Europe during the 1920s and 1930s. Designers developed Art Deco as a reaction against Art Nouveau, a style that favored natural lines and shapes. Designers used geometric shapes, smooth lines, and streamlined forms. They used a variety of natural materials that included jade, silver, ivory, and rock, as well as industrial materials such as plaster, chrome, and stainless steel.

Baroque Term used to describe a style that developed mainly in Italy around 1580 and influenced many forms of art in Europe for more than a century. The Baroque movement spread to western Europe and Latin America, undergoing modifications as it migrated. Artists rebelled against the restrained, orderly, and symmetrically balanced art of the Renaissance period. Painters and sculptors used dramatic details and ornate forms to convey grandeur, realism, illusion, movement, and emotion. Architects designed buildings to create an illusion of great space. The Baroque style can be found in the works of Giovanni Lorenzo Bernini, Caravaggio, and Diego Velázquez.

Bartlett, Jennifer (1941–) American installation artist, painter, printmaker, and sculptor born in Long Beach, California. Bartlett is renowned for her visual images that appear to move back and forth. Her 1976 piece titled *Rhapsody* contains 988 variations of mountains, trees, oceans, and houses on painted steel panels. In 1997, she was commissioned to create a display for Ronald Reagan Airport in Washington, D.C. For that work, Bartlett reworked paintings as glass collages, using gold, silver, and platinum leaf and paint on glass panels that are displayed in the airport public concourse. *Images by this artist: Student Edition p. 106.*

Bearden, Romare [BEER•duhn, roh•MAIR] (1911–1988) American artist best known for his vibrant collages depicting African American life and culture. Bearden was born in Charlotte, North Carolina. His family moved to New York City when he was a child, and Bearden grew up during the height of the Harlem Renaissance. Bearden graduated from New York University with an education degree in 1935, the same year he began to paint. For years he worked at nine-to-five jobs, studying and practicing his art in his spare time. Bearden held his first solo exhibitions in the 1940s. He received critical praise but made few sales, and he continued to study art and experiment with medium and style. Bearden achieved his greatest success in the 1960s, when he began producing colorful semi-abstract collages assembled from newspaper and magazine photographs, often enlarged, and painted paper on canvas. From the 1960s until his death in 1988, Bearden worked productively and was widely recognized as an important contemporary artist. *Images by this artist: Student Edition pp. 116–117; Art Print 15.*

DID YOU KNOW?

While he developed his artistic talent, Romare Bearden worked as a semi-professional baseball player, a newspaper political cartoonist, and a New York City social worker. He was also a successful songwriter who had several of his songs recorded by popular artists.

Bell, Charles (1935–1995) American photorealist and still-life painter. Born in Tulsa, Oklahoma, and based in New York City, Bell created almost 200 works of art during his lifetime. Bell painted his subjects as much as ten times their actual size, and he used the clearest and brightest colors that can be attained in oil painting. *Images by this artist: Student Edition p. 58.*

Benton, Thomas Hart (1889–1975) Painter and muralist who was part of the American Regionalist movement of the 1930s. Benton, who was born in Neosho, Missouri, studied for a year at the Art Institute of Chicago and then in Paris and New York. His early works were abstracts, but by 1920, he had rejected modernism and begun painting straightforward, recognizable scenes based on American history, daily life, folktales, and song lyrics. He used strong colors and dark, dramatic outlines, depicting people and objects with distorted, almost cartoon-like features. Benton received commissions to paint numerous murals for public buildings, including the New School for Social Research in New York City, the Missouri State Capitol in Jefferson City, and the Truman Presidential Museum & Library in Independence, Missouri. He settled in Kansas City, Missouri, in the mid-1930s and is said to have died with a paintbrush in his hand. *Images by this artist: Student Edition p. 44.*

DID YOU KNOW?

At five feet three inches tall, Thomas Hart Benton was so small that he is said to have bought his clothes from boys' shops his entire life.

Borg, Carl Oscar (1879–1947) Swedish-born painter best known for his paintings of California landscapes and the Native Americans of the Southwest. Borg was born in Dals-Grinstad and immigrated to the United States in 1901. Phoebe Hearst, a wealthy arts patron, arranged for Borg to live with local Native Americans. He painted scenes of their ceremonies and everyday lives. Borg taught at the California Art Institute and the Santa Barbara School of Art. *Images by this artist: Student Edition p. 91.*

Botero, Fernando [boh•TAY•roh] (1932–) Colombian painter and sculptor best known for his depictions of rotund human and animal figures and his design of monumental bronze sculptures. Botero was born in Medellín. As a child, he was inspired by pre-Columbian art, Spanish colonial art, and the murals of Diego Rivera. While studying art in Madrid, Botero painted copies of masterpieces that hung in local museums and sold them to tourists. In his own work, he experimented with proportion and size and developed his own unique style of painting. Botero used flat, bright colors and boldly outlined forms mimicking the style of Latin American folk art. He eliminated the appearance of brushstrokes and gave his paintings a smooth appearance. Botero gained international recognition, and his paintings and sculptures command high prices. *Images by this artist: Student Edition p. 34.*

Bronze Age Cultural period during which bronze became the principal metal used to make tools and weapons. The Bronze Age flourished between 3500 and 3000 B.C. in the Near East and Southeast Asia. However, it did not develop in all regions at the same time. The Bronze Age of the Aztecs, for example, occurred in the fifteenth century. The development of metal use coincided with the rise of urbanization and the requirement for specialized laborers such as artisans. Around 3000 B.C., Aegean artisans began producing pottery, marble figures, and jewelry. They built palaces with wall paintings called frescoes and painted symbols of daily life such as flowers, children, and animals on their pottery.

Calder, Alexander [CAWL•der] (1898–1976) American sculptor and painter best known as the creator of the mobile—a type of kinetic, or moving, sculpture. Calder was born in Pennsylvania. He became expert at single-line drawing, a technique that led him to make wire sculptures that were three-dimensional extensions of his drawings. In Paris in 1926, Calder created a miniature circus of moving toys, which attracted such artists as Joan Miró, Piet Mondrian, and Marcel Duchamp. A visit to Mondrian's studio in 1930 inspired Calder's switch to pure abstraction in his work. He created what he called "moving Mondrians," pieces in which metal shapes, delicately balanced and suspended from wires or cords, move with the air currents. Duchamp dubbed these moving sculptures "mobiles." Nonmoving variations were "stabiles." From the late 1930s until his death, Calder produced mobiles and stabiles—many of them tremendous in size—for public spaces around the world. *Images by this artist: Student Edition p. 104.*

DID YOU KNOW?

Beginning in 1972, Alexander Calder designed and painted the outside of two full-sized passenger jets for Braniff International Airlines.

Carroll, Mary Ann (1940–) African American painter who was the only female member of a Florida folk art group called the Highwaymen. This group, led by artist A. E. Backus in the 1950s, painted Florida landscapes to make extra money. They sold their exotic, intensely colored artworks from the trunks of their cars. Early buyers included motel and office building workers in need of cheap decoration. The pieces quickly became popular with local shops and tourists looking for inexpensive Florida-themed gifts. Interest grew in the Highwaymen as a folk art movement, and their works are credited with shaping Florida's popular image. Carroll was born and raised in central Georgia before a family move took her to Fort Pierce, Florida. Carroll, who was already a talented hobby artist, learned oil painting in 1959. Like the rest of the Highwaymen, she discovered that painting paid far better than other work available to them. *Images by this artist: Art Print 11.*

Chihuly, Dale [chih•HOO•lee] (1941–) American artist renowned as a maker of art glass. Born in Tacoma, Washington, Chihuly enrolled in the first glass program in the country at the University of Wisconsin. He continued his studies at the Rhode Island School of Design, where he established a glass program. He cofounded the Pilchuck Glass School in Washington, which became known as the international center for the development of glass as a fine art. Chihuly created many series of glass works, including *Baskets, Persians,* and *Seaforms.* He also designed several architectural installations, including the Chihuly Bridge of Glass in Tacoma, Washington. *Images by this artist: Student Edition p. 38.*

Christo and Jeanne-Claude (1935–) Husband-and-wife artistic team known for their installation art. Christo Javacheff was born in Bulgaria on the same day that Jeanne-Claude (formerly de Guillebon) was born in Casablanca. The pair specializes in *empaquétage*—wrapping objects in materials ranging from canvas to plastic. Their work is distinguished by its gigantic size. An example is *Running Fence*—an 18-foot-tall ribbon of fabric that extended twenty-four miles through two counties in California in the 1970s. *Images by these artists: Student Edition p. 99.*

Cliff, Clarice (1899–1972) English pottery designer known for her "Bizarre" ware household pottery. Cliff was born in the Staffordshire pottery district of central England. She left school at age thirteen to learn freehand pottery painting as an apprentice and by age seventeen was employed at the AJ Wilkinson, Ltd.

pottery company. In 1928, Cliff launched what she called "Bizarre" ware, a line of white pottery in unusual geometric shapes hand-painted in vibrant, almost abstract, florals and landscapes. A huge hit in British department stores, "Bizarre" ware and Clarice Cliff were household names throughout the 1930s. Since her death, her coffee and tea services, vases, sugar sifters, platters, and other pieces have become extremely popular collectibles. *Images by this artist: Student Edition p. 126.*

Cubism Movement in twentieth-century painting and sculpture developed jointly by Pablo Picasso and Georges Braque from around 1907 to 1914. Cubists reacted against the Impressionists' use of color and their style of painting from a single viewpoint. Cubists paint a subject in multiple viewpoints. The Cubist style is divided into two categories—analytical and synthetic. In analytical Cubism, painters use monochromatic colors and fragmented geometric shapes to place subjects in different presentations in a composition. Synthetic Cubists use color and the technique of collage to give texture and illusion to the painting. Other artists who have worked in the Cubist style include Robert Delaunay and Juan Gris.

Dada Twentieth-century artistic and literary movement originating in Switzerland in 1916 that protested traditional values and pretension in the art world and focused on the absurd. It flourished from 1916 to 1922 in Switzerland, New York, and Berlin. Dadaists were not united by a common style. They organized to protest World War I, traditional art, and the established values of society. Artists practiced Dada to shock and provoke the public with absurd and illogical works of art. Dadaists abandoned traditional forms of painting and sculpture and replaced them with collage, photomontage, objects, and ready-mades, or items chosen by the artist and put into an artistic context. They believed that art should be a group activity and involve accident and chance, rather than fine materials and craftsmanship. The Dada style can be found in the works of Kurt Schwitters, Man Ray, and Marcel Duchamp.

Davis, Stuart (1894–1964) American painter who combined elements of European avant-garde art, especially Cubism, with American themes—everyday objects and places, jazz music, mass-produced products, and lettered signs—into a distinctly American contemporary style. Davis was born in Philadelphia where, through his art enthusiast parents, he got to know Robert Henri and others who later led the Ashcan School of painting. At the age of nineteen, Davis was the youngest exhibitor in the fabled Armory Show of 1913, where his watercolors hung alongside those of contemporary European masters including Wassily Kandinsky, Paul Gauguin, Vincent van Gogh, and Henri Matisse. Davis's mature works also included murals (several of which were commissioned in the late 1930s by the WPA's Federal Art Project), collages, and prints. *Images by this artist: Art Print 10.*

Delaunay, Robert [duh•loh•NAY] (1885–1941) French painter, considered one of the earliest to paint purely abstract, or nonrepresentational, works. Delaunay's paintings combined the fragmented forms of Cubism with his own contribution—the use of vibrant color and a sense of dynamic, rhythmic motion. He may be best known for his series of "color Cubism" paintings of the Eiffel Tower. Delaunay's study of the effects of color on the senses led him, with his wife, painter and designer Sonia Delaunay, to develop a style known as Orphism. Orphists emphasized the effects of color and contrasts between colors over representation. *Images by this artist: Student Edition p. 46.*

Delaunay, Sonia [duh•loh•NAY] (1885–1979) Russian-born painter, printmaker, and designer who spent her youth in St. Petersburg. At the age of twenty, Delaunay moved to Paris, where she studied painting and printmaking, visited galleries, and studied the work of well-known artists of the day. Collaborating with her husband, French painter Robert Delaunay, Sonia Delaunay produced abstract paintings that emphasized the harmonious juxtaposition of pure color over representation. During the 1920s, she designed sets and costumes for stage and screen and dressed celebrities. The Great Depression hurt her business, and in the 1930s, Delaunay turned back to painting. She continued to paint, exhibit, and design, and remained an active supporter of abstract art until her death. *Images by this artist: Student Edition p. 114.*

Dougherty, Patrick (1945–) American sculptor known for his huge, swirling constructions of woven tree saplings, installed in locations around the world, most of them outdoors. Dougherty was born in Oklahoma and raised in North Carolina, which is still his home. He was in his thirties before he took up art as a career, sculpting first in clay and then turning to sticks as a plentiful, renewable resource. His sculptures, which he describes as three-dimensional drawings made with sticks instead of pencil lines, have a life span of one to two years before they begin to dry out and break apart; they are then recycled into wood chips and compost. *Images by this artist: Art Print 6.*

Dove, Arthur G. (1880–1946) American painter, considered one of the first abstract painters in the United States. Dove worked as a freelance magazine illustrator, traveling to Paris, where he studied the work of artists who included Paul Cézanne and Henri Matisse. He translated landscapes and nature scenes into small-scale abstracts in muted colors. Dove lived most of his life in New York City. *Images by this artist: Student Edition p. 61.*

Duncanson, Robert Scott (1821?–1872) African American painter best known for his landscapes. Duncanson is thought to be the first African American artist to make a living by painting as well as the first to become internationally known. Duncanson was born in New York, but was educated in Canada. As an adult, Duncanson returned to the United States and taught himself to paint by producing portraits and copying works by the Hudson River School of landscape artists. He exhibited in Cincinnati and painted eight large landscape murals in the house that is now Cincinnati's Taft Museum. Duncanson traveled widely and became known in Europe and Canada as well as in England and Scotland, where he spent the Civil War years. *Images by this artist: Student Edition p. 87.*

Egyptian art Art of ancient Egypt, from about 3000–300 B.C. The purpose of Egyptian art was to glorify kings and honor the deceased by burying them with personal belongings. Evidence of this idea was discovered in the early 1920s when King Tut's tomb was opened, revealing personal treasures that included jewelry, weapons, and a mask made of gold and decorated with gems. Egyptian art is renowned for the sculptures and wall paintings that adorned the tombs within the pyramids. The wall paintings depicted the pursuits of the king and his family. Egyptians used a unique system of writing called hieroglyphs, in which symbols represented ideas and sounds. These symbols were often carved in stone and were an important feature of Egyptian art.

Expressionism Late nineteenth- and early twentieth-century artistic movement that is reflected in European art, film, music, literature, and theater of the time. Artists practiced Expressionism to convey emotion, in contrast with Realism. Painters use jarring colors, rapid brushwork, and jagged lines to express emotions such as joy, sadness, fear, or horror. Expressionism can be found in the works of artists such as Vincent van Gogh, Wassily Kandinsky, Franz Marc, and Paul Klee.

Fauvism Early twentieth-century artistic movement originating in France. Fauvism flourished in Paris from 1905 to 1907. It is considered the first avant-garde European art movement. Like the Impressionists, Fauvists painted scenes directly from nature, but they rejected the way Impressionists used color. Fauvist painters use pure, brilliant, luminous colors straight from the tube and then aggressively apply them to the canvas in broad, flat areas. They also use rough brushstrokes, thick outlines, and contrasting hues, and they often leave areas of the canvas exposed. Painters practice Fauvism to create a feeling of space and light. The Fauvist style can be found in the work of Henri Matisse.

Folk art Natural art style that conveys simplicity in art while expressing the beliefs and interests that a group of people share. Folk art has been created in numerous countries for hundreds of years, but American folk art gained popularity from 1780 to 1860. It represents everyday life and includes pottery, carving, needlework, weaving, quilting, and other decorative art forms. This art style can be found in the works of Grandma Moses and Horace Pippin.

Freshman-Brown, Louise American painter, photographer, educator, and mixed-media artist. Freshman-Brown studied painting and printmaking at Syracuse University. She is best known for collages that mix photographs and other media to depict widely varying images, from bright florals, landscapes, and underwater scenes to dark and brooding assemblages relating the darker themes of human behavior. *Images by this artist: Student Edition p. 132.*

Gauguin, Paul [goh•GAN] (1848–1903) French painter whose innovative style influenced the development of modern art. Gauguin was born in Paris. By young adulthood, he had lived in Lima, Peru and spent six years sailing the world in a merchant marine service. Between 1871 and 1883, Gauguin lived a typical middle-class life in Paris. He worked as a stockbroker, married, had five children, and developed an interest in collecting art and painting. In 1891, Gauguin left France on a government grant to paint the people and customs of Tahiti. Three years after his death, a Paris exhibition of nearly 300 of his paintings brought his work to the attention of a new generation of artists. His bold use of color and rejection of Realism inspired both the Fauvist and Expressionist movements. *Images by this artist: Art Print 1.*

DID YOU KNOW?

In 1888, Paul Gauguin spent two months in Arles, France, where he worked with Vincent van Gogh. The two appreciated each other's art but quarreled bitterly about almost everything else.

Gehry, Frank O. (1929–) Canadian-born architect and designer renowned for designing buildings that resemble free-form sculptures constructed with inexpensive materials. Born in Toronto, Gehry immigrated to California with his family in 1947. He studied architecture at the University of Southern California and city planning at Harvard University. Gehry designed the Experience Music Project museum in Seattle, Washington. He constructed a fabricated steel frame wrapped in colorful sheet metal around the building. As a result, the museum had the shape of a guitar. Gehry has won many prestigious awards, including the Pritzker Architectural Prize in 1989. *Images by this artist: Student Edition p. 131.*

Gogh, Vincent van *See* Van Gogh, Vincent.

Gordon, Arturo (1883–1944) Chilean-born painter known for his use of bright colors and the treatment of light as an independent element in his paintings. Gordon studied art under several great masters and was part of a group of painters who rejected the artistic style of Academic Naturalism that dominated Chilean art. Gordon's style of using partial disintegration of forms, colored shadows, and an emphasis on luminosity has been compared to French Impressionism. In addition to landscapes, Gordon painted scenes from the daily life of the poor, festivals, popular dances, and religious subjects. *Images by this artist: Student Edition p. 86.*

Gris, Juan [GREES] (1887–1927) Spanish painter, sculptor, stage designer, graphic artist, and major figure in Cubism. Gris was born in Madrid, the thirteenth of fourteen children. When he was about eighteen, Gris moved to Paris, where one of his neighbors was the young Pablo Picasso. For four years, Gris supported himself by producing illustrations for newspapers and magazines. He did not begin painting seriously until 1910, but by 1912, he was recognized as a leading painter of the Cubist movement. Between 1913 and 1914, Gris developed his own style of Cubism, called synthetic Cubism. Where Picasso and other Cubists started with objects and broke them down into shapes, Gris started with shapes and transformed them into recognizable objects. Gris was plagued by a variety of health problems. He died in France at the age of forty. *Images by this artist: Student Edition p. 112. See also* **Cubism.**

Grooms, Red (1937–) American painter, sculptor, filmmaker, and performance artist. Grooms is best known for the "sculpto-pictoramas" he has created since the 1970s. They are large assemblages of cartoon-like, three-dimensional figures arranged into elaborate scenes from city life. Born Charles Rodgers Grooms in Nashville, Tennessee, Grooms's red hair earned him his nickname. Grooms began painting at an early age and exhibited at a local gallery while he was still in high school. In the 1950s and 1960s, Grooms collaborated on a series of unscripted, nonverbal performances called "happenings." He also produced more than a dozen short films and has made prints and bronze sculptures. Many of Grooms's works depict scenes from life in New York City, where he still lives and works. *Images by this artist: Student Edition p. 92.*

Gunter, Jack American egg tempera painter from Washington state. Gunter has also worked in photography, ceramics, and pottery and exhibits his art in a museum-like setting at the Pilchuck School near his home. In 1995, he co-created a panoramic mural that portrayed turn-of-the-century Stanwood, Washington, in a fun, humorous way. *Images by this artist: Student Edition p. 59.*

Harlem Renaissance Cultural movement inspired by a group of artists, writers, and musicians in the New York City neighborhood of Harlem during the1920s. The goal of the Harlem Renaissance was to use art as a means of change. The movement represented social and intellectual freedom, and its supporters encouraged African Americans to celebrate their heritage while searching for new methods of self-expression. The Harlem Renaissance gained recognition with scholarships and philanthropic grants but declined during the Great Depression, when many of Harlem's residents relocated. This art movement is illustrated by the work of Romare Bearden.

Hepworth, Dame Barbara (1903–1975) British sculptor who was one of the earliest abstract sculptors in England and among the most influential sculptors of the mid-1900s. Hepworth worked in wood, stone, and later in metal, especially bronze. She is best known for smooth, gently curved forms in which hollowed out spaces or holes through the solid masses are as important as the solid masses themselves. Hepworth often brought attention to those voids by painting inside them, stretching strings or wires across them, or placing smaller objects inside them. She was internationally known by the 1950s and received numerous commissions for large public works. *Images by this artist: Student Edition p. 37.*

Hiroshige, Ando (other first names also include Ichiryusai or Ichiryusu or Utagawa) [hee•roh•shee•gay] (1797–1858) Japanese painter and printmaker, renowned for his full-color landscape prints. Hiroshige was born in Edo, Japan (present-day Tokyo). As a child, Hiroshige liked to sketch. The prints of the great artist Katsushika Hokusai inspired him to become an artist. His most successful print series, titled *Fifty-three Stages on the Tokaido,* was made from sketches about life along the Tokaido highway connecting the ancient Japanese cities of Edo and Kyoto. Hiroshige's technique of using sweeping brushstrokes to suggest vast landscapes influenced the Impressionist movement. *Images by this artist: Student Edition p. 88.*

Homer, Winslow (1836–1910) American painter, illustrator, and lithographer, known as the era's leading representative of Realism. Homer was born in Boston and grew up in Cambridge, Massachusetts. In 1855, he became a lithographer's apprentice; he then moved on to work as a freelance magazine illustrator. In 1859, the magazine *Harper's Weekly* hired Homer and eventually made him an artist-correspondent covering the Civil War. After the war, Homer focused on oil painting. His early oils were inspired by his wartime illustrations and were somber in color. His masterpiece from the period, titled *Prisoners from the Front,* was praised as the most powerful painting to come out of the Civil War. During the 1860s and 1870s, Homer began painting in watercolor, choosing rural or idyllic scenes of farm life as his subjects. He eventually moved to the Maine coast, and the sea became the leading subject of his paintings. He also traveled to Canada and the Caribbean to paint seascapes. Homer's paintings are characterized by their directness, realism, objectivity, and splendid color. *Images by this artist: Student Edition pp. 96–97; Art Print 12.*

DID YOU KNOW?

Winslow Homer was twenty-four years old when he received his first important assignment with *Harper's Weekly*. He had to sketch Abraham Lincoln's first inauguration.

Hopper, Edward (1882–1967) American painter and illustrator best known for his realistic paintings of American life, and one of the founders of the American Scene movement. Hopper was born in Nyack, New York. He studied painting under Robert Henri, a Realist painter and leader of the Ashcan School. Around 1920, Hopper and other artists, including Thomas Hart Benton and Grant Wood, joined together in a Nationalist school dedicated to painting American scenes. His artistic style included the use of strong patterns of light and shade, simple large geometric forms, bright cool colors, and the omission of distracting details in his compositions. *Images by this artist: Student Edition p. 82. See also* **American Scene Painting.**

Hudson River School Nineteenth-century artistic movement originating in American art. The Hudson River School flourished primarily in New York City from 1825 to 1870. It is an association of artists who rejected European styles of painting and represented the first native movement of American Art. The Hudson River School artists painted landscapes using realistic compositions, accurate details, and sketches to paint romantic views of wilderness areas. Some artists use contrasts of light and dark called luminism to convey emotion.

Impressionism Late nineteenth-century artistic movement that flourished in France from 1860 to 1900. The Impressionists were a group of artists with different styles who exhibited their work together. They reacted against traditional painting techniques and the Romantics' belief that paintings should portray emotion. Impressionists attempt to capture the visual impression made by a scene, usually a landscape or city scene painted outdoors. Their primary goal is to show the effect of natural light and color on a subject and quickly transmit it to the canvas. Painters use unmixed bright, soft colors applied with swift, loose brushstrokes to intensify luminosity and brilliance. The Impressionist style can be found in the works of Claude Monet, Pierre-Auguste Renoir, Edgar Degas, and Mary Cassatt.

Japanese Ukiyo-e [oo•kee•oh•ay] Genre that existed in Tokyo from the seventeenth to the nineteenth centuries. *Ukiyo-e* translates to "pictures of the floating world" and refers to freedom from the cares of the world. Screen paintings were the original artworks done in this style, but the woodblock prints were the medium for which Ukiyo-e gained recognition. These prints were renowned for their rich quality and designs as well as for their vibrant colors, even though the first prints were produced in black and white. The prints gained popularity as interest in everyday urban life and personal experience grew. They showed scenes from the theater, restaurants, and other forms of entertainment. The prints influenced Edgar Degas and the movements of Impressionism, Post-Impressionism, and Art Nouveau. This art style can be found in the work of Ando Hiroshige.

Jimenez, Nicario Peruvian mixed-media folk artist. Jimenez was born in a peasant community in the Andes mountains and was raised in Ayacucho, Peru. Known as "the Artist of the Andes," Jimenez produces a contemporary version of the centuries-old retablo art form. Retablos are portable boxes filled with rows of figurines arranged into scenes that tell a story. The figures are made from a dough-like mixture of boiled potatoes and clay or plaster. Once dry, they are painted and assembled into ornately decorated boxes. Unlike ancient retablos, which often told stories about saints or other religious figures, Jimenez's retablos relate stories of the history, culture, and current events of his people. Today, Jimenez lives and works in Naples, Florida. *Images by this artist: Student Edition pp. 136–137.*

Johnson, William H. (1901–1970) American painter best known for his vivid, primitive scenes of African American life, culture, and history. Johnson was born in Florence, South Carolina. He showed artistic talent at an early age, and when he dropped out of school to help support his family, he earned money by drawing cartoons for local newspapers. At age seventeen, he followed an uncle to New York City. Johnson worked at odd jobs until he had saved enough money to enroll in art school. His work impressed supporters, who paid for his further training, including a three-year stint in Paris. There, he learned from the popular artists of the day and exhibited Expressionist-style paintings. He returned to the United States in 1930, where his work won prestigious awards. Johnson's style evolved to include bold, contrasting colors; heavy, black outlines; and figures with exaggerated, even cartoonish features. *Images by this artist: Student Edition p. 35.*

Kahlo, Frida (1907–1954) Mexican painter noted for her self-portraits and primitive artistic style. Kahlo was born in Coyoacan, Mexico. She never planned to become an artist, wanting instead to go to medical school. However, devastating injuries in a traffic accident left her permanently disabled. During her slow recovery, Kahlo taught herself to paint. She painted mostly self-portraits and still lifes. In 1929, Kahlo married Diego Rivera, Mexico's most famous artist. Rivera encouraged Kahlo to focus on her Mexican heritage as the subject of her paintings. In her second self-portrait, Kahlo portrayed herself in traditional Mexican folk dress. She used bright colors in her paintings to create a mixture of realism and fantasy. Throughout her life, she refused to let her physical problems interfere with her art. *Images by this artist: Student Edition p. 66.*

DID YOU KNOW?

As a result of her accident, Frida Kahlo endured thirty-two operations. At one exhibit of her paintings, Kahlo was too ill to leave her bed, so she had it moved into the gallery in order to become a part of the exhibit.

Kandinsky, Wassily [kan•DIN•skee, vuh•SEEL•yee] (1866–1944) Russian-born painter and writer who is renowned as one of the most important pioneers of abstract art. Kandinsky was born in Moscow. He admired the work of Paul Gauguin and was also influenced by an exhibition of Islamic art, which does not permit showing images of human figures. In 1910, he painted his first abstract watercolor. Kandinsky, along with artist Franz Marc, founded an Expressionist art movement called the Blue Rider group. His early paintings were expressive, colorful compositions with figures. In his later work, figures gradually disappeared. Describing how he came to understand the power of nonrepresentational art, or art without figures, Kandinsky said that one night he failed to recognize one of his paintings because it was upside down. Seeing it that way, he began to appreciate how light transformed the shapes and colors. He decided that the figures in a painting should not be recognizable. *Images by this artist: Student Edition pp. 30–31; Art Print 2.*

Klee, Paul [KLAY] (1879–1940) Swiss-born painter, printer, teacher, and writer, best known for creating a modern artistic style combining elements of fantasy and satire. Klee was born near Bern to parents who were musicians, and he studied art at the Academy of Fine Arts in Munich, Germany. He continued his artistic education by visiting Italy and Paris. While in Germany, Klee met Expressionist artists Wassily Kandinsky and Franz Marc. He began to participate in their Blue Rider art group, where he was exposed to the use of bright colors and a childlike way of painting. Klee painted on paper or small canvases using a variety of materials, including chalk and crayons. He used bright colors as well as figures, numbers, and letters as symbols. In his abstract pieces, however, he used only colors and shapes. Klee is remembered as one of the most individualistic figures of twentieth-century art. During his life, he produced more than 9,000 works. *Images by this artist: Student Edition p. 102; Art Print 14.*

Kriesel, Johanna American designer. Kriesel studied art history in Italy and designed many of the zany props for Disney's *Bill Nye the Science Guy* television show. She has also designed websites for various companies and, since 1997, has worked at Linnea Designs, where she recently completed projects for the Discovery Channel and the World Wildlife Fund. *Images by this artist: Student Edition p. 139.*

Locker, Thomas (1937–) American landscape painter and children's book illustrator born in New York City. Locker has illustrated approximately thirty books, some of which he also wrote. His drawings, brought to life with vibrant colors and unique textures, express his love of nature. Locker's artwork has been exhibited in well-known galleries in London and in cities in the United States. He received his bachelor's degree in art history from the University of Chicago and his master's degree in painting from American University. *Images by this artist: Student Edition p. 12.*

Malevich, Kasimir [muh•LAY•vich, kuh•ZEE•mir] (1878–1935) Russian painter who pioneered geometric abstract art. Born in Kiev, Malevich taught himself to paint when he was a child. In art school, Malevich studied modern art. His early paintings showed the influence of Cubism and Futurism. Malevich later moved away from representational art and developed a form of abstract painting that uses geometric simplicity, with the elements of color, line, and shape shown on a white background. He added tilting rectangles, colors, and overlapping forms to his paintings. After experimenting with this style for a few years, Malevich gave up abstract painting and pursued writing and teaching. *Images by this artist: Student Edition p. 121.*

Matisse, Henri [mah•TEES, ahn•REE] (1869–1954) French painter, sculptor, and graphic artist. Matisse is widely considered the greatest French painter of the twentieth century and one of the major figures of contemporary art. Matisse did not become interested in art until he was in his twenties when, against his father's wishes, he left law school to become an artist. He studied in Paris, where the work of Paul Cézanne, Claude Monet, Paul Gauguin, and other revolutionary artists influenced him. Matisse experimented with their styles as he developed his own. He emphasized color and line over the realistic depiction of people and objects. A 1913 New York show that introduced Matisse and other contemporary European artists to the United States only enhanced his reputation, and he was soon one of the world's best-known—and best-paid—living artists. Until about 1920, Matisse divided his time between a studio in Paris, another in Nice on the French Riviera, and his family home in the Paris suburbs. By the 1940s, Matisse's eyesight was failing, and arthritis limited the use of his hands. During this time, he experimented with what he called "drawing with scissors," producing compositions of cut paper that today are among his most recognizable works. *Images by this artist: Student Edition pp. 22, 26. See also* **Fauvism.**

DID YOU KNOW?

Henri Matisse suffered from an attack of appendicitis in 1890. While he was recovering, his mother gave him a set of oil paints to help him pass the time. "Henceforth," he later wrote, "I did not lead my life. It led me."

Meem, John Gaw (1894–1983) American architect who was a principal designer and promoter of Southwestern regional architecture. Meem was born in Pelota, Brazil, to American parents who were serving as missionaries there. Meem contracted tuberculosis in 1920 and recuperated in a sanatorium in Santa Fe, New Mexico, where he first developed an interest in architecture. When he recovered, Meem traveled to Denver, Colorado, to work and study. By 1924, he had opened an architectural firm in Santa

Fe, where he worked for thirty-six years. Meem combined elements from Pueblo and Spanish colonial architecture to develop the classic Santa Fe style, which he translated into churches, homes, government offices, and university buildings throughout New Mexico. *Images by this artist: Student Edition p. 130.*

Milici, Reynard (1942–) Photorealist born in Brooklyn, New York. Milici received his bachelor of fine arts degree from Connecticut's Hartford Art School. He is best known for his portrayal of townscapes. *Images by this artist: Student Edition p. 94.*

Miró, Joan [mee•ROH, hoh•AHN] (1893–1983) Spanish painter, sculptor, printmaker, etcher, and lithographer best known as one of the leaders of Surrealism. Miró was born in Barcelona and worked as an accountant for two years before deciding to become a full-time artist. In 1919, Miró visited Paris, where he studied the paintings of Pablo Picasso and the Fauvists. He also associated with the Surrealists and joined their movement. Miró's artistic technique combined elements of folk art, the bright colors of Fauvism, and the expressive lines and odd geometric forms of Cubism. Miró's Surrealist painting *Harlequin's Carnival* features humorous insect-like creatures dancing and playing instruments. He said, "I begin painting and as I paint the picture begins to assert itself, or suggest itself, under my brush." Miró wanted his artwork to be available to the public. In 1947, he painted a large mural for the Terrace Hilton Hotel in Cincinnati. He also painted a mural for Harvard University. Miró continued to experiment with new media, and he took up stained-glass design when he was in his eighties. *Images by this artist: Student Edition p. 41. See also* **Surrealism.**

Mondrian, Piet [MAWN•dree•ahn, PEET] (1872–1944) Dutch painter who specialized in pastels, oils, and watercolors. Mondrian experimented with the techniques of different art movements, including Impressionism, Symbolism, and Cubism. In 1917, he cofounded the *De Stijl* group, from which the abstract style of Neo-plasticism stems. Neo-plasticism focuses on the use of primary colors, straight lines, and basic geometric shapes. Mondrian felt that the combination of these features suggested a sense of balance and harmony. His paintings are characterized by smooth surfaces and are free of visible brushstrokes. *Images by this artist: Art Print 17.*

Monet, Claude [moh•NAY] (1840–1926) French painter renowned as the leader of the Impressionist movement. Born in Paris, Monet spent his childhood in Le Havre, France. In 1862, he moved back to Paris to study art. There, he met several other artists, including Pierre-Auguste Renoir. In 1874, Monet and his friends held an independent exhibition of their paintings, including Monet's landscape titled *Impression: Sunrise*. That apparently inspired one art critic to call the entire exhibition Impressionist, which gave the movement its name. The Impressionists attempted to capture a visual impression of a scene, especially the effect natural light has on the setting. Monet painted the same view many times to capture the light at different times of the day, as can be seen in his *Rouen Cathedral* series. Monet once said, "I want the unobtainable. Other artists paint a bridge, a house, a boat, and that's the end. They are finished. I want to paint the air which surrounds the bridge, the house, the boat, the beauty of the air in which the objects are located, and that is nothing short of impossible." Despite failing eyesight, Monet continued to paint until his death. *Images by this artist: Student Edition p. 84; Art Print 4. See also* **Impressionism.**

Moore, Henry (1898–1986) English artist regarded as one of the greatest sculptors of the twentieth century. Moore was born in Castleford, a coal-mining town near Leeds. He admired Michelangelo and wanted to become a sculptor. Moore liked to visit the British Museum to study the art of the indigenous peoples of Africa and Mexico. He worked in wood, stone, cement, and bronze. His study of ancient American art helped him develop his style. Moore rejected the classic Renaissance treatment of human form. Smooth, organic shapes and holes in the solid mass of his sculptures characterize his work. Moore became an important figure in the English Surrealist movement. In 1948, he won the International Sculpture Prize. *Images by this artist: Student Edition pp. 70–71; Art Print 9.*

Moses, Grandma (Anna Mary Robertson) (1860–1961) American painter best known for her folk art paintings. Grandma Moses was born Anna Mary Robertson in Greenwich, New York. Robertson had no formal art training. She married Thomas Salmon Moses in 1887, and the couple became farmers. Moses loved to work in needlepoint, and she won prizes for her embroidery. After her husband's death in 1927, she began to paint full time. Her first art exhibition was held in a drugstore in Hoosick Falls, New York, where an art collector discovered her work. In 1940, an exhibition in Manhattan titled *What a Farm Wife Painted* launched her career. Five years later, Hallmark bought the rights to reproduce her paintings on Christmas cards, making her an instant celebrity. Moses published her autobiography, *My Life's History,* in 1952. At the age of one hundred, she illustrated *'Twas the Night Before Christmas* by Clement Moore. *Images by this artist: Art Print 8.*

Murillo, Bartolomé Esteban [moo•REE•yoh, bar•toh•loh•MAY ehs•TAY•vahn] (1618–1682) Baroque-period Spanish painter renowned for his religious paintings. Murillo was born in Seville. In 1645, Murillo visited artist Diego Velázquez in Madrid. Velázquez permitted Murillo to study the paintings in the royal collection. After his visit, Murillo created eleven paintings of saints for a church in Seville. These paintings brought him fame. His human portrayal of figures and his use of color and light show the strong influence of Velázquez. Murillo also became well known for portraits, paintings of children, and everyday scenes. *Images by this artist: Student Edition p. 24.*

Nadelman, Elie [NAH•duhl•muhn, AY•lee] (1882–1946) Polish-born sculptor and draftsman known for his smoothly stylized, almost caricature-like human forms. At the beginning of World War I, Nadelman moved to New York City and became an international celebrity. He lived and worked in grand style until a series of crises—including the Great Depression—ruined him both emotionally and financially. In his last years, Nadelman produced mostly small, decorative pieces in papier-mâché, plaster, and ceramic, but he did so in seclusion, selling little and refusing to exhibit. *Images by this artist: Art Print 3.*

Nevelson, Louise (1899–1988) American sculptor, painter, and printmaker known for her large monochromatic abstract sculptures and assemblages. Nevelson was born in Kiev, Ukraine, but her family moved to Rockland, Maine, in 1905. At the age of ten, Nevelson decided to become a sculptor. However, she did not begin studying art seriously until the age of thirty. She studied at the Art Students League under Hans Hofmann, who taught her the artistic techniques of Cubism and collage. In 1933, Nevelson assisted Diego Rivera in painting murals. Surrealism, African art, and pre-Columbian art influenced her work. Her early sculptures were done in wood, terra-cotta, bronze, and plaster. She also began creating assemblages in which she used found objects such as chair backs, furniture legs, moldings, and spindles. In 1976, Nevelson wrote her autobiography, titled *Dawns and Dusks,* in which she said that determination was the key to her success. In 2000, the United States government issued five commemorative stamps in her honor. *Images by this artist: Student Edition p. 134.*

O'Keeffe, Georgia (1887–1986) American painter renowned for her abstract paintings and still-life compositions. Born in Sun Prairie, Wisconsin, O'Keeffe became interested in art after she saw a pen-and-ink drawing of a Grecian maiden in one of her mother's books. O'Keeffe studied art at many prestigious schools, including the Art Institute of Chicago and Columbia University. She worked as a teacher and commercial artist but after 1918 began to paint full time. O'Keeffe's life changed when she married photographer Alfred Stieglitz in 1924. She learned about photography and began to use in her work certain elements of the photographic process, such as objectivity, cropped images, isolated detail, and magnified close-ups. O'Keeffe moved to New Mexico and was inspired by the state's beautiful landscapes. In New Mexico, she painted abstracts and still lifes of flowers, animal bones, mountains, and other natural forms. Near the end of her life, O'Keeffe lost her sight, but she did not give up her art. She pursued pottery instead. *Images by this artist: Student Edition p. 48.*

Oldenburg, Claes [OHL•duhn•berg, KLAHS] (1929–) Swedish-born sculptor who became a leader of the Pop Art movement. Oldenburg was born in Stockholm. His father, a diplomat, moved the family to Chicago in 1936. After graduating from Yale University in 1950, Oldenburg worked as a reporter before going on to study at the Art Institute of Chicago. He became an American citizen in 1953 and later moved to New York City. He became a keen observer of common aspects of city life, such as store windows, advertising, graffiti, and trash. Oldenburg began to think about how he could turn street objects into art. He turned his inspiration into "The Store," where he re-created the environment of neighborhood shops and sold painted plaster copies of objects such as food and articles of clothing. Oldenburg's art poked fun at American material culture. Oldenburg also created abstract outdoor monuments of common objects made of steel. After 1970, Oldenburg worked mostly on public commissions. In 1977, he received the American Institute of Architects Award. *Images by this artist: Student Edition p. 42. See also* **Pop Art** and **van Bruggen, Coosje.**

Ong, Diana (1940–) American multimedia artist. Born in New York City, Ong has produced works in watercolors and acrylics as well as etchings, woodcuts, silkscreens, computer art, and ceramic art. Ong's artworks have been exhibited in more than thirty countries and have also appeared on hundreds of book jackets by publishers around the world. In many of her works, she has combined several media. *Images by this artist: Student Edition p. 36.*

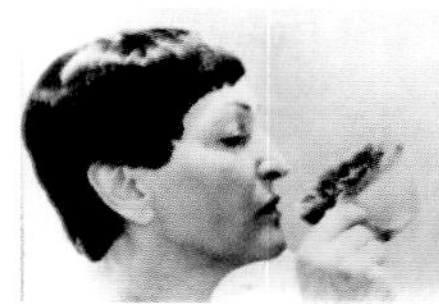

Oppenheim, Meret [AHP•en•hym, MER•et] (1913–1985) German-born Swiss painter and sculptor known for her Surrealist sculptures. Born in Berlin, Oppenheim moved to Paris in 1932, where she studied with Surrealist painter Man Ray. She also studied art in Germany and was influenced by Paul Klee. With the encouragement of artist Alberto Giacometti, Oppenheim produced her first Surrealist sculpture, titled *Giacometti's Ears*. She went on to create assemblages made from everyday objects. Oppenheim's most famous sculpture is a fur-lined teacup and saucer titled *Object. Images by this artist: Student Edition p. 54. See also* **Surrealism.**

Photorealism Depiction of ordinary life with the sharp detail and impersonality of a photograph. Photorealistic artists often paint from photographs and combine more detail into a scene than the camera would capture, such as exaggerated sharpness of focus, multiple layers of reflection in shiny surfaces, or an impossible point of view—the same building or intersection seen simultaneously from two different viewpoints, for example. Photorealism was prominent in the United States and Britain during the late 1960s and 1970s and included the paintings of Richard Estes, Chuck Close, Janet Fish, and Charles Bell.

Picasso, Pablo [pih•KAHS•soh] (1881–1973) Spanish painter, sculptor, printmaker, ceramicist, and illustrator renowned for pioneering the artistic style of Cubism. Picasso was born in Malaga, Spain. His father, an art teacher, recognized Picasso's early talent and gave him art lessons. At fifteen, Picasso completed in one day the one-month qualifying examination to enter the Academy of Fine Arts in Barcelona. After one year, he left school and went to Paris. There, he painted the poor and social outcasts of the city using blue tones to express their sadness. In 1904, Picasso changed his style and began to paint happy circus performers in pink tones. After studying Paul Gauguin's paintings of non-Western cultures and the artistic style of ancient Iberian sculpture, Picasso became inspired to experiment with the element of distortion. In 1907, he collaborated with fellow artist Georges Braque to produce a new artistic style called Cubism. Cubists try to show all sides of an object at once by using geometric forms. *Images by this artist: Student Edition p. 108. See also* **Cubism.**

DID YOU KNOW?

Picasso invented an important artistic technique called collage. Collage is an artistic form that attaches flat, ready-made materials to the surface of a canvas or sculpture. Picasso invented collage when he created *Still Life with Chair Caning*.

Polacco, Patricia (1944–) American children's author and illustrator who was born in Lansing, Michigan. Polacco, who earned a Ph.D. in art history, began her art career as a painter and a sculptor. However, coming from a long line of storytellers, she decided to try her hand at this craft. Her first book, *Meteor!,* was not published until she was in her forties. Many themes in her books stem from her own childhood experiences. Polacco is inspired by her relationships with people of various ages and cultures. She feels it is important for children to understand and accept people from backgrounds different from their own. *Images by this artist: Student Edition p. 111.*

Pont-Aven, School of School of artists that developed in the 1860s as an art colony in the southwest of Brittany, France. Pont-Aven offered affordable living conditions combined with rich landscape beauty and lack of industrialization. The Pont-Aven School of artists reached its peak in the late 1880s and early 1890s, led by the influential Paul Gauguin. This group of artists aimed to reinterpret nature, guided by their imaginations. Strong use of color, form, and line were prevalent in their art. Artists of the Pont-Aven School were known for their vibrant, decorative style. They rejected Impressionist, Pointillist, and Neo-Impressionist techniques. When Gauguin left for Tahiti, the other members became interested in the newly developing Symbolism. With an array of art galleries, studios, schools, and museums, Pont-Aven continued to attract artists into the 1990s.

Pop Art Movement in painting, sculpture, and printmaking that began in Britain in the 1950s and shifted to the United States in 1960. Pop Art focused on images from popular culture, including advertising, comic strips, and brand-name packaged goods. Highly impersonal and often employing commercial and applied art techniques, Pop Art developed as a reaction against the seriousness and highly personal nature of Abstract Expressionism, which it surpassed as the dominant American avant-garde art form in the mid-1960s. Inspired by Dada, which broke new ground in both subject matter and technique, Pop Art is sometimes called Neo-Dada. Major Pop artists include Roy Lichtenstein, Jasper Johns, Claes Oldenburg, and Andy Warhol.

Post-Impressionism General term for trends in modern art that developed as a reaction against Impressionism and Neo-Impressionism. The three major Post-Impressionist artists were Paul Cézanne, Vincent van Gogh, and Paul Gauguin, but Henri Matisse and Pablo Picasso were also involved for part of their careers. All produced early work that was Impressionist in style but later developed styles that used flat areas of bright color and emphasized solid structures and simplified forms. Most Post-Impressionist work was created between 1886 and 1905, but the term was not in general use until 1910.

Potthast, Edward (1857–1927) American painter and lithographer known as one of the most important American Impressionists of the nineteenth century. Potthast was born in Cincinnati, Ohio, a city known for its art community at the turn of the century. Potthast worked as an illustrator in New York before he began to paint full time. He chose as his subjects New York families enjoying themselves at local beach resorts. Potthast's paintings *Sailing Time* and *Afternoon Fun* show how New Yorkers spent their leisure time at the turn of the century. *Images by this artist: Student Edition p. 68. See also* **Impressionism.**

Renoir, Pierre-Auguste [REN•wahr, PYAIR•oh•GOOST] (1841–1919) French painter and co-founder of Impressionism. Renoir was born in Limoges, France. He showed an interest in art at an early age and spent time copying Rococo masterpieces in the Louvre. In 1862, Renoir began studying classical painting and met fellow art students Claude Monet, Alfred Sisley, and Jean-Frederic Bazille. Together, these young artists revolted against the rules of the classical art style. They founded a group of painters known as the Impressionists. Outdoor scenes, an emphasis on natural light, quick brushstrokes, and bright colors characterized this new style. Unlike other Impressionist painters, who painted only landscapes, Renoir painted individual human figures and family group portraits. Renoir traveled to Italy in 1880 to study the Renaissance masters. After that trip, he began to once again paint in a classical style. *Images by this artist: Student Edition p. 62. See also* **Impressionism.**

Rios, Eli and Zeferino Texas designers best known for their customized cowboy boots made for President Dwight D. Eisenhower in 1953. The boots featured designs that included the United States Capitol, the Great Seal of the United States, and sunflowers from Eisenhower's home state of Kansas. *Images by these artists: Student Edition p. 76.*

Rivera, Diego [ree•VAY•rah, DYAY•goh] (1886–1957) Mexican painter known for his murals and as the co-founder of the Mexican School of Painting. Rivera was born in Guanajuato, Mexico. As a young boy, he wanted to paint all the time. To accommodate his son, Rivera's father covered the walls of a room in their house with paper so that Diego could paint on them. At the age of ten, Rivera received a scholarship to study art in Mexico City. Later, he went to France and also toured Italy to study the fresco techniques of the Renaissance artists. He wanted to paint murals on the walls of public buildings to make art accessible to all people. For his murals, Rivera chose older methods of painting. He used fresco, a technique where paint is placed on wet plaster, and also encaustic painting, a method that uses heat to fuse wax colors onto a surface. He developed his own style using large, simplified figures and bold colors. Rivera's best-known mural is at the National Palace in Mexico City. It depicts the history of Mexico from ancient to modern times. In 1929, Rivera married Frida Kahlo, an accomplished Mexican painter. *Images by this artist: Student Edition pp. 52, 78.*

Rousseau, Henri [roo•SOH, ahn•REE] (1844–1910) French painter renowned for his modern primitive-style paintings. Born in Laval, France, Rousseau came from a working-class family. His family could not afford art lessons, but he taught himself to paint. He did not begin painting full time until he retired at the age of forty-nine. At first, critics ridiculed his work, but he believed in himself and continued painting. Rousseau liked to paint jungle landscapes and wild animals. His best-known jungle landscape is entitled *Tiger in a Tropical Storm.* His inspiration came from walks through Paris gardens and from looking at photographs of wild animals in books. He painted each detail and varnished the surfaces of his paintings to a high gloss. *Images by this artist: Student Edition p. 66.*

Sagar, Beatricia American artist who grew up in New York but now lives in Miami. Sagar is known for her segmented paintings, some of which are vertical or square in format. She refers to the vertical works as "Totem Paintings." Each section of a painting reflects a journey in time, with different colors and images representing transitions. Her goal is to make all of the sections within a painting relate to one another, bringing a sense of harmony to her art. *Images by this artist: Student Edition p. 128.*

Santiago, Pepe Mexican folk artist with a vivid imagination who specializes in woodcarving. He is famous for creating *alebrijes,* or brightly colored animals carved out of wood that are linked to Mexican culture. No two *alebrijes* are alike, and they take many days to complete. They range in size from 2 inches up to 4 feet. *Images by this artist: Art Print 18.*

Schwitters, Kurt (1887–1948) German painter and sculptor considered a leading figure of the German Dada movement and one of the greatest masters of collage. Schwitters was born in Hanover, Germany, and studied there and at the Dresden Academy. He experimented with Expressionist and Cubist styles until 1918, when he first assembled collages from discarded items, including stamps, strings, bus tickets, and other refuse. He used several of his homes for his art, covering the walls, floors, and ceilings with bizarre arrangements of found objects. *Images by this artist: Student Edition p. 119.*

Spanish-Pueblo Architectural style, pioneered by John Gaw Meem in New Mexico, that enjoyed its greatest popularity between 1905 and 1940. Sometimes called Spanish colonial, Spanish-Pueblo architecture combines traits of Spanish and southwestern Native American structures. Characteristics of a Spanish-Pueblo structure include a flat roof with visible rafters called *vigas* that project through the exterior walls near the roofline; thick, round-edged, earth-toned stucco walls meant to imitate the adobe walls of the Indian pueblo; stepped levels; deep-set doors and windows; and a low parapet, or portion of an exterior wall that extends upward past the roofline.

Stewart, David American painter who works in modern and realistic styles. Stewart received a degree in art history and anthropology from the University of Texas. He also studied at the Art Students League in New York. Stewart uses his knowledge of history and culture to make his paintings more intriguing. For example, the Ming dynasty is a major subject in many of his works. Stewart spent time painting in New Mexico. However, he returned to his home in North Carolina to get inspiration from the Blue Ridge Mountains and the Great Smoky Mountains. *Images by this artist: Student Edition p. 134.*

Stuart, Gilbert (1755–1828) American portrait painter, best known for his unfinished portrait of George Washington, a version of which has appeared on the United States one-dollar bill since 1869. Stuart was born in Rhode Island and trained in London, where he established his first studio. He returned to the United States in 1793 and was renowned as the nation's leading portrait painter. His works are known for realistic, glowing faces that give the viewer a sense of the sitter's character as well as his or her outward appearance. Stuart is credited with developing a uniquely American portrait style, and his notable sitters include John Adams, Abigail Adams, and Thomas Jefferson. *Images by this artist: Art Print 7.*

DID YOU KNOW?

The original of Gilbert Stuart's famous portrait of George Washington—the image that comes to mind when countless people think of him today—was left unfinished at the request of Martha Washington, who thought it was a particularly bad representation of her husband.

Surrealism Movement in visual art and literature that flourished in Europe in the 1920s and 1930s. Surrealist, or "Super Realist," art was seen as a way to give expression to the unconscious part of the mind. Some Surrealists might use spontaneous techniques as a means to unleash their own subconscious. Others might force viewers to expand their sense of what is real by challenging them with a seemingly incomprehensible scene. Surrealist painters, whose specific styles varied widely, included René Magritte, Salvador Dalí, and Joan Miró.

Tamayo, Rufino [tah•MAH•yoh, roo•FEE•noh] (1899–1991) Mexican painter, printmaker, and sculptor born in Oaxaca, Mexico. Tamayo combined modern European painting styles with Mexican folk themes. He attended the School of Fine Arts in Mexico City. However, he did not like the traditional art program and left to study independently. From 1921 to 1926, he made drawings of pre-Columbian art for the National Museum of Art in Mexico City. Tamayo used small canvases, vibrant colors, and the techniques of the Cubists, Surrealists, and other modern European painters to create his semi-abstract style. He chose the folklore, history, people, and landscapes of Mexico as his subjects. He also painted murals. Tamayo's mural titled *Birth of Nationality and Mexico* is in the National Palace of Fine Arts in Mexico City. Tamayo's work received international recognition, including the Legion of Honor Medal from the French government. *Images by this artist: Art Print 13.*

Taylor, Harriet Peck (1954–) American illustrator and children's author who was born in Lake Forest, Illinois. Taylor's subjects often include animals and Native American folklore. She paints in batik, an ancient Indonesian art form that uses dyes and wax on cotton fabric. Taylor received her bachelor of fine arts degree in painting and her bachelor of arts in education from the University of Colorado. *Images by this artist: Student Edition p. 64.*

Thomas, Alma Woodsey (1891–1978) African American painter and teacher known for her abstract style of painting that is associated with the Washington Color Field Painters. Thomas was born in Columbus, Georgia. Her interest in art began on her grandfather's plantation in Alabama, where she molded objects from riverbank clay. Thomas attended Howard University and became the first graduate of its fine arts department in 1924. She also earned a master of fine arts degree from Columbia Teacher's College. She taught art in the Washington Public Schools while painting part time. Thomas used large canvases filled with dense, irregular patterns and bright colors. She had her first major exhibition at the age of eighty and was the first African American woman to have a solo show at the Whitney Museum of American Art. *Images by this artist: Student Edition pp. 50–51; Art Print 5.*

Trotter, Josephine British painter of landscapes, still lifes, and interior scenes. Trotter began her career as a portrait painter. She works *en plein air,* applying paint directly onto the canvas while viewing the landscape. Her vigorous brushstrokes and rich colors bring life and energy to her paintings. Trotter's inspiration comes from her external environment, and she spends some of her free time exploring landscapes and towns near her Oxfordshire home. *Images by this artist: Student Edition p. 49.*

Valdez, Patssi American painter, printmaker, photographer, graphic artist, and costume and stage designer known for her multifaceted artwork that depicts her childhood experiences, the traditional Chicano lifestyle, and everyday urban life. Valdez's art career began when she was a student at Garfield High School in East Los Angeles. She was the only female member of a Chicano art group called ASCO. The group experimented with street performances, photographic montage, pageantry, and conceptual art. In 1999, an exhibition titled *Patssi Valdez: A Precarious Comfort* opened at the Mexican Museum in San Francisco. It was the first retrospective exhibition of the work of a contemporary Chicano artist from Southern California. *Images by this artist: Student Edition p. 107.*

Van Bruggen, Coosje [vahn BROO•guhn, KOH•sha] (1942–) American sculptor who was born in Groningen, the Netherlands. Van Bruggen earned a master's degree in art history from the University of Groningen. She has been working with her husband, sculptor Claes Oldenburg, since 1976. Their first project together, titled *Trowel I,* can be seen in the sculpture garden of the Kröller-Müller Museum in the Netherlands. Many of their artworks are displayed in parks and gardens in urban settings. *Images by this artist: Student Edition p. 42. See also* **Oldenburg, Claes.**

Van Gogh, Vincent [van GOH] (1853–1890) Dutch painter born in the small village of Groot-Zundert, Holland, renowned as one of the greatest Post-Impressionist artists. In 1869, van Gogh became an apprentice in his uncle's art business and later pursued his interest in religious studies. He became a missionary and went to live in the coal-mining district of southern Belgium. There, he decided to become an artist, and he began to draw pictures chronicling the miners' harsh living conditions. After studying drawing in Brussels and watercolor with Anton Mauve, van Gogh began to paint in oils. He moved to a desolate area of the Netherlands, where he painted the remote landscape and local peasants. In 1885, he produced his first masterpiece based on the daily life of peasants, titled *The Potato Eaters*. The works of Rubens, the Japanese printmakers Hiroshige and Katsushika Hokusai, and the French Impressionists influenced his work. In 1888, he went to paint in southern France; his works created there reflect the sunlight, landscapes, and vivid colors of the countryside. In France, he began to exhibit erratic behavior. Paul Gauguin joined him, they argued, and after cutting off his own earlobe, van Gogh was hospitalized for mental illness. He spent the last nineteen months of his life fighting this illness. *Images by this artist: Student Edition p. 101. See also* **Post-Impressionism.**

DID YOU KNOW?

Vincent van Gogh sold only one painting during his lifetime. In 1987, his painting *Irises,* which he painted while in a hospital, sold for $53.9 million. The buyer called it "the most important painting in the world."

Warhol, Andy [WAWR•hawl] (1928?–1987) American painter, printmaker, sculptor, filmmaker, and writer, best known as a leading figure in the Pop Art movement. Warhol was born in Pennsylvania. He studied pictorial design at the Carnegie Institute of Technology and worked as a successful commercial illustrator in New York City before he began to paint in the late 1950s. Warhol is best known for his images of common objects such as soup cans, dollar bills, and soda bottles. His art showed the emptiness of American material culture, and it ridiculed the values of the American middle class. In 1962, he exhibited a group of paintings titled *32 Campbell's Soup Cans*. Warhol explained that one of the reasons he painted soup cans was that he liked to eat soup. He said, "I paint things I always thought beautiful, things that you use every day and don't think about." He worked in a studio called the Factory, where he and his staff mass-produced his paintings, using a mechanical stencil process called silkscreen printing. Later in life, he spent his time making portraits of famous people, including Marilyn Monroe and Mick Jagger. Warhol's successful process of mass-producing his work made him a leading innovator in the Pop Art movement. *Images by this artist: Student Edition p. 141. See also* **Pop Art.**

Washington, Anna Belle Lee (1924–2000) American folk artist who was born and raised in Detroit. Washington pursued painting as a hobby when she moved to St. Simon's Island, Georgia, in 1984. She found her inspiration in books, people-watching, and visiting African American churches. Many of her paintings depict the landscapes of Georgia, as well as the history of St. Simon's Island. The people in her paintings do not have facial features, and many viewers feel they can see themselves in her painted subjects. The interpretation of her art relies solely on the imagination of the audience. *Images by this artist: Student Edition p. 124.*

Wesselmann, Tom (1931–) American painter, sculptor, and printmaker who became an important exponent of Pop Art. Wesselmann was born in Cincinnati, Ohio. He was influenced by Abstract Expressionism and the work of Willem de Kooning and Jackson Pollock. Later, he began to develop his own style, which led him to Pop Art. In 1959, Wesselmann began to make collages and assemblages that included items such as television sets. He also painted landscapes, portraits, and still lifes. Wesselmann developed two new art forms: drop outs, where negative shapes become positive shapes, and cutouts, which use laser-cut metal to create three-dimensional drawings. *Images by this artist: Student Edition p. 118. See also* **Pop Art.**

Westphal, Katherine (1919–) American textile and mixed-media artist born in Los Angeles, California. Westphal's experimental new approaches, which she developed with her husband, Ed Rossbach, are credited with changing the face of contemporary fiber art, if not creating the field altogether. Westphal's works include hand-printed and commercially produced textile designs, elaborate quilts, kimonos and other "wearable art" objects, and three-dimensional constructions of fabric, embroidery, and found objects. *Images by this artist: Art Print 16.*

Scope & Sequence

PERCEPTION: DEVELOP AND ORGANIZE IDEAS FROM THE ENVIRONMENT	GRADE 1	2	3	4	5
Use Sensory Knowledge and Life Experiences to Identify Ideas					
About self	•	•	•	•	•
About family, school, community	•	•	•	•	•
About visual symbols, life events		•	•	•	•
Elements of Art					
Line					
Identify and discuss line as an element of art	•	•	•	•	•
Examine and explore line in art	•	•	•	•	•
curved, straight, diagonal	•	•	•	•	•
vertical, horizontal		•	•	•	•
outline; contour; expressive		•	•	•	•
crosshatch; sketched			•	•	•
actual; implied				•	
continuous					•
Shape					
Identify and discuss shape as an element of art	•	•	•	•	•
Recognize shape as two-dimensional	•	•	•	•	•
Examine and explore shape in art	•	•	•	•	•
geometric; organic/free-form; repeated; symbols/pictures	•	•	•	•	•
symbols/letters; positive, negative					•
Color					
Identify and discuss color as an element of art	•	•	•	•	•
Examine and explore color in art	•	•	•	•	•
primary, secondary, neutral	•	•	•	•	•
warm, cool	•	•	•	•	•
intermediate, complementary		•	•	•	•
monochromatic, dominant				•	•
analogous; hue; saturation; intensity					•
Space					
Identify and discuss space as an element of art	•	•	•	•	•
Examine and explore space in art	•	•	•	•	•
three-dimensional; horizon line	•	•	•	•	•
foreground, background		•	•	•	•
overlapping; illusion of depth		•	•	•	•
placement; proportion		•	•	•	•
atmospheric perspective; linear perspective; vanishing point				•	•
middle ground, positive, negative				•	•
points of view					•
Value					
Identify and discuss value as an element of art	•	•	•	•	•
Examine and explore value in art	•	•	•	•	•
dark, light	•	•	•	•	•
brightness		•	•	•	•
shadows; gray scale; color gradations	•	•	•	•	•
shades, tints	•	•	•	•	•
contrast		•	•	•	•

	GRADE				
	1	2	3	4	5
Texture					
Identify and discuss texture as an element of art	•	•	•	•	•
Recognize texture as simulated (drawn or painted on a surface) and real (tactile); distinguish between visual and tactile textures	•	•	•	•	•
Examine and explore texture in art	•	•	•	•	•
visual, tactile; repeated lines	•	•	•	•	•
values				•	•
Form					
Identify and discuss form as an element of art	•	•	•	•	•
Recognize form as three-dimensional	•	•	•	•	•
Examine and explore form in art	•	•	•	•	•
geometric, organic	•	•	•	•	•
Principles of Design					
Pattern/Repetition					
Identify and discuss pattern as a principle of design	•	•	•	•	•
Recognize repetition of art elements to create pattern	•	•	•	•	•
Examine and explore pattern in art	•	•	•	•	•
Proportion					
Identify and discuss proportion as a principle of design			•	•	•
Emphasis					
Identify and discuss emphasis as a principle of design	•	•	•	•	•
Identify emphasis by indicating what parts of an artwork are most important	•	•	•	•	•
Examine and explore emphasis in art	•	•	•	•	•
center of interest; color; contrast	•	•	•	•	•
visual weight		•	•	•	•
Balance					
Identify and discuss balance as a principle of design	•	•	•	•	•
Understand balance as a composition that achieves equilibrium in the eyes of the viewer		•	•	•	•
Examine and explore balance in art	•	•	•	•	•
symmetrical	•	•	•	•	•
radial; asymmetrical; midline		•	•	•	•
vertical axis; visual weight				•	•
horizontal axis; exact symmetry, near symmetry					•
Rhythm					
Identify and discuss rhythm as a principle of design	•	•	•	•	•
Understand that rhythm is achieved by repeating elements in artwork	•	•	•	•	•
Examine and explore rhythm in art (repetition; movement)	•	•	•	•	•
Movement					
Identify and discuss movement as a principle of design		•	•	•	•
Examine and explore movement on two-dimensional surfaces		•	•	•	•
Unity					
Identify and discuss unity as a principle of design	•	•	•	•	•
Examine and explore unity in art	•	•	•	•	•
Variety					
Identify and discuss variety as a principle of design	•	•	•	•	•
Examine and explore variety in art (variety in line, color, texture, shape)	•	•	•	•	•

CREATIVE EXPRESSION/PERFORMANCE: EXPRESS IDEAS THROUGH ORIGINAL ARTWORKS	GRADE 1	2	3	4	5
Safety in Art Processes					
Display an awareness of and respect for art tools and materials	•	•	•	•	•
Demonstrate the proper care for and use of tools, materials, and art area	•	•	•	•	•
Follow art safety rules and procedures	•	•	•	•	•
Develop and Apply Art Knowledge and Skills					
Apply elements (line, shape, color, form, texture, value, space) in original artworks	•	•	•	•	•
Apply design principles (pattern, rhythm, movement, unity, variety, balance, proportion, emphasis) in original artworks	•	•	•	•	•
Creative Expression					
Create artworks based on personal observations and experiences	•	•	•	•	•
Integrate a variety of ideas about self, life experiences, family, and community in original artworks	•	•	•	•	•
Combine information from personal observations, experiences, and imagination to express ideas about self, family, and community in original artworks	•	•	•	•	•
Organization and Composition					
Compare relationships between design and everyday life	•	•	•	•	•
Use design skills to develop effective compositions in original artworks		•	•	•	•
Production					
Follow directions and solve problems	•	•	•	•	•
Produce artworks using a variety of art media appropriately	•	•	•	•	•
Produce drawings, paintings, prints, constructions, clay/ceramics, textiles/fiberart	•	•	•	•	•
Produce art that reflects knowledge of a variety of cultures		•	•	•	•
HISTORICAL/CULTURAL HERITAGE: UNDERSTAND ART HISTORY AND CULTURE					
Understanding the Visual Arts in Relation to History and Cultures					
Historical Background					
Understand that art reflects values, beliefs, traditions, expressions, or experiences in a historical context	•	•	•	•	•
Recognize or describe art as a visual record of humankind	•	•	•	•	•
Recognize that media, tools, materials, and processes available to artists have changed through history	•	•	•	•	•
Relate art to different kinds of jobs in everyday life	•	•	•	•	•
Identify main ideas expressed in art	•	•	•	•	•
Recognize a variety of artworks as being from various historical eras		•	•	•	•
Investigate major themes in historical/contemporary eras			•	•	•
Identify the roles of art in American society				•	•
Cultural Influences					
Understand that art reflects values, beliefs, traditions, expressions, or experiences in a cultural context	•	•	•	•	•
Compare and contrast art from various cultures	•	•	•	•	•
Recognize a variety of artworks as being from various cultures	•	•	•	•	•
Determine ways in which artworks reflect or express cultural themes	•	•	•	•	•
Acknowledge and appreciate the artistic contributions of various ethnic groups in our culture	•	•	•	•	•
Compare ways individuals and families are depicted in art	•	•	•	•	•
Identify stories and constructions in art		•	•	•	•
Identify the characteristics of art from other cultures, and value the images, symbols, and themes distinguishing a specific culture		•	•	•	•
Artists and Artistic Styles					
Identify and discuss the artworks of a particular artist	•	•	•	•	•

	GRADE				
	1	2	3	4	5
Value the diverse contributions of artists	•	•	•	•	•
Recognize various artistic styles	•	•	•	•	•
Recognize artists' roles in history and society (to inform, define, interpret, enlighten, entertain; to raise questions and cause reflection; to provide a visual record of humankind; to communicate values, beliefs, feelings; to reveal social and political customs)	•	•	•	•	•
Learn that art is universal, made by people in all cultures throughout history	•	•	•	•	•
Recognize that artists are influenced by artists of the past		•	•	•	•

Understanding the Visual Arts in Relation to the Environment and Everyday Lives

Art in the Environment

	1	2	3	4	5
Develop an awareness of art in natural and human-made environments	•	•	•	•	•
Respond to art elements and design principles (formal structure) found in natural and human-made environments	•	•	•	•	•
Identify art that reflects, celebrates, or communicates sensitivity to natural and human-made environments	•	•	•	•	•

Art in the Community

	1	2	3	4	5
Recognize art as an important part of daily life	•	•	•	•	•
Recognize that art can contribute to the quality of daily life	•	•	•	•	•
Develop awareness of the historical relationship between art and daily life	•	•	•	•	•
Recognize the function of visual arts in the family, the neighborhood, and the community		•	•	•	•
Recognize the importance of art careers		•	•	•	•

RESPONSE/EVALUATION: MAKE INFORMED JUDGMENTS ABOUT ARTWORKS

Apply Simple Criteria to Make Informed Judgments About Art

	1	2	3	4	5
Analyze art elements in art	•	•	•	•	•
Analyze design principles in art	•	•	•	•	•
Analyze media, processes, techniques in art	•	•	•	•	•
Form conclusions about artworks	•	•	•	•	•
Analyze and interpret moods, meanings, symbolism, themes, stories, constructions in art		•	•	•	•

Evaluate Personal Artworks

	1	2	3	4	5
Identify general intent in art	•	•	•	•	•
Identify expressive qualities in art	•	•	•	•	•
Form conclusions about art	•	•	•	•	•
Interpret meaning in art	•	•	•	•	•

Evaluate Artworks by Peers and Others

	1	2	3	4	5
View and respond to original art and reproductions	•	•	•	•	•
Use art vocabulary in discussions about artworks	•	•	•	•	•
Recognize characteristics that make artworks similar and different	•	•	•	•	•
Distinguish characteristics of style in art	•	•	•	•	•
Respond to evidence of skill and craftsmanship found in art	•	•	•	•	•
Respect the differences in others' responses to and perceptions of art	•	•	•	•	•
Identify ideas/moods in original artworks, portfolios, and exhibitions by peers and others	•	•	•	•	•
Recognize that the aim of criticism is to clarify the meaning of and to share discoveries about art			•	•	•

CONNECTIONS BETWEEN AND AMONG THE ARTS AND OTHER CONTENT AREAS

	1	2	3	4	5
Discover and identify connections between the visual arts and other disciplines	•	•	•	•	•
Construct meaning and express ideas, feelings, experiences, and responses through connections to the other subjects	•	•	•	•	•
Analyze and interpret similarities and differences between characteristics of the visual arts and other disciplines		•	•	•	•

Index

D

E

F

G

Cross-Curricular
Themes and Topics

READING	Examples of Artworks and Artist's Workshop Activities from *Art Everywhere*, Grade 3	
Biographies	Wassily Kandinsky, pp. 30–31 Alma Woodsey Thomas, pp. 50–51 Henry Moore, pp. 70–71 Winslow Homer, pp. 96–97	Romare Bearden, pp. 116–117 Nicario Jimenez, pp. 136–137 Art Print 7: *George Washington (Lansdowne Portrait)*
Celebrations	*Baile en Tehuantepec,* p. 52 Native American children in traditional dress, p. 56 Traditional dancers in Korea, p. 57	Teenagers dancing at an Austin festival, p. 57 Artist's Workshop: Mood Painting, p. 53 Art Print 16: *Unveiling of the Statue of Liberty*
Citizenship/Patriotism	Cowboy boots, p. 76 Texas cowboy boot, p. 77 *Mural (America),* p. 79	*World Series,* p. 134 Art Print 7: *George Washington (Lansdowne Portrait)* Art Print 16: *Unveiling of the Statue of Liberty*
Communities	*Wild West,* p. 28 *Baile en Tehuantepec,* p. 52 Native American children in traditional dress, p. 56 Traditional dancers in Korea, p. 57 Teenagers dancing at an Austin festival, p. 57 African mask, p. 72 Huichol yarn mask, p. 72 Mola panel, p. 74 Cowboy boots, p. 76 Texas cowboy boot, p. 77	*The Market,* p. 78 *Mural (America),* p. 79 Mural showing waterfront activities, p. 81 *Looking Along Broadway Towards Grace Church,* p. 92 Egyptian hieroglyphics, p. 126 Artist's Workshop: Community Mural, p. 79 Art Print 16: *Unveiling of the Statue of Liberty* Art Print 18: Lizard Alebrije
Cooperation	*Games We Played,* p. 124 Art Print 8: *Taking in Laundry*	Art Print 15: *Brass Section (Jamming at Minton's)*
Creativity/ Problem Solving	*Torn Notebook,* p. 42 *Object,* p. 54 *The Boat Builders,* p. 97 Ornamental Municipal Gardens in Angers, France, p. 98 *Surrounded Islands,* p. 99 *Myxomatose,* p. 104 *Clown,* p. 112	Artist's Workshop: Garden Design, p. 99 Artist's Workshop: Grid Drawings, p. 107 Artist's Workshop: Graphic Design, p. 139 Art Print 5: *Iris, Tulips, Jonquils and Crocuses* Art Print 6: *From the Castle's Kitchen* Art Print 14: *Caprice in February* Art Print 17: *Broadway Boogie Woogie*
Cultures/Traditions	*Wild West,* p. 28 Brazilian Tapestry (Six Patterns), p. 32 *Woman pouring, Portuguese still life,* p. 46 *Baile en Tehuantepec,* p. 52 Native American children in traditional dress, p. 56 Traditional dancers in Korea, p. 57 Teenagers dancing at an Austin festival, p. 57 African mask, p. 72	Huichol yarn mask, p. 72 Mola panel, p. 74 Chariot of the Sun, p. 122 Egyptian hieroglyphics, p. 126 Artist's Workshop: Mexican Yarn Mask, p. 73 Art Print 16: *Unveiling of the Statue of Liberty* Art Print 18: Lizard Alebrije

Geography	*My Back Yard,* p. 48 Illustration from *Coyote Places the Stars,* p. 64 *The Lighthouse at Two Lights,* p. 82 *Valley Pasture,* p. 87	*Fuji from Kogane-Ga-Hara, Shimosa,* p. 88 The Colorado River in the Grand Canyon, p. 90 *Grand Canyon,* p. 91 Art Print 11: *Poinciana Tree (#150)*
Jobs/Careers	*I Myself Portrait-Landscape,* p. 66 *The Market,* p. 78 Illustration from *Appelemando's Dreams,* p. 111	Architect's model, p. 131 *Weaver's Workshop,* p. 137
Seasons	*Autumn Still Life,* p. 35 *My Back Yard,* p. 48 *Winter Palace,* p. 49 *Fall Begins,* p. 50 *Ice and Clouds,* p. 61 *Landscape—Haystacks in the Snow,* p. 84	*Grainstacks in Bright Sunlight,* p. 84 *Morning in the Village after Snowstorm,* p. 121 *Sun Shines,* p. 128 Artist's Workshop: Seasonal Drawing, p. 49 Art Print 8: *Taking in Laundry*
Self-Discovery	*I Myself Portrait-Landscape,* p. 66 *The Rocker,* p. 70 Cowboy boots, p. 76 Texas cowboy boot, p. 77 *Mural (America),* p. 79 Artist's Workshop: Expressive Line Drawing, p. 29	Artist's Workshop: Indoor Scene Painting, p. 47 Artist's Workshop: Mood Painting, p. 53 Artist's Workshop: Self-Portrait, p. 67 Artist's Workshop: Abstract Self-Portrait, p. 113 Artist's Workshop: Clay Pinch Pot, p. 127

SOCIAL STUDIES	Examples of Artworks and Artist's Workshop Activities from *Art Everywhere*, Grade 3	
HISTORY • understanding how communities have changed over time	*Wild West,* p. 28 *The Market,* p. 78 Chariot of the Sun, p. 122 Egyptian hieroglyphics, p. 126	*Mercedes-Benz Type C111 prototype,* p. 141 Artist's Workshop: Community Mural, p. 79 Art Print 2: *Houses in Munich*
• understanding the importance of events across time and place	*Wild West,* p. 28 *Snoopy—Early Sun Display on Earth,* p. 51 Mola panel, p. 74 *Mural (America),* p. 79	Artist's Workshop: Community Mural, p. 79 Art Print 7: *George Washington (Lansdowne Portrait)* Art Print 16: *Unveiling of the Statue of Liberty*
• understanding how individuals have contributed to communities	*I Myself Portrait-Landscape,* p. 66 *Gospel Song,* p. 116 *The Piano Lesson (Homage to Mary Lou),* p. 117	*Art Festival,* p. 136 *Weaver's Workshop,* p. 137 Art Print 7: *George Washington (Lansdowne Portrait)*
• understanding/comparing past and present	*Two Women at a Window,* p. 24 *Wild West,* p. 28 *Wreck of the Ole '97,* p. 44 Mola panel, p. 74 *Mural (America),* p. 79 Chariot of the Sun, p. 122	Egyptian hieroglyphics, p. 126 Santa Fe Museum of Fine Arts, p. 130 Guggenheim Bilbao, p. 131 *Mercedes-Benz Type C111 prototype,* p. 141 Art Print 7: *George Washington (Lansdowne Portrait)* Art Print 16: *Unveiling of the Statue of Liberty*
GEOGRAPHY • understanding climate, landforms, natural resources, and natural hazards	*My Back Yard,* p. 48 *Winter Palace,* p. 49 *Ice and Clouds,* p. 61 Illustration from *Coyote Places the Stars,* p. 64 *Landscape—Haystacks in the Snow,* p. 84	*Grainstacks in Bright Sunlight,* p. 84 The Colorado River in the Grand Canyon, p. 90 *Grand Canyon,* p. 91 *Morning in the Village after Snowstorm,* p. 121 Artist's Workshop: Seasonal Drawing, p. 49

• **understanding regions**	*My Back Yard,* p. 48 Illustration from *Coyote Places the Stars,* p. 64 The Colorado River in the Grand Canyon, p. 90	*Grand Canyon,* p. 91 Art Print 11: *Poinciana Tree (#150)*
ECONOMICS • **understanding goods, services, and businesses**	*The Market,* p. 78 *The Boat Builders,* p. 97 *Weaver's Workshop,* p. 137	Cactus Brand Oranges—Highland Fruit Growers Association, Promotional literature posters, p. 138 Artist's Workshop: Graphic Design, p. 139
GOVERNMENT AND CITIZENSHIP • **understanding patriotic identity and characteristics of good citizenship**	Mola panel, p. 74 Cowboy boots, p. 76 Texas cowboy boot, p. 77 *Mural (America),* p. 79	*World Series,* p. 134 Artist's Workshop: Community Mural, p. 79 Art Print 7: *George Washington (Lansdowne Portrait)* Art Print 16: *Unveiling of the Statue of Liberty*
• **understanding democratic institutions**	Cowboy boots, p. 76 Texas cowboy boot, p. 77 *Mural (America),* p. 79 *World Series,* p. 134	Artist's Workshop: Community Mural, p. 79 Art Print 7: *George Washington (Lansdowne Portrait)* Art Print 16: *Unveiling of the Statue of Liberty*
CULTURE • **understanding the significance of ethnic and/or cultural celebrations**	*Baile en Tehuantepec,* p. 52 Native American children in traditional dress, p. 56 Traditional dancers in Korea, p. 57	Teenagers dancing at an Austin festival, p. 57 Artist's Workshop: Mood Painting, p. 53 Art Print 16: *Unveiling of the Statue of Liberty*
• **identifying examples of cultural heritage from different communities**	Brazilian Tapestry (Six Patterns), p. 32 *Woman pouring, Portuguese still life,* p. 46 Native American children in traditional dress, p. 56 Traditional dancers in Korea, p. 57 Teenagers dancing at an Austin festival, p. 57 African mask, p. 72 Huichol yarn mask, p. 72 Mola panel, p. 74	Cowboy boots, p. 76 Texas cowboy boot, p. 77 Chariot of the Sun, p. 122 Egyptian hieroglyphics, p. 126 Santa Fe Museum of Fine Arts, p. 130 *Art Festival,* p. 136 *Weaver's Workshop,* p. 137 Art Print 18: Lizard Alebrije

SCIENCE	Examples of Artworks and Artist's Workshop Activities from *Art Everywhere*, Grade 3	
LIFE SCIENCE Animals	*Kat,* p. 36 Illustration from *Coyote Places the Stars,* p. 64 *Fuji from Kogane-Ga-Hara, Shimosa,* p. 88	*The Pigeons,* p. 108 Art Print 1: *Still Life with Three Puppies* Art Print 18: Lizard Alebrije
Plants	*Fruit,* p. 34 *Lime Mist Ikebana with Cascading Oxblood Leaf,* p. 38 Ornamental Municipal Gardens in Angers, France, p. 98	Artist's Workshop: Garden Design, p. 99 Art Print 4: *Water Lilies (Nympheas)* Art Print 5: *Iris, Tulips, Jonquils and Crocuses* Art Print 11: *Poinciana Tree (#150)*
Ecosystems	*My Back Yard,* p. 48 Illustration from *Coyote Places the Stars,* p. 64	*Valley Pasture,* p. 87 Art Print 4: *Water Lilies (Nympheas)*

EARTH SCIENCE Weather	*My Back Yard,* p. 48 *Winter Palace,* p. 49 *Fall Begins,* p. 51 *Ice and Clouds,* p. 61 *Landscape—Haystacks in the Snow,* p. 84	*Grainstacks in Bright Sunlight,* p. 84 *Morning in the Village after Snowstorm,* p. 121 Artist's Workshop: Seasonal Drawing, p. 49 Art Print 8: *Taking in Laundry*
Land, Water, and Environmental Changes	Illustration from *Coyote Places the Stars,* p. 64 *Fuji from Kogane-Ga-Hara, Shimosa,* p. 88 The Colorado River in the Grand Canyon, p. 90 *Grand Canyon,* p. 91	*Surrounded Islands,* p. 99 *Boats on the Beach,* p. 101 Artist's Workshop: Landscape Drawing, p. 89 Art Print 10: *Marine Landscape*
PHYSICAL SCIENCE Simple Systems, Forces, Motion	*Wreck of the Ole '97,* p. 44 *Dazzling Dozen,* p. 58 *Myxomatose,* p. 104	Chariot of the Sun, p. 122 Art Print 10: *Marine Landscape* Art Print 12: *Snap the Whip*

MATHEMATICS	**Examples of Artworks and Artist's Workshop Activities from *Art Everywhere*, Grade 3**	
GEOMETRY Line	*Interior in Yellow and Blue,* p. 26 *Prades, the Village,* p. 41 Artist's Workshop: Crayon Etching, p. 27	Artist's Workshop: Expressive Line Drawing, p. 29 Art Print 17: *Broadway Boogie Woogie*
Shapes and Solids	Brazilian Tapestry (Six Patterns), p. 32 *Fruit,* p. 34 *Flowers,* p. 35 *Autumn Still Life,* p. 35 *Kat,* p. 36 *Three Forms,* p. 37	*Carrousel Pierrot,* p. 38 *Lime Mist Ikebana with Cascading Oxblood Leaf,* p. 38 Artist's Workshop: Shape Design, p. 33 Artist's Workshop: Still-Life Painting, p. 35 Artist's Workshop: Organic Form Sculpture, p. 39
Symmetry	African mask, p. 72 Huichol yarn mask, p. 72 Ornamental Municipal Gardens in Angers, France, p. 98 *Red House Painting,* p. 106	*Fenye's House Dining Room,* p. 107 Artist's Workshop: Mexican Yarn Mask, p. 73 Artist's Workshop: Grid Drawing, p. 107
NUMBERS Fractions	*Portrait of Virginia,* p. 66 *I Myself Portrait-Landscape,* p. 66	Artist's Workshop: Texture Weaving, p. 55 Artist's Workshop: Self-Portrait, p. 67
Problem/Solution	Architect's model, p. 131	Artist's Workshop: Grid Drawing, p. 107
MEASUREMENT Length and Area	*Red House Painting,* p. 106 Architect's model, p. 131 Artist's Workshop: Texture Weaving, p. 55	Artist's Workshop: Grid Drawing, p. 107 Art Print 17: *Broadway Boogie Woogie*
Time and Temperature	*Winter Palace,* p. 49 *Fall Begins,* p. 50 *Ice and Clouds,* p. 61 *Landscape—Haystacks in the Snow,* p. 84	*Grainstacks in Bright Sunlight,* p. 84 *Morning in the Village after Snowstorm,* p. 121 Artist's Workshop: Seasonal Drawing, p. 49

Texas Essential Knowledge and Skills

This correlation shows where the Texas Essential Knowledge and Skills are developed in the *Teacher Edition* for grade 3.

ART

(3.1) **Perception.** The student develops and organizes ideas from the environment.

	The student is expected to:	**Teacher Edition pages**
(A)	identify sensory knowledge as a source for ideas about visual symbols; and	xxii, 22, 30, 31, 39, 50, 90, 116, 117, 127
	identify sensory knowledge as a source for ideas about self; and	22, 62, 96, 101, 102, 113, 116, 127
	identify sensory knowledge as a source for ideas about life events; and	29, 49, 82, 102, 116, 127, 137
	identify life experiences as sources for ideas about visual symbols; and	30, 31, 50, 57, 76, 77, 79, 116, 127
	identify life experiences as sources for ideas about self; and	41, 47, 62, 67, 71, 75, 77, 79, 96, 101, 111, 116, 127, 137
	identify life experiences as sources for ideas about life events; and	49, 53, 68, 69, 71, 75, 79, 111, 116, 127, 137
(B)	identify art elements such as color, texture, form, line, space, and value and art principles such as emphasis, pattern, rhythm, balance, proportion, and unity in artworks.	26, 28, 29, 32, 33, 34, 36, 38, 40, 41, 46, 48, 50, 52, 54, 56, 58, 59, 60, 61, 66, 68, 70, 72, 73, 74, 76, 78, 80, 81, 86, 90, 94, 95, 96, 98, 100, 101, 106, 108, 109, 110, 112, 114, 115, 118, 120, 121, 126, 128, 132, 133, 134, 138, 140, 141

(3.2) **Creative expression/performance.** The student expresses ideas through original artworks, using a variety of media with appropriate skill.

	The student is expected to:	**Teacher Edition pages**
(A)	create artworks based on personal observations;	22d, 35, 39, 67, 82d, 89, 91
	create artworks based on personal experiences;	29, 47, 49, 53, 69, 79, 95, 97, 102d, 111, 117, 120, 127, 137
(B)	develop a variety of effective compositions, using design skills; and	35, 59, 69, 91, 97, 115, 133
(C)	produce drawings using a variety of art materials appropriately.	22d, 27, 31, 42d, 49, 59, 62d, 67, 69, 82d, 89, 95, 97, 99, 102d, 107, 109, 111, 120, 122d, 139
	produce paintings using a variety of art materials appropriately.	42d, 47, 51, 53, 57, 79, 87, 91, 93, 113, 115, 117, 120
	produce prints using a variety of art materials appropriately.	37, 120, 122d, 129, 140
	produce constructions using a variety of art materials appropriately.	82d, 102d, 120, 122d, 131, 135, 137

	produce ceramics using a variety of art materials appropriately.	22d, 39, 71, 77, 120, 127, 137
	produce fiberart using a variety of art materials appropriately.	22d, 55, 73, 75, 119, 120

(3.3) **Historical/cultural heritage.** The student demonstrates an understanding of art history and culture as records of human achievement.

The student is expected to:		Teacher Edition pages
(A)	compare content in artworks from the past for various purposes such as telling stories and documenting history;	56, 66, 69, 90, 96, 122, 126, 127, 130
	compare content in artworks from the past for various purposes such as telling stories and documenting traditions;	56, 96, 122, 126, 130, 136
	compare content in artworks from the present for various purposes such as telling stories and documenting history;	64, 69, 74, 90, 118, 122, 127, 130
	compare content in artworks from the present for various purposes such as telling stories and documenting traditions;	64, 74, 90, 122, 130
(B)	compare selected artworks from different cultures; and	56, 72, 73, 78, 93, 136
(C)	relate art to different kinds of jobs in everyday life.	80, 100, 110, 111, 130, 138, 139, 140

(3.4) **Response/evaluation.** The student makes informed judgments about personal artworks and the artworks of others.

The student is expected to:		Teacher Edition pages
(A)	identify general intent in personal artworks; and	35, 39, 47, 55, 61, 67, 69, 79, 93, 127, 129, 139
	identify expressive qualities in personal artworks; and	29, 31, 53, 67, 113, 117, 127
(B)	apply simple criteria to identify main ideas in original artworks by peers.	37, 57, 77, 87, 91, 111, 131
	apply simple criteria to identify main ideas in portfolios by peers.	37, 57, 77, 91, 111, 131
	apply simple criteria to identify main ideas in exhibitions by peers.	37, 49, 57, 77, 91, 100, 111, 131
	apply simple criteria to identify main ideas in original artworks by major artists.	31, 41, 44, 45, 47, 51, 60, 70, 71, 81, 97, 110, 117, 121, 124, 137
	apply simple criteria to identify main ideas in portfolios by major artists.	31, 51, 70, 71, 97, 116, 117, 137
	apply simple criteria to identify main ideas in exhibitions by major artists.	31, 51, 71, 97, 117, 137

READING

(3.1) **Listening/speaking/purposes.** The student listens attentively and engages actively in various oral language experiences.

The student is expected to:		Teacher Edition pages
(C)	participate in rhymes, songs, conversations, and discussions (K–3);	xvi, 22, 30, 36, 50, 56, 62, 70, 76, 82, 90, 96, 102, 110, 116, 122, 130, 136

(3.2) Listening/speaking/culture. The student listens and speaks to gain knowledge of his/her own culture, the culture of others, and the common elements of cultures.

The student is expected to:	Teacher Edition pages
(A) connect experiences and ideas with those of others through speaking and listening (K–3); and	56–57, 96–97, 111, 116–117, 136
(B) compare language and oral traditions (family stories) that reflect customs, regions, and cultures (K–3).	111

(3.3) Listening/speaking/audiences. The student speaks appropriately to different audiences for different purposes and occasions.

The student is expected to:	Teacher Edition pages
(C) ask and answer relevant questions and make contributions in small or large group discussions (K–3);	xvi, 22, 30, 36, 50, 56, 62, 70, 76, 82, 90, 96, 102, 110, 116, 122, 130, 136

(3.4) Listening/speaking/communication. The student communicates clearly by putting thoughts and feelings into spoken words.

The student is expected to:	Teacher Edition pages
(A) use vocabulary to describe clearly ideas, feelings, and experiences (K–3);	41, 61, 81, 101, 121, 141

(3.6) Reading/fluency. The student reads with fluency and understanding in texts at appropriate difficulty levels.

The student is expected to:	Teacher Edition pages
(A) read regularly in independent-level materials (texts in which no more than approximately 1 in 20 words is difficult for the reader) (3);	xvi, 26, 28, 32, 34, 38, 42d, 46, 48, 52, 54, 58, 62d, 64, 66, 68, 72, 74, 78, 82d, 86, 88, 92, 94, 98, 102d, 106, 108, 110, 112, 114, 118, 122d, 126, 128, 132, 134, 138

(3.7) Reading/variety of texts. The student reads widely for different purposes in varied sources.

The student is expected to:	Teacher Edition pages
(B) read from a variety of genres for pleasure and to acquire information from both print and electronic sources (2–3);	xvi, 26, 28, 32, 34, 38, 42d, 46, 48, 52, 54, 58, 62d, 64, 66, 68, 72, 74, 78, 82d, 86, 88, 92, 94, 98, 102d, 106, 108, 110, 112, 114, 118, 122d, 126, 128, 132, 134, 138

(3.8) Reading/vocabulary development. The student develops an extensive vocabulary.

The student is expected to:	Teacher Edition pages
(B) develop vocabulary through reading (2–3);	26, 28, 32, 34, 38, 46, 48, 52, 54, 58, 66, 68, 72, 74, 78, 86, 88, 92, 94, 98, 106, 108, 112, 114, 118, 126, 128, 132, 134, 138
(C) use resources and references such as beginners' dictionaries, glossaries, available technology, and context to build word meanings and to confirm pronunciation of words (2–3);	23, 43, 63, 83, 103, 115, 123

(3.9) Reading/comprehension. The student uses a variety of strategies to comprehend selections read aloud and selections read independently.

	The student is expected to:	Teacher Edition pages
(E)	draw and discuss visual images based on text descriptions (1–3);	69, 133
(F)	make and explain inferences from texts such as determining important ideas, causes and effects, making predictions, and drawing conclusions (1–3);	25, 26, 28, 32, 34, 38, 40, 45, 46, 47, 48, 52, 54, 58, 59, 60, 61, 85, 86, 88, 92, 94, 98, 100
(G)	identify similarities and differences across texts such as in topics, characters, and themes (3);	136
(H)	produce summaries of text selections (2–3);	125, 126, 127, 128, 129, 132, 134, 138, 140, 141
(I)	represent text information in different ways, including story maps, graphs, and charts (2–3);	25, 45, 60, 65, 85, 100, 105, 120, 125, 140, 145
(J)	distinguish fact from opinion in various texts, including news stories and advertisements (3); and	105, 106, 108, 112, 114, 118, 119, 120
(K)	practice different kinds of questions and tasks, including test-like comprehension questions (3).	40, 60, 80, 100, 120, 140

(3.10) Reading/literary response. The student responds to various texts.

	The student is expected to:	Teacher Edition pages
(A)	respond to stories and poems in ways that reflect understanding and interpretation in discussion (speculating, questioning), in writing, and through movement, music, art, and drama (2–3);	22, 42, 62, 82, 102, 122
(B)	demonstrate understanding of informational text in various ways such as through writing, illustrating, developing demonstrations, and using available technology (2–3);	25, 45, 85, 105, 125

(3.11) Reading/text structures/literary concepts. The student analyzes the characteristics of various types of texts.

	The student is expected to:	Teacher Edition pages
(B)	distinguish fiction from nonfiction, including fact and fantasy (K–3);	xx
(C)	recognize the distinguishing features of familiar genres including stories, poems, and informational texts (1–3);	xx
(E)	understand and identify literary terms such as title, author, illustrator, playwright, theater, stage, act, dialogue, and scene across a variety of literary forms (texts) (3–5);	110–111
(H)	analyze characters, including their traits, feelings, relationships, and changes (1–3);	65
(I)	identify the importance of the setting to a story's meaning (1–3); and	65
(J)	recognize the story problem(s) or plot (1–3).	65

(3.12) Reading/inquiry/research. The student generates questions and conducts research using information from various sources.

The student is expected to:		Teacher Edition pages
(C)	recognize and use parts of a book to locate information, including table of contents, chapter titles, guide words, and indices (1–3);	xx–xxi, R10–R12
(D)	use multiple sources, including print such as an encyclopedia, technology, and experts, to locate information that addresses questions (2–3);	35, 47, 53, 79, 87, 89, 93, 99, 109, 119, 135
(E)	interpret and use graphic sources of information, including maps, charts, graphs, and diagrams (2–3);	22, 42, 62, 82, 102, 113, 137, R3
(H)	demonstrate learning through productions and displays such as oral and written reports, murals, and dramatizations (2–3);	29, 69, 79, 93, 133

(3.13) Reading/culture. The student reads to increase knowledge of his/her own culture, the culture of others, and the common elements of culture.

The student is expected to:		Teacher Edition pages
(A)	connect his/her own experiences with the life experiences, language, customs, and culture of others (K–3);	56–57, 72–73, 74–75, 78–79, 96–97, 135

(3.14) Writing/purposes. The student writes for a variety of audiences and purposes and in various forms.

The student is expected to:		Teacher Edition pages
(A)	write to record ideas and reflections (K–3);	29, 38, 41, 46, 49, 52, 54, 58, 68, 71, 86, 88, 107, 108, 113, 128, 132, 138
(B)	write to discover, develop, and refine ideas (1–3);	26, 33, 34, 61, 75, 92, 93, 114, 120
(C)	write to communicate with a variety of audiences (1–3); and	39, 67, 79, 99, 113, 119
(D)	write in different forms for different purposes such as lists to record, letters to invite or thank, and stories or poems to entertain (1–3).	27, 28, 32, 35, 39, 47, 48, 53, 55, 59, 66, 67, 69, 72, 73, 78, 79, 81, 87, 89, 94, 95, 97, 98, 101, 106, 109, 115, 118, 126, 127, 129, 133, 134, 135, 139, 141

(3.17) Writing/grammar/usage. The student composes meaningful texts applying knowledge of grammar and usage.

The student is expected to:		Teacher Edition pages
(E)	edit writing toward standard grammar and usage, including subject-verb agreement; pronoun agreement, including pronouns that agree in number; and appropriate verb tenses, including *to be,* in final drafts (2–3).	41, 61, 81, 101, 121, 141

(3.18) Writing/writing processes. The student selects and uses writing processes for self-initiated and assigned writing.

The student is expected to:		Teacher Edition pages
(A)	generate ideas for writing by using prewriting techniques such as drawing and listing key thoughts (2–3);	41, 61, 81, 101, 121, 141
(D)	edit for appropriate grammar, spelling, punctuation, and features of polished writing (2–3);	41, 61, 81, 101, 121, 141

MATHEMATICS

(3.2) Number, operation, and quantitative reasoning. The student uses fraction names and symbols to describe fractional parts of whole objects or sets of objects.

The student is expected to:	Teacher Edition pages
(C) use fraction names and symbols to describe fractional parts of whole objects or sets of objects with denominators of 12 or less;	67

(3.8) Geometry and spatial reasoning. The student uses formal geometric vocabulary.

The student is expected to:	Teacher Edition pages
name, describe, and compare shapes and solids using formal geometric vocabulary.	22d, 32, 33, 34, 36, 37, 38, 72, 73, 106, 134, 138

(3.9) Geometry and spatial reasoning. The student recognizes congruence and symmetry.

The student is expected to:	Teacher Edition pages
(A) identify congruent shapes;	72, 74
(B) create shapes with lines of symmetry using concrete models and technology; and	72, 106, 107
(C) identify lines of symmetry in shapes.	72, 73, 107

(3.11) Measurement. The student selects and uses appropriate units and procedures to measure length and area.

The student is expected to:	Teacher Edition pages
(A) estimate and measure lengths using standard units such as inch, foot, yard, centimeter, decimeter, and meter;	55, 95
(C) use concrete models of square units to determine the area of shapes.	107

(3.12) Measurement. The student measures time and temperature.

The student is expected to:	Teacher Edition pages
(B) use a thermometer to measure temperature.	49

(3.13) Measurement. The student applies measurement concepts.

The student is expected to:	Teacher Edition pages
measure to solve problems involving length, area, temperature, and time.	49, 95

SCIENCE

(3.2) Scientific processes. The student uses scientific inquiry methods during field and laboratory investigations.

The student is expected to:	Teacher Edition pages
(B) collect information by observing and measuring;	49, 59
(C) analyze and interpret information to construct reasonable explanations from direct and indirect evidence;	49, 55
(E) construct simple graphs, tables, maps, and charts to organize, examine and evaluate information.	49

(3.4) Scientific processes. The student knows how to use a variety of tools and methods to conduct science inquiry.

The student is expected to:	Teacher Edition pages
(A) collect and analyze information using tools including calculators, microscopes, cameras, safety goggles, sound recorders, clocks, computers, thermometers, hand lenses, meter sticks, rulers, balances, magnets, and compasses;	49, 59, 106

(3.5) Science concepts. The student knows that systems exist in the world.

The student is expected to:	Teacher Edition pages
(A) observe and identify simple systems such as a sprouted seed and a wooden toy car; and	109
(B) observe a simple system and describe the role of various parts such as a yo-yo and string.	109

(3.6) Science concepts. The student knows that forces cause change.

The student is expected to:	Teacher Edition pages
(B) identify that the surface of the Earth can be changed by forces such as earthquakes and glaciers.	89, 90–91

(3.7) Science concepts. The student knows that matter has physical properties.

The student is expected to:	Teacher Edition pages
(A) gather information including temperature, magnetism, hardness, and mass using appropriate tools to identify physical properties of matter;	55, 59

(3.8) Science concepts. The student knows that living organisms need food, water, light, air, a way to dispose of waste, and an environment in which to live.

The student is expected to:	Teacher Edition pages
(A) observe and describe the habitats of organisms within an ecosystem;	35

(3.11) **Science concepts.** The student knows that the natural world includes earth materials and objects in the sky.

The student is expected to:		Teacher Edition pages
(A)	identify and describe the importance of earth materials including rocks, soil, water, and gases of the atmosphere in the local area and classify them as renewable, nonrenewable, or inexhaustible resources;	37, 47, 71
(D)	describe the characteristics of the Sun.	87

SOCIAL STUDIES

(3.1) **History.** The student understands how individuals, events, and ideas have influenced the history of various communities.

The student is expected to:		Teacher Edition pages
(A)	describe how individuals, events, and ideas have changed communities over time;	22, 26, 30, 51, 76, 90, 96–97, 116–117, 126–127, 130–131
(B)	identify individuals such as Pierre-Charles L'Enfant who have helped to shape communities;	22, 26, 30, 76, 90, 116–117, 130–131

(3.3) **History.** The student understands the concepts of time and chronology.

The student is expected to:		Teacher Edition pages
(A)	use vocabulary related to chronology, including ancient and modern times and past, present, and future times;	29, 122, 126–127, 130–131, 136–137
(C)	describe historical times in terms of years, decades, and centuries.	90, 126–127, 130–131, 136–137

(3.4) **Geography.** The student understands how humans adapt to variations in the physical environment.

The student is expected to:		Teacher Edition pages
(A)	describe and explain variations in the physical environment including climate, landforms, natural resources, and natural hazards;	53, 90–91
(B)	compare how people in different communities adapt to or modify the physical environment;	35, 77, 90–91
(C)	describe the effects of physical and human processes in shaping the landscape; and	90–91
(D)	identify and compare the human characteristics of selected regions.	53, 74, 91, 131

(3.5) **Geography.** The student understands the concepts of location, distance, and direction on maps and globes.

The student is expected to:		Teacher Edition pages
(B)	use a scale to determine the distance between places on maps and globes;	113

(C)	identify and use the compass rose, grid, and symbols to locate places on maps and globes;	53, 113, 137

(3.12) Culture. The student understands ethnic and/or cultural celebrations of the United States and other nations.

The student is expected to:		**Teacher Edition pages**
(A)	explain the significance of selected ethnic and/or cultural celebrations in Texas, the United States, and other nations such as St. Patrick's Day, Cinco de Mayo, and Kwanzaa; and	56–57, 79, 137
(B)	compare ethnic and/or cultural celebrations in Texas, the United States, and other nations.	56–57

(3.14) Culture. The student understands the importance of writers and artists to the cultural heritage of communities.

The student is expected to:		**Teacher Edition pages**
(A)	identify selected individual writers and artists and their stories, poems, statues, paintings, and other examples of cultural heritage from communities around the world; and	22, 24, 26, 28, 30, 32, 34, 36, 38, 42, 44, 46, 48, 50, 52, 58, 62, 64, 66, 68, 70, 72, 74, 76, 78, 82, 84, 86, 88, 90, 92, 96, 98, 102, 104, 106, 108, 110, 111, 112, 114, 116, 124, 128, 130, 132, 134, 136
(B)	explain the significance of selected individual writers and artists and their stories, poems, statues, paintings, and other examples of cultural heritage to communities around the world.	22, 24, 26, 28, 30, 32, 34, 36, 38, 42, 44, 46, 48, 50, 52, 58, 62, 64, 66, 68, 70, 72, 74, 76, 78, 82, 84, 86, 88, 90, 92, 96, 98, 102, 104, 106, 108, 110, 112, 114, 116, 122, 124, 126, 128, 130, 132, 134, 136, 138

(3.16) Social studies skills. The student applies critical-thinking skills to organize and use information acquired from a variety of sources including electronic technology.

The student is expected to:		**Teacher Edition pages**
(A)	obtain information, including historical and geographic data about the community, using a variety of print, oral, visual, and computer sources;	35, 47, 69, 79, 89, 100, 119, 133
(C)	interpret oral, visual, and print material by identifying the main idea, identifying cause and effect, and comparing and contrasting;	44, 45, 47, 48, 54, 58, 61, 81, 84, 85, 86, 88, 92, 93, 94, 95, 96, 98, 100, 101, 107
(D)	use various parts of a source, including the table of contents, glossary, and index, as well as keyword computer searches, to locate information;	xx–xxi, 35, 89
(E)	interpret and create visuals including graphs, charts, tables, timelines, illustrations, and maps;	25, 35, 40, 43, 45, 49, 60, 63, 65, 69, 80, 83, 85, 93, 100, 103, 105, 120, 123, 139, 140

(3.17) Social studies skills. The student communicates effectively in written, oral, and visual forms.

The student is expected to:		**Teacher Edition pages**
(A)	express ideas orally based on knowledge and experiences;	24, 40, 41, 47, 49, 53, 57, 62, 67, 68, 69, 72, 78, 79, 82, 84, 89, 96, 101, 104, 110, 111, 113, 116, 117, 120, 121, 127, 137
(B)	create written and visual material such as stories, poems, pictures, maps, and graphic organizers to express ideas; and	22d, 27, 28, 29, 31, 33, 35, 37, 39, 40, 42d, 43, 45, 47, 49, 53, 55, 59, 60, 62d, 63, 65, 66, 67, 69, 73, 75, 79, 80, 82d, 85, 86, 89, 93, 95, 99, 102d, 103, 107, 109, 111, 113, 115, 119, 125, 129, 133, 135, 139, 140